Building Clouds with Windows Azure Pack

Bring the benefits of Azure Pack to your cloud service and discover the secrets of enterprise class solutions

Amit Malik

[PACKT] enterprise
PUBLISHING
professional expertise distilled

BIRMINGHAM - MUMBAI

Building Clouds with Windows Azure Pack

Copyright © 2016 Packt Publishing

All rights reserved. No part of this book may be reproduced, stored in a retrieval system, or transmitted in any form or by any means, without the prior written permission of the publisher, except in the case of brief quotations embedded in critical articles or reviews.

Every effort has been made in the preparation of this book to ensure the accuracy of the information presented. However, the information contained in this book is sold without warranty, either express or implied. Neither the author, nor Packt Publishing, and its dealers and distributors will be held liable for any damages caused or alleged to be caused directly or indirectly by this book.

Packt Publishing has endeavored to provide trademark information about all of the companies and products mentioned in this book by the appropriate use of capitals. However, Packt Publishing cannot guarantee the accuracy of this information.

First published: January 2016

Production reference: 1220116

Published by Packt Publishing Ltd.
Livery Place
35 Livery Street
Birmingham B32PB, UK.

ISBN 978-1-78588-247-0

www.packtpub.com

Credits

Author
Amit Malik

Reviewer
Efim Idelman

Commissioning Editor
Kartikey Pandey

Acquisition Editor
Manish Nainani

Content Development Editor
Onkar Wani

Technical Editor
Murtaza Tinwala

Copy Editor
Yesha Gangani

Project Coordinator
Bijal Patel

Proofreader
Safis Editing

Indexer
Rekha Nair

Production Coordinator
Melwyn Dsa

Cover Work
Melwyn Dsa

About the Author

Amit Malik is an IT enthusiast and technology evangelist from Delhi, India. He specializes in Virtualization, Cloud, and emerging technology space. He has an intense knowledge in building cloud solutions with Microsoft Windows Azure Pack.

Amit holds various industry admired certifications from all major OEM's in Virtualization and Cloud space including MCSE for Private Cloud.

Amit has designed and built numerous virtualization and private cloud solutions comprising the product lines of Microsoft, VMware, and Citrix.

Apart from these, he can be found working on emerging technologies including VDI, hyper convergence, Software Defined Infrastructure solutions including networking and storage, Containers, Big Data, IoT, and other similar technologies. Amit is interested in building products and doing product management in near future for related technology space.

You can always reach Amit on LinkedIn (`https://in.linkedin.com/in/amitmalik99`) or email (`contact2amitmalik@gmail.com`)

Acknowledgement

One day I saw a dream, some sort of drafts, samples, and rough notes, dreams really come true. I am an author now and I am living my dream!

First of all, special thanks to my family for providing encouragement and patience throughout the writing of this book. Special thanks to Mrs. Puspanjali Patnaik, who always gave me full freedom to learn and practice anything I have ever wanted in the initial years of my career.

In general, I would also like to thank my friends, colleagues, and all the people who have ever attended any of my trainings and sessions or interacted with me on technologies in any medium. Your feedback inspired me for authoring this book.

I extend my thanks to Packt Publishing for giving me this opportunity to write my first book and Onkar Wani, Shubhangi Dhamgaye, Murtaza Tinwala, Yesha Gangani, and Ruchita Bhansali from Packt for their tremendous support throughout this journey. Big thanks to my reviewer Efim Idelman for taking time out of his schedule to help me in improving the content of this book. Last but not the least, thanks to Karan Singh for introducing and providing me guidance during the writing of this book.

About the Reviewer

Efim Idelman has over 10 years of experience in Microsoft System Management products starting from SMS 2003 and MOM 2005 to the most current. Starting as a support engineer in Microsoft enterprise manageability team, Efim has advanced through different roles, and most recently, he is working as a senior product manager on Hybrid Cloud offerings in one of Canada's largest telecommunication companies. During his career, Efim was responsible to provide support and consultation for Microsoft enterprise management products such as System Center, Windows server, Virtualization and Azure. With great passion for services and solutions, Efim shifted into products and solutions development working with a number of organizations and building several cloud-based offerings. Efim has great experience in delivering end-to-end cloud services mainly focusing on the hosted service provider's space as well as the enterprise. Efim can be reached at https://ca.linkedin.com/in/efimide

www.PacktPub.com

Support files, eBooks, discount offers, and more

For support files and downloads related to your book, please visit www.PacktPub.com.

Did you know that Packt offers eBook versions of every book published, with PDF and ePub files available? You can upgrade to the eBook version at www.PacktPub.com and as a print book customer, you are entitled to a discount on the eBook copy. Get in touch with us at service@packtpub.com for more details.

At www.PacktPub.com, you can also read a collection of free technical articles, sign up for a range of free newsletters and receive exclusive discounts and offers on Packt books and eBooks.

PACKTLIB

https://www2.packtpub.com/books/subscription/packtlib

Do you need instant solutions to your IT questions? PacktLib is Packt's online digital book library. Here, you can search, access, and read Packt's entire library of books.

Why subscribe?

- Fully searchable across every book published by Packt
- Copy and paste, print, and bookmark content
- On demand and accessible via a web browser

Free access for Packt account holders

If you have an account with Packt at www.PacktPub.com, you can use this to access PacktLib today and view 9 entirely free books. Simply use your login credentials for immediate access.

Instant updates on new Packtbooks

Get notified! Find out when new books are published by following @PacktEnterprise on Twitter or the *Packt Enterprise* Facebook page.

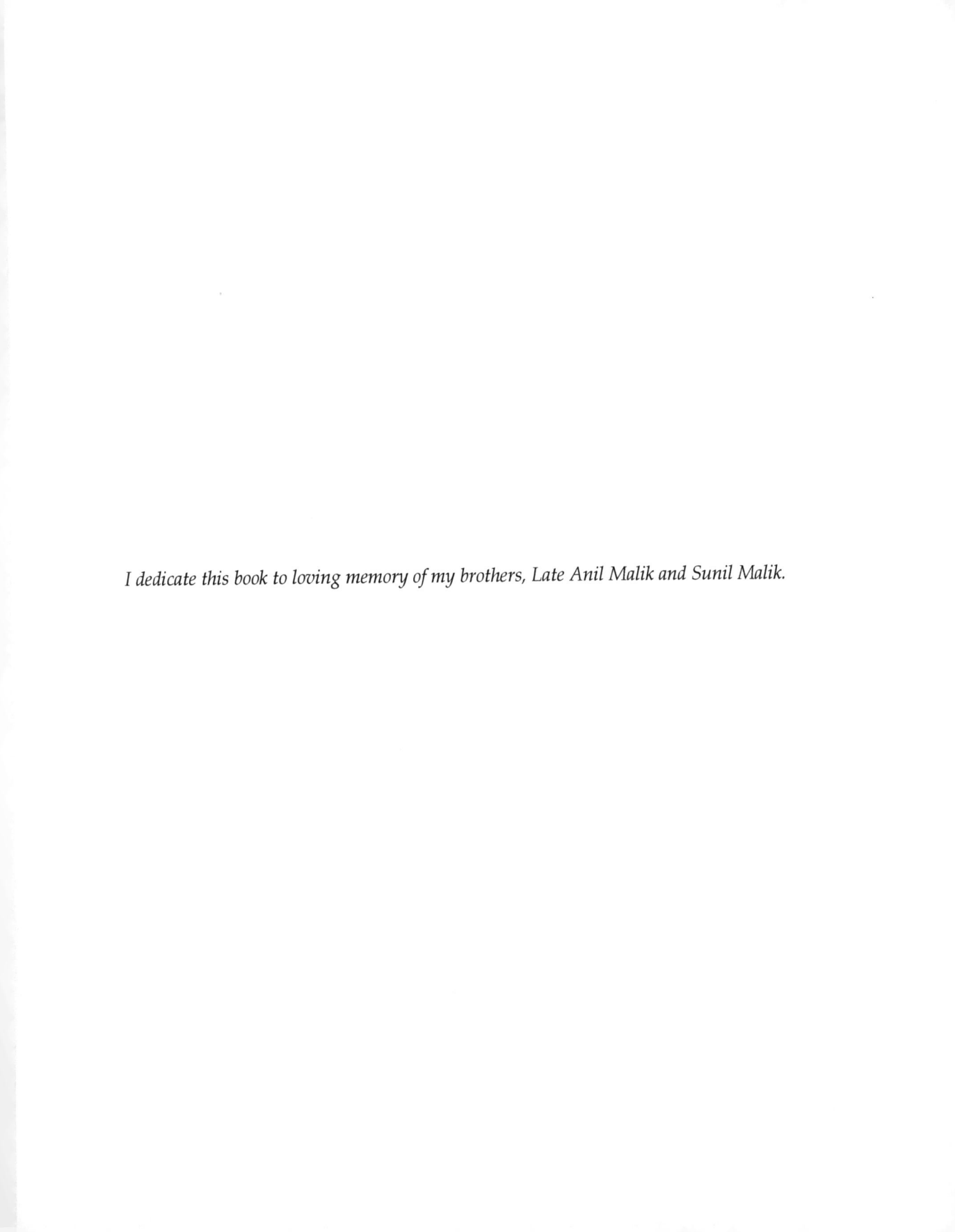

I dedicate this book to loving memory of my brothers, Late Anil Malik and Sunil Malik.

Table of Contents

Preface	**xi**
Chapter 1: Know Windows Azure Pack and Its Architecture	**1**
Microsoft Cloud OS vision	1
What is Windows Azure Pack?	2
Windows Azure Pack for an organization's private cloud	3
Windows Azure Pack for cloud service providers	5
Windows Azure Pack capabilities and offerings	7
Windows Azure Pack components and functionalities	9
Windows Azure Pack cloud solution building blocks	13
Windows Azure Pack cloud IaaS offering solution components	14
WebSites cloud solution components (PaaS offering)	14
DBaaS offering solution components (SQL and MySQL)	15
Service bus offering solution components	15
Custom resource providers	16
Windows Azure Pack deployment models	16
Express deployment architecture	17
Distributed deployment architecture	18
Minimal production deployment sample architecture	20
Scaled production deployment sample architecture	22
Scaling Windows Azure Pack cloud deployment	23
Integrating Windows Azure Pack and System Center Suite for IaaS services	**24**
Summary	**26**

Table of Contents

Chapter 2: Getting the Cloud Fabric Ready — 27
Cloud fabric infrastructure planning — 28
- Choosing the hardware — 28
- Sizing the hardware — 29
- Choosing hypervisor's deployment options and editions — 31
  - Windows Server editions — 31
  - Choosing the right edition for your cloud — 32
  - Free Microsoft Hyper-V Server 2012 R2 — 32
- Choosing the system center deployment options and edition — 33
  - System Center editions — 34
- Cloud management infra and tenant workload infrastructure — 35
- Core MS infrastructure services planning — 35

Hyper-V deployment best practices — 36
- Hyper-V installation best practices — 36
- Hyper-V networking best practices — 38
- Hyper-V storage deployment best practices — 38
- Hyper-V virtual machine deployment best practices — 39
- Hyper-V cluster and mobility deployment best practices — 40

Setting up virtual machines for cloud management fabric — 41
Planning and deploying SQL Server for cloud management DB — 42
- Choosing the database server version and deployment model — 42
- Installing and configuring SQL Server 2012 SP2 — 45
  - Installation procedure — 45
- Post installation tasks — 50

Planning and deploying SCVMM 2012 R2 — 50
- The VMM architecture and deployment model — 50
  - VMM deployment models — 51
- Installing System Center Virtual Machine Manager 2012 R2 — 52
  - Installation prerequisites — 52
  - Software prerequisite — 53
  - Installation procedure — 53
  - Post-installation tasks — 57
- Highly available SCVMM architecture and deployment — 58

Planning and configuring hypervisor compute layer with SCVMM — 59
- Planning and creating SCVMM host groups — 59
- Creating host groups — 60
- Adding virtual machine hosts in host groups — 62
  - Adding Hyper-V host in a host group — 62

[ii]

Planning and configuring cloud network fabric with SCVMM — 63
Network Virtualization — 65
Configuring networking fabric in SCVMM — 66
- Logical networks — 66
- MAC address pool — 73
- Load balancers — 73
- VIP template — 73
- Logical switches — 73
- Port profiles — 73
- Port classifications — 73
- Network service — 73

Planning and configuring cloud storage fabric with SCVMM — 74
Cloud storage deployment options in VMM — 74
Configuring storage fabric in VMM — 76

Planning and Deploying Service Provider Foundation — 78
SPF architecture and deployment options — 78
Installing Service Provider Foundation 2012 R2 — 79
- Installation prerequisites — 80
- Software prerequisites — 80
- Installation procedure — 81
- Post-installation tasks — 83

Summary — 84

Chapter 3: Installing and Configuring Windows Azure Pack — 85
Windows Azure Pack deployment models review — 85
Installing and configuring Windows Azure Pack — 86
WAP installation prerequisite — 86
Installing Windows Azure Pack: Portal and API Express — 88
Configuring Windows Azure Pack Express Deployment — 91
Validating a successful deployment — 94

Installing Windows Azure Pack in a Distributed architecture — 96
Required firewall ports for WAP components — 97
Customizing WAP portal's accessibility and certificates — 98
Configure portal's DNS names — 100
Getting SSL certificates for WAP websites — 102
Configuring site binding to use new URL's, port and SSL — 105
Updating changes in the Windows Azure Pack database — 106
Verifying portal customizations — 108

Registering Service Provider Foundation with WAP — 108
Summary — 111

Table of Contents

Chapter 4: Building VM Clouds and IaaS Offerings — 113
VM Clouds overview — 114
Registering SCVMM with Windows Azure Pack — 114
- Building a SCVMM cloud for Windows Azure Pack cloud — 116
- Requirements for Windows Azure Pack VM Clouds — 117
- Creating a cloud in SCVMM — 117
  - Verifying a SCVMM cloud in the Windows Azure Pack portal — 123
Preparing OS images for a cloud catalogue (Windows and Linux VMs) — 124
- Planning VM images — 125
- Preparing a Sysprepped virtual disk for Windows OS virtual machine — 126
- Preparing VHDX for a Linux OS virtual machine — 128
IaaS virtual machine offerings – standalone VM versus VM Role — 129
- Standalone virtual machine — 129
- VM Role — 130
Building standalone VM IaaS offerings — 131
- Requirements for using VM templates for Windows Azure Pack — 131
- Creating a SCVMM virtual machine template for Windows Azure Pack standalone VM Cloud offerings — 131
- Testing the VM template functionality — 135
The VM Role architecture — 137
- Resource definition packages — 138
- Resources extension packages — 138
- Getting VM Role gallery resources — 139
- Dealing with gallery items – available tools — 139
Building VM Role IaaS offerings using gallery resources — 140
- Downloading gallery items using Microsoft Web PI — 140
- Preparing and importing gallery resources in Windows Azure Pack and SCVMM — 142
  - Importing resource extension packages in SCVMM — 142
  - Configuring virtual hard disks properties for VM Role — 143
  - Importing the Resource Definition package in Windows Azure Pack — 146
Using GRIT (Gallery Resource Import) tool — 148
- GRIT functionalities — 148
- Using GRIT for dealing with gallery resource — 148
Developing VM Role gallery resource using VM Role Authoring tool — 151
- Getting the VM Role Authoring tool — 152
- Developing sample gallery resource – VM Role — 152
- The virtual machine Role example kit — 160

[iv]

Table of Contents

Accessing tenant virtual machines – Windows Azure Pack Console Connect	**161**
Windows Azure Pack Console Connect architecture	161
Preparing certificates for Console Connect deployment	162
Deploying Console Connect	163
Importing trusted certificates (Console Connect) to management servers	163
Setting up Remote Desktop Services Gateway	164
Registering RDS Gateway server in Windows Azure Pack	165
Securing the Console Connect deployment	166
Summary	**167**
Chapter 5: Assigning Cloud Services – Plans, Add-Ons, Tenant Accounts, and Subscriptions	**169**
Windows Azure Pack plans and add-ons – overview and planning	**169**
Planning Windows Azure Pack Cloud plans	170
Planning Windows Azure Pack plans	172
Planning Windows Azure Pack Cloud add-ons	173
Creating and managing Windows Azure Pack plans and add-ons	**173**
Creating a WAP plan	173
Publishing, configuring, advertising, and cloning a WAP plan	177
Creating and managing add-ons	180
Linking an add-on to a plan	182
Creating and managing tenants' user accounts	**182**
Creating user accounts for tenants	183
Configuring notification settings and rules	184
Configuring additional accounts management settings	186
Tenant subscriptions – an overview and management	**187**
Subscription management operations – administrators	187
Adding a new subscription to the tenant's user account	188
Summary	**189**
Chapter 6: Experiencing the Cloud Services – the Tenant's Point of View	**191**
Tenant registrations and account management	**191**
Sign up and plan subscription	192
Tenant account and subscriptions management operations	194
Creating and managing virtual networks	**197**
Creating a virtual network	197
Managing and extending a virtual network	199

[v]

Standalone VM – provisioning and management	**201**
Creating a standalone virtual machine	201
Management operations – standalone virtual machine	203
Virtual machine Role – provisioning and management	**205**
Creating a VM Role	205
Management operations – virtual machine Role	206
Summary	**209**
Chapter 7: Delivering PaaS – WebSites Cloud and Service Bus	**211**
Overview and capabilities of the WebSites cloud	**212**
WAP websites capabilities from the service provider's point of view	212
WAP websites overview and capabilities from a tenant's point of view	214
WAP WebSites – architecture	**215**
WebSites cloud service roles	215
WAP Websites – database roles	216
Planning the WebSites cloud platform	**216**
Planning for resiliency	216
Planning for capacity	217
Domain versus workgroup for WebSites server roles	218
Preparing the installation of Windows Azure Pack WebSites cloud	**219**
Preparing Windows servers	219
Preparing DNS records	219
Preparing a SQL server for the WebSites cloud database	220
Preparing SSL certificates	220
Preparing file servers	221
Installing and configuring the WebSite cloud	**222**
Installing and configuring controller and management servers	222
Registering the Websites Management Server with Windows Azure Pack	228
Installing and configuring frontend, web worker and publisher roles	229
Customizing the WebSite cloud source control and the web gallery feed settings	**232**
Configuring source control	232
Web Gallery feed settings	233
WebSites cloud – management operations	**234**
The utilization dashboard	234
Roles – configuration and management	234
WebSites – monitoring and operations	235
Configuring WebSites cloud settings	236

Table of Contents

The block list – IP filtering	237
Websites cloud platform credentials	238
Websites IP SSL	239
Authoring WebSite cloud plans	**239**
Websites cloud plans overview and service models	239
Creating a plan for WebSites cloud offerings	240
WebSites cloud – a tenant's experience	**242**
Creating Websites – Quick Create and the Web App Gallery	243
Management operations – tenants' websites	245
Windows Azure Pack Service Bus	**249**
Understanding Service Bus queues	250
Understanding Service Bus topics	250
The Service Bus architecture	251
Installing and configuring the Service Bus cloud farm	251
Registering the Service Bus cloud with Windows Azure Pack	255
Authoring a Service Bus plan	257
Service Bus – a tenant's experience	258
Provisioning and accessing a Service Bus namespace and features	258
Creating topics and queues	260
Summary	**261**
Chapter 8: Delivering Database as a Service	**263**
Windows Azure Pack DBaaS offerings overview and capabilities	**264**
Shared and dedicated database services	264
The architectural components of WAP DBaaS	265
Planning the DBaaS platform fabric	**266**
Planning the database server's groups	266
Planning the SQL Server's fabric deployment	267
Planning the MySQL Server's fabric deployment	268
Implementing SQL DBaaS	**268**
Creating SQL groups	269
Adding SQL Servers to groups	270
Implementing the MySQL resource provider fabric	**271**
Installing and configuring MySQL servers	272
Creating MySQL groups	274
Adding MySQL Servers to groups	275
SQL and MySQL DBaaS management operations – service providers	**276**

Enabling DB QoS – the SQL resource governor	**278**
Implementing SQL resource governor for WAP	278
Creating SQL groups and adding SQL Servers	279
Resource templates	279
Authoring DBaaS plans	**282**
Creating plans for SQL and MySQL DBaaS	282
Add-ons for SQL and MySQL DBaaS plans	284
DBaaS – tenant experience	**286**
Database provisioning and access	286
Database management operations – tenants	288
Dedicating DBaaS offerings	**289**
DBaaS VM Role gallery items (IaaS and database software)	289
Dedicated groups and plans	290
Summary	**290**

Chapter 9: Automation and Authentication – Service Management Automation and ADFS — 291

SMA – overview and architecture	**292**
An overview of SMA	292
The architecture of SMA	293
Planning the SMA infrastructure	**295**
Planning for availability	295
Planning for performance and capacity	296
Installing and configuring SMA	**297**
SMA installation prerequisites	297
Installing the SMA web service, runbook worker, and PowerShell module	298
Installing web worker roles	302
Post installation tasks	303
Integrating SMA with Windows Azure Pack	**304**
Dealing with SMA assets	**305**
Asset types and functionalities	306
Adding and managing assets	307
Dealing with SMA runbooks	**311**
Sample runbooks	311
Creating a runbook	312
Authoring a runbook	313
Using assets in runbook PowerShell workflows	314
Scheduling a runbook	315

Dealing with jobs	315
Configuring the runbook logging	316
Linking runbooks with VM cloud actions	317
Enabling ADFS authentication for WAP portals	**319**
ADFS authentication architecture and overview – admin and tenant portals	319
Adding the WAP portal as a relying party	320
Configuring WAP websites to use ADFS	322
Summary	**323**

Chapter 10: Extending WAP Capabilities with Partners' Solutions — 325

Microsoft Azure Stack	**326**
Windows Azure Pack updates	**327**
Windows Azure Pack Partner Ecosystem	**328**
Offer VMware with WAP – vConnect by Cloud Assert	**329**
Konube Integrator – connect with public clouds	**330**
Apprenda – Enterprise PaaS solutions	**330**
BlueStripe's performance center for WAP	**331**
Usage and billing by Cloud Assert	**332**
Cloud Cruiser for WAP	**333**
Request Management by GridPro	**333**
Odin – WAP APS packages	**334**
Cisco ACI – application centric infrastructure	**335**
5nine cloud security	**335**
Team access control for WAP	**336**
Nutanix hyper-converged infrastructure for WAP clouds	**336**
A NetApp storage for Microsoft Clouds	**336**
Summary	**337**
Index	**339**

Preface

Microsoft Azure is the fastest growing public cloud and offers a comprehensive list of services, which continues to increase the list with time.

In 2013, Microsoft released Windows Azure Pack, which is a collection of Microsoft Azure Pack technologies and enables organizations and services providers to build cloud solutions providing consistent experience with one of the world's largest public cloud. Since then, Windows Azure pack has continued to enhance every quarter by adding more services and capabilities.

Windows Azure Pack, or WAP, integrates with proven Microsoft technologies such as Windows Server and System Center and provides cloud offerings including IaaS and PaaS services. Offered services aren't limited to Microsoft technologies as they offer a wide range of other vendor's and open source technologies such as Linux operating systems and MySQL Database. While cloud computing has already been a reality now and is no more a future technology, Windows Azure Pack provides a solid platform with extensible architecture to build a private cloud or service provider's cloud.

This book focuses on enabling readers to build a cloud solution with Windows Azure Pack. This includes a mix of design, implementation and management principles, and steps for building a cloud. Following this book, readers will be able to build their own cloud solution on-premises offering a wide range of services and capabilities.

You will learn about the following aspects of the cloud platform and offerings covered in the book:

- Learning overview, architecture, and capabilities
- Planning for service providers and Organization's private cloud
- Deployment and management of tasks
- Tenant or user experience

What this book covers

Chapter 1, *Know Windows Azure Pack and Its Architecture*, will introduce you to Microsoft's Cloud OS Vision and the role of Windows Azure Pack in enabling it. It then covers Windows Azure Pack capabilities, Service offerings and concludes how WAP is a great platform for building a private or a hosting service provider's cloud. It also covers the architecture, building blocks, and deployment models for a WAP-based cloud solution.

Chapter 2, *Getting the Cloud Fabric Ready*, will focus on building the fabric layer for building a cloud solution. This chapter covers planning and configuration of compute, virtualization, network, and storage fabric for our cloud. It also covers deploying system center components including SCVMM and SPF.

Chapter 3, *Installing and Configuring Windows Azure Pack*, will include installation and configuration of Windows Azure Pack components. It also covers configurations of portals for customized URL's and certificates.

Chapter 4, *Building VM Clouds and IaaS Offerings*, will cover building IaaS Offerings including Virtual Machines (Windows and Linux), Virtual networks, and more. It includes building the platform for providing IaaS Services and then developing offerings for self-service automated services deployment.

Chapter 5, *Assigning Cloud Services – Plans, Add-Ons, Tenant Accounts, and Subscriptions*, will cover mechanism on assigning cloud services to tenants by leveraging WAP Plans and Add-Ons. It will also cover a tenant's user account and subscriptions management.

Chapter 6, *Experiencing the Cloud Services – the Tenant's Point of View*, will enable us to experience the services build earlier as a tenant. It will cover the cloud services provisioning and management as a tenant.

Chapter 7, *Delivering PaaS – WebSites Cloud and Service Bus*, will cover the planning and deployment of PaaS offerings (WebSites and Service Bus). This will also cover building websites and service bus cloud offerings and then experiencing the services as a tenant.

Chapter 8, *Delivering Database as a Service*, will cover the planning and deployment of DBaaS offerings (SQL and MySQL). This will also cover building SQL and MySQL database cloud and then experiencing the services as a tenant.

Chapter 9, *Automation and Authentication – Service Management Automation and ADFS*, will enable us to learn about SMA and its capabilities to add automation to cloud deployment, services offerings, and operations. It then covers leveraging ADFS for authentication in Windows Azure Pack portals.

Chapter 10, *Extending WAP Capabilities with Partners' Solutions*, will introduce you to Microsoft Azure Stack and the WAP updates model. It will also introduce you to many other solutions developed by partners to extend WAP capabilities and offerings.

What you need for this book

While all the aspects of the book don't require you to have any infrastructure or software component running, the following software are required along with sufficient hardware to build a cloud solution covered in this book:

- Windows Server 2012 R2
- Microsoft SQL Server (2008 and above)
- System Center 2012 R2
- Windows Azure Pack
- MySQL Server

Who this book is for

This book targets cloud and virtualization professionals who are willing to get hands-on exposure to Windows Azure Pack. It will help virtualization customers adopt cloud architecture, and it will also help the existing cloud providers to understand the benefits of Azure Pack. Similarly, the book will also help cloud professionals from other platforms such as VMware/OpenStack to appreciate and evaluate Azure Pack. If you are experienced in Server Virtualization and looking forward to learning about building an on-premises cloud solution, this book is for you. If you already know or have experience with other on-premises cloud solution, such as VMware cloud products, OpenStack, and more, and looking forward to seeing what Windows Azure Pack has to offer in cloud computing space, this book is for you. If you are an existing virtualization user and looking forward to adopting cloud in your IT operations, this book is for you. Same goes for cloud service provider offering IaaS and PaaS services.

Conventions

In this book, you will find a number of text styles that distinguish between different kinds of information. Here are some examples of these styles and an explanation of their meaning.

Code words in text, database table names, folder names, filenames, file extensions, pathnames, dummy URLs, user input, and Twitter handles are shown as follows: "Also Verify if system databases such as `master`, `tempdb` are created "

A block of code is set as follows:

```
[default]
exten => s,1,Dial(Zap/1|30)
exten => s,2,Voicemail(u100)
exten => s,102,Voicemail(b100)
exten => i,1,Voicemail(s0)
```

When we wish to draw your attention to a particular part of a code block, the relevant lines or items are set in bold:

```
[default]
exten => s,1,Dial(Zap/1|30)
exten => s,2,Voicemail(u100)
exten => s,102,Voicemail(b100)
exten => i,1,Voicemail(s0)
```

Any command-line input or output is written as follows:

```
# cp /usr/src/asterisk-addons/configs/cdr_mysql.conf.sample
    /etc/asterisk/cdr_mysql.conf
```

New terms and **important words** are shown in bold. Words that you see on the screen, for example, in menus or dialog boxes, appear in the text like this: "Web PI provides a single click option which is **Windows Azure Pack: Portal and API Express**"

> Warnings or important notes appear in a box like this.

> Tips and tricks appear like this.

Reader feedback

Feedback from our readers is always welcome. Let us know what you think about this book—what you liked or disliked. Reader feedback is important for us as it helps us develop titles that you will really get the most out of.

To send us general feedback, simply e-mail feedback@packtpub.com, and mention the book's title in the subject of your message.

If there is a topic that you have expertise in and you are interested in either writing or contributing to a book, see our author guide at www.packtpub.com/authors.

Customer support

Now that you are the proud owner of a Packt book, we have a number of things to help you to get the most from your purchase.

Downloading the color images of this book

We also provide you with a PDF file that has color images of the screenshots/diagrams used in this book. The color images will help you better understand the changes in the output. You can download this file from

https://www.packtpub.com/sites/default/files/downloads/Building_Clouds_with_Windows_Azure_Pack_ColorImages.pdf.

Errata

Although we have taken every care to ensure the accuracy of our content, mistakes do happen. If you find a mistake in one of our books—maybe a mistake in the text or the code—we would be grateful if you could report this to us. By doing so, you can save other readers from frustration and help us improve subsequent versions of this book. If you find any errata, please report them by visiting http://www.packtpub.com/submit-errata, selecting your book, clicking on the **Errata Submission Form** link, and entering the details of your errata. Once your errata are verified, your submission will be accepted and the errata will be uploaded to our website or added to any list of existing errata under the Errata section of that title.

To view the previously submitted errata, go to https://www.packtpub.com/books/content/support and enter the name of the book in the search field. The required information will appear under the **Errata** section.

Piracy

Piracy of copyrighted material on the Internet is an ongoing problem across all media. At Packt, we take the protection of our copyright and licenses very seriously. If you come across any illegal copies of our works in any form on the Internet, please provide us with the location address or website name immediately so that we can pursue a remedy.

Please contact us at copyright@packtpub.com with a link to the suspected pirated material.

We appreciate your help in protecting our authors and our ability to bring you valuable content.

Questions

If you have a problem with any aspect of this book, you can contact us at questions@packtpub.com, and we will do our best to address the problem.

1
Know Windows Azure Pack and Its Architecture

In this chapter, we will learn about Microsoft Cloud OS vision and the role of Windows Azure Pack within it. This chapter will help in understanding Windows Azure Pack cloud solution overview, capabilities, and service offerings with building blocks. Later, we will cover the architecture of Windows Azure Pack components and their deployment models in test and production environments.

We will be covering the following topics in this chapter:

- Microsoft Cloud OS vision
- What is Windows Azure Pack?
- Windows Azure Pack capabilities and offerings
- Windows Azure Pack architectural components and functionalities
- Windows Azure Pack cloud solution building blocks
- Windows Azure Pack deployment models
- Integrating Windows Azure Pack and System Center Suite for IaaS services

Microsoft Cloud OS vision

The Cloud OS is Microsoft's hybrid cloud solution comprised of Windows Server, Windows Azure, System Center, Windows Intune, and SQL Server. Microsoft Cloud OS vision enables one consistent platform and experience of cloud services hosted inside Microsoft Azure Public Cloud data center, in a customer's on-premises data center, or in a service provider data center. Cloud OS essentially does the same traditional infrastructure operations such as provisioning servers and applications, but with cloud scale capabilities and efficiencies.

Windows Azure Pack adds major contribution towards enabling Cloud OS vision, which brings Microsoft Azure's capabilities and experience inside an organization's private cloud and service provider cloud. This provides one true, consistent platform to deliver cloud services using Microsoft technologies.

It can be summarized in the following quote from Microsoft's Whitepaper, "Unified Management for Cloud OS: System Center 2012 R2":

> *"The Microsoft vision for a new era of IT provides one consistent platform for infrastructure, applications, and data: the Cloud OS. The Cloud OS spans your datacenter environments, service provider datacenters, and Windows Azure, enabling you to easily and cost-effectively cloud optimize your business."*

> More information on Microsoft Cloud OS can be found at http://www.microsoft.com/en-in/server-cloud/cloud-os/.

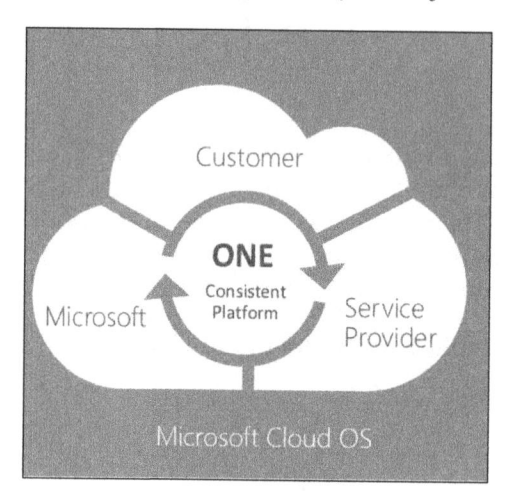

What is Windows Azure Pack?

Windows Azure Pack is a Microsoft solution which integrates with Windows Server 2012 R2, System Center Suite, SQL, and IIS Servers. Together, these provide an enterprise class cloud solution for both organizations and service providers. Windows Azure Pack brings the capabilities of Microsoft Public Cloud, that is, Microsoft Azure's capabilities to your data center.

Windows Azure Pack consists of a collection of Azure technologies which enables organizations to have enterprise class self-service and multitenant cloud along with consistent Microsoft Azure Public Cloud experience. Eliminating the confusion, Windows Azure Pack runs independently with Microsoft Azure Cloud, and is deployed in your own organization's data center; managed and operated by your organization only.

Windows Azure Pack provides cloud service offerings including virtual machines (Infrastructure as a Service), **Database as a Service (DBaaS)**, **Platform as a Service (PaaS)** and many more along with custom offering enabled architecture which gives flexibility to provide anything as a service (XaaS).

Windows Azure Pack can primarily be used in the following use cases:

- By an organization as a private cloud solution
- By a cloud service provider, that is, cloud reseller, as a Hosted Cloud Platform

Amazingly, Windows Azure Pack is available at no extra cost for Microsoft customers.

> Licensing for other Microsoft components like Windows Server, System Center, SQL Server, and so on has to be considered for cloud management and workload infrastructure.

Windows Azure Pack for an organization's private cloud

In today's era of cloud computing, IT departments of organizations are turning into IT service providers for their different teams and LOBs. In traditional computing models, different teams approach their IT departments for their IT needs, which becomes quite a lengthy process involving several levels of approvals, procurement of HW/SW, implementations, services, schedules, and much more. In this model, infrastructure readiness itself takes considerable amount of time and resources, resulting in various constraints when it comes to application deployment. The situation gets even worse when it comes to test and development environment-related requests.

A private cloud helps in eliminating these challenges drastically. For example, with a private cloud solution a development team can request for a VM with required specification and middleware components using an easy to use self-service portal without getting into manual e-mail threads with IT infra provider departments. In such a private cloud infrastructure, a development team can expect to have a server ready for applications usage in a matter of minutes, whereas in a traditional model it could have taken days.

Windows Azure Pack is the platform that can help the organization in getting all those private cloud benefits and capabilities in a very efficient manner. Let's have a look at few of the major requirements and characteristics of any private cloud and their solutions using Azure Pack:

- **Familiar technologies and operational simplicity**: One of the important aspects of any private cloud solution is that the solution has to be managed by the organization's IT personnel only. Technology should be familiar and easily manageable. Windows Azure Pack integrates with Microsoft products such as Windows Servers, System Center, SQL, IIS, and so on, which are already being used across the world by organizations for their IT needs.

- **Self service portal and automated provisioning**: Windows Azure Pack provides the same tenant portal for self-service which is being used by customers of Microsoft's public cloud along with automated provisioning using SPF, SMA, and SCVMM. These roles will be covered in upcoming topics.

- **Effective utilization of existing infrastructure**: Windows Azure Pack can leverage existing infrastructure to provision workload, along with effective utilization using proven Hyper-V and SCVMM capabilities such as dynamic memory, dynamic optimization, differencing disks, and many more.

- **Support for software defined infrastructure technologies**: Windows Azure Pack can leverage software-defined infrastructure components such as SDN and SDS. This can significantly help in being hardware agnostic and avoiding proprietary expensive hardware purchases. An example includes using a SDS product with commodity hardware servers and disk enclosures instead of enterprise class storage array.

- **Dynamic control and chargeback**: Different teams and line of businesses have different IT needs; for example, an HR department may need more storage to store data whereas Finance may need more computing power along with storage. Built-in Windows Azure Pack plans and usage services can be leveraged to have better control over different business resources usage along with chargeback for financial management.

- **Support of multi-vendor operating systems and applications**: As Windows Azure Pack cloud is integrated with Hyper-V and System Center, it supports a wide range of operating systems comprising various Windows and Linux flavors, virtualization vendors (Hyper-V by default, VMware by partner provided solutions), and application/database products.

- **Custom cloud services**: Every organization may have some specific custom needs limited only to a particular entity or team. Windows Azure Pack customer offering gives organizations flexibility to design and develop their custom services and integrate them with Windows Azure Pack for cloud enablement.

> All features or self-service capabilities may not be available while using VMware as a hypervisor. This will be covered in detail in *Chapter 10, Extend Windows Azure Pack Capabilities with Partner Solutions*.

Windows Azure Pack for cloud service providers

Windows Azure Pack gives the flexibility to cloud service providers (such as resellers/hosting service providers) to provide Microsoft Azure Cloud a consistent experience as well as capabilities to their customers. In this scenario, Windows Azure Pack components run in a service provider's data center and provide services to external or internal customers.

Windows Azure Pack provides service providers the ability to build their own cloud to host services at a lower cost and with proven Azure technologies, enabling them to win more and more business. This brings a win-win situation for cloud providers as well as for Microsoft as the Microsoft Azure technology footprint is expanding in cloud markets beyond Azure data centers.

A cloud service provider's main focus is to provide a true multitenant, self-service cloud along with extreme automation possibilities, which differs from organizational private cloud needs which we discussed earlier. Let's have a look at some major requirements of a service provider's cloud solutions and their fulfillment using Windows Azure Pack:

- **To win more and more cloud business**: This is not a direct technical requirement from a cloud solution, but one of the most important aspects of any service provider's business. The service provider needs to win the customer's confidence to get their workload running in the provider's cloud. Windows Azure Pack is built using the same technologies that power one of the leading public clouds, Microsoft Azure, to serve customers worldwide. This will help service providers to offer proven technologies to their customers at a lower cost, enabling more and more business.

- **True multitenant offerings**: The cloud service provider will have to serve varying needs of different customers. True multitenant architecture with respect to portal, offerings, QoS (Quality of Service), and so on is must for any provider's cloud platform. Windows Azure Pack enables these features with tenant portals, Windows Azure Pack plans and subscriptions, and so on.

- **Networking isolation and extension capabilities**: A customer's workload running in same data center will have different networks, security needs and requirements to be completely isolated from each other. Windows Azure Pack's virtual network, using network virtualization, provides complete isolation of networks for a customer's workloads. Windows Azure Pack's site to site VPN capabilities, using network virtualization gateways, enables customers to extend their on-premises network to a service provider's cloud network for hybrid scenarios.

- **Wide range of cloud offerings (IaaS, PaaS, and so on)**: Windows Azure Pack cloud solution supports a wide range of in-built self-service IaaS, PaaS, and DBaaS offerings along with capabilities to add custom service offerings.

- **Usage and billing**: Windows Azure Pack cloud solution has usage and metering capabilities which can be used along with SCOM (System Center Operations Manager) chargeback or other third party usage and billing solutions like Cloud Assert and others to provide an enterprise class cloud billing solution.

- **Extreme automation possibilities**: With Service Management Automation (SMA) integration with Windows Azure Pack, service providers can have their own automation workflows (written in PowerShell workflows) exclusively written for their environments, enabling a completely automated cloud solution. Along with SMA, standard Microsoft automation solutions such as System Center Orchestrator and Windows PowerShell can be leveraged to automate operations.
- **Optimized resource usage**: Windows Azure Pack cloud solution leverages proven enterprise class Hyper-V Virtualization technologies which enables maximum usage of hardware and software resources.
- **Custom offerings**: Windows Azure Pack provides the option to add custom offerings integrated with its portal, which enables service providers to add custom unique offerings apart from default offerings.

Windows Azure Pack capabilities and offerings

Windows Azure Pack, along with System Center and Hyper-V, provides enterprise class IaaS (Infrastructure as a Service), PaaS (Platform as a Service), and DBaaS (Database as a Service) capabilities. The following are the primary features and capabilities that Windows Azure Pack provides once it is deployed:

- **Management portal for cloud admins**: Windows Azure Pack Service management portal for administrators provides facilities to create and manage a cloud offerings catalogue, resource providers, tenants user accounts, plans and subscriptions, and much more. This portal will be used by cloud admin of organization or service providers.
- **Management portal for tenants**: The service management portal for tenants is used by tenant admins for self-service capabilities. Using this portal, tenants can provision, manage, and monitor cloud services available to them such as IaaS, websites, and databases.
- **Service management REST API**: The service management API is the core of capabilities that the management portal delivers. It can be used to provide custom resource offerings and portal integrations.
- **Virtual machines**: This is one of the core offerings using Windows Azure Pack. It provides Windows and Linux Virtual Machines based on Hyper-V and System Center. It includes VM gallery items for different OS flavors, VM roles for automated services provisioning post VM deployment, and scaling options.

- **Virtual networks**: Windows Azure Pack tenant portal provides self-services capabilities to tenant admin to create their own virtual network along with required IP schema and VPN configurations. It works using System Center and Hyper-V Network Virtualization technologies. Virtual networks also provide site to site VPN capabilities, which can extend customers' on-premises network to cloud providers' network for hybrid cloud requirements.

- **Databases**: This offering enables DBaaS capabilities for MS SQL servers and MySQL database servers. Tenants can create databases using tenant service management portals, which can be used by web servers or by any other applications for database needs.

- **Websites**: Windows Azure Pack provides a scalable shared web hosting platform which can be leveraged by service providers or organizations to run web workloads. This is consistent with Microsoft Azure Public Cloud websites capabilities. Along with supporting ASP.NET, PHP, and Node.js applications, Website Cloud provides gallery items built-in for popular web applications such as WordPress and integration with custom developed applications and systems.

- **Automation:**: Windows Azure Pack includes capabilities to have custom automation enabled in environments using integration with Service Management Automation (SMA), which is part of the System Center orchestrator product. With SMA integration, custom runbooks and workflows can be written and executed in an automated manner.

- **Custom offerings**: Windows Azure Pack architecture allows integration of additional custom services into the service catalogue. These capabilities allow the cloud service providers to provide anything as a service. Organizations and service providers can design and develop custom resource providers for custom offering enablement.

- **Service bus**: This service enables the provision of a reliable asynchronous messaging service between distributed applications. Service bus solves the challenges of communicating between on-premises applications and the outside world by allowing on-premises web services to project public endpoints.

> Windows Azure Pack is supported in English, German, Spanish, French, Italian, Japanese, Chinese simplified, Chinese traditional, Brazilian, Portuguese, Korean, and Russian languages.

Windows Azure Pack components and functionalities

Now that we understand what is Windows Azure Pack, along with its capabilities and service offerings, it's time to get technical and deep dive into bits and pieces that make Windows Azure Pack.

Windows Azure Pack is made up of a collection of sites and API endpoints, which are responsible for their different functions. Windows Azure Pack components can be categorized in two categories as follows:

- Mandatory components
- Optional/dependency components

Mandatory components must be installed in every Windows Azure Pack deployment whereas optional components deployment depends upon use cases.

> Windows Azure Pack components use SQL server database to store its configuration and run time data that is highly dependent upon database availability.

Windows Azure Pack components are as follows:

Mandatory components:

- Service management API:
    - Admin API
    - Tenant API
    - Tenant public API

- Authentication sites:
    - Admin authentication site
    - Tenant authentication site

- Service management portals:
    - Management portal for administrators
    - Management portal for tenants

Optional or dependency components:

- Resource provider's extensions (VM Cloud, websites, and so on)
- Service bus
- Automation and extensibility
- PowerShell APIs
- SQL server and MySQL server extension
- Usage extensions (service)
- Usage extension (collector)
- Monitoring extension
- Partner enabled solutions extensions (for instance, vConnect, GridPro, and so on)
- Customer resource provider's extension
- Windows Azure Pack BPA (Best Practice Analyzer)

Let's understand the roles and functionalities of the preceding components:

- **Service management API**: A collection of service management REST API. APIs are the core endpoints that facilitate Windows Azure Pack cloud services access through management portals and PowerShell modules. We can see APIs as a backbone to the management portals and PowerShell modules to enable cloud services integration with the rest of the cloud fabric.

   There are total of three API interfaces differentiating upon their functions as follows:

   - **Admin API**: Admin API is responsible for administrative tasks being performed in Windows Azure Pack through management portals or PowerShell modules. This API is usually hosted inside corporate LAN networks, that is, they are not exposed to the public Internet.
   - **Tenant API**: Tenant API is responsible for tenant administrative tasks like configuring and managing services being performed through tenant management portals or PowerShell modules. This API isn't exposed to the public Internet.
   - **Tenant public API**: Tenant public API also enables tenants to configure and manage cloud services they are subscribed to. Normally, it is publicly exposed. This enables tenants to have custom automation capabilities using Azure Pack PowerShell Modules on their subscriptions from the Internet.

Apart from cloud services provisioning and management, tenant public API enables tenants to have custom automated tasks configured on their cloud workload without involvement of an admin portal plus SMA.

- **Authentication sites**: Authentication sites enable authentication services to manage interfaces for cloud administrators and tenants. When cloud admin or tenant users open their respective portals, they are redirected to authentication sites to complete sign in using their Windows AD credentials or ASP.NET credentials as applicable. **Active Directory Federation Services (ADFS)** authentication can be also be used instead of available default authentication. Upon successful login, the page is redirected to their respective management portals. There are a total of two authentication sites:
    - **Admin authentication site**: This site is responsible for providing authentication services to admin management interfaces. By default, it uses Windows authentication as an authentication source. It can also be configured to support ADFS as an authentication source. This site is normally not exposed to the public Internet.
    - **Tenant authentication site**: This site is responsible for providing authentication services to tenant management interfaces. By default, it uses ASP.NET membership providers to authenticate users. It can also be configured to support ADFS as an authentication source. Usually, this site is exposed to the public Internet to support tenant access across the Internet.

- **Service management portals**: Service management portals are websites built upon HTML5 that are used by admins and tenants for cloud service provisioning and management. These portals provide a similar experience to Microsoft Azure Public Cloud portal. There are total two service management portals:
    - **Management portal for administrators**: In this portal, cloud admins configure and manage resource providers such as IaaS clouds, websites' clouds, catalogue gallery items, plans and user subscriptions, database resource providers, and many more. This portal is restricted to be accessed by cloud administrators and usually isn't exposed to the public Internet.
    - **Management portal for tenants**: This is the self-service interface for tenants to provision, manage and monitor cloud services such as websites, virtual machine, databases, and so on. This portal can also be used by tenants to sign up and subscribe to available Azure Pack plans. Usually, this portal is exposed to the public Internet.

- **Optional components**: Optional components are usually required to enable resource providers' extension and any other third party solutions/custom offerings integration. The following are a few important optional component roles and their functionalities:
    - **Virtual machines cloud**: This allows Windows Azure Pack to provide **IaaS (Infrastructure as a Service)** services for Windows and Linux virtual machines and virtual networks. Virtual machine cloud requires SPF (Service provider foundation) and **SCVMM (System Center Virtual Machine Manager)** to function.
    - **WebSite cloud extension**: This extension allows Windows Azure Pack to provide WebSites as a Service (PaaS) functionality to tenants. It can be co-installed with other Windows Azure Pack internal components. To provide functionality, it needs to be integrated with website cloud resource provider fabric, which will be discussed in detail in *Chapter 7, Delivering PaaS – WebSites Cloud and Service Bus*.
    - **SQL and MySQL resource provider**: This extension enables Database as a Service functionalities for tenants. MS SQL server and MySQL databases can be provided using Windows Azure Pack and database resource provider fabric.
    - **Usage extensions (API and collector)**: Windows Azure Pack provides a service which can collect usage of services offered by the cloud in order to have an enterprise class billing and metering system. This service can be used by partners to develop custom billing solutions and integrate with Windows Azure Pack Usage for automated and consistent billing models. Collector service collects usage data from every resource provider such as VM Cloud, websites, and so on, and stores the data in a usage database. Usage API, that is, a usage service that can be used to fetch this data by customer billing solutions.
    - **Service bus extension**: This extension enables reliable messaging services between distributed applications. This is similar to Microsoft Azure Service Bus functionality. It provides queued and topic based publish or subscribe functionalities.
    - **Partner provided and custom offering extension**: This extension includes partner provided extensibility solution to Windows Azure Pack such as request management by GridPro, vConnect by CloudAssert for VMware integration, and so on. Developers can also have their own custom extension to add custom cloud offerings.

Windows Azure Pack cloud solution building blocks

Windows Azure Pack cloud solution has different fabric components for each cloud offering required to deliver a particular service. Windows Azure Pack components discussed above would remain consistent and have integration with other system centers and other Microsoft components to provide functionality such as IaaS and PaaS.

Usually, each offering requires an extension which can be installed with Windows Azure Pack components and is responsible for portal integration and extension (admin and tenant integration). This extension communicates with resource providers' fabric components (such as SCVMM, SQL Servers, and so on) directly or indirectly to provision and manage services.

The following screenshot illustrates major components of a Windows Azure Pack cloud solution providing IaaS, DBaaS, and PaaS services.

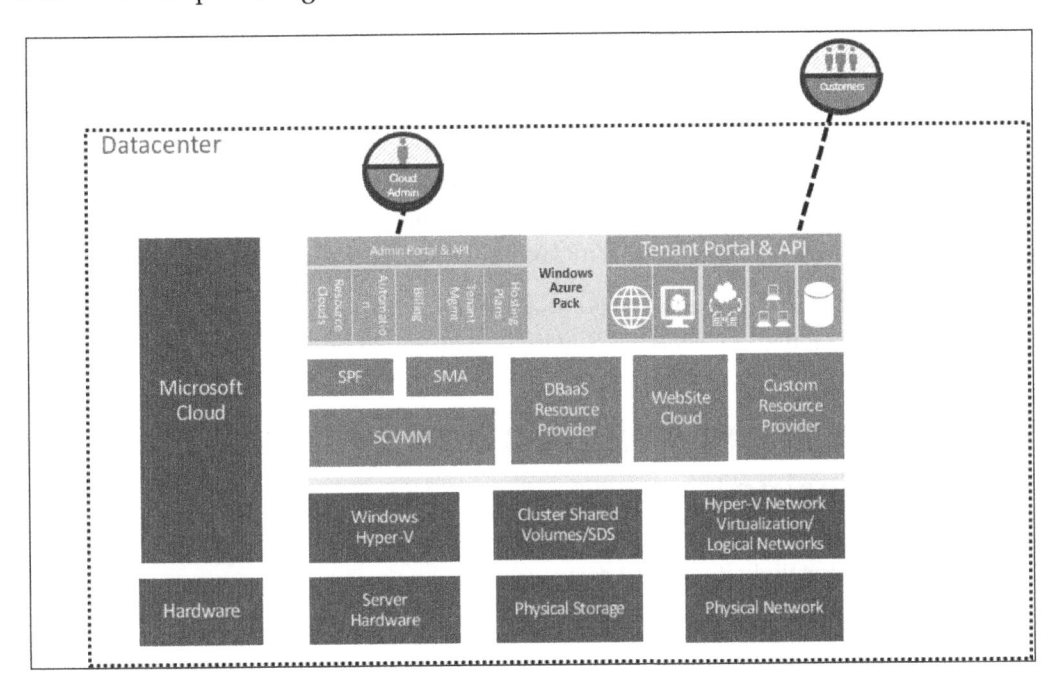

Windows Azure Pack cloud IaaS offering solution components

To enable IaaS offering comprising Windows and Linux virtual machines, virtual networks Windows Azure Pack cloud solution requires the following components to be deployed and integrated:

- Windows Azure Pack components
- Service Provider Foundation (SPF)
- System Center Virtual Machine Manager 2012 R2 (SCVMM)
- Hyper-V 2012 R2 Hosts and Clusters (for cloud management and workload)
- SQL database server for Windows Azure Pack, SPF, and SCVMM
- Windows/Linux virtual machine templates and gallery items
- Compute, network, and storage availability
- Service Management Automation (SMA-optional)

Windows Azure Pack VM Clouds services use SPF to communicate with SCVMM to provision and manage virtual machine resources. All tasks performed by admin or tenants for virtual machines are passed to SCVMM for execution by SPF, that is, SPF is responsible for getting the work done by SCVMM. SMA is integrated with Windows Azure Pack and SPF to add custom automation capabilities to the cloud. IaaS offering also includes virtual network self-service provisioning by tenants provided by SCVMM using Hyper-V network virtualization.

Detailed building procedures for IaaS Cloud will be discussed in *Chapter 2, Getting the Cloud Fabric Ready* and *Chapter 4, Building VM Clouds and IaaS Offerings*.

WebSites cloud solution components (PaaS offering)

WebSites cloud require the following components to be deployed in order to provide PaaS capabilities for websites cloud services.

Windows Azure Pack communicates to websites management servers for website cloud related operations.

Website's server roles comprise:

- Windows Azure Pack components
- WebSites controller
- Management server
- Web worker
- Front end
- File server
- Publisher
- SQL DB service for Website Cloud API database, runtime database, and application databases

Deployment and architecture of the preceding components will be discussed in *Chapter 7, Delivering PaaS – WebSites Cloud and Service Bus*.

DBaaS offering solution components (SQL and MySQL)

Adding DBaaS offerings in Windows Azure Pack cloud consists of the following components:

- Windows Azure Pack components
- SQL server for tenants workload (standalone or cluster using SQL HA or Always On)
- MySQL server for tenants workload

Windows Azure Pack database extension API communicates with database server directly to provision and manage databases for tenants. Deployment and architecture of these components will be discussed in *Chapter 8, Delivering Database as a Service*.

Service bus offering solution components

Service bus is another PaaS offering using Windows Azure Pack cloud which helps developers in building and running message-driven applications. This is consistent with Microsoft Azure service bus and provides similar scalability and resiliency. Solution components for service bus offerings include the following components:

- Windows Azure Pack components
- Service Bus Farm (built on Windows Server 2012 R2)
- SQL server database for service bus

Deployment and architecture of service bus will be discussed in *Chapter 8, Delivering Database as a Service*.

Custom resource providers

Windows Azure Pack enables capabilities to allow custom resource providers to add additional services to the cloud catalogue. Components of custom providers will depend on its architecture, but will usually contain resource providers' applications servers along with its database, and integrate it with Windows Azure Pack using its custom extensions.

In common scenarios, custom resource providers' solutions includes the following components:

- Windows Azure Pack components
- Custom resource provider Windows Azure Pack admin and tenant extension
- Custom resource provider fabric

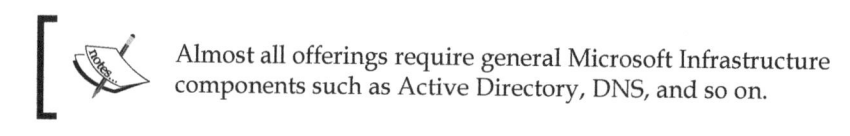

> Almost all offerings require general Microsoft Infrastructure components such as Active Directory, DNS, and so on.

Windows Azure Pack deployment models

Windows Azure Pack components, both mandatory and optional can be deployed in various architectures depending upon use case. All components require Windows Server 2012 or 2012 R2 as an operating system and can be deployed in virtual or physical machines. Virtual machines are recommended to take advantage of Hypervisor level protection and other capabilities. All components can be deployed in a redundancy manner by having two or more servers for each components, eliminating any single point of failure. Windows Azure Pack components use Microsoft SQL Server for its database needs, which can also be protected against failures using SQL high availability techniques.

Mainly there are two deployment architectures for Windows Azure Pack components, with further deployment topologies available for varying needs:

- Express deployment architecture
- Distributed deployment architecture

Express deployment architecture

In express deployment architecture all Windows Azure Pack mandatory components are installed on a single machine, whereas optional components can be installed on the same machine or a different machine. This model isn't a recommended model for production deployments and should be used for test and evaluation purposes only.

Windows Azure Pack Express installation is done via Microsoft Web Platform Installer. For express deployment Web PI provides a single click option which is **Windows Azure Pack: Portal and API Express**, this will install all Windows Azure Pack mandatory and optional components as per requirement on a single machine.

In the express deployment model, MS SQL Server (Express) can also be installed on this same server or on a separate server.

> The Microsoft Web Platform Installer (Web PI) is a free tool that makes getting the latest components of the Microsoft Web Platform such as IIS, SQL Server Express, Windows Azure Pack, and so on. Web PI also helps in installing these components in an easier way. Web PI can be download from http://www.microsoft.com/web/downloads/platform.aspx

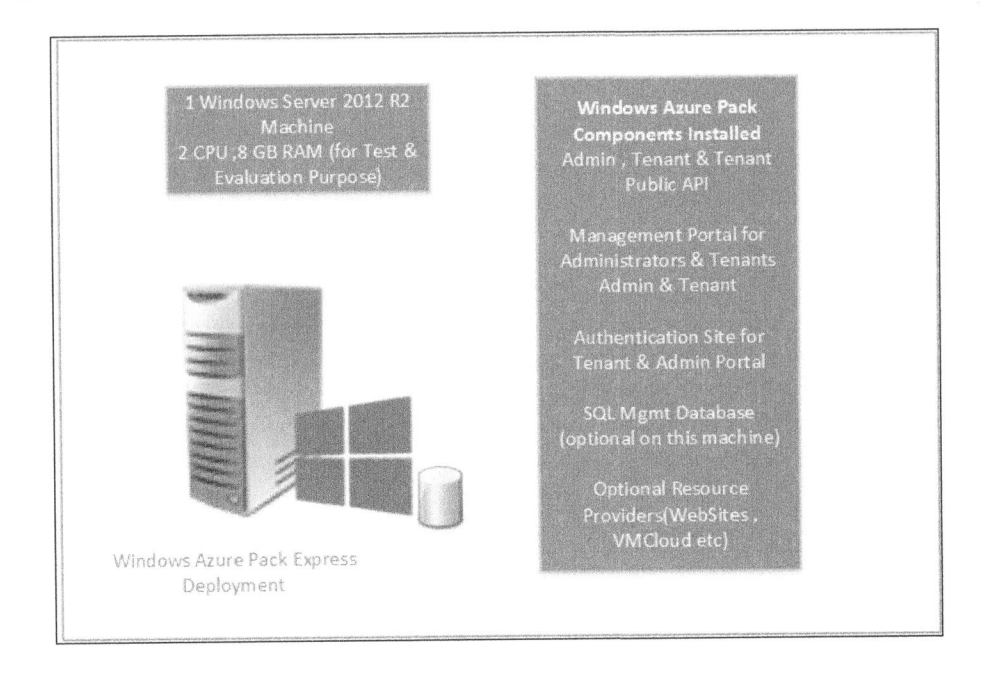

Windows Azure Pack Express Deployment

- 1 Windows Server 2012 R2 Machine
- 2 CPU, 8 GB RAM (for Test & Evaluation Purpose)

Windows Azure Pack Components Installed
- Admin, Tenant & Tenant Public API
- Management Portal for Administrators & Tenants Admin & Tenant
- Authentication Site for Tenant & Admin Portal
- SQL Mgmt Database (optional on this machine)
- Optional Resource Providers (WebSites, VMCloud etc)

The previous diagram illustrates the components which get installed on a machine in a Windows Azure Pack express deployment model. Minimal hardware requirements for express deployment is two CPUs, 8GB Memory (without dynamic memory) with 40GB of available disk space. Detailed deployment procedure for express deployment architecture shall be covered in *Chapter 3, Installing and Configuring Windows Azure Pack*.

> Express deployment is only for test and evaluation purposes and should not be used in a production environment.
>
> Though Windows Azure Pack components can be installed on Windows Server 2012 or 2012 R2 OS, all features like ADFS, SMA support and so on, may not be available while deployed on Windows 2012. It is recommended to use Windows Server 2012 R2 with latest patches and updates to get all functionalities and features.

Distributed deployment architecture

Distributed deployment architecture enables installation of Windows Azure Pack roles on different servers for reliability and scalability. In this deployment model each component can be installed on a separate server or co-located with other roles as per functionality and requirement. Redundancy servers can be added for each role with load balancer to eliminate single point of failure at each layer.

The distributed deployment model is recommended for production deployment and provides scale-out capabilities. The diagram which will come next illustrates a sample distributed deployment architecture without any high availability.

In the following sample architecture, Windows Azure Pack components which will be accessed from the Internet (tenant admin portal, authentication site and tenant public API) are installed on three different servers in a separate network zone (aka DMZ Internet facing) which is separated with a firewall from other network zones. The rest of Windows Azure Pack mandatory components and Internet facing components are kept in separate network zone considering security best practices. All servers can be deployed as virtual machines on any Hypervisor hosts.

Minimal Hardware Configuration Requirement for Each Windows Azure Pack Server	
CPUs	2
RAM	8GB (no dynamic memory)
Available disk space	40GB

Chapter 1

> Hardware requirements, high availability and scalability for resource providers' servers to be in line with product specific guidelines are shown in the following screenshot:

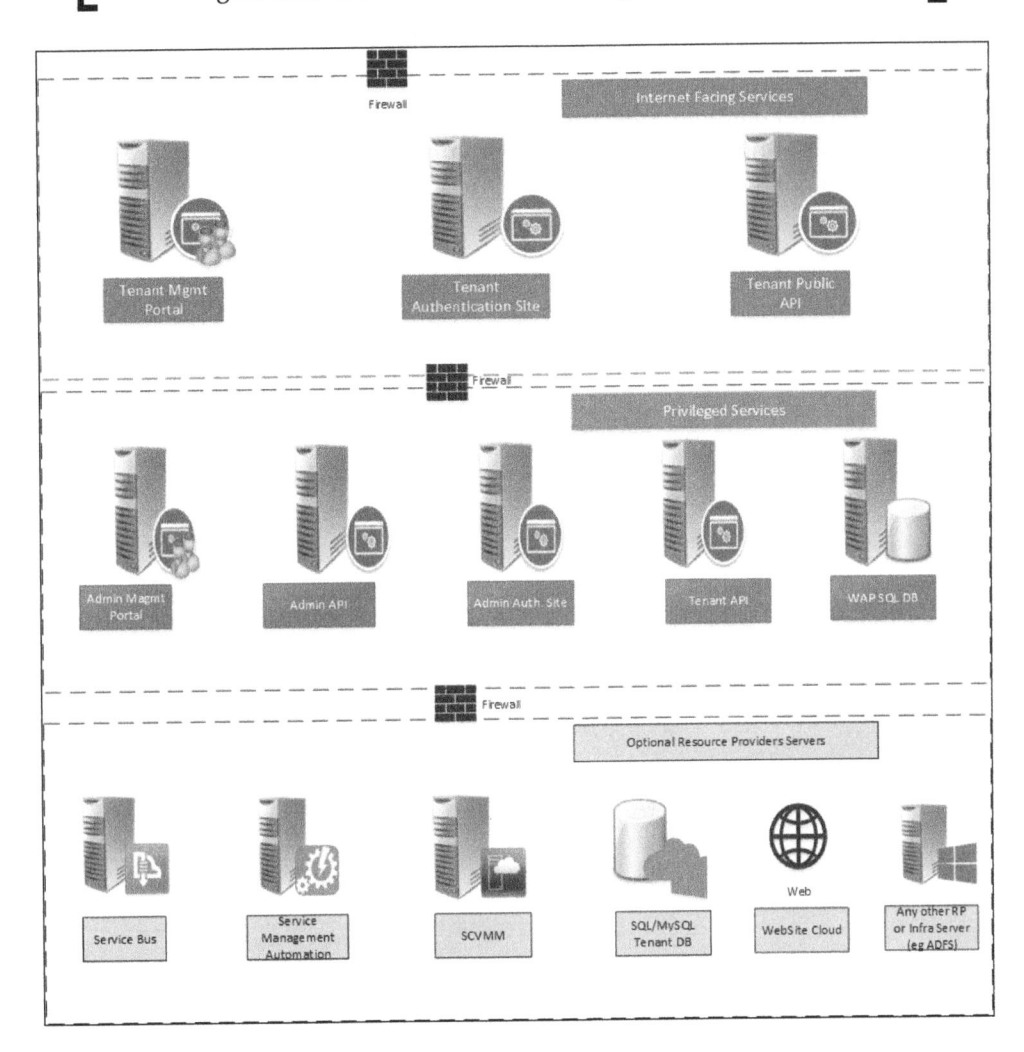

Internet Facing Services: Tenant Mgmt Portal, Tenant Authentication Site, Tenant Public API

Privileged Services: Admin Mgmt Portal, Admin API, Admin Auth. Site, Tenant API, WAP SQL DB

Optional Resource Providers Servers: Service Bus, Service Management Automation, SCVMM, SQL/MySQL Tenant DB, WebSite Cloud (Web), Any other RP or Infra Server (eg ADFS)

> In all deployment models, standard Microsoft Infrastructure Services such as Active Directory, DNS and Fabric should be deployed as per product specific best practices. These architecture diagrams are limited to Windows Azure Pack components deployment.

Minimal production deployment sample architecture

Distributed deployment architecture provides flexibilities to users to design and deploy Windows Azure Pack components as per their needs in terms of resiliency, scalability and security. One of the most common production deployment models is having production ready architecture with minimal footprint and no single point of failure. The following diagram illustrates a sample architecture with minimal deployment with resiliency.

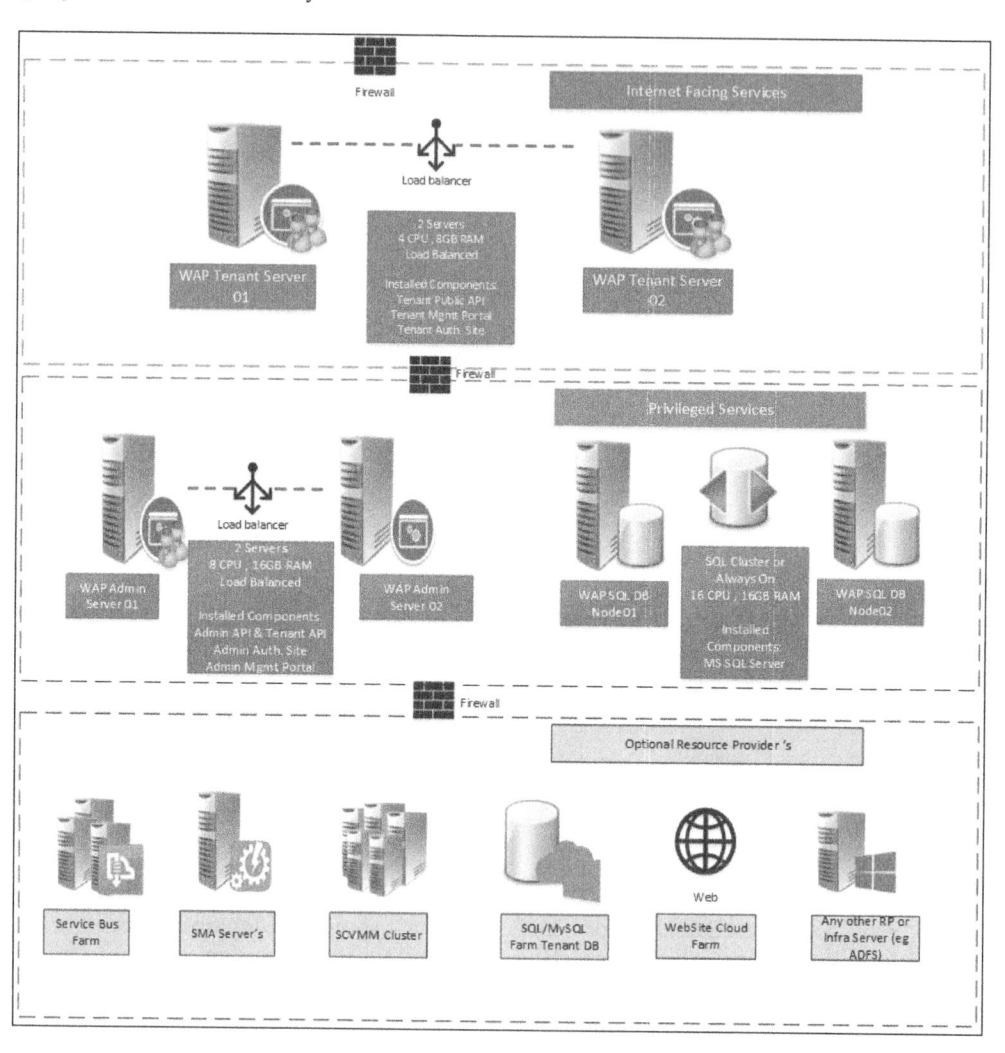

In the preceding sample architecture, the number of VMs required for Windows Azure Pack components is six (excluding infra and RP servers). All Windows Azure Pack required components are segregated in three types primarily based upon functionality and placement in network zones.

Windows Azure Pack tenant servers: Tenant servers includes management portal for tenants, tenant public API and tenant authentication site. Two servers are load balanced to provide resiliency and scalability. Since these servers will be Internet facing, they have to be placed in a DMZ network zone.

Hardware Configuration Requirement for Each Windows Azure Pack Tenant Server	
CPUs	4
RAM	8GB (no dynamic memory)
Available disk space	40GB

Windows Azure Pack admin servers: Admin servers include management portal for administrators, admin API, and tenant API and admin authentication site.

Two servers are load balanced to provide resiliency and scalability. Since these servers will not be Internet facing, they have to be placed in an internal network zone.

Hardware Configuration Requirement for Each Windows Azure Pack Admin Server	
CPUs	8
RAM	16GB (no dynamic memory)
Available disk space	40GB

Windows Azure Pack DB servers: In this sample, 2 Node SQL Cluster / AlwaysOn is considered to provide the database for Windows Azure Pack and System Center components. Hosted in an internal network zone, this cluster provides resiliency for a cloud management fabric database.

Hardware Configuration Requirement for SQL DB Nodes	
CPUs	16
RAM	16GB (no dynamic memory)
Available disk space	40GB + DB Disk (subject to size or cloud)

Resource providers sizing and availability best practices should be deployed as per product specific guidelines.

This architecture is suitable for SMB organizations and cloud providers as it provides minimal production deployment feasibility as well as customization possibilities in case of specific needs.

Scaled production deployment sample architecture

In this sample architecture, each component of Windows Azure Pack solution shall be deployed on separate dedicated servers along with redundancy to eliminate any single point of failure. This architecture is best suited for large scale enterprises and cloud service providers. The diagram that will come next illustrates the components deployment model and placement along with minimal configurations.

To deploy Windows Azure Pack components in this architecture, a total of 16 virtual machines are required in this architecture comprising eight failover/LB clusters.

Minimal Hardware Configuration Requirement for Each Windows Azure Pack Server	
CPUs	2
RAM	8GB (no dynamic memory)
Available disk space	40GB

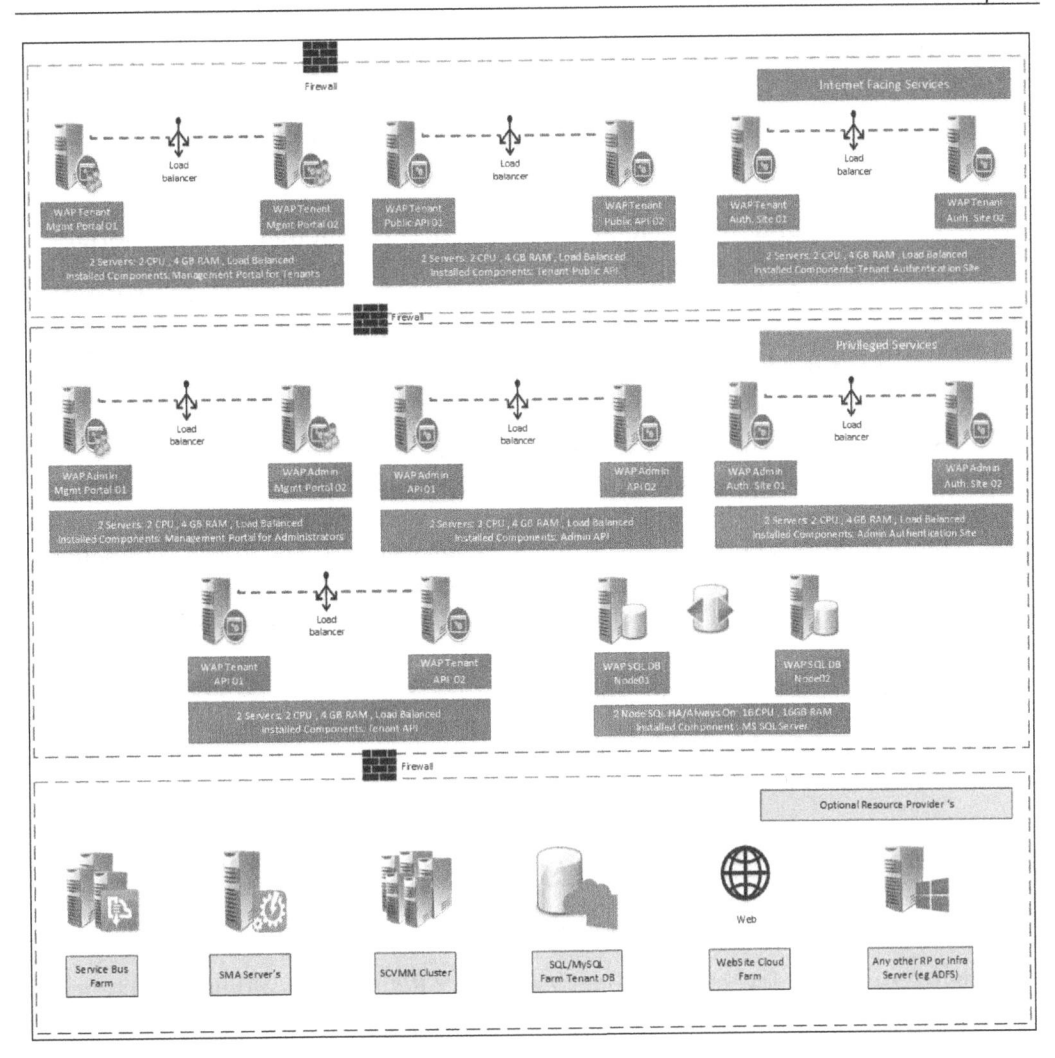

Scaling Windows Azure Pack cloud deployment

Scalability is one the most important aspects of any cloud solution. A cloud solution must support scalability without minimal changes and service disruption as soon as infrastructure size changes. Windows Azure Pack has capabilities to be scaled as and when required. Windows Azure Pack has to be deployed in a distributed model in order to support scaling; the best option would be having dedicate servers for each component in order to scale with minimal efforts.

Know Windows Azure Pack and Its Architecture

In common scenarios scaling is required, particularly for tenant related components as tenant workload is likely to be increase with time.

There are some considerations which should be taken care of while scaling Windows Azure Pack deployment, as follows:

- **Tenant API and management portal scaling**: Tenant management portal needs to be scaled along with tenant API and vice versa. While you scale management portal for tenant, you will also need to scale tenant APIs.
- **Scaling tenant authentication sites**: Tenant authentication has to be scaled corresponding to ADFS servers. Tenant authentication sites have to be deployed in correspondence with ADFS in this scenario.
- **Scaling workload infrastructure**: Scaling of tenant workload infrastructure depends upon the workload fabric being used. In case of IaaS workload, System Center and Hyper-V provides highly scalable capabilities by adding more compute, network and storage resources non-disruptively. The same applies for DBaaS and PaaS services as well. In most scenarios, additional resources can be added as and when required without disruption.

> See product specific guidelines (such as SQL Servers, IIS, Service Bus, and so on) while scaling resource providers' workload infrastructures.

Integrating Windows Azure Pack and System Center Suite for IaaS services

Windows Azure pack leverage System Center 2012 R2 products along with Hyper-V in order to provide infrastructure as a service offering. System Center Suite is a set of multiple tightly integrated products which helps in having unified management and provisioning for your entire data center or cloud infrastructure. System Center Suite of products supports both Microsoft and non-Microsoft infrastructure integration.

System Center components are responsible for delivering IaaS services in Windows Azure Pack cloud. System Center products, which can be integrated with Windows Azure Pack are as follows:

- **System Center Service Provider Foundation**: SPF adds multi-tenancy to System Center products. Available as a part of System Center Orchestrator media, it provides an extensible OData API over a REST web service enabling programmatic multi-tenant interface to System Center Virtual Machine Manager. Windows Azure Pack uses SPF to integrate with SCVMM for IaaS workload provisioning and life cycle management.

- **System Center Virtual Machine Manager**: SCVMM is the management solution for virtualization infrastructure provisions and managing compute (Virtualization Hosts), network, and storage resources to deploy virtual machines and services. VMM also enables software defined networking capabilities using Hyper-V Network Virtualization. Windows Azure Pack uses SCVMM to provision and manage clouds, virtual machines, virtual networks and other IaaS services.

- **System Center Service Management Automation (optional – for custom automation capabilities)**: SMA is an automation solution for Windows Azure Pack cloud infrastructures. It enables provisioning, monitoring and life cycle management of resources in a Windows Azure Pack cloud solution. It is available as a part of System Center Orchestrator.

- **System Center Operations Manager (optional – for monitoring and usage metering)**: SCOM is a monitoring and usage metering solution. It can be used in a Windows Azure Pack cloud for real-time monitoring of infra resources (using SCOM Console) and usage metering (using partner solutions such as CloudAssert, Cloudcruiser, and so on).

> Other System Center products can also be integrated with Windows Azure Pack using partner provider solutions (for example, GridPro enables System Center Service Manager integration with Windows Azure Pack for request management solution). While some components may not be able to integrate with Windows Azure Pack directly for having self-service, these can be utilized in cloud infrastructure to add capabilities as per product specific functionalities.

Other System Center product capabilities in a cloud management solution include:

- **System Center Configuration Manager**: In a Windows Azure Pack based cloud, SCCM deployment would help in compliance management, asset intelligence and inventory, patching solution and device management. SCCM has to be managed using SCCM management console and doesn't have any Windows Azure Pack portal integration functionalities at this point of time.

- **System Center Data Protection Manager**: DPM is an enterprise class backup solution. It can be leveraged for backup and recovery of cloud management and workload resources. DPM provides features such as VM and application centric backup with granular recovery capabilities. DPM can also archive backup data to Microsoft Azure which enables hybrid scenarios.

- **System center Service Manager**: It provides an IT service management solution for cloud infrastructure. SCSM is built on frameworks by **Microsoft Operations Framework (MOF)** and **Information Technology Infrastructure Library (ITIL)**. It provides a built in process for handling incident and change management, change control and life cycle management. GridPro provides a way to integrate SCSM with Windows Azure Pack for enabling effective request management solutions.

- **System Center Endpoint Protection**: Endpoint protection is an antimalware and security solution for the Microsoft platform. It can be used with SCCM for enterprise class endpoint management solutions.

- **System Center App Controller**: App controller provides self-service experience for VMM infrastructure along with support of provisioning workload in Microsoft Azure.

- **System Center Orchestrator (SCORCH)**: SMA and SPF (discussed above) are part of the SCORCH product and are tightly integrated with Windows Azure Pack for delivering IaaS services. Apart from SMA and SPF, Orchestrator provides workflow management solutions for data centers. Orchestrator can automate data center operations of deployment and management of resources.

Summary

In this chapter, we learned about Microsoft Cloud OS vision and how Windows Azure Pack contributes towards that. We got to know about capabilities and service offerings Windows Azure Pack provides along with an overview and functionalities of its architectural pieces.

We understood the building blocks of Windows Azure Pack cloud solution offerings with required and optional components details.

We also covered the deployment models of Windows Azure Pack components and discussed several sample architectures for test and production ready cloud infrastructures. We discussed the role of System Center products in delivering IaaS services with Windows Azure Pack cloud.

In the next chapter we will setup the cloud fabric which will be utilized by Windows Azure Pack for cloud management and tenant workloads.

2
Getting the Cloud Fabric Ready

Fabric is one of the most important and crucial part of any traditional data center or cloud solution. Cloud fabric essentially includes, but is not limited to compute, network, storage, and hypervisors. Well designed and deployed fabric infrastructure is the way towards smooth operations of any cloud or traditional data center. In this chapter, we will cover all aspects of planning and deploying cloud fabric for our Windows Azure Pack-based cloud solution. It will help you understand fabric requirements and deployment practices for a WAP-based cloud solution. We will also include installation and configuration of major components such as SQL DB, SCVMM, SPF, and so on. We will be covering planning guidelines for both organizations' private cloud as well as for service providers' cloud. This fabric infrastructure will be used to deliver IaaS services in our WAP cloud.

We will cover the following topics in this chapter:

- Cloud fabric infrastructure planning
- Hyper-V deployment best practices
- Setting up virtual machines for cloud management fabric
- Planning and deploying SQL Server for cloud management DB
- Installing and configuring **System Center Virtual Machine Manager (SCVMM)**
- Planning and configuring cloud compute hypervisor layer with SCVMM
- Planning and configuring cloud network with SCVMM
- Planning and configuring cloud storage with SCVMM
- Planning and deploying System Center Service Provider Foundation

Cloud fabric infrastructure planning

Planning a cloud fabric infrastructure involves practice and involvement of business and technical decision makers. Cloud fabric has to be planned in such a manner that ensures that services are available for the business in a reliable and efficient manner. Current infrastructure assessment, forecasting and future resource planning, cloud service catalogues, along with strategic vision and financials are the key facts to consider while planning for cloud infrastructure. Let's have a look at the foundation and basic principles for planning a WAP-based cloud fabric infrastructure for delivering IaaS services.

Choosing the hardware

While choosing hardware for your cloud infrastructure, there is a long list of precautions to be taken care of. The following are some of these precautions:

- Follow the Microsoft certified hardware and software supportability and compatibility list. It is not a mandatory requirement as a WAP-based solution can be installed on almost any x86 based virtualization supported hardware, however, it is recommended to go with Microsoft certified hardware to avoid any glitches at a later stage in production. Getting support could be challenging sometimes while using non-supported hardware.
- While going for commodity hardware, check for compatibility and features of individual pieces of server such as NIC cards and so on.
- Use latest hardware supporting new features such as RDMA and other hardware offloading capabilities to take advantage of all capabilities of your hypervisor and cloud layer.
- Check for the scalability flexibilities, sufficient number of processors, memory, PCI slots can be helpful in increasing resources as and when required.
- Hardware failure happens, it's a good idea to check for hardware vendor support and SLAs in case of hardware failure part replacement and more.
- While comparing multiple hardware options for your cloud, include data center physical requirements (space, power, cooling, and so on) as one of the parameters, physical requirements usually become constraints in the real world.

While all preceding points are valid, today's data center technologies trends include software defined strategy. Using commodity hardware with best of breed software runs the data centers. It is fairly possible and good to use commodity hardware in your WAP cloud solution, though building the commodity hardware has to be planned very carefully.

For example, using non-supported disk drives leads to IOPS related performance issues, and the same goes for NIC speed and features. Follow the industry best practice guideline along with Microsoft Hyper-V compatibility and features support while designing commodity hardware.

Choosing a combination of both proprietary and commodity hardware is also not uncommon; organizations can choose to run critical workload on proprietary hardware to ensure performance and support, whereas use commodity hardware for less critical or test and development workloads.

Enabling commodity hardware options is helping small and midsized businesses (SMBs) to utilize enterprise class virtualization and cloud technologies for their IT needs in a limited budget. The same goes for the cloud service providers, small vendors with budget constraints can also get into the cloud services market using commodity hardware.

> The Microsoft supportability and compatibility list can be accessed at https://www.windowsservercatalog.com/.

Sizing the hardware

After choosing the hardware, the next thing which comes is sizing. Sizing for a cloud fabric for a private cloud and service provider cloud is an altogether different science with a common foundation of data center infrastructures sizing practice. Projecting future needs is the most important aspect while sizing any cloud hardware that is cloud should be able to handle hardware needs for the next X years, depending upon businesses strategy. Microsoft provides MAP toolkit (Microsoft Assessment and Planning) which can be utilized by organizations and service providers for accessing current infra and planning for target infrastructure.

Let's have a look at few major sizing best practices and procedures for both private clouds and service providers' cloud.

Sizing the cloud hardware for private cloud:

- Assess current workload requirements and plan hardware as per Hyper-V Server Virtualization sizing guidelines pertaining to virtual CPUs, memory, and more.
- Utilize MAP toolkit to assess current running workload in traditional computing.

- Perform server consolidation planning if P2V or hardware refresh is also planned.
- List down the expected new workload requirements (like new application planned in the near future and so on.)
- List down the expected resources increment in the coming X years in terms of compute, network, and storage.
- Analyze isolated infrastructure requirements if any (a few apps may need to be isolated from each other in terms of network/server due to compliance and more.)
- Factor for **Business Continuity and Disaster Recovery (BCDR)** planning.
- Bring all collected details together and size the hardware as per Hyper-V virtualization and IT infrastructure sizing guidelines.
- Add hardware requirements for cloud management infrastructure depending upon workload to be managed.

Sizing the cloud hardware for service provider cloud:

- Access customer needs and technological requirements in service providers' technology space
- Define technology offering and flexibilities in terms of infra and apps with their fabric requirements
- Set business goals like having X number of resources/customers in the coming X years as per service provider's strategy
- Bring all collected details and strategy decisions together and size the hardware as per Hyper-V virtualization and IT infrastructure sizing guidelines
- Add hardware requirements for cloud management infrastructure depending upon the workload to be managed as planned here.

> Sizing the hardware for cloud or any traditional data center is an altogether different detailed study and practice. The above mentioned guidelines are to help readers in understanding the base foundation for cloud fabric hardware planning. Refer to product and practice specific technical and economical guidelines for a production sizing.

Choosing hypervisor's deployment options and editions

Microsoft added a variety of all enterprise class virtualization features to Windows Server 2012. With Windows Server 2012 / R2 Hyper-V becomes the enterprise class proven virtualization platform supporting greater flexibility and scalability.

Microsoft Windows Server 2012 R2 Hyper-V provides an enterprise class virtualization platform for WAP-based cloud solution. Hyper-V can be deployed in three ways:

- Windows Server 2012 R2 Server with GUI with Hyper-V role
- Windows Server 2012 R2 Server Core with Hyper-V role
- Hyper-V Server 2012 R2 (free)

The **Server with GUI** option installs and configures all user interface options, such as server manager, desktop experience, and so on. It installs Windows Server also in the same traditional manner with all features and functionality available.

The **Server Core** version is a stripped down version of full installation, in this no GUI components gets installed. It has to be managed via a command line, PowerShell or remote server management options. Benefits of deploying the Server Core version includes but is not limited to less resource consumption, less disk footprint, better security by reducing attack surface of eliminated components in comparison to the Server with GUI option, and so on.

It is recommended to deploy Server Core in a cloud infrastructure for hypervisor's as these servers shall be used for running VMs only. This can take advantage of server core deployment benefits in large infrastructures.

With Windows Server 2012 and R2, it is possible to switch between full editions and core edition after deployment. Administrators can choose to install the Server with GUI initially and switch to the core version post configuration for easy deployment.

Windows Server editions

There are multiple editions of Windows Server such as Essentials, Foundation, and so on, but majorly for any virtualization needs below two editions are used:

- Windows Server Standard edition
- Windows Server Data center edition

Both Standard and Data center editions of Windows Server is licensed on processor basis, one license per two processors. Both Standard and Data center editions provide the same set of features, the difference lies in the virtualization rights. Standard edition allows you to run two virtual machines with Windows Server OS, in the case of Data center edition the number goes unlimited. Taking a scenario Windows Server 2012 R2 Standard edition licensed hypervisor hosts allows you to create two virtual machines with Windows Server 2012/R2 Standard Guest OS without purchasing any additional licensing. Licensing downgrade rights apply for running VM with Windows Server 2008 R2 OS.

Choosing the right edition for your cloud

Choosing the right edition depends upon the type and number of operating systems in the cloud infrastructure. It's recommended to go with the Data center edition if virtualized workload incudes Windows as Guest OS majorly. Standard edition can be helpful and budgetary while the number of virtual machines with Windows OS isn't high.

As a best possible solution, in a large infrastructure combination of both Standard and Data center editions can be utilized depending on the OS of virtualized workload.

While for organizations it will depend on workload nature if it is Windows or non-Windows to choose the right edition, server providers can use a combination of both Data center/Standard edition to service customers' requests for both Windows and non-Windows infra requirements.

> Refer to the Windows Server 2012 product and edition comparison guide on http://www.microsoft.com/ for detailed comparison between various Windows editions.

Free Microsoft Hyper-V Server 2012 R2

Microsoft Hyper-V Server 2012 R2 (also known as Standalone Hyper-V) is a free (yes, completely free) edition of Microsoft's proprietary hypervisor. It is a stripped down version of Windows Server operating system comprising only hypervisor and virtualization capabilities, Windows Server drivers, and supporting components such as cluster capabilities. Free Hyper-V version doesn't include any additional Windows feature apart from hypervisor, making it available with less footprint, management burden, and attack surface.

Free Hyper-V Server 2012 R2 provides free access to Hyper-V virtualization capabilities only, virtual machine guest OS licensing has to be separately considered. If you are running Windows Server OS inside a virtual machine, it's a good idea to use Standard or Data center edition depending upon the count of Windows VMs. This edition can be helpful in scenarios where Guest OS inside VMs wouldn't be Windows.

A major use case of free Hyper-V Server is to be utilized by organizations or service providers for hosting non-Windows workloads.

> Ensure to check for the supportability of the free Hyper-V version while extending WAP cloud solution with custom offerings or partner provided solutions.

Microsoft Hyper-V is the best choice for a WAP-based cloud solution, though there are integration possibilities with other hypervisor's vendors such as VMware and Citrix. See product specific guidelines to choose the edition and deployment model along with the supportability matrix of features while choosing VMware or Citrix.

Choosing the system center deployment options and edition

Microsoft System Center 2012 R2 is the core management component for delivering cloud services in a WAP-based cloud solution. System Center products can be deployed in multiple ways such as:

- Physical or virtual machines
- Standalone or high availability mode (product dependent)

System Center components requires Windows Server as an operating system to run. It can be in a virtual machine or a physical server. Since we virtualize every piece of our cloud management and tenant workload, it doesn't make sense to keep system center components on physical servers unless there is some specific requirement or exception.

For both organizations and service providers, it is recommended to deploy system center components inside virtual machines to take the advantage of hypervisor level HA and other capabilities.

Along with hypervisor HA, deploying servers in Guest OS or app level HA adds additional benefits such as application level failure detection and load balancing.

System Center products can be deployed in OS/app level cluster or redundant mode.

Organizations or service providers can choose a combination of standalone or HA mode products depending upon their availability business and technical requirements.

System Center editions

System Center is available as a suite in two editions. When you buy a System Center suite you are entitled to use all components (except SCCM) depending upon licensing.

The two editions of the System Center suites are as follows:

- System Center Standard edition
- System Center Data center edition

Licensing is required only for a number of endpoints being managed by system center components. There is no licensing required for running the system center components. Licensing is available in a similar fashion with Windows Server that is a processor-based licensing (two products per license). There is no difference in terms of features with Standard and Data center editions; the difference lies in the number of virtual instances you can manage with Standard and Data center editions. With Standard edition, two **OSEs** (**Operating System Environments**) can be managed by the System Center and is unlimited in the case of Data center edition. Microsoft licensing policy may change from time to time and depending upon agreements such as EA/SA and so on. It is recommended to touch base with Microsoft for planning licenses and editions.

> Refer the *How to buy System Center 2012 R2* page on Microsoft's official website to know more on licensing and comparisons.

Choosing the right edition for System Center for organizations and service providers directly corresponds to the edition chosen for Windows Server. It's good to go with System Center Data center edition to manage Windows Server Data center edition and vice versa to enable a consistent feature set and flexibilities.

> The licensing details given are up to the date of writing this chapter; licensing policies may change in future, and it is advised to consult while planning for licensing and editions.

Cloud management infra and tenant workload infrastructure

A cloud infrastructure is usually segregated in two categories, cloud management and tenant workload. Let's have a look at these two:

- **Cloud Management Infrastructure**: Management infrastructure or management cluster is used to host virtual machines for cloud management components such as Windows Azure Pack server and system center components. It is recommended to have a separate hypervisor cluster dedicatedly for hosting cloud management workload. The sizing of the management cluster would depend upon the number of services offered and the size of tenant workload to be managed.

- **Tenant Workload Infrastructure**: Tenant workload infrastructure is used for hosting customers' cloud resources such as virtual machines and databases. Tenant workload infrastructure has to be designed keeping available cloud services, QoS and SLAs in mind.

Core MS infrastructure services planning

Microsoft's WAP-based cloud solution uses core Microsoft core infrastructure services such as Active Directory, DNS, DHCP, and so on for foundation operations such as authentication and more. These core infrastructure services have to be deployed with product specific guidelines and industry best practices to ensure availability and efficiency . Let's have a look at the core services and the deployment best practices:

- **Active Directory**: Microsoft AD is the most critical component of most of MS infrastructure solutions including WAP cloud solution. AD is used for authentication, authorization along with other capabilities in WAP cloud. AD deployment can be planned with redundancy (deploying additional domain controllers) and security best practices. Regular backup and disaster recovery should be planned for Active Directory infrastructure.

- **DNS**: Usually co-located with AD, DNS provides name resolution for the entire cloud. DNS failure may cause entire cloud failure, hence it needs to be planned to ensure every time availability and security from attacks. Regular backup and DR should be planned.

- **NTP**: Another crucial component of any cloud or any IT solution, NTP ensures time synchronization among all cloud resources. Time lag may cause the entire cloud solution to fail as well as incorrect billing. The NTP device must be highly available as well as accurate. All components should be configured to use the same NTP device. Domain joined Windows operating systems utilize the domain controller (PDC role) for time synchronization.

> Follow Microsoft's guidelines while virtualizing domain controllers holding NTP role. See https://technet.microsoft.com/en-us/library/virtual_active_directory_domain_controller_virtualization_hyperv%28v=ws.10%29.aspx to know more.

- **DHCP**: Dynamic Host Configuration Protocol can be utilized for Dynamic IP address allocation and management. The deployment of DHCP should be highly available and efficient for serving cloud IP address requirements.
- **Other infrastructure supporting services (PXE Boot server, IPAM and so on)**: Depending upon deployment and use cases other MS services such as PXE boot and deployment server for bare metal provisioning or network boot, WSUS or SCCM for patch management, IPAM for IP address management, jump servers for centralized access, security products should be deployed in an efficient and highly available manner as applicable.

> Planning and deployment options for cloud network and storage shall be discussed in the coming topics in this chapter.

Hyper-V deployment best practices

Hypervisor is the core foundation of WAP-based cloud infrastructure as every virtual machine including management workload VMs such as WAP admin/tenant portal VM, SCVMM, SPF will be running inside a VM on Hyper-V host only. Let's have a look at a few of the deployment best practices of Hyper-V Server.

It is recommended to maintain symmetry in terms of configuration, best practices applied across all Hyper-V hosts. SCVMM and AD group policies can be used to configure and manage Hyper-V configurations and policies across all the hosts.

Centralized management is the key element in every cloud solution.

Hyper-V installation best practices

Though Windows Server 2012 R2 Hyper-V installation is quite straightforward. It's recommended to follow best practices of Hyper-V installation for a smooth and stable virtualized infrastructure.

Best practices for hypervisor installation are as follows:

- **Supported hardware and latest hardware firmware**: It is recommended to use supported hardware for proven performance and stability. Always ensure to update the firmware of the server's hardware or chassis or blades as applicable.
- **Install OS using hardware vendor provided tools**: Major server hardware vendors provide their proprietary tools for installing operating system such as HP intelligent provisioning. This ensures that the hypervisor is deployed with proper hardware-specific drivers and integration tools.
- **Choose correct deployment option**: In a cloud infrastructure, it is recommended to use the Server Core version to utilize the benefits of the Server Core deployment, such as less disk footprint and attack surface, which reduces management and updates burden. If you deploy the Server with GUI, it is advised to remove all unnecessary components.
- **Latest device drivers**: Use the latest device drivers for hardware devices regardless of the proprietary and commodity hardware.
- **Windows updates**: Ensure to update the hypervisor with the latest patches and service packs that are available. It is recommended to have patch management solutions deployed for ensuring the continuous deployment of the latest hot fixes.
- **Page file**: Hyper-V server automatically manages page file size as per the physical memory that is installed in the system. It should be set to **System Managed**.
- **Windows firewall**: Configure Windows firewall rules as per environmental requirements. An organization may choose to disable the firewall if the port level access is being managed by network firewalls.
- **Hypervisor hardening and VA**: Apply standard security policies as per the organization's defined standard. Perform necessary vulnerability assessments and remediation as per the organization's policies.
- **Naming convention and domain**: Ensure to follow the proper hostname convention and join the domain wherever applicable. For cluster nodes, it is required to join hosts to the domain.

Hyper-V networking best practices

Best practices for Hyper-V networking are as follows:

- **Separate network for Hyper-V and VM network traffic**: A separate physical and logical network should be considered for management traffic such as host management and live migration, and another for virtual machine traffic as per the VM network zone such as internal, DMZ, and so on.
- **Configure redundancy at physical network path**: Configure at least two NIC adaptors connecting to two different network switch in each network team. Ensure not to have any single point of failure.
- **Configure teaming and load balancing policies**: Windows Server 2012 / R2 provides multiple load balancing policies(Hyper-V port, address hash, dynamic balancing, and so on) which provides maximum performance and reliability for Hyper-V network. Ensure to configure proper NIC teaming load balancing policies.
- **Separate network for IP storage traffic**: It is recommended to use a separate physical and logical network for IP based storage traffic such as iSCSI, SMB, and so on.
- **Implement network QoS**: Use the Hyper-V network **Quality of Service (QoS)** feature to ensure that no single VM becomes the network bandwidth constraints for other VMs. It becomes important to implement QOD in a WAP-based cloud solution to ensure providing request network bandwidth to tenants' virtual machines as per their plan and subscription.
- **Monitor network usage**: Monitor Hyper-V network virtualization continuously to plan to get insight of network usage and plan for future scalability.
- **Use SDN (Software Defined Networking)**: This is not a Hyper-V networking best practice, but looking at cloud solution using SDN, aka network virtualization, can enable automated provisioning, management and flexibilities for cloud networking.

Hyper-V storage deployment best practices

Best practices for Hyper-V storage deployment are as follows:

- **Ensure redundancy for storage path**: Use multipath IO for storage paths. Eliminate any single point of failure at server port, storage port, or SAN switch and so on. Configure multipathing policies as per SAN provider guidelines for reliability and efficiency.

- **Using vhdx**: New virtual disk file format that is vhdx was introduced with Windows Server 2012. VHD provides multiple benefits over older format VHD in terms of performance and reliability. Use vhdx instead of vhd unless exceptionally required.
- **Size volumes and CSV properly**: Sizing workload VMs is important in terms of capacity and IOPS. Oversized volumes may cause performance and outage issues.
- **Implement storage QoS**: Use Hyper-V storage quality of service feature to ensure that no single VM becomes the storage performance constraints for other VMs with respect to IOPS. It is a must for a WAP-based cloud solution to ensure providing requested storage IOPS to tenants' virtual machines as per their plan and subscription.
- **Monitor storage usage**: Monitor Hyper-V storage continuously for capacity and performance to plan to get insight of network usage and plan for future scalability.
- **Use SDS/SMI-S/SMP integrations**: This is not a Hyper-V storage best practice, but from a cloud prospective it is recommended to use SDS (Software Defined Storage), SMI-S provider array integration for better provisioning, management and automation for cloud storage.

Hyper-V virtual machine deployment best practices

Best practices for Hyper-V virtual machine deployment are as follows:

- **Properly sizing of VM Compute**: A greater number of virtual CPUs doesn't guarantee more performance, assign CPUs to VMs as per actual application requirements. The same goes for memory. Ensure not to oversize or undersize virtual machines.
- **Use Generation-2 VM**: Generation 2 VMs provide multiple features over Generation-1 VMs such as UEFI boot, synthetic hardware, faster installation and booting time and more. It is recommended to use Generation-2 VMs unless specifically required.
- **Use dynamic memory**: It is recommended to use dynamic memory to make the most out of physical RAM available in your server. Using dynamic memory in a large cloud environment can help in increasing host density. It is recommended to plan carefully while using dynamic memory to avoid any performance hit on any of the virtual machines or hosts.

- **Use non-uniform memory access (NUMA) if supported**: NUMA helps virtual machines having multiple virtual CPUs assigned to scale and perform better by facilitating it to use local cache and memory bus of the CPU executing its instruction. NUMA is dependent upon hardware architecture.
- **Remove unused virtual hardware**: It's recommended to use unused virtual hardware such as a floppy drive and so on.
- **Use proper integration services**: Integration service are installed inside guest operating systems to make those virtualization aware and avail features such as graceful shutdown from Hyper-V manager, time sync, data exchange and so on. All the latest Windows operating systems by default include integration service, for non-Windows OS it may be required to manually install integration services.
- **Monitor virtual machine usage**: Monitor VM usage continuously for compute and take necessary corrective action for oversized and undersized virtual machines.

Hyper-V cluster and mobility deployment best practices

Best practices for Hyper-V cluster and mobility deployment are as follows:

- **Cluster Validation Report**: Microsoft Windows' failover cluster provides features to examine the nodes with respect to Hyper-V configuration, inventory, network, storage and system configuration before deploying a cluster. Any error or warning produced by validation check should be remediated with the necessary corrective actions. Successfully validated cluster is the key to smooth Hyper-V HA functionalities.
- **Use SCVMM to deploy and manage highly available virtual machines**: This isn't particularly related to Hyper-V cluster best practice, but for a cloud solution it is recommended to deploy and manage Hyper-V cluster and mobility via SCVMM.
- **Use separate network for live migration**: It is recommended to use separate physical and logical network live migration traffic for reliability and performance.
- **Cluster Aware Updating**: It is recommended to use CAU for patching and upgrading cluster nodes. With this organizations and service providers can ensure no outages to end customers during the patching of hypervisors. WSUS can be integrated with VMM to automate updates to Hyper-V hosts.

Setting up virtual machines for cloud management fabric

Enough of planning and best practices, it is time to get things in action. Let us setup virtual machines to host our cloud infrastructure. These VMs shall host cloud management infrastructure and be hosted on the cloud management cluster.

Create a user in Active Directory for joining these servers into the Active Directory domain.

> Add one redundant VM for each type of VM below, except WAP server (see *Chapter 1, Know Windows Azure Pack and Its Architecture*, for WAP HA), to provide highly available fabric. See product specific guidelines for configuring HA for respective components.

Sr. Num	VM Name	Compute Configuration	Purpose of VM
1	WAPMGT-SQLDB-01	4 CPU, 12 GB RAM	Host SQL databases for entire WAP solution database needs
2	WAPMGTSCVMM-01*	4 CPU, 12 GB RAM	System Center Virtual Machine Manager
3	WAPMGT-SCSPF-01	2 CPU, 8GB RAM	Service Provider Foundation
4	WAPMGT-SCSMA-01	2 CPU, 8 GB RAM	Service Management Automation
5	WAPMGT-ACRDG-01	2 CPU, 8 GB RAM	Remote Desktop Gateway Server for providing Azure Console Connect
6	WAPMGT-WAPSR-01	2 CPU, 8 GB RAM	Windows Azure Pack (Express Installation Model)

> These VM configuration used in this book is only for evaluation purpose, follow guidelines discussed in *Chapter 1, Know Windows Azure Pack and Its Architecture* and this chapter along with product specific documentation for production deployment.

All VMs mentioned above shall be configured with the following common settings:

- 127 GB disk (dynamic expanding disk)
- Windows Server 2012 R2 DC/STD edition operating system
- Single NIC card connected to Hyper-V virtual switch (external)
- Dynamic memory not being used
- All integration services available
- Highly available in a Hyper-V cluster (recommended, not mandatory)

The post VM deployment steps are as follows:

- Active Windows operating system
- Assign static IPv4 address
- Assign hostname as per naming convention
- Join the server to domain
- Turn off Windows firewall or create firewall rules as applicable

Planning and deploying SQL Server for cloud management DB

All components of Windows Azure Pack and system center uses SQL Server database to store its configuration, run time data, historical usage data etc. Failure of the database is directly proportional to the failure of respective components.

Choosing the database server version and deployment model

In a bare minimum deployment, this SQL Server for management databases shall be used by the following components:

- Windows Azure Pack components
- SCVMM
- SPF
- SMA

While choosing the database version a deployment model, supportability and compatibility has to be aligned with respect to each of the components mentioned previously.

Windows Azure Pack supports the following MS SQL Server versions for managing databases:

- MS SQL Server 2008 Service Pack 3
- MS SQL Server 2008 R2 Service Pack 2
- MS SQL Server 2012 Service Pack 1
- MS SQL Server 2012 Service Pack 2
- MS SQL Server 2014

System Center 2012 R2 has different SQL Server version support differentiating upon components. Taking the common and latest, MS SQL 2012 SP1 is the supported SQL version for Windows Azure Pack and all System Center products, MS SQL 2012 SP2 and MS SQL 2014 is supported for WAP components and all System Center 2012 R2 components except app controller. Organizations or cloud providers can choose between SQL 2012 SP1, SQL 2012 SP2 and SQL 2014 depending upon the components installed.

> SQL Support matrix for System Center 2012 R2 can be accessed at https://technet.microsoft.com/en-us/library/dn281933.aspx

The deployment model in SQL Server can be deployed in multiple ways with respect to placement, failover, and so on. WAP management database deployment is supported in following ways:

- Standalone SQL Server deployment
- SQL Server failover cluster
- SQL Server AlwaysOn availability groups

Choosing the right deployment model for your cloud management databases depends upon deployment strategy. Standalone deployment works fine but becomes a single point of failure. Failure in the management database will cause failure of all cloud management components functionalities.

SQL Cluster (active/passive) and SQL AlwaysOn availability group can be used to add redundancy for management databases eliminating any single point of failure.

While both options provide redundancy for SQL Server, AlwaysOn adds greater flexibility and reliability by enabling clusters without any shared storage and protection at database level, which is at instance level in case of SQL Cluster.

More on SQL Cluster versus SQL can be found at https://msdn.microsoft.com/en-us/library/ff929171.aspx.

> SQL cluster functionalities is available in MS SQL Standard edition where AlwaysOn requires Enterprise edition license.

While installing SQL for management databases, the following features are required to be installed. Default collation will work when deploying for English language. See product specific guidelines for other languages:

- Common features:
    - Database engine
    - Management tools

- Product specific features:
    - Full text search (for SC operations Manager and Service Manager)
    - Reporting services (for SC operations Manager and Service Manager)
    - Analysis services (For SC Service Manager)

Additional consideration while deploying SQL Server for WAP and System Center 2012 R2 include:

- Deploy additional SQL Server/instances in a large production setup to avoid any performance issues.
- Reporting services instances cannot be shared between components.
- Configure pre-size and automatically grow along with monitoring for efficient and undisrupted management databases.
- SQL authentication needs to be enabled on the SQL Server before installing Windows Azure Pack components. If Windows authentication is planned for configuration, the current user has to be added as an administrator on the SQL Server.
- SQL AlwaysOn availability groups functionality is not supported for a named instance for System Center Service Manager Database, it is supported for default server instance only.

> SQL Express Edition can be used WAP in Express deployment. For WAP distributed deployment and system center components Standard edition is the minimum edition supported. Choose SQL edition depending upon the features and HA model discussed above.

Installing and configuring SQL Server 2012 SP2

For the purpose of evaluation in this book, we shall be using SQL Server 2012 SP2 standalone installation as the DB server. This database server shall be used by all WAP and system center components.

- Installation prerequisite:
    - A set of hardware and software prerequisite has to be met before deploying SQL Server
- Software requirements:

    Install the following components on SQL Server VM before installing SQL Server:
    - .NET 3.5 SP1 Framework
    - Windows PowerShell (installed by default)
    - Network protocol and libraries (like shared memory, named pipe, TCP IP — available by default)
- Active Directory accounts requirements:
    - Create a user account in AD for SQL Server administration and services login account

Account Name	Purpose	Permissions
Sqldbadmin	SQL DB administrator user	Member of local administrator group on SVMM + DB admin
Sqldb-svc	Service account for SQL Server Service	Member of local administrator group on SVMM + DB admin

- Add created user accounts in the local administrator's group on SQL Server Windows OS.

Installation procedure

The following is the installation procedure to be followed:

1. Download MS SQL Server 2012 SP1 installation media and mount on SQL VM.
2. Execute the setup file from installation media and select **Standalone installation**.

Getting the Cloud Fabric Ready

3. SQL setup will start a valid validation check for installing the SQL Server setup support file. All tests must report green to green to proceed further.
4. Enter the product key (embedded in licensed media) or select evaluation mode installation option as applicable.
5. Accept the license terms and proceed further to install setup files.
6. Verify the setup support rules result. All results must pass successfully to proceed further.
7. Select **SQL Server Feature Installation** on the **Setup Role** page.

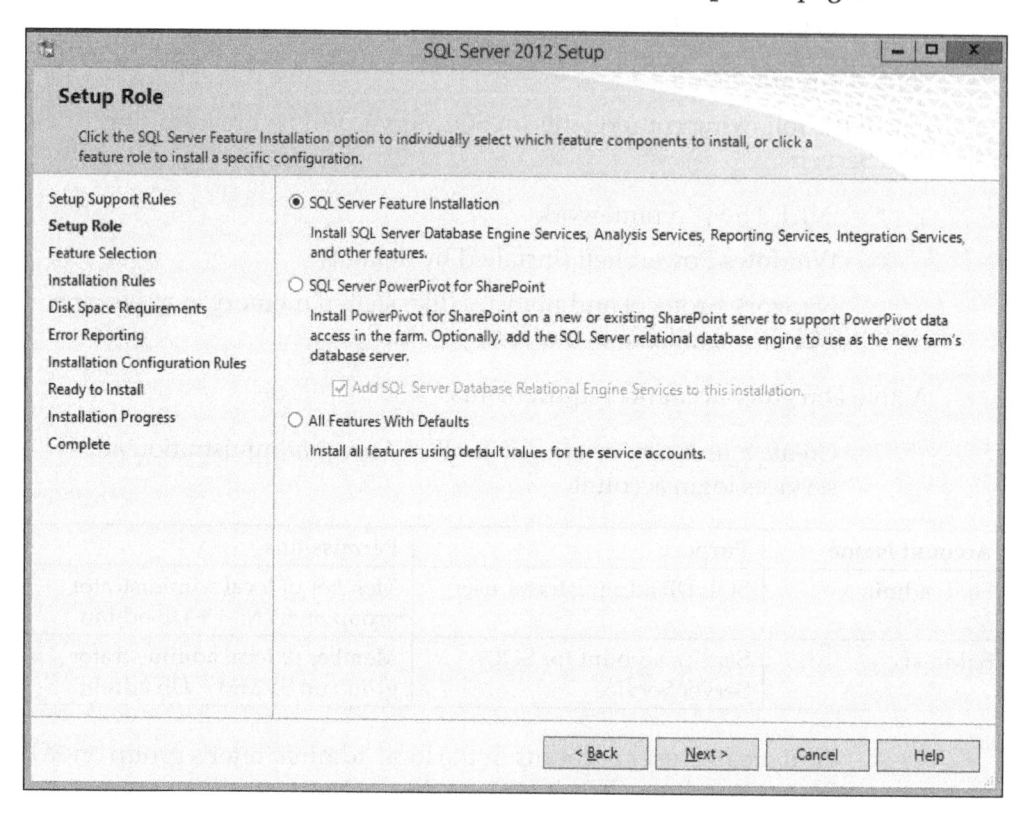

![SQL Server 2012 Setup - Setup Role screen showing SQL Server Feature Installation option selected]

8. Select **Database Engine Services**, **Client Tools Connectivity** and **Management Tools - Basic** on the **Features** page (select features as per product specific requirements discussed in the last topic).

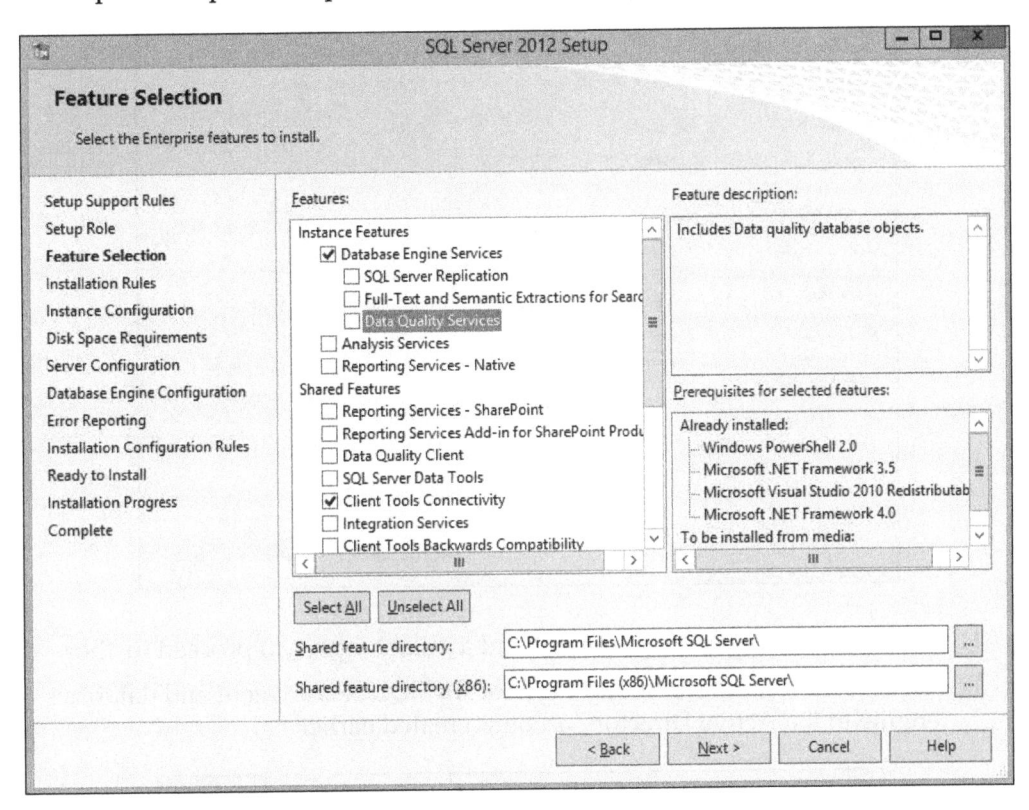

9. Verify the installation rules status, all rules must pass successfully in order to proceed further.

10. Change the instance name to a name of your choice. For the purpose of evaluation we are using the **Default instance**.

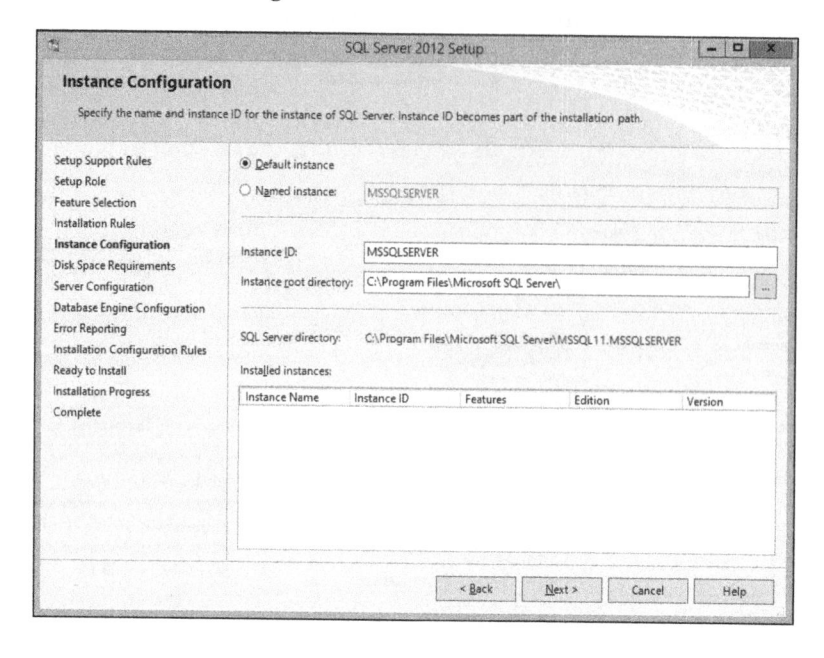

11. Verify the disk space requirement and available space to proceed further.
12. Change the default service account for the SQL Server agent and database engine to the Active Directory account created earlier.

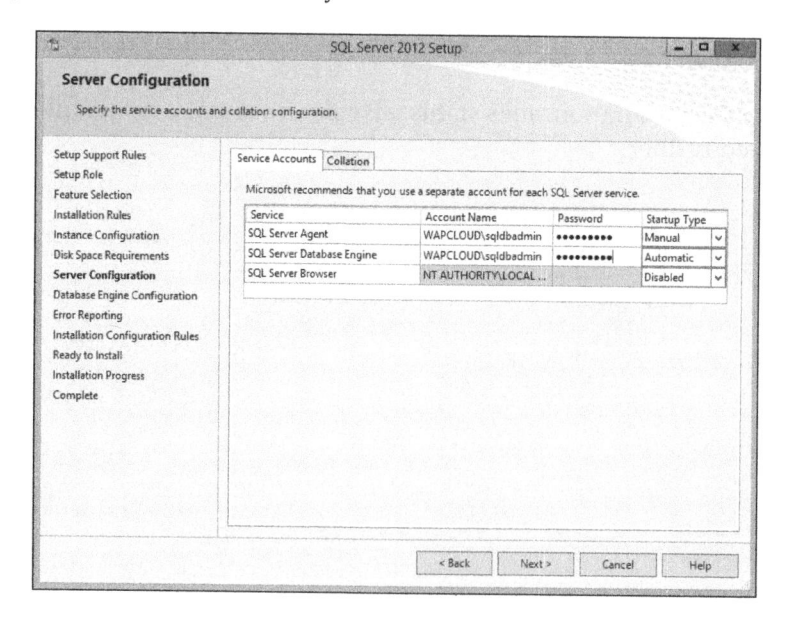

13. Select **Mixed Mode** authentication on the **Database Engine Configuration** page. Provide "sa" as the password and add the current logged in user (SQLDBADMIN) into SQL administrators. Change the data directories location to different drives if applicable.

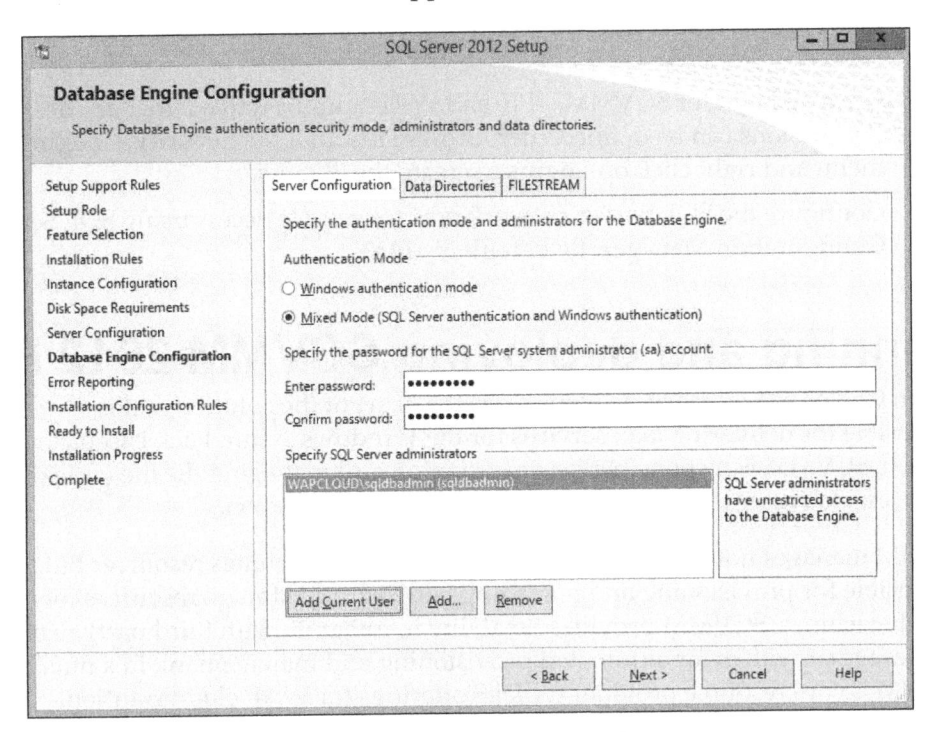

14. Choose the error reporting option if you wish to participate in error reporting to Microsoft.
15. Verify the installation configuration rule status. Each rule must pass successfully to proceed further.
16. Verify the installation option selected summary.
17. SQL Setup will start installing SQL DB Server as per the inputs provided.
18. Close the wizard once installation finishes successfully, review setup logs in case of any errors.

Post installation tasks

Configure the following tasks after successfully installing SQL Server 2012 SP1:

1. Login into SQL Server using SQL Management Studio and verify successful installation. Also verify whether the system databases such as `master`, `tempdb` are created.
2. Create a login for SCVMM, SPF, and WAP admin Active Directory user. Permissions can be defined later. Browse through the **Security** | **Logins** menu and right click on **Logins** to create the SQL user.
3. Configure the SQL Server network port for remote access using SQL Server Configuration Manager. By default it's **1433**.

Planning and deploying SCVMM 2012 R2

System Center virtual machine manager is the heart of the solution and is responsible for delivering IaaS services for the Windows Azure Pack based cloud solution. SCVMM is responsible for provisioning and managing the life cycle of IaaS resources such as virtual machines, virtual networks and so on.

SCVMM manages not only the hypervisor and virtual machines resources but also is responsible for provisioning and managing network and storage resources for cloud virtual machines. SCVMM provides flexibility to integrate with third party network and storage providers for automated provisioning and management. In a nutshell, SCVMM is core resource provider for IaaS offerings for WAP cloud solution.

SCVMM comes as a part of system center suite. WAP communicates with SCVMM for IaaS services via **SPF** (**Service Provider Foundation**). In this section we will cover VMM architecture and deployment models along with installation walkthrough.

The VMM architecture and deployment model

VMM server is made up of multiple components which can be deployed together on a single server or on a different server in a distributed fashion to achieve scalability and availability. VMM requires a SQL Server database to store all configurations and run time data. Components of overall VMM working solutions are as follows:

- **VMM Management Server**: This server is responsible for the execution of all tasks SCVMM is participating in. It installs System Center Virtual Machine management services which communicates with all other system center VMM and non-system center components for provisioning and controlling the fabric. This can be protected from SPOF by deploying in HA mode on the top of Microsoft Failover Cluster.

- **VMM Management Console**: Management console is used by administrators for connecting to VMM management services and performing administrative tasks. It gets installed on VMM management server by default, you can also install it in your management endpoints for SCVMM administration. .
- **VMM Database**: VMM database is a Microsoft SQL Server provided database which stores VMM configuration such as hosts, networks, virtual machine, and so on, along with run time data. VMM is highly dependent on this database to function, it is highly recommended to protect this database using SQL HA techniques in production deployment.
- **VMM library and library server**: VMM library stores all resources that are used to deploy VMs or services. VMM library typically includes VHDs, templates, ISO files, network and storage profiles and so on. VMM library is stored in a file share hosted on a library server.
- **VMM Agent**: VMM agent is not a server component, it facilitates communication between hypervisor and VMM. VMM agent gets installed on hypervisor while adding hosts in VMM. It can also be manually installed in case of any isolated environmental restrictions.

All components here except VMM database (provided by SQL) are available in SCVMM 2012 R2 installation media.

VMM deployment models

SCVMM works on a distributed architecture which enables it to provide multiple flexible deployment options. Organizations can choose to increase components such as management server or library server for scalability needs. Majorly, SCVMM can be deployed in three ways:

- **Standalone deployment**: In standalone deployment all server components of VMM (VMM management server, VMM console, VMM library server and VMM SQL database) are installed on a single server. This deployment model facilitates a minimum deployment footprint and is suitable for test and non-production architectures. It doesn't provide any redundancy for any of the components.
- **Distributed deployment**: In a distributed deployment, organizations can choose to install a management server, library server and database server of three or more different servers to achieve availability and scalability. VMM database can be protected using SQL high availability techniques

- **SCVMM in high availability mode**: SCVMM supports deployment in cluster mode using Windows Failover Cluster. Virtual machine management server can be protected using HA deployment mode, along with protected DB using SQL HA techniques. This is recommended for production deployment eliminating any single point of failure.

Installing System Center Virtual Machine Manager 2012 R2

For the purpose of evaluation in this book, we shall be deploying VMM Management Server, VMM Console and VMM Library Server and share on a single machine. Cloud Management SQL database server shall be utilized for hosting VMM database.

Installation prerequisites

Multiple Active Directory accounts with specific permission are required for SCVMM to work. Let's have a look at the recommended accounts and permissions for SCVMM usage.

AD user account and group for SCVMM:

Account Name	Purpose	Permissions
Scvmmadmin	SCVMM admin user for administrative tasks	Member of local administrator group on SVMM + DB Admin
Scvmmsvc	Service account for SCVMM service	Member of local administrator group on SVMM + DB Admin
Scvmm-runasadmin	Run as account for SCVMM operation	Admin permissions on SCVMM and other resources being managed such as Hyper-V hosts.
Scvmm-admins	Security group for administrators	Admin permissions on SCVMM

Add SCVMM admin and service account as a part of "scvmm-admin" security group

Software prerequisite

VMM takes care of installing most of the software prerequisites except Windows Access and development kit (Windows ADK) and SQL database related tools. Install the following components as a part of the software prerequisite for deploying System Center Virtual Machine Manager 2012 R2:

- Features from Windows assessment and development toolkit:
    - Deployment tools
    - Windows pre-installation environment (Windows PE)
- SQL Server connectivity tools:
    - SQL Server 2012 command line utilities
    - Microsoft SQL Server native client

Apart from installing, VMM has the following software components requirements which the setup takes care of during installation:

- Windows Remote Management (WinRM 2.0) Service
- Microsoft .NET framework 4 or 4.5
- Windows PowerShell 2.0

> Windows ADK can be download from https://www.microsoft.com/en-in/download/details.aspx?id=39982, SQL connectivity tools can be downloaded from http://www.microsoft.com/en-in/download/details.aspx?id=29065. These are also available in SQL Server 2012 installation media.

Installation procedure

For evaluation purposes, we shall be deploying VMM Management Server, VMM console and library server on a single machine.

1. Download MS System Center 2012 R2 Virtual Machine Management installation media and mount on SCVMM VM.

Getting the Cloud Fabric Ready

2. Execute the setup file from installation media and click **Install**.

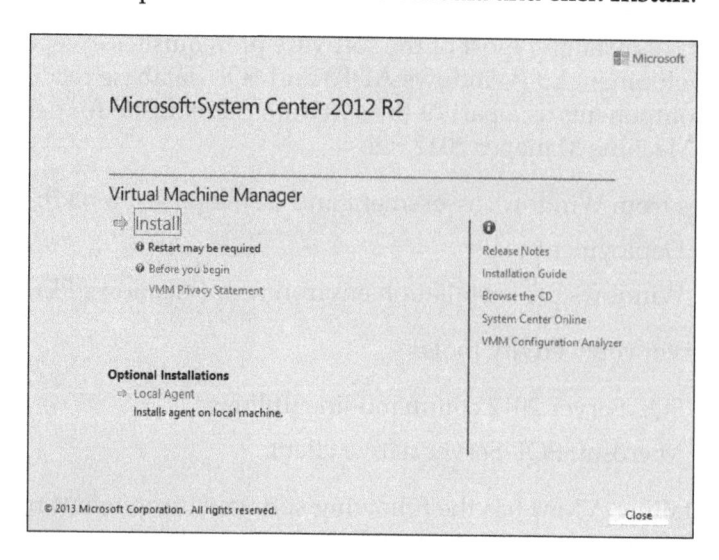

3. Select the **VMM Management Server** feature to install, it will automatically select **VMM console** as well.

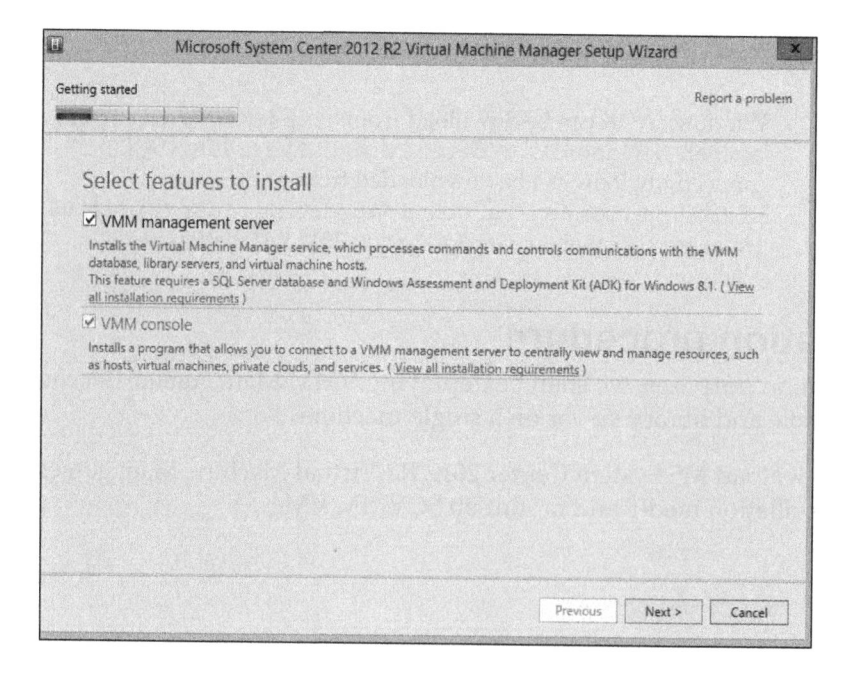

4. Enter the name and organization details along with the product key provided by Microsoft for your system center licenses. VMM will be installed in evaluation mode if no product key is specified. You can choose to provide the product key at a later stage as well, post installation.

5. Accept the evaluation/product license terms and proceed further.

6. Choose **Yes** or **No** to participate in the **Customer Experience Improvement Program**.

7. Turn on or off for Microsoft Update, with turning it on you can update VMM using automatic updates.

8. Specify the SCVMM installation location, by default it is in `C:\Program Files\Microsoft System Center 2012 R2\Virtual Machine Manager`.

9. Clicking **Next** will start the prerequisite check and will return with an error or warning if any of the prerequisites defined in the previous section aren't completed. Complete any pending prerequisites if any and proceed further.

10. Provide the database configuration on this page. You can choose to use existing DB created in SQL instance for VMM or may choose to create a new database. Change the SQL port if changed in SQL post-installation tasks.

11. Verify Database configuration and proceed further.

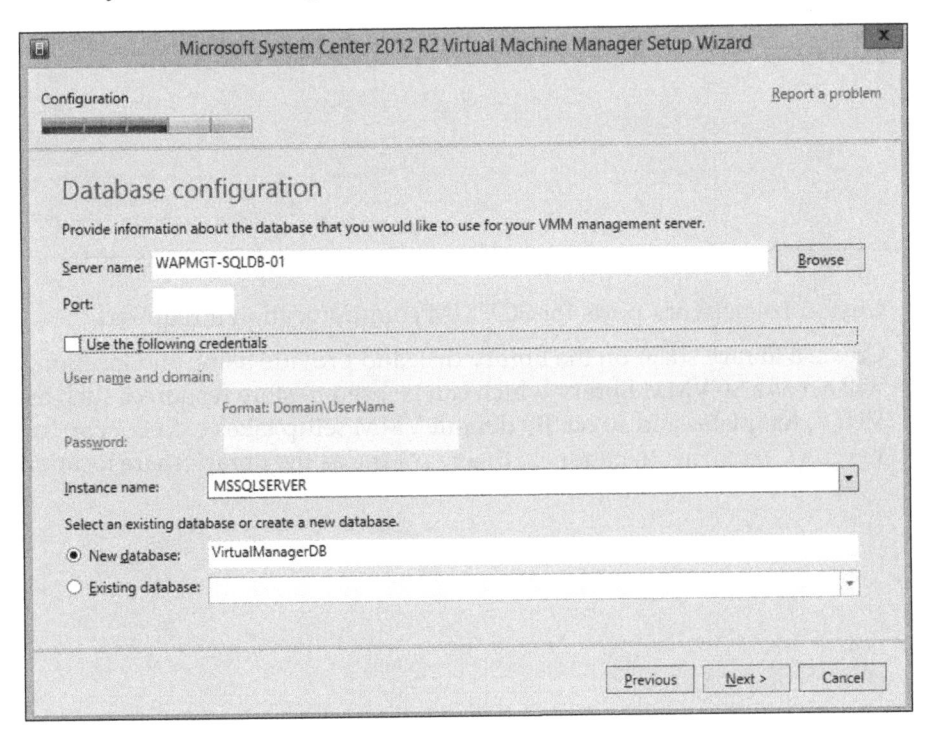

12. Configure the service account for SCVMM services login. For SCVMM in HA mode, this has to be a domain account. Provide the location to store the Distributed Encryption key location in AD if deploying in HA mode. More on deployment in HA mode is covered in the next section.

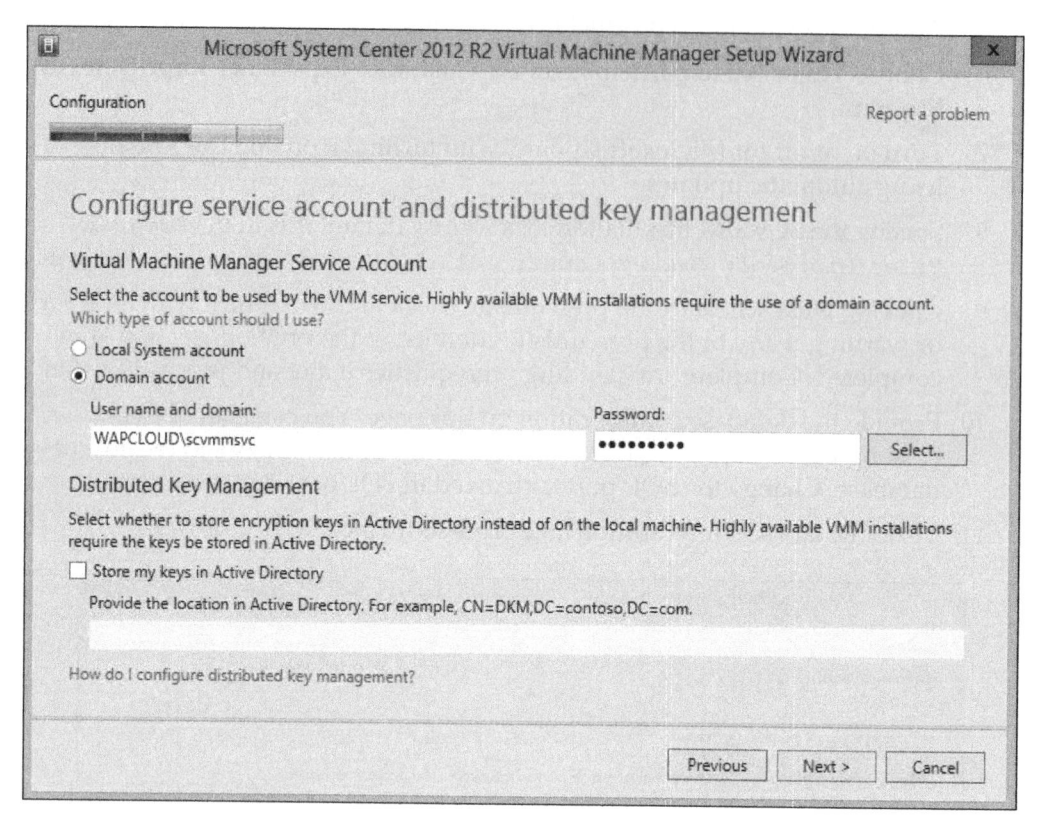

13. Customize network ports for SCVMM communication if required.
14. Create a library share on the library disk and provide name and location. This will act as a SCVMM library which can be used to store resources such as VHDs, templates and so on. By default VMM setup takes `C:\Program Data\Virtual Machine Manager Library Files` as the library share location.

Chapter 2

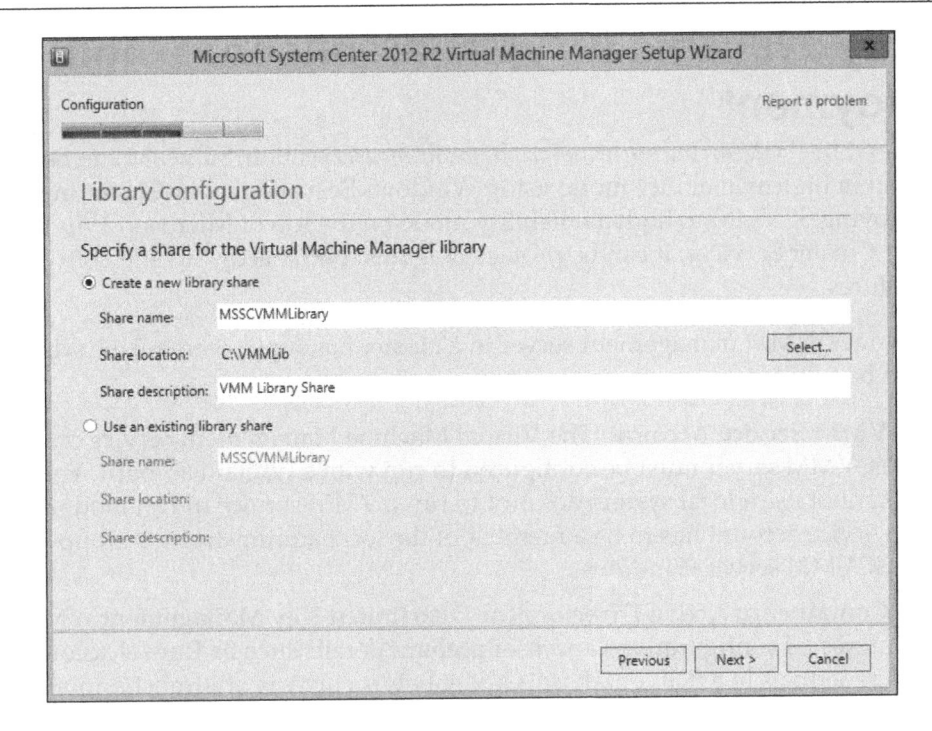

Library configuration

Specify a share for the Virtual Machine Manager library

- Create a new library share
  - Share name: MSSCVMMLibrary
  - Share location: C:\VMMLib
  - Share description: VMM Library Share
- Use an existing library share
  - Share name: MSSCVMMLibrary
  - Share location:
  - Share description:

15. Review the installation configuration summary and start installation.
16. Close the Wizard on successful installation.

> VMM Installation logs are located at %SystemDrive%\ProgramData\ VMMLogs\
>
> There is a known issue of installation failing while having –SCVMM in computer name of SCVMM server. You can try renaming the server by removing "-" from hostname or changing it to scvmm or any other characters.

Post-installation tasks

Following are the post installation tasks:

1. Verify successful VMM installation by logging into VMM server using VMM console.
2. Add SCVMM-admins group to SCVMM administrator in VMM console settings.
3. Create RunAs accounts for hypervisor and more related operations.
4. Update SCVMM with the latest updates and patches.

Highly available SCVMM architecture and deployment

As covered in *VMM architecture and deployment models* section, SCVMM can be deployed in high availability mode using Windows Server Failover Clustering. By deploying SCVMM in high availability mode on the top of Microsoft Windows Failover Cluster Services, it can be protected against both hardware and software level failures.

Deploying SCVMM management server in a cluster has some prerequisite which needs to be fulfilled:

- **VMM Service Account**: The Virtual Machine Management service on the SCVMM server must be configured to run with a domain account. You cannot use a local system account to run a VMM service in HA mode. This service account has to be a member of the local administrator's group on SCVMM server Windows.
- **Container in Active Directory for Distributed Key Management**: VMM stores all configurations and user account details such as RunAs account credentials in a SQL database. Credentials security is of utmost importance in every scenario, and SCVMM takes care of security by storing these credentials in encrypted form.

There are two ways to encrypt these credentials:

- **DPAPI**: DPAPI uses computer hardware ID (on which SCVMM is installed) to encrypt the credentials.
- **DKM**: In the case of DKM SCVMM, it stores the encrypted keys in a container in Active Directory. These encryption keys aren't tied to any physical parameter of any of SCVMM server.

In a clustered deployment, SCVMM Virtual Machine Management service shall be running on multiple nodes which make DPAPI encryption technique unusable. For cluster deployment DKM is mandatory to be used.

As a prerequisite of deploying SCVMM in a cluster, a container needs to be created in Active Directory prior to installing SCVMM. This container will be used to store the encrypted keys for various SCVMM credentials.

Steps to deploy a highly available VMM Management Server are as follows:

1. Complete the prerequisite for VMM service account and AD container.
2. Join VMM servers to Windows Server Failover Cluster.

3. Execute the SCVMM installation setup; the setup automatically detects that setup is running on cluster node and gives the option to deploy VMM in highly available mode.
4. Follow the SCVMM installation guidelines given in the last topic.
5. Provide a cluster name and DKM container location when asked.
6. Add other SCVMM node by executing the setup, the setup will automatically detect the cluster and SCVMM configuration deployed.
7. Once deployed successfully, Failover Cluster Manager can be used to view cluster status and switch services as and when required.

Planning and configuring hypervisor compute layer with SCVMM

In this section we will learn to plan and configure hypervisor resources such as Hyper-V hosts and clusters, VMware and Citrix hypervisors. In a WAP-based cloud solution the hypervisor layer has to be in control of SCVMM for IaaS services provisioning and lifecycle management.

In this section we will cover various ways of adding and managing a hypervisor layer in SCVMM.

Planning and creating SCVMM host groups

In a large scale cloud deployment comprising hundreds of Hyper-V hosts and thousands of virtual machines or more, managing the hosts effectively in terms of resource provisioning and controlling becomes challenging. SCVMM host groups can be used to avoid such challenges, it provides flexibilities to group multiple hypervisor hosts and uses as a single entity for resource provisioning and management.

Host group planning would have a different foundation and strategy for organizations and service providers. A few common options are as follows:

- Site or geo location
- Performance and capabilities such as fault tolerance and so on
- Isolated environment of the web zone environment such as DMZ
- Dedicated host groups for large tenants in a service provider's cloud
- Host groups with or without BC and DR
- Cloud management infra and tenant workload infra
- Many more

We can add Hyper-V hosts or clusters and VMware/Citrix hosts in a host group and define various settings at host group level such as:

- General settings.
- Placement rules.
- Host reserve settings (CPU, memory, network and storage bandwidth, and so on.)
- Dynamic optimization.
- Power optimization.
- Network and storage resources and quota.
- PRO configuration.
- Custom properties.

Host groups can be nested to providers' greater level of hierarchy and management. By default child host groups inherit parent host group settings and policies, which can be overridden at child host group level. Hypervisor hosts can be moved from one host group to another.

You can create SCVMM cloud consisting of multiple host groups. SCVMM cloud will be discussed in detail in *Chapter 4, Building VM Clouds and IaaS Offerings*.

Creating host groups

Following are the steps to create host groups:

1. Login to SCVMM server using VMM console and open fabric workspace.
2. Expand **Servers** in the **Fabric** menu, right click on **All Hosts**.

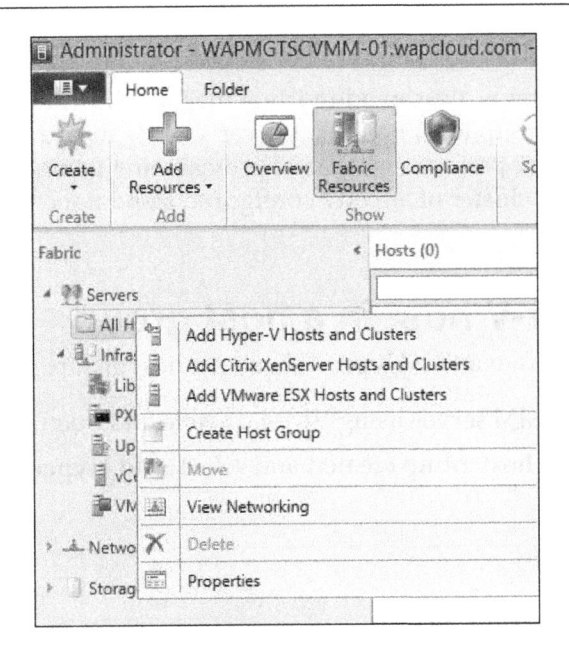

3. Click **Create Host Group** and provide the host group friendly name.
4. Configure host group properties.

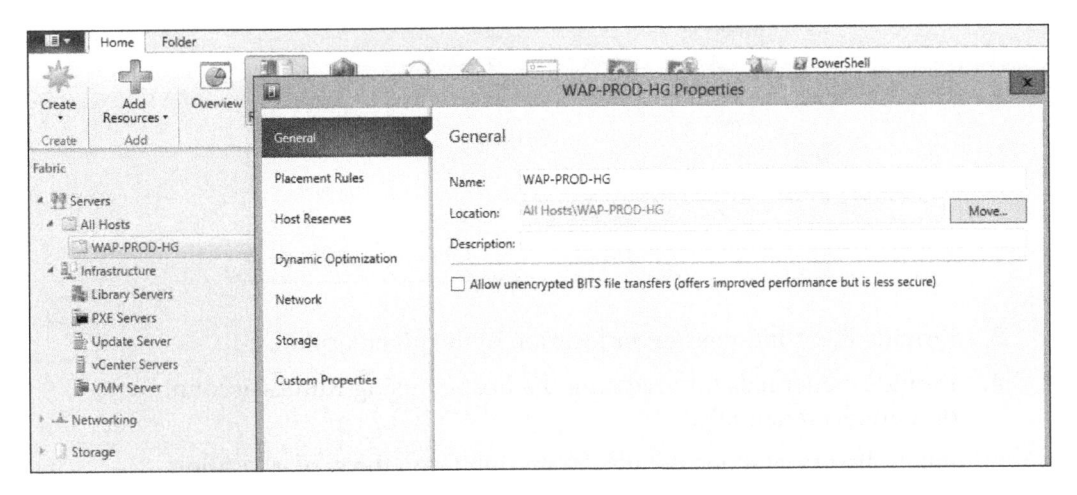

Adding virtual machine hosts in host groups

After creating host groups, we can add virtual machine hosts in their respective group to apply host group level policies. We can choose to add already configured hypervisor or cluster or perform bare metal provisioning using SCVMM. We can also create a Hyper-V cluster of already configured standalone Hyper-V hosts using SCVMM.

Adding Hyper-V host in a host group

Following are the steps to add a Hyper-V host in a host group:

1. Login to SCVMM server using VMM console and open fabric workspace.
2. Right click on host group created and select **Add Hyper-V Hosts and Clusters**.

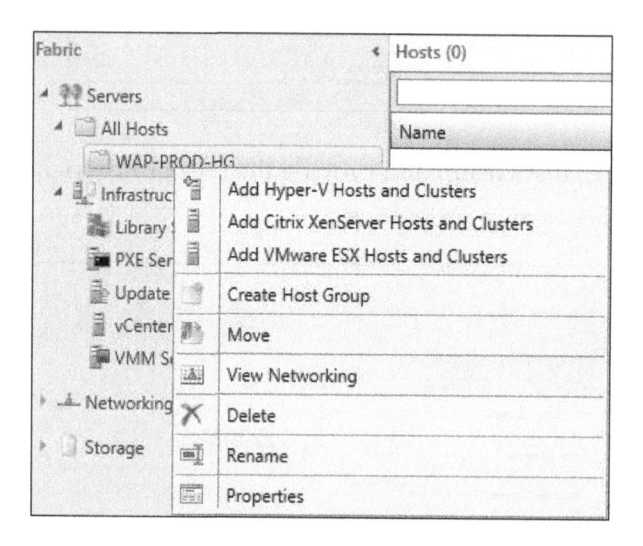

3. Provide the Windows Server location in the given option.
4. Provide credentials for accessing the host by using RunAs account or manual credentials.
5. Fill in discovery scope details depending upon the server location provided earlier.
6. Select target host groups and host setting.

7. Review the configuration summary and finish the wizard to add the host.

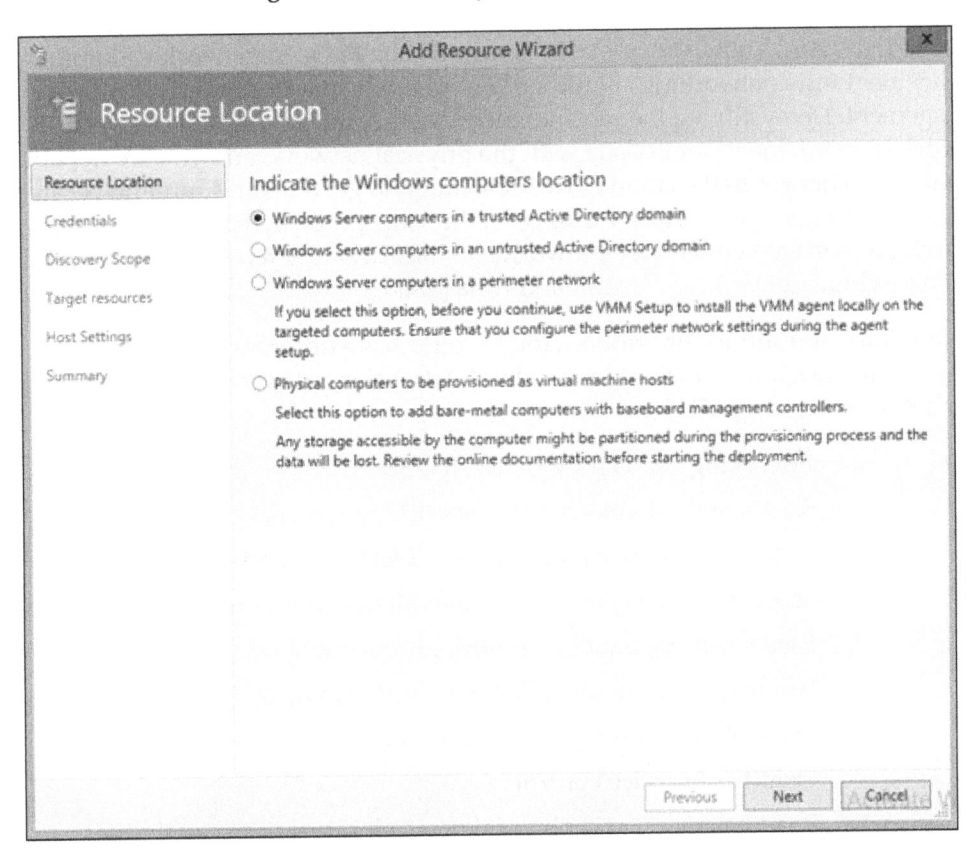

Planning and configuring cloud network fabric with SCVMM

Cloud network is the most crucial and complex piece of any private or service provider's cloud. Cloud network has to be efficient and flexible enough to handle daily changing networking needs of tenants and businesses. Software defined networking is a key pillar of providing automated and flexible networking for tenants with complete isolation and extensibilities. In this section we will learn various cloud network solution components for both private cloud and service providers' cloud in a WAP cloud.

Getting the Cloud Fabric Ready

Before getting into tenant workload networking needs, it is crucial to note that networking for cloud management infra and tenant workload infrastructure should be kept separate. Also known as Control Plane and Data Plane in networking languages, management infra networking should be kept separate in terms of provisioning and management. Demystifying the recommendation, assume a scenario where cloud network is down due to some issue with the physical network, and you are not able to make any changes to the cloud network solution to get it up and running because network controller VM was also running on the same problematic network. Follow the same cloud management and tenant workload infrastructure recommendation while designing cloud networking Control and Data plane.

Private cloud and service providers' cloud would have different networking requirement, let's have a look at major cloud networking requirement for both and their solution in our WAP cloud:

- Cloud networking needs for a private cloud:
    - Secure and reliable virtual networking with easy management
    - Isolated network capabilities for **T&D environments**
    - Separate zone separated by firewall depending upon network traffic
    - Faster and automated network provisioning
    - IP address automated allocation and managed
    - Extensibility to support custom needs
    - Quality of service control
    - Load balancing and physical network integration capabilities
    - Hardware independent configurations
- Cloud networking needs for a service provider's cloud:
    - Complete isolation between different tenants' networks while using the same physical network
    - Extensibility to support hybrid networking model with a tenant's on-premises deployment
    - Automated provisioning and tenant controlled management
    - Advanced address translation capabilities with limited resources such as gateways and more for public facing services
    - No IP range usage constraints

- Easily manageable and open to dynamic changes
- Quality of service as per the tenant's plans and subscriptions
- All enterprise class networking features such as load balancing and physical network integrated or hardware independent configurations

WAP along with system center and Hyper-V provides true cloud networking capabilities for requirements of private clouds and service providers' cloud. Networking capabilities of SCVMM such as logical networks and switches, network load balancing integration, network virtualization (the BIG thing), network virtualization gateways, port profiles along with automation and self-service experience of Windows Azure Pack provide solutions to all these requirements of organizations and service providers.

Network Virtualization

Network Virtualization allows us to create multiple independent networks on the same physical hardware, traveling and routing on the same physical NIC cards and network switches/routes with complete isolation to each other. Network Virtualization is the foundation of one of the most modern networking technologies today, that is Software Defined Networking. Network Virtualization enables transforming of traditional physical network devices such as routers, firewalls, and load balancers into software. Software Defined Networking enables all networking features from layer 2 to 7 with isolation and multi-tenancy. Network Virtualization is a must have technology for cloud service providers in order to facilitate flexible isolated networking for tenants without any dependency on each other.

Hyper-V **Network Virtualization using General Routing Encapsulation** (**NVGRE**) mechanism is used to facilitate virtualized networks for virtual machines. Windows Azure Pack with SCVMM and Hyper-V provides true self service automated virtual networks for private and service providers' cloud solutions. Hyper-V and VMM provides Network Virtualization gateways to enable virtualized network traffic communication with physical networks and the outside world.

Each VM connected to a virtualized network has two IP associated with it, one from the virtual network known as **customer address** (**CA**) and the other from a cloud **provider's address** (**PA**). Hyper-V Network Virtualization encapsulates the CA address network packet using PA, source and destination IP and virtual network ID while transmitting the packet so that it can travel on a physical network. On the receiver end it decapsulates the packet and transmits the packet with the CA address only in the other virtual machine.

Network Virtualization works at Hyper-V virtual switch level on Hyper-V hosts. Hyper-V virtual switch on Server 2012 onwards can be extended to provide additional functionalities apart from default layer 2 responsibilities. Additional extension can be programmed and implemented on a virtual switch for additional features for network and security such as network filtering, virtual firewalls, and so on. This enables a true Software Defined Network infrastructure.

There is no separate dedicated NIC requirements for implementing network virtualization, we can use same NIC or virtual switch for both types of traffic including traditional networks as well as virtualized networks.

> The provider address doesn't need to be the IP of physical NIC or team, in VMM it comes from the IP pool configured in the logical network.

Configuring networking fabric in SCVMM

In this section we will configure networking fabric in SCVMM for traditional and virtualized networks. There are multiple network resources when it comes to configuring networking fabric in VMM:

- Logical network
- MAC address pools
- Load balancers
- VIP templates
- Logical switches
- Port profiles
- Port classifications
- Network service
- VM networks (available in VM and services workspace)

Logical networks

A logical network in SCVMM is the top level hierarchy of SCVMM network fabric. It can be used to represent a network site, or a different network domain. Logical networks can consist of multiple virtual machine networks. Multiple logical networks can be created such as production network, T&D logical network. Logical networks can be assigned to hosts and host groups.

In a traditional network, create logical network corresponding to a physical network in your environment such as DMZ, backup, internal and so on. One virtual machine network per logical network shall be created in this scenario.

Network Virtualization is enabled at logical network level.

Creating a logical network

The following steps have to be followed to create a logical network:

1. Login to VMM server using VMM console and select fabric workspace.
2. Expand **Networking** and click on **Logical Networks**.
3. Right click on **Logical Networks** and click on **Create Logical Network**.

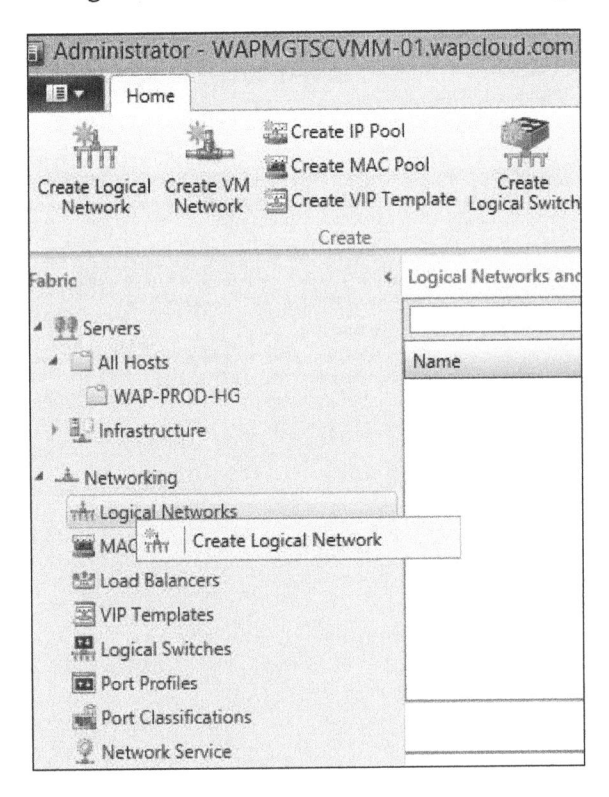

4. Type the name of the logical network such as **WAP-CLOUD-PROD**, along with the optional description for easy identification in case of large deployments. Select **One connected network** or VLAN based network or PVLAN network as per your network topology.

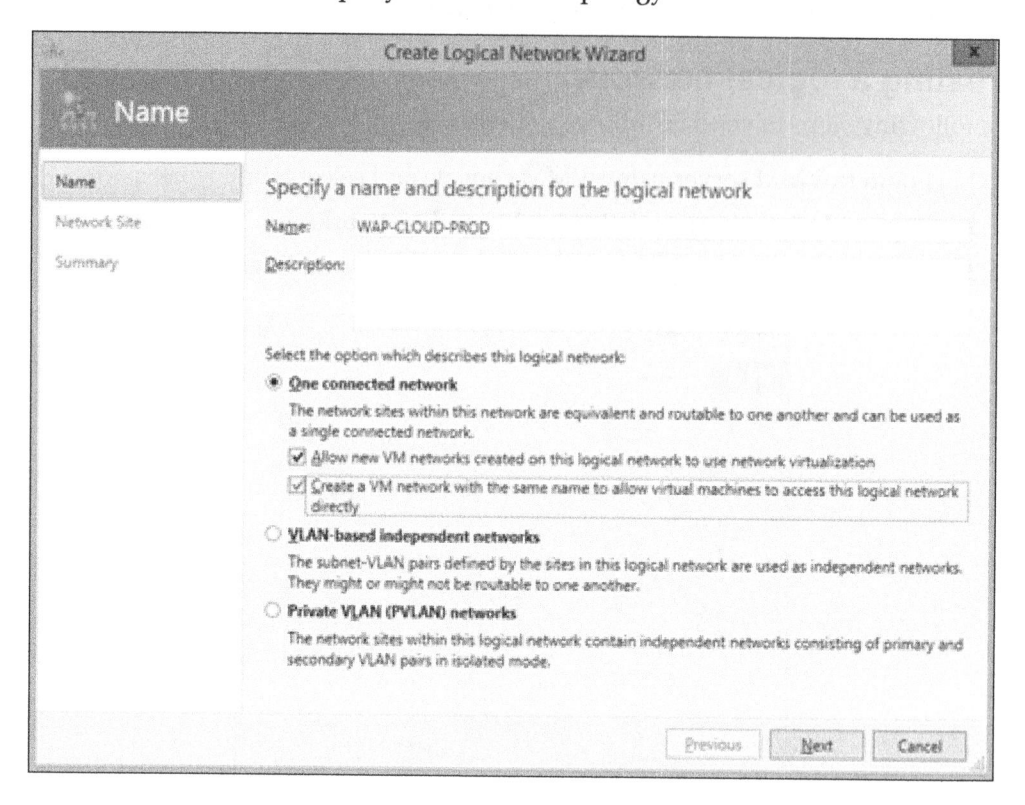

5. Click **Next** and add the network site in the logical network. Select a host group that can use this logical network along with the **VLAN** ID and **IP subnet**.

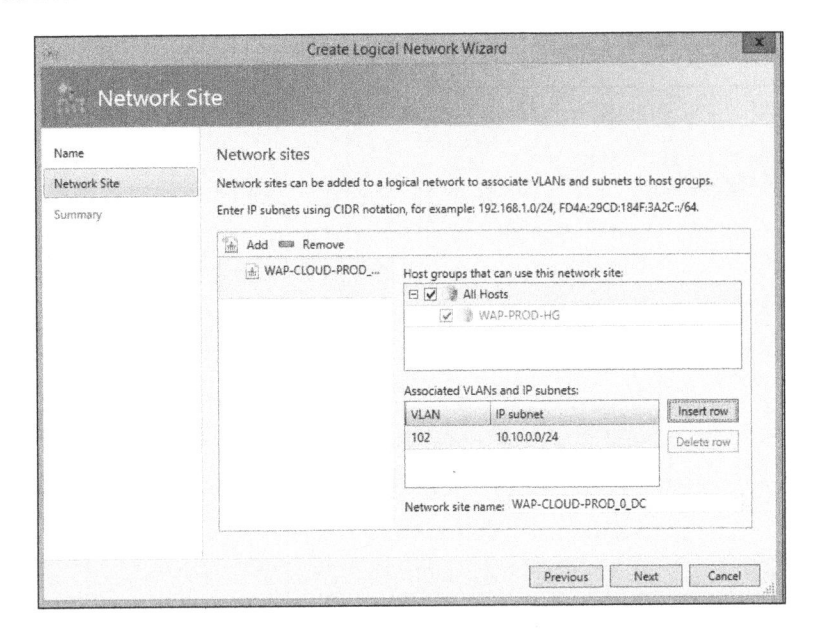

6. Review the configurations on the **Summary** page and click **Finish** to create the network.

Creating an IP pool for the newly created logical network

IP pools are created to provide a usable IP address range to VMM for IP allocation. IP pools assigned to a logical network are also used to provide PA (provider address) in Network Virtualization.

1. Open **Fabric | Networking** in VMM console.

2. Expand the logical network and right click on the logical network to select **Create IP Pool**.

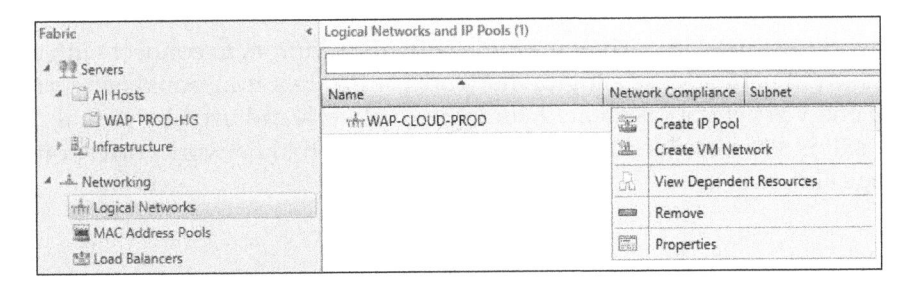

3. Provide the IP pool name and description and select the logical network we created.
4. On **Network Sites**, click **Use an existing network site**.
5. Next enter a usable IP range.

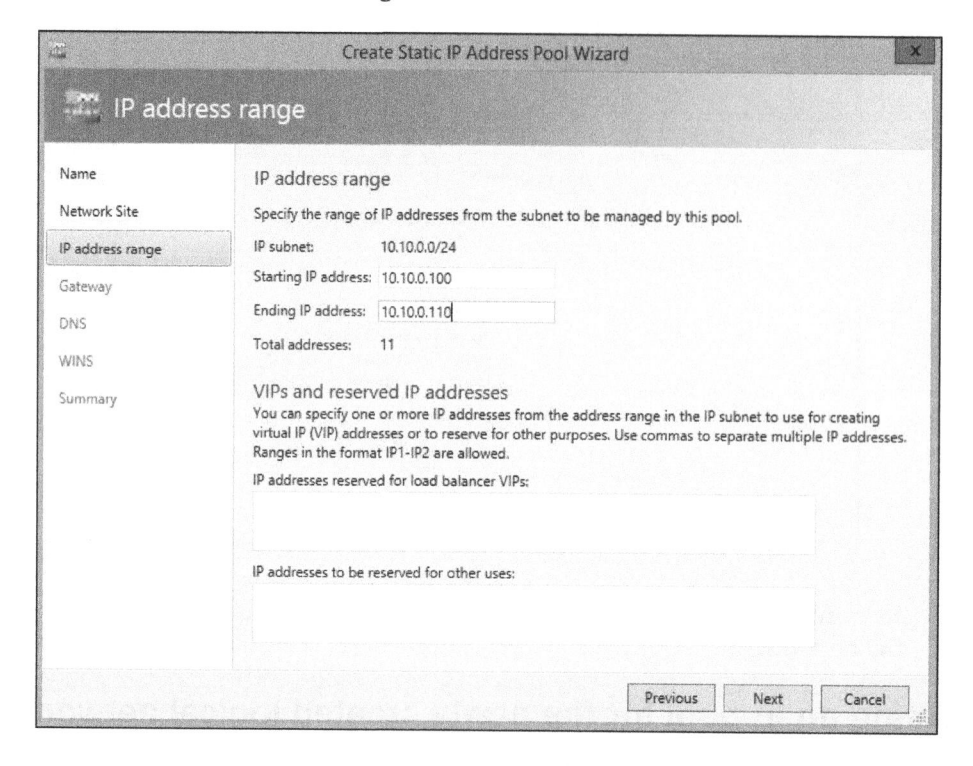

6. Provide a gateway for the given IP range.
7. Configure DNS, DNS Suffix and WINS settings if any.
8. Review the settings on the **Summary** page and create the IP pool.

Creating a Virtualized VM Network and IP Pool on the Logical Network

VM networks are used by virtual machine network adaptors to connect with a virtualized VM network use a logical network for PA. In a traditional network scenario one VM network is created per logical network and used by virtual machines. It is also possible to automatically create virtual network corresponding to the logical network.

Create a VM network

The following are the steps to create a VM network:

1. Login to the VMM console and select **Logical Network**.
2. Right click on **Logical Network** and select **Create VM network**.
3. Provide name and description for VM network for identification. Select corresponding logical network.
4. Configure the Isolation setting, click **Isolation using Hyper-V network virtualization** for isolated networks.

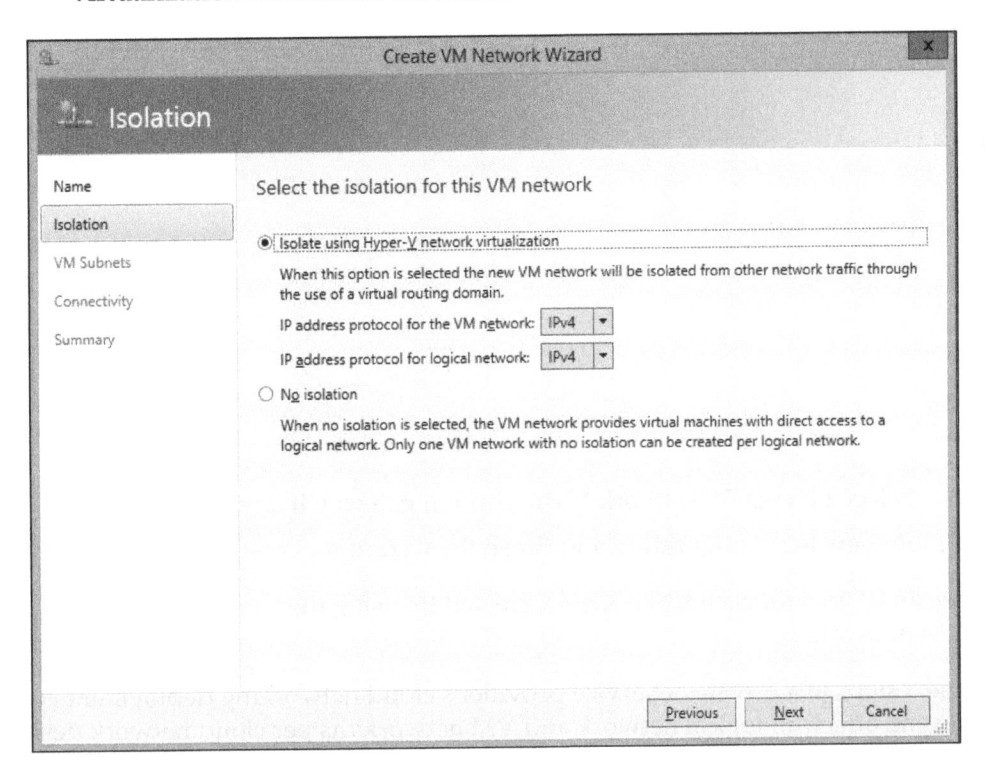

5. Provide the Virtual Network **Name** and **Subnet**.

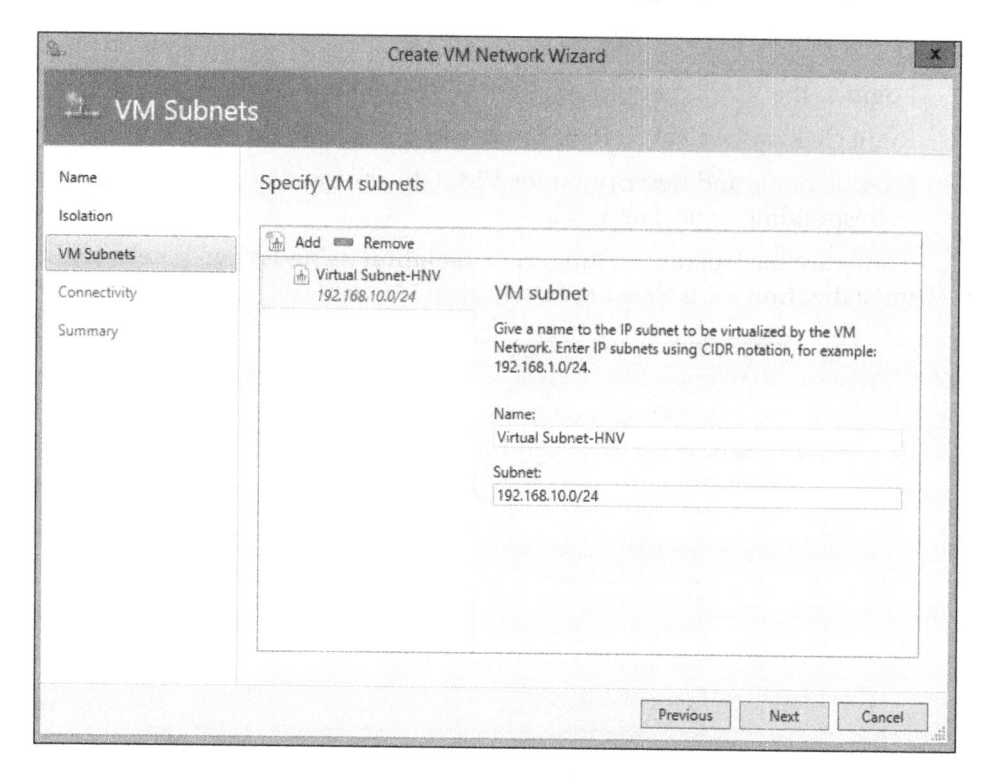

6. Select a Hyper-V Network Virtualization gateway if any.
7. Review the configuration and finish the wizard for creating the VM network.

Create an IP pool for each VM network created by using the Create IP Pool wizard for VM network.

The next steps in a private or service provider's cloud networking deployment is to create and attach all logical network and VM networks as per cloud network design and attach to host groups accordingly.

[VM Network management wizard is available in the "VM and Services" workspace in VMM Console, not in fabric workspace.]

Apart from logical networks, VM networks and IP pools, VMM provides multiple other network resources mentioned above to add greater management control and flexibility on your cloud's network fabric.

MAC address pool

MAC address pool allows you to provide a custom static MAC address for your virtual machine. While the VMM given MAC address pool is created by default, you can always create a new one as per requirement.

Load balancers

By using load balancing, you can easily distribute traffic between multiple servers for a scaled application. SCVMM has inbuilt support of using Microsoft NLB as a native load balancing provider, you can also add custom configurations for supported third party load balancer integration such as F5, Citrix and more. Custom configuration providers need to be installed for third party integration.

VIP template

VIP templates are configurations which are utilized by load balancers for virtual IP needs. They can be used for configuring VIP configuration for load balancing traffic rules such for HTTPS and so on.

Logical switches

These enable centralized networking deployment on your Hyper-V hosts. Logical switches can be configured to use specific port mapping, classifications and extensions.

Port profiles

Port profiles enable deploying consistent network settings such as QoS, and advanced security features across all Hyper-V hosts.

Port classifications

Port classifications can be used to classify ports such as 10GB networks, low bandwidth networks.

Network service

In network services, third party network devices can be integrated with SCVMM such as TOR switches and so on.

Planning and configuring cloud storage fabric with SCVMM

Microsoft Windows Azure Pack based cloud solution support both block based storage and file based storage configured with VMM for storing virtual machines and other cloud IaaS resources.

Storage requirements and solutions are likely to be different for private clouds and service provider clouds. While it is common to see traditional enterprise class SAN storage solutions in private clouds, software defined storage solutions on commodity hardware are also in use for both private and service provider cloud solution. VMM supports a wide range of storage solution integration for automated provisioning and management solving storage challenges for both private clouds and service provider clouds.

In the case of block based storage, VMM can take advantage of **Storage Area Network (SAN)** using Fibre Channel, iSCSI and SAS storage connectivity solutions for storing virtual machines and resources.

For file based storages, VMM can be integrated with storage solutions supporting SMB 3.0 protocol for file based storage access. Windows server file server provides SMB capabilities, enabling shared storage capabilities without purchasing expensive storage array solutions.

Cloud storage deployment options in VMM

There are various options available in VMM to store virtual machines and other cloud resources. Every storage appears to Hyper-V hosts as local or remote storage, local storage stands for storage devices locally attached or assigned to hosts where remote storage defines remotely connected LUNs. Let's have a look at major options for providing storage fabric in a VMM environment.

- **Directly attached storage (DAS)**: This is storage disks connected directly to hypervisor hosts, commonly in a form of disk drive inside a server chassis connected via inbuilt RAID controller or SAS based JBOD connectivity. This is dedicated to each host and isn't shared. This doesn't provide any high availability or host failure tolerance, hence is not recommended for production usage.

- **Traditional SAN arrays**: Enterprise class storage solutions from leading vendors such as EMC, NetApp, Hitachi and so on, comes under this category. These solutions can be used to store virtual machines on LUNs using FC/iSCSI and other connectivity mechanisms. VMM can be integrated with iSCSI target arrays by supporting both static and dynamic discovery.

- **Storage solutions with SMI-S or SMP providers**: Storage solutions which support integration with SCVMM using SMI-S or SMP protocol comes under this category. SMI-S enables automated storage provisioning and management using VMM console enabling a true automated cloud solution. It is recommended to integrate any supported existing traditional storage with VMM in a private cloud for automation at storage layer. See vendor specific guidelines for configuring SMI-S for VMM integration.
- **File storage (SMB 3.0)**: With Windows Server 2012 R2 Hyper-V supports storing virtual machines on file shares accessible via SMB protocol. Windows Server based file server clusters can be deployed and integrated with VMM for storing cloud virtual machines and resources.
- **Scale out file server**: Scale out file server is a Windows Server feature which ensures continuous availability of file share storage across multiple hosts simultaneously. SOFS can take advantages of JBOD connected for file server nodes to provide always available file shares to Hyper-V hosts. SOFS uses SMB protocol for providing storage access. SOFS can be easily provisioned and managed using System Center Virtual Machine Manager.
- **Software Defined Storage (Microsoft Storage Spaces)**: In today's era of Software Defined infrastructure, Microsoft provides Windows storage spaces which can be utilized for delivering storage solutions on commodity hardware without purchasing expensive storage arrays. This can be utilized by cloud service providers for providing shared storage features and capabilities without investing in traditional storage solutions. Microsoft storage space groups physical disks together in a storage pool which can be used to create space for data storage requirements. It can be configured to protect failure at each level by maintain multiple copies of data. Storages spaces can be used to provide shared storage capabilities by using multiple nodes connected to JBOD trays.

> A list of supported storage solutions for VMM integration can be found at http://social.technet.microsoft.com/wiki/contents/articles/16100.system-center-2012-vmm-supported-storage-arrays.aspx

Getting the Cloud Fabric Ready

Configuring storage fabric in VMM

Let's have a look at the various configurable parameters available in VMM for storage fabric.

- **Storage classifications**: Storage classification can be used to provide a friendly name or container to storage resources available such as gold storage, silver storage differentiating upon factors such as capacity, performance, resiliency and more. This can ease daily administrative tasks while assigning storage by representing complex architecture in a simplified way. You can associate storage pools with classification for mapping resources with a friendly name. To create a storage classification you need to perform the following steps:

    1. Login to VMM console and open **Fabric** workspace.
    2. Right click on **Storage | Classification and Pools** to create classification.
    3. Provide a friendly name and description and click **Add**.

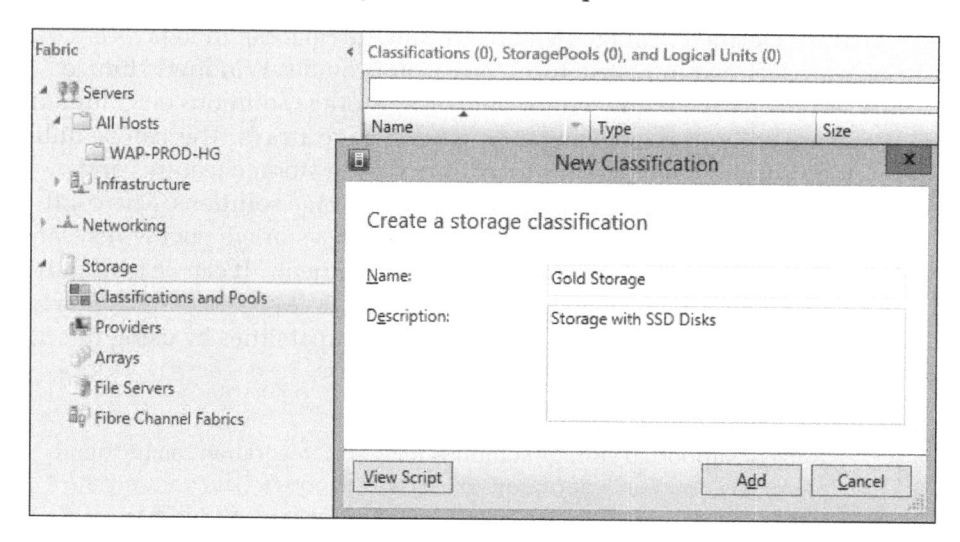

- **Storage provider**: Storage provider provides options to add storage devices in VMM for automated LUN provisioning and management. VMM 2012 R2 provides flexibility to add the following storage solutions:
    - Windows based file server
    - SAN or NAS device discovered and managed by a SMI-S provider
    - SAN device managed by native SMP providers
    - Fibre channel fabric discovered and managed by SMI-S providers

By integrating storage devices in VMM, we can provision and assign LUNs to Hyper-V hosts using VMM console, provisioning and management of storage devices can be performed using VMM, which allows the flexibility of having completed automated storage deployment and management.

- Adding a storage device in VMM:
    1. Launch VMM console and connect to VMM server with admin permissions.
    2. Open fabric workspace, right click on **Providers** under the **Storage** section.
    3. Select **Add Storage Devices**, and select the type of device from the given option.

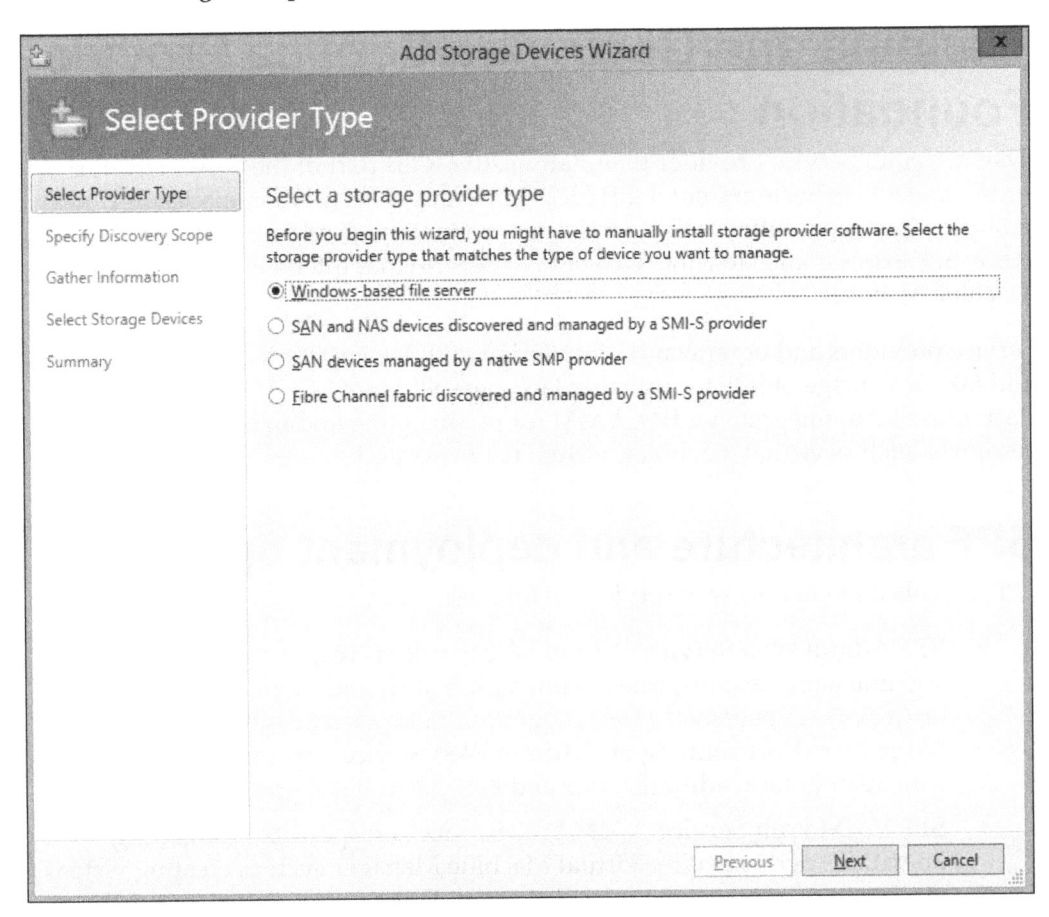

4. Provide discovery scope, credentials and more details depending upon the storage provider type.
5. Select an available storage device and finish the wizard to add.
6. Verify the array listed in the VMM storage fabric workspace.

- Post storage device integration tasks:
    - Create storage pools and LUNs
    - Map the storage pool with classification created earlier
    - Assign LUNs and storage pools to the hosts
    - Manage and monitor storage resources

Planning and Deploying Service Provider Foundation

System Center Service Provider Foundation 2012 R2 is part of the System Center suite, available in System Center 2012 R2 Orchestrator installation media. SPF add multi-tenancy capabilities to System Center products such as SCVMM, SMA and more. SPF exposes an extensible OData Web Service that interacts with Virtual Machine Manager.

Service providers and organization can design and develop their own cloud portals, and take advantage of SPF for utilizing IaaS capabilities of SCVMM. Windows Azure Pack uses SPF to integrate with SCVMM for provisioning and managing cloud IaaS resources such as virtual machines, virtual networks and so on.

SPF architecture and deployment options

SPF is a collection of four web services as follows:

- **SPF Admin Web Service**: Admin Web Service is responsible for creating and managing tenants, roles, stamps (SCVMM) and more. It can be accessed on https://SPFSERVER:8090/SC2012R2/Admin/Microsoft.Management.Odata.svc. User running SPF Admin Web Service application pool must be a member of local administrator and SPF_Admin local group on SPF server.
- **SPF VMM Web Service**: VMM Web Service is responsible for getting operations performed by Virtual Machine Manager such as creating virtual machines, networks, user roles and more. This service is also responsible to maintain and replicating change performed at components such as WAP and SCVMM. It can be accessed on

- `https://SPFSERVER:8090/SC2012R2/VMM/Microsoft.Management.Odata.svc`. The user running SPF Admin Web Service application pool must be a member of the local administrator, `SPF_VMM` local group and VMM administrators on SPF and VMM server respectively.
- **SPF Usage Service**: Usage Web Service integrates with System Center Operations Manager Data warehouse and is used by WAP or third party billing providers for gathering resources usage data. A user account running Usage Service must be a part of the local administrator and `SPF_Usage` group on the SPF server along with access on the SC Operations Manager data warehouse database.
- **SPF Provider Service**: Provider Web Service is used by resource providers for delivering IaaS services. Provider services provide Microsoft ASP.NET Web API and not OData as in the case of other web services. Provider Service also uses the VMM and admin service. Users running the SPF Provider Web Service application pool must be a member of local administrator and SPF_Provider, SPF_VMM, and SPF_Admin local groups on the SPF Server.

System Center Service Provider Foundation can be deployed in two ways:

- **Standalone Single Server deployment**: In case of standalone deployment, only one server will be deployed in a solution with no redundancy. This is not recommended for production and is used for test and evaluation purposes only. All web services are always installed on the same server.
- **Highly available scaled deployment**: SPF support highly available deployment with the use of load balancers. Hardware LBs or Microsoft NLB can be used for providing load balancing between multiple SPF servers. Multiple SPF servers can be deployed behind a load balancer pointing to a highly available database for providing HA capabilities to SPF deployment at each layer. This is the recommended deployment model for a production scenario.

Installing Service Provider Foundation 2012 R2

Like every other system center or Microsoft product, SPF also has a set of prerequisites which need to be met before starting installation. SPF installation binaries are included in System Center 2012 R2 Orchestrator media.

Installation prerequisites

The following are the installation prerequisites.

Create SPF service accounts as follows (Active Directory Accounts):

Account name	Purpose	Permissions
Spfsvc	SPF service account for running IIS application pool	Member of local administrator + SPF local groups + SCVMM admin + SQLDB sysadmin
Spflocal	Local account for SPF integration	Member of local administrator + SPF local groups + SCVMM admin

Separate service accounts can also be created for admin, provider, usage and VMM application pool if required.

Software prerequisites

The following software needs to be installed before starting Service Provider Foundation installation:

Windows features:

- Management OData Internet Information Services (IIS) extension
- NET Framework 4.5 features, WCF Services, and HTTP activation
- For Web Server (IIS) server install the following components of IIS:
    - Basic authentication
    - Windows authentication
    - Application deployment ASP.NET 4.5
    - Application development ISAPI extensions
    - Application deployment ISAPI filters
    - IIS Management scripts and Tools Role Service
- Web Services:
    - WCF data services 5.0 for OData V3
    - ASP.NET MVC 4
- Virtual Machine Manager 2012 R2 Console
- Certificates SPF creates self-signed certificate, CA provided SSL certificates should be created for production deployments

> The local account is used by Windows Azure Pack for registering SPF.

Installation procedure

The following is the installation procedure:

1. Login to SPF server and mount System Center Orchestrator media.
2. Run `SetupOrchestrator.exe` from the mounted media.
3. Click **Service Provider Foundation** under the **Standalone installation** section.
4. This will launch the **SPF Installation wizard**, click **Install** to proceed further.
5. Accept the agreement and proceed.
6. Setup will check for prerequisite check, proceed if all checks are completed successfully. Review errors in case of any failure.
7. Provide database **Server** IP and **Port number** along with **Database name**.

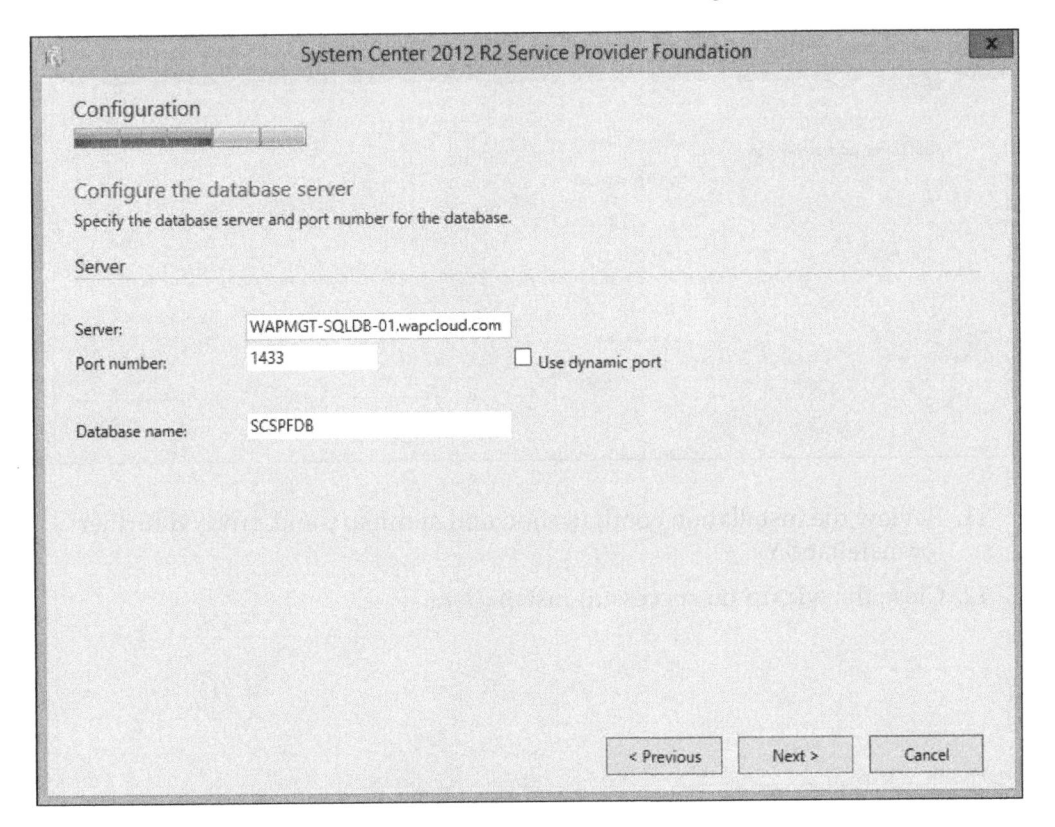

Getting the Cloud Fabric Ready

8. Provide the installation folder for SPF files and a port number. (By default `C:\intepub` and `8090`). Select **Generate self signed certificate** or provide pre-created SSL for SPF.

9. SPF automatically creates local groups on the SPF server for administrative permissions, provide SPF Admin service account and admin account, SCVMM-Admins group and SPF local account.

10. Provide service account details for each service that is, admin web, VMM, usage and provider.

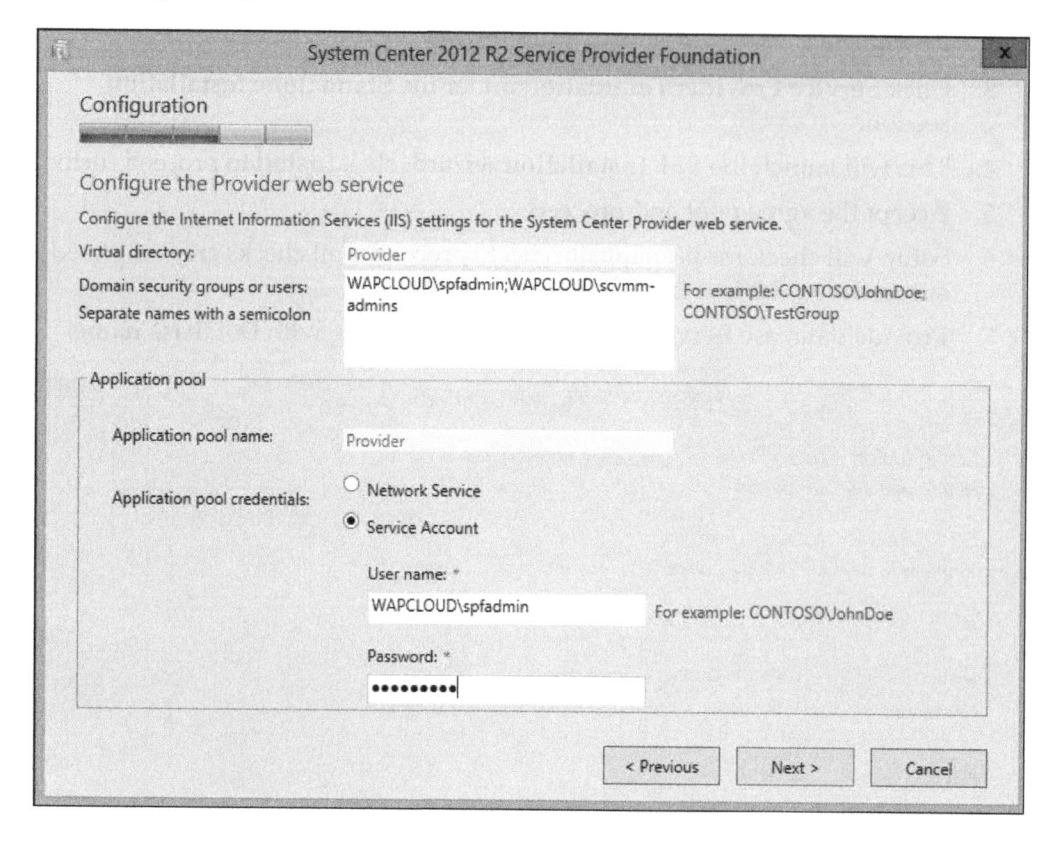

11. Review the installation configuration and summary and proceed further for installation.

12. Close the wizard on successful installation.

Post-installation tasks

The following are the post installation tasks:

1. Verify successful installation and application pools status in IIS.

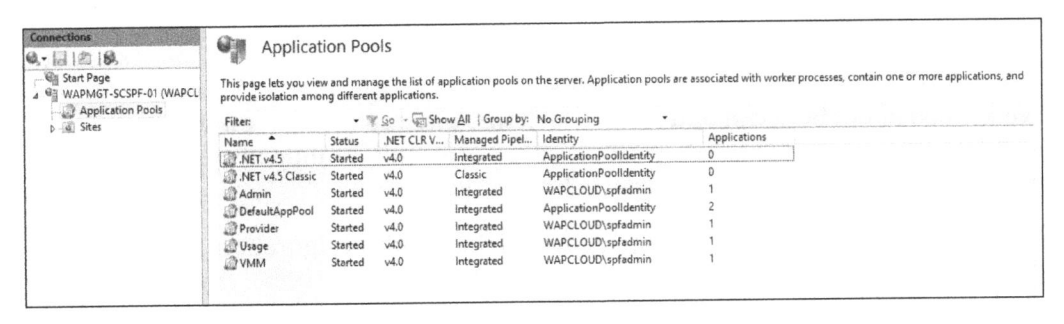

2. Verify local groups created in the SPF server, add `spflocal user` in all groups.

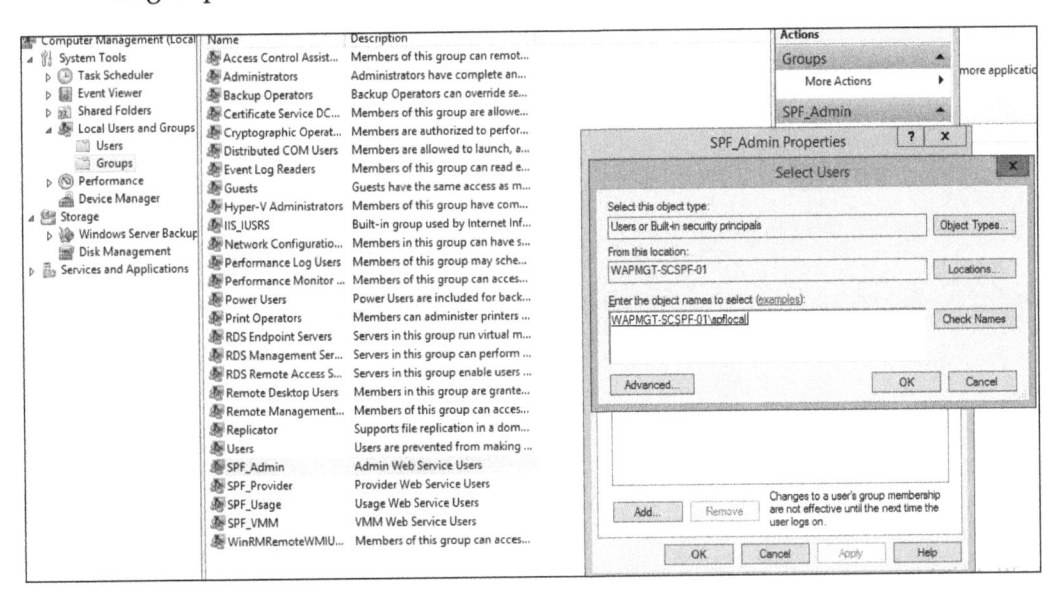

3. Enable **Basic Authentication** for the SPF website, this is a requirement for WAP integration.

Summary

In this chapter we learned about planning for cloud fabric for private cloud needs and service providers. We covered infrastructure planning at each layer starting from hardware to hypervisors, network and storage. Hyper-V deployment best practices were also covered which will help in deploying a reliable and stable hypervisor layer.

We learned about SCVMM and SPF architecture and has installation walkthrough for both products. We learned about planning and configuration of compute, network and storage for cloud fabric in SCVMM.

In the next chapter we will be covering installation and configuration of Windows Azure Pack portals, API's and authentication sites.

3
Installing and Configuring Windows Azure Pack

In the previous chapter, we covered planning and configuration of Cloud Fabric Infrastructure, which is used to host the Cloud Fabric management and tenant workloads. Moving ahead, in this chapter we shall cover the installation and configuration of Windows Azure Pack websites, APIs, and authentication sites. We shall also cover post deployment steps such as customizing portal names and certificates as per enterprise and service providers' needs.

We will be covering the following topics in this chapter:

- Windows Azure Pack deployment model review
- Installing and configuring Windows Azure Pack
- Installing Windows Azure Pack in a distributed model
- Required firewall ports for WAP components
- Customizing WAP portals' accessibility and certificates summary
- Registering the Service Provider Foundation with WAP

Windows Azure Pack deployment models review

In *Chapter 1*, *Know Windows Azure Pack and Its Architecture*, we covered the architecture and various deployment models for an organization's private cloud and a service provider's cloud needs. Let's have a review of possible and recommended deployment models before starting actual installation of **Windows Azure Pack (WAP)**.

- **Express Deployment Architecture**: In Express Deployment Architecture, all components of WAP (portals, APIs, and authentication sites) are installed on a single Windows Server 2012/Windows Server 2012 R2. It doesn't provide any high availability and is suitable only for testing, development, and deployments. For the purpose of evaluating WAP in this book, we shall be following the Express Deployment model.
- **Distributed Deployment Architecture**: In Distributed Deployment Architecture, WAP roles such as Admin/Tenant portals or API's. authentication sites are deployed in a distributed manner involving multiple Windows servers to provide scalability and high availability in a secure manner. Distributed Deployment Architecture can be customized as per requirement, such as adding a **high availability** (**HA**) layer only for particular roles instead of all. This is suitable for production deployments.

Installing and configuring Windows Azure Pack

Microsoft Web Platform Installer (WEB PI) is used to install Windows Azure Pack components in both Express and Distributed Architectures. Microsoft Web Platform is a free tool available, which is used to download and install latest components of Microsoft Web platform-related components such as IIS, .NET, web development tools, web applications, Windows Azure Pack, and so on. Web PI automatically detects the operating system on which it's executed and displays only compatible solutions available for download and installation.

Before downloading and starting Web Platform installer, we need to ensure that Windows Azure Pack installation prerequisites are completed. Let's finish up the prerequisites before starting the installation.

WAP installation prerequisite

For the purpose of evaluation, we are installing Windows Azure Pack in the Express Deployment model. The following hardware and software prerequisites have to be met before starting the installation. Please follow *Chapter 1*, *Know Windows Azure Pack and Its Architecture*, for details on hardware requirements and for the deployment model of Express and Distributed Deployment Architectures.

- Active Directory user accounts:
  - Create the following user accounts and groups in Active Directory for Windows Azure Pack components authentication:

Account Name	Purpose	Permissions
Wapsvc	Service account for WAP Web Services	Member of local administrator group on WAP servers and WAP Admins Group Member
Wapadmin	Administrator account to manage WAP Cloud	Member of local administrator group on WAP servers + WAPAdmins Group Member
Wapadmins	WAP Administrators Group	Member of local administrator group on WAP servers

- Hardware requirements:
  - Windows Server 2012 R2 VM or physical server
  - 8 GB RAM (no dynamic memory)
  - 50 GB of available disk space
- Software requirements:
  - Windows Server 2012 / 2012 R2 operating system. All the latest features and support are available with Windows Server 2012 R2. See the feature compatibility guide if deploying on Windows Server 2012.
  - Microsoft Web Platform Installer 5, available at http://www.microsoft.com/web/downloads/platform.aspx.
  - Microsoft .NET Framework 3.5 Service Pack. Install using the server manager and add features wizard.
  - IIS (Internet Information Service). Component of Windows Server OS. Web Platform installer can install it automatically before WAP installation. Add Management Console manually later.
  - Microsoft .NET Framework 4.5 Extended with ASP.NET for Windows 8. It can be installed using the Server Manager's Add Feature wizard. WEB PI can also automatically install this before starting WAP installation.
  - Internet Explorer enhanced security configuration for administrators should be disabled. Use Server Manager to disable it.

> Installing .NET Framework 3.5 on Windows Server 2012 or 2012 R2 requires specifying an alternate location for .NET files in the Add Roles and Features wizard. Visit https://technet.microsoft.com/en-in/library/dn482071.aspx for more information on this.

Installing Windows Azure Pack: Portal and API Express

We can start installing Windows Azure Pack after successful completion of the prerequisites.

Follow the following steps to install WAP Express:

1. Log on to the WAP server.
2. Start Microsoft Web PI (Microsoft Web Platform Installer).
3. Search **Windows Azure Pack: Portal and API Express**. Web PI will automatically detect that it's running and Windows Server 2012 R2 will display only compatible products for download and installation.
4. Search for **Windows Azure Pack: Portal and API Express**. This will automatically download and install all WAP components that are a part of Express Deployment.

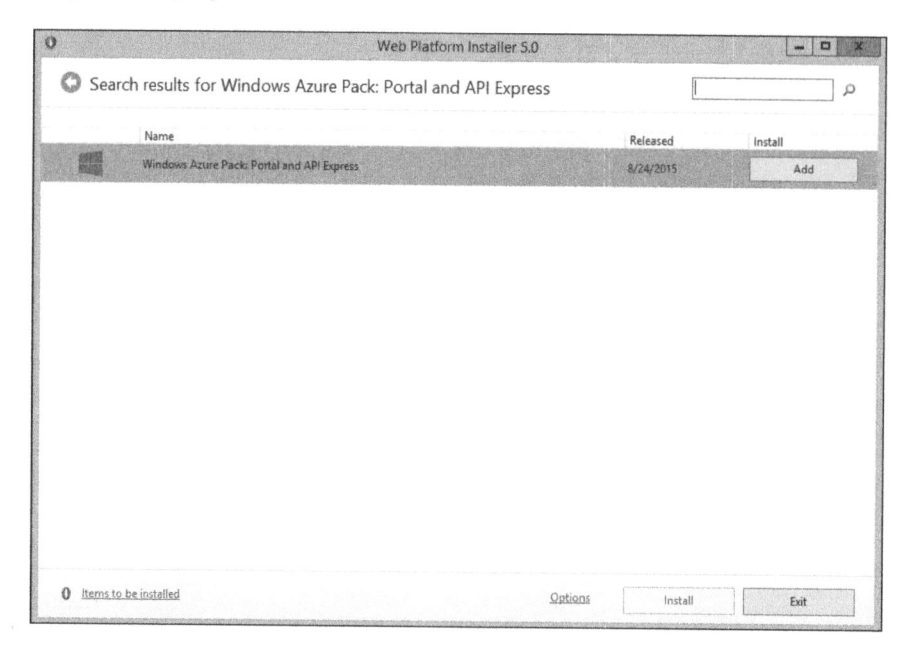

Chapter 3

5. Click **Add** to select the highlighted entry for download and installation.
6. Select **Install** to proceed further.
7. Web PI wizard will show the prerequisites and optional components that can be installed. You may choose to remove extra components such as partner provided extensions if you are not planning to use them.

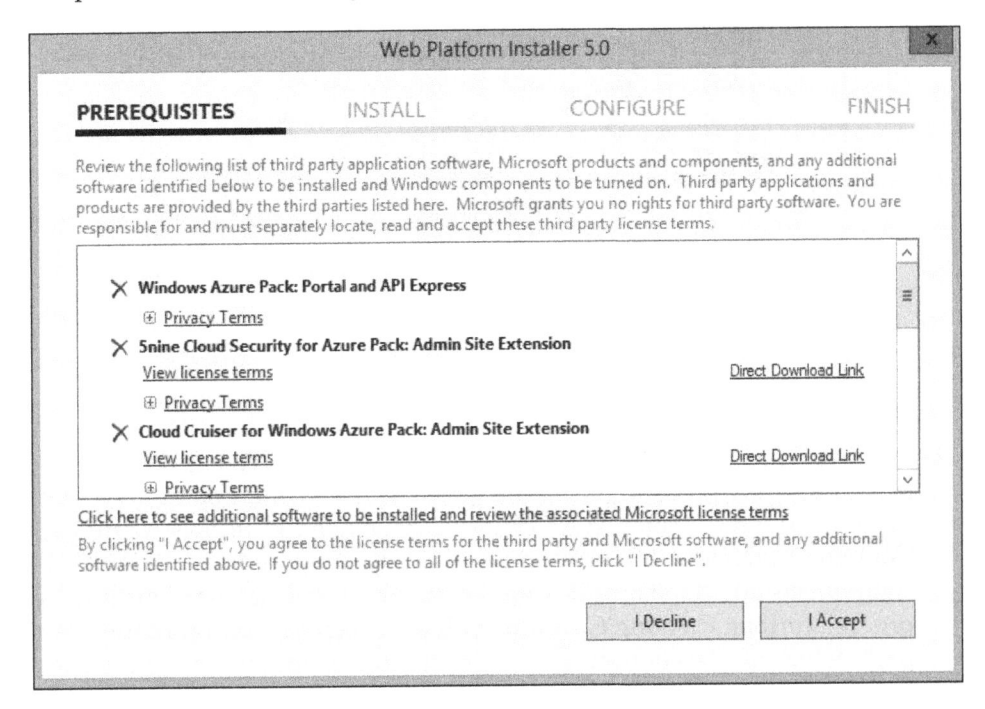

8. Remove any extra or not used components and click **I Accept** to proceed further.
9. Select Microsoft updates settings as per your requirement. It is recommended to enable Microsoft updates to keep WAP and other components updated with the latest features and fixes using the Windows Update Console itself.

Installing and Configuring Windows Azure Pack

10. Wizard will start downloading and installing WAP components and prerequisites, as shown in the following screenshot:

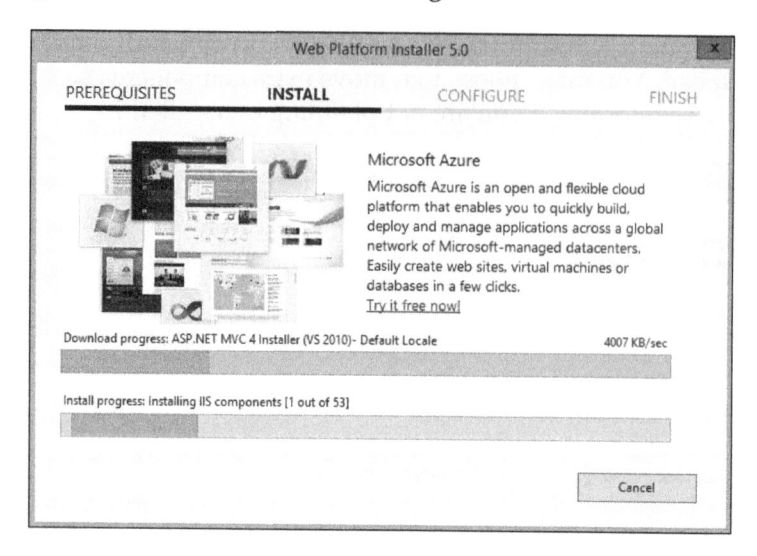

11. Successful installation will take you to the **CONFIGURE** page, which provides details on configuring the WAP installed components, as shown in the following screenshot. WAP creates a site named Windows Azure Pack Configuration Site in IIS for configuration and integration of all the WAP components and databases during the initial setup. Click on **Continue** to proceed further. Clicking **Continue** will also open the configuration site page, which can be configured now or closed to configure the settings later.

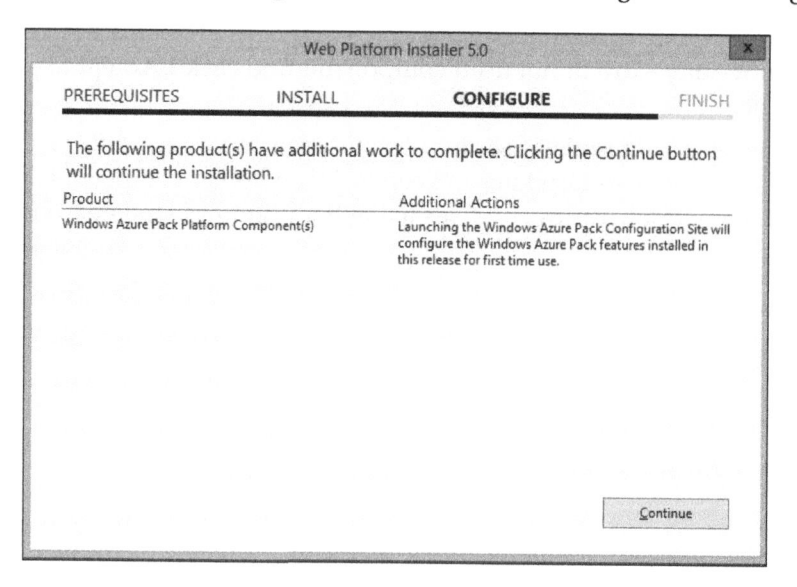

12. Review the installed components summary and finish the wizard. See installation logs in case of any errors. Exit the Web PI Console.
13. Installed components can be verified in the Programs and Features (`appwiz.cpl`) management console.

> Microsoft Web PI always contains the latest available version along with updates of Windows Azure Pack components.

Configuring Windows Azure Pack Express Deployment

In the preceding topic, we only installed those WAP components that were not ready to be used yet. Now, we need to configure all the WAP components (installed on a single server) by integrating with its management database and so on. Windows Azure Pack Configuration Site is used to configure the installation. You can open WAP Configuration Site by opening IE and its URL, or by using the Start menu icon.

Steps to configure a WAP Express installation are as follows:

1. Launch Internet Explorer with **Run as administrator**.
2. Open Windows Azure Pack Configuration Site accessible at `https://localhost:30101/`.
3. If any SSL warning comes up, click **continue** to this website.
4. Click **configure now** to proceed further.

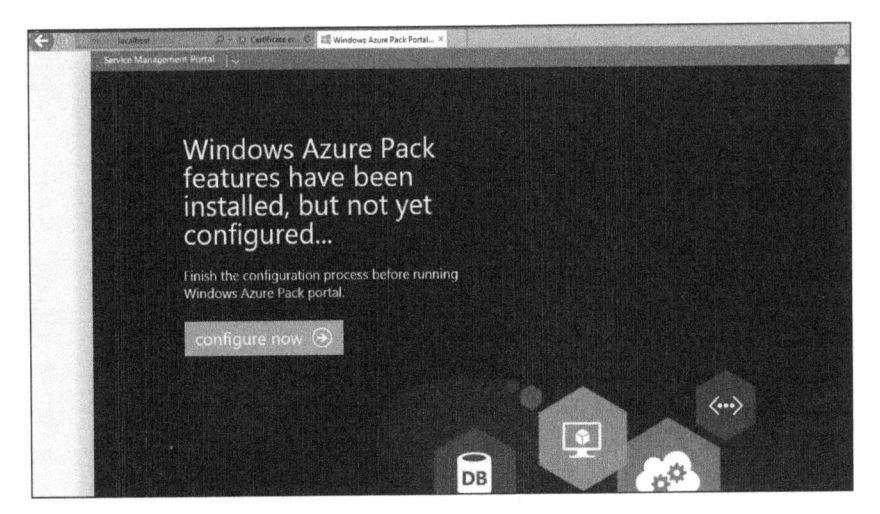

Installing and Configuring Windows Azure Pack

5. Provide the required information in the **Database Server Setup** wizard:
   - **SERVER NAME**: FQDN of the SQL Server used to the host cloud management database.
   - **AUTHENTICATION TYPE**: Windows Authentication or SQL authentication.
   - **DATABASE SERVER ADMIN USERNAME** and **DATABASE SERVER ADMIN PASSWORD**: The wizard will automatically detect if the username and password is correct before proceeding further.
   - **Configuration Store Passphrase**: WAP uses encryption and decryption to store and retrieve secret data from the configuration stored on SQL. This passphrase will be used to encrypt and decrypt the data. The same passphrase has to be used while configuring all the servers in a Distributed Deployment.

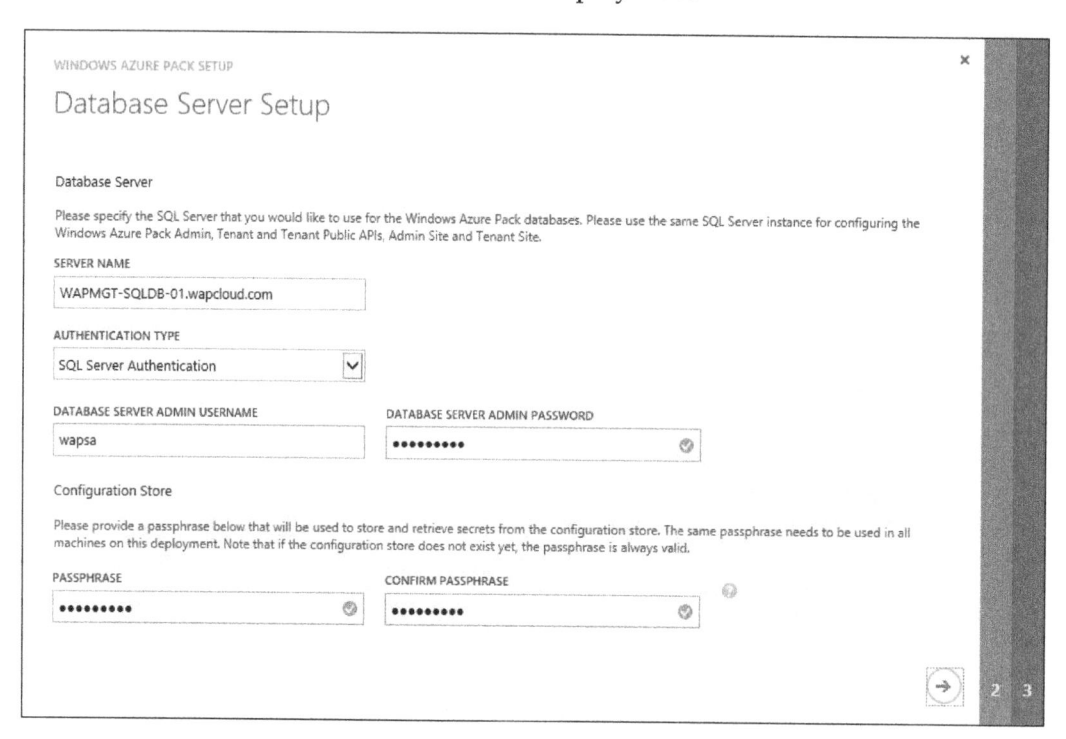

WINDOWS AZURE PACK SETUP

Database Server Setup

Database Server

Please specify the SQL Server that you would like to use for the Windows Azure Pack databases. Please use the same SQL Server instance for configuring the Windows Azure Pack Admin, Tenant and Tenant Public APIs, Admin Site and Tenant Site.

SERVER NAME

`WAPMGT-SQLDB-01.wapcloud.com`

AUTHENTICATION TYPE

`SQL Server Authentication`

DATABASE SERVER ADMIN USERNAME

`wapsa`

DATABASE SERVER ADMIN PASSWORD

`•••••••••`

Configuration Store

Please provide a passphrase below that will be used to store and retrieve secrets from the configuration store. The same passphrase needs to be used in all machines on this deployment. Note that if the configuration store does not exist yet, the passphrase is always valid.

PASSPHRASE

`•••••••••`

CONFIRM PASSPHRASE

`•••••••••`

Chapter 3

6. Select yes or no to participate in the **Customer Experience Improvement Program**.
7. Review the components to be configured and click the checkmark at the bottom right-hand side.

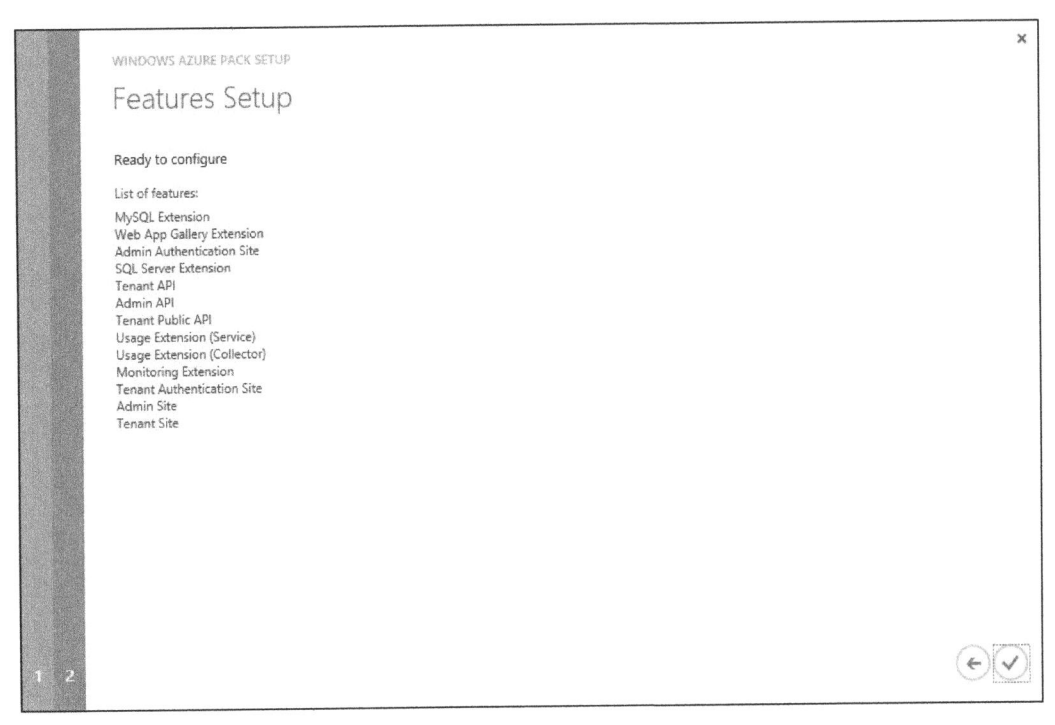

```
WINDOWS AZURE PACK SETUP
Features Setup

Ready to configure

List of features:
MySQL Extension
Web App Gallery Extension
Admin Authentication Site
SQL Server Extension
Tenant API
Admin API
Tenant Public API
Usage Extension (Service)
Usage Extension (Collector)
Monitoring Extension
Tenant Authentication Site
Admin Site
Tenant Site
```

8. **WINDOWS AZURE PACK SETUP** will start configuring each role. It will take a few minutes for the configuration to finish. Hit **finish** once the configuration is completed and is successful for all components.
9. The configuration is completed. Now you can proceed further to verify the deployment and to the next steps.

Installing and Configuring Windows Azure Pack

> 💡 Log out and login back to the WAP server post completion of the configuration. This creates the necessary security permissions to log into portals.

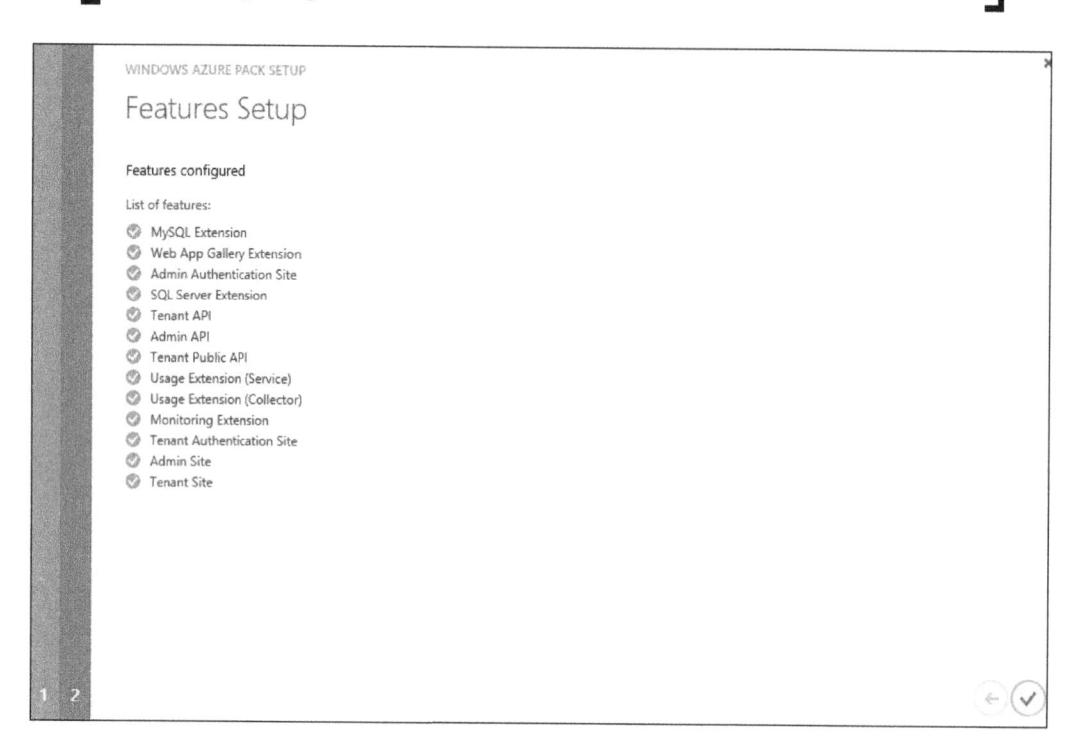

```
WINDOWS AZURE PACK SETUP

Features Setup

Features configured

List of features:
  ✓ MySQL Extension
  ✓ Web App Gallery Extension
  ✓ Admin Authentication Site
  ✓ SQL Server Extension
  ✓ Tenant API
  ✓ Admin API
  ✓ Tenant Public API
  ✓ Usage Extension (Service)
  ✓ Usage Extension (Collector)
  ✓ Monitoring Extension
  ✓ Tenant Authentication Site
  ✓ Admin Site
  ✓ Tenant Site
```

Validating a successful deployment

After completion of the configuration wizard, it's good to quickly run some tests to verify if deployment and database integration is completed successfully. Perform the following checks to verify if deployment is successful:

- Verify if all Internet Information Services (IIS) websites and applications are created on the WAP server. Use **Internet Information Services (IIS) Manager** to verify this. Install IIS Manager using Server Manager if not installed.

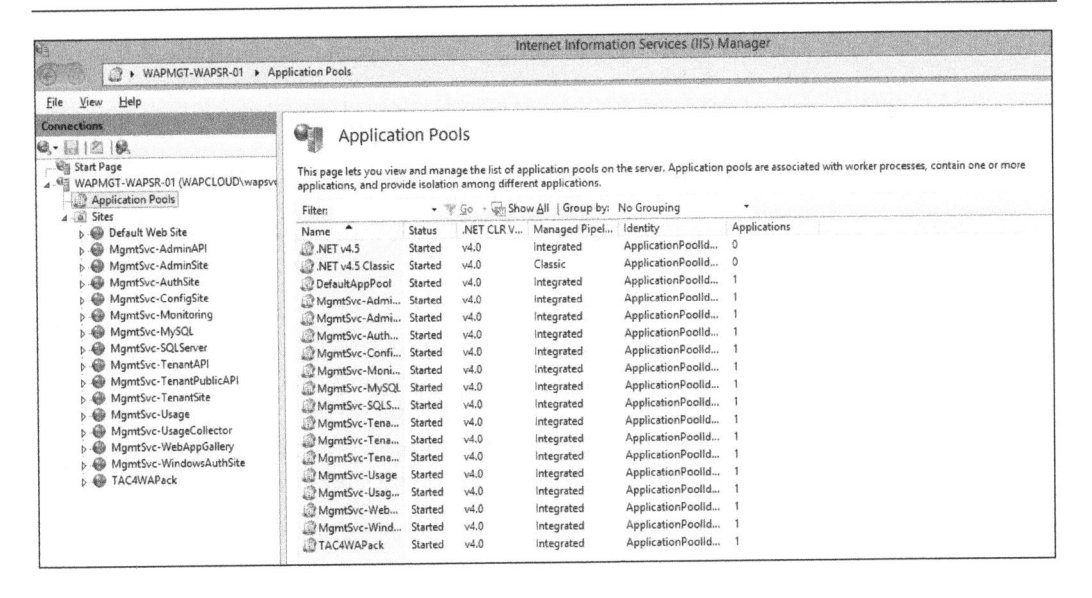

- Verify if all WAP databases are created on the SQL server specified during setup. Use SQL Management Studio to access the SQL Management Server. Access the WAP database server and expend databases to see all the databases created on the server:

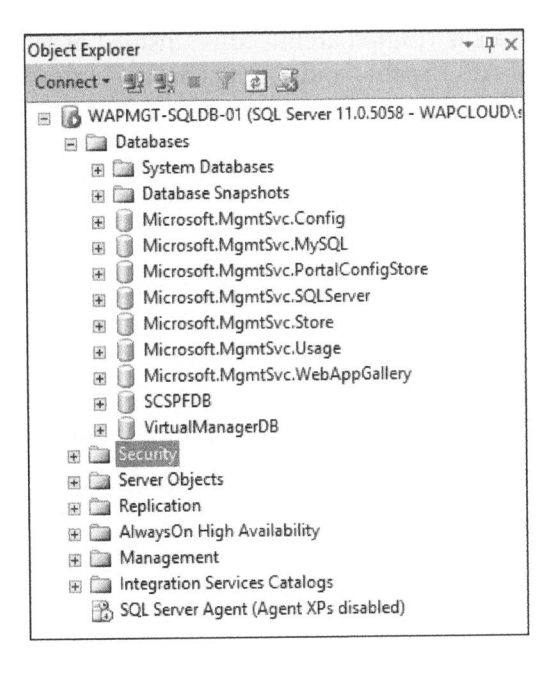

- Verify login to the Admin portal and the Tenant portal accessibility. Try logging into the Admin portal:

  Admin portal URL: `https://WAPServer:30091`

  Tenant portal URL: `https://WAPServer:30081`

- Run Microsoft Best Practice Analyzer for Windows Azure Pack to identify any gaps in deployment.

> The account used to install WAP components has to be used for logging into the Admin portal. Additional co-administrators can be added by adding users in MgmtSvc Operators local group on the WAP server.
> Microsoft Best Practice Analyzer for Windows Azure Pack can be downloaded and installed using Microsoft Web Platform Installer (WebPI).

Installing Windows Azure Pack in a Distributed architecture

Installation of Windows Azure Pack in a Distributed architecture is similar to Express installation. In a Distributed architecture, instead of selecting Windows Azure Pack: Portal and API Express, individual components such as Admin site and Admin authentication sites are selected and installed on multiple servers.

Microsoft Web Platform Installer (Web PI) is used to select individual components and installation of each of them on all the WAP servers. Let's have a look at the steps to deploy WAP in a Distributed architecture.

1. Complete the hardware and software prerequisite on all WAP servers (see *Chapter 1, Know Windows Azure Pack and Its Architecture*, for various deployment topologies of WAP in a Distributed architecture, last topic for software prerequisites).

2. Verify required firewall ports allowed in Windows or network firewalls.

3. Deploy any load balancers (physical or logical) for WAP virtual machines as per architecture.

4. Install and run Microsoft Web Platform Installer on WAP servers in a sequential manner.

5. Follow the given sequence to install and configure WAP components on multiple servers:
   1. Install and configure WAP Service Management APIs (Admin API, Tenant API, and Tenant Public API)
   2. Install and configure WAP Management portals (Admin site, Tenant site, and so on)
   3. Install and configure authentication sites (Admin Authentication site and Tenant Authentication sites)
   4. Install and configure other components such as resource providers, and so on
6. During configuration, provide SQL server details and the passphrase. Note down the passphrase as it has to be exactly the same while configuring all other components. It is a good idea to make a note of it, as there is no way to recover the passphrase if lost.
7. Configure load balancers to distribute traffic and DNS records.
8. Customize the portal and authentication site's URL and ports for load balanced names.
9. Replace self-signed certificates with trusted SSL certificates for websites.
10. Test deployment and complete post deployment best practices such as running BPA.

Changing portal URLs and ports, and replacing SSL certificates, is covered in further topics.

> By default, Windows Azure Pack portals uses HTTPS. If you try to open portals on HTTP, it will result in a page cannot be displayed error. To accept HTTP traffic for portals, create additional binding in IIS for each website pointing to port 80 along with the default HTTPS.
>
> Web.Config of each portal already has a rule of redirecting HTTP traffic to HTTPS, which comes into action after adding binding for port 80.

Required firewall ports for WAP components

The following networks ports have to be allowed in networks or any other external firewalls to enable communication between WAP components and websites access by admins or tenants.

Windows Azure Pack automatically creates rules in Windows firewall (if enabled) for these ports. Note that the following list includes only the default ports used by WAP components; add other ports if using any customized ports.

WAP Service	Port Number	Scope
Admin API	30004	Any IP required to access Admin API. It is usually cloud management IP range.
Management portal for Admins	30091	Any IP required to access admin portal. It is usually cloud management IP range.
Windows authentication site (used for admin portal authentication)	30072	Any IP required to access admin portal. It is usually cloud management IP range.
Configuration site	30101	Local WAP components subnet. This will be accessed during initial setup.
Monitoring site	30020	Any IP required to access monitoring services. It is usually cloud management range.
MySQL Resource Provider	30012	Any IP address using specified service.
SQL Server or MySQL Resource Provider	30010	Any IP address using specified service.
Tenant API	30005	Any IP address using specified service.
Tenant public API	30006	Any IP address using specified service. Usually all Internet IP ranges.
Management portal for tenants	30081	Any IP address using specified service. Usually all Internet IP ranges.
Tenant authentication site	30071	Any IP address using specified service. Usually all Internet IP ranges.
Usage	30022	Any IP address using specified service.
WebAppGallery	30018	Any IP address using specified service.

Customizing WAP portal's accessibility and certificates

By default, WAP websites use server hostnames as website URL, default port number, and self-signed certificates. In this topic, we will change the website's name, that is, URL, default port (such as 30081 to 443 for tenant portal) and SSL certificate with internal or public certificates as required. It is recommended to customize these portals' configuration for better security and user experience.

Assume a user experience of a tenant portal, also known as a customer portal, with complex enough URL and a custom port to add with disturbing security warnings of untrusted SSL certificates. Windows Azure Pack provides flexibilities to change URLs and ports along with trusted SSL certificates for WAP websites for improved security and smooth end user experience.

Before getting things into action, let's understand which websites come into the picture for the user logins (Admin or Tenant) WAP portal use claim-based authentication mechanism during the login process, as follows:

1. The user opens their respective portals such as admin portal or tenant portal by entering the WAP server's hostname with the port.
2. The admin site redirects the webpage to the respective authentication site webpage.
3. The user enters their credentials with a mechanism such as Windows Authentication/ASP.NET Authentication, or ADFS. Upon successful authentication, the user is provided with a security access token and redirected to the portal webpage again.
4. The admin portal webpage accepts the security token of the user and display the portal as per services/permissions available with the user.

As we learned, four websites plays a role in getting a user authenticated and getting their personalized portal as per role. In order to provide smooth user experience, we need to customize names, ports, and have trusted certificates for the following WAP websites:

- Admin management portal
- Admin authentication site
- Tenant management portal
- Tenant authentication site

For an organization's private cloud, in most cases all these websites will be accessible from inside the organizations only, which makes it feasible to use an internal **CA** (**Certification Authority**) provided SSL certificates for all websites.

In a service provider scenario, the Tenant portal will be accessible over the public Internet; whereas the Admin portal is likely to be accessed inside the provider's network only. In such cases, SSL certificates issued by public CA should be used for the Tenant management portal and Authentication site, whereas an internal CA can be leveraged for the Admin portal and Admin authentication site.

This makes the recommendation clear that internal CA provided SSL certificates should be used for portal and authentication sites to be used inside corporate LAN, where any public portal or authentication sites should be assigned SSL certificates issued by Public trusted CAs.

Overall, the following recommendations have to be performed for user accessible websites to improve user experience and security:

- Use simpler URLs for Admin and Tenant websites
- Use standard ports such as 443 (HTTPS) to avoid any complexity in URLs
- Use trusted SSL certificates to avoid any SSL related security warnings

To implement the preceding recommendations, the following operations have to be performed in a WAP Cloud solution:

1. Create DNS records for new URLs (in internal DNS and Public DNS servers.)
2. Generate and import trusted SSL certificates for each website.
3. Configure website bindings to use new URLs, ports, and certificates.
4. Update the Windows Azure Pack Configuration database with new URLs and ports.

Configure portal's DNS names

By default, WAP management portals and authentication sites use the following ports.

The following are WAP websites' default URLs and ports:

Site Name	URL	Port
Management Portal for Administrator	https://WAPServer:30091	30091
Admin Authentication Site	https://WAPServer:30072	30072
Management Portal for Tenants	https://WAPServer:30081	30081
Tenant Authentication Site	https://WAPServer:30071	30071

For evaluation purposes, we shall be changing URLs and ports as per the following table. Organizations and service providers may choose their own names and ports as per their choice.

Site Name	URL	Port
Management Portal for Administrator	`https://admin.wapcloud.com`	443
Admin Authentication Site	`https://adminauth.wapcloud.com`	443
Management Portal for Tenants	`https://manage.wapcloud.com`	443
Tenant Authentication Site	`https://manageauth.wapcloud.com`	443

"`A`" records and "`PTR`" records need to be created in internal and external DNS servers for the preceding names pointing to the WAP server. Changes in Public DNS servers are required if any of the services are accessible over the Internet like tenant portals and authentication sites.

DNS Manager can be used to create records in the internal DNS server. Use the following steps to create the records:

1. Open DNS Manager on the DNS server.
2. Right click on **DNS Zone** and create a new record button.
3. Provide the name and IP of portal and WAP server, as follows:

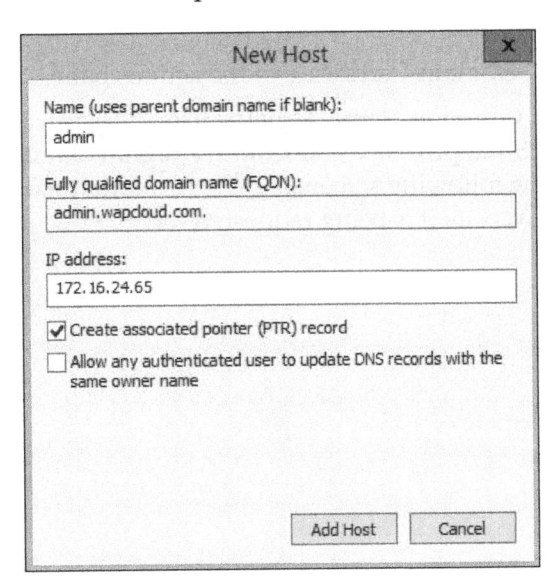

4. Select **Create associated pointer (PTR) record**.
5. Create all required records using the same method.

Getting SSL certificates for WAP websites

Getting SSL certificates for WAP management portals and authentication sites is similar to getting SSL for any other websites running on any web server. SSL certificates are usually requested and assigned online by any CA authority, or offline by creating a certificate request file at the IIS server and then submitting a certificate request file to Public CA providers to get the required SSL.

Active Directory Certificate Services, that is, internal Enterprise CA can be used to assign certificates for portals accessible inside corporate networks only, such as management portals for administrators and so on. For the purpose of evaluation, we shall be using internal Windows ADCS Services as a CA to assign certificates to the websites.

Assuming that you already have an Enterprise CA configured inside your organization (Active Directory Certificate Services), the following are the steps required to request and assign SSL certificates for WAP websites:

1. Log on to WAP server and open IIS Manager.
2. Select Your IIS server name and then **Server Certificates** on the homepage.
3. The **Server Certificates** window will display all existing self-signed or other certificates being used in the IIS server.
4. Click **Request Domain Certificate** in the actions pane.
5. Providing the **Common Name**, **Organization**, **Organizational Unit**, **City/locality**, **State/province** and **Country/region** details as requested, as shown in the following screenshot. The **Common name** would be the FQDN of the website it is being requested for.

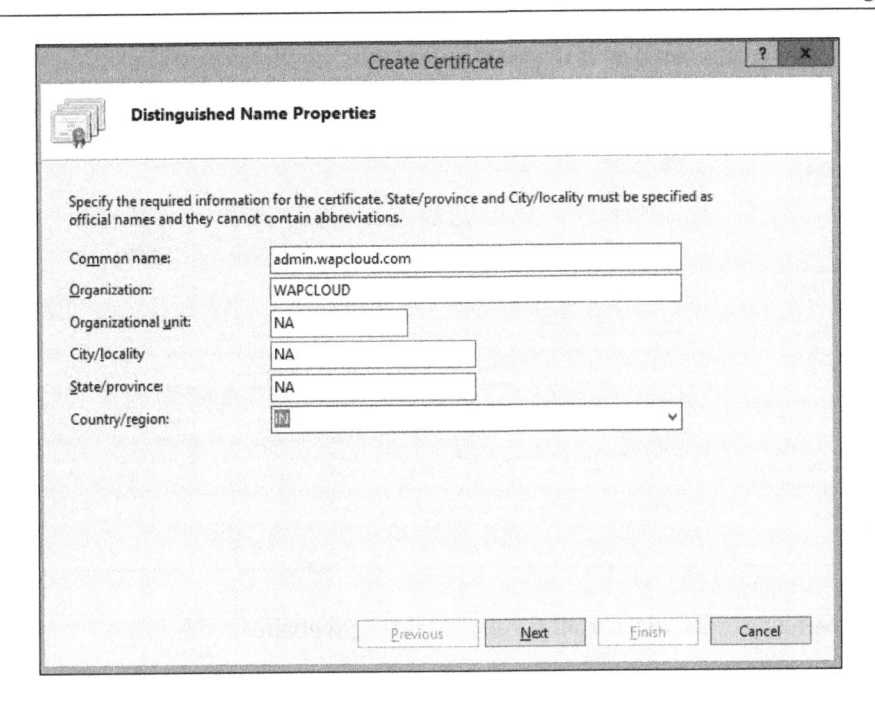

[Screenshot: Create Certificate – Distinguished Name Properties dialog with Common name: admin.wapcloud.com, Organization: WAPCLOUD, Organizational unit: NA, City/locality: NA, State/province: NA, Country/region: IN]

6. Specify the CA name and server name where ADCS is running and configured. Assign a friendly name for the certificate for easy identification and management.

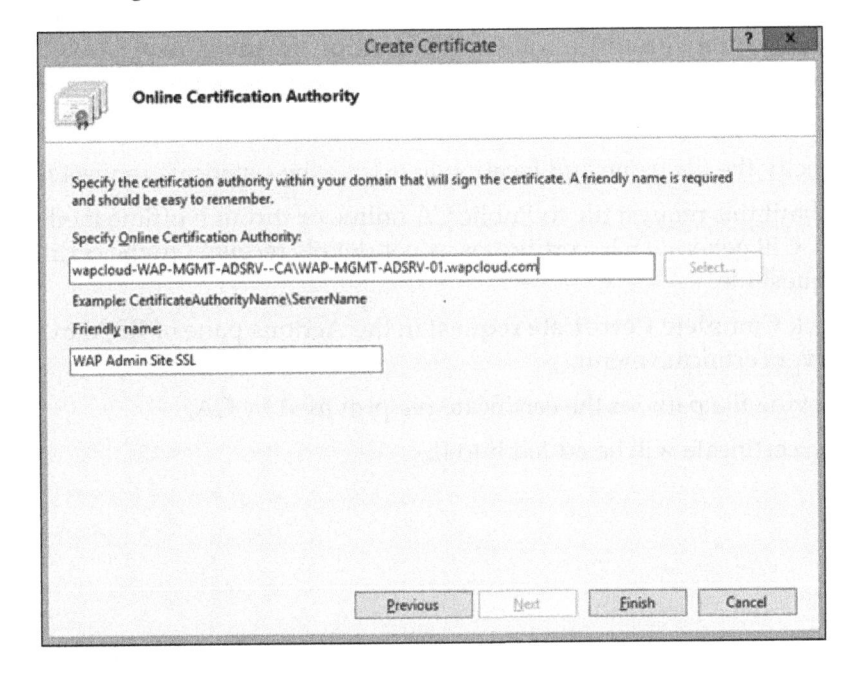

[Screenshot: Create Certificate – Online Certification Authority dialog with Specify Online Certification Authority: wapcloud-WAP-MGMT-ADSRV--CA\WAP-MGMT-ADSRV-01.wapcloud.com, Friendly name: WAP Admin Site SSL]

Installing and Configuring Windows Azure Pack

7. Clicking on **Finish** will request and import certificates in IIS, as shown in the following screenshot:

8. Request certificates for all three remaining websites.

To request the SSL certificate from a Public CA, perform the following steps:

1. Open **IIS Manager** | **IIS Server Home** | **Server Certificates**.
2. Click **Create Certificate Request** in the **Actions** pane.
3. Provides the **Common Name**, **Organization**, **Organizational Unit**, **City/locality**, **State/province** and **Country/region** details as requested. The **Common name** would be the FQDN of the website it is being requested for.
4. Select **Cryptographer service provider** and **Bit length** as per the Public CA.
5. Specify the file name and location to extract the certificate request file.
6. Submit this request file to Public CA online or through offline method. CA will generate SSL certificates as per details received in the certificate request file.
7. Click **Complete Certificate request** in the **Actions** pane of IIS Manager's server certificate menu.
8. Provide file path for the certificate file provided by CA.
9. The certificate will be added into IIS.

Configuring site binding to use new URL's, port and SSL

Now, we need to configure WAP websites to use these new names, ports, and SSL certificates. Follow these steps to do this:

1. Open IIS Manager on the WAP server and browse through the websites.
2. Select **MgmtSvc-AdminSite** to select Management portals for the administrator site.
3. Click on **Bindings** on the **Actions** pane.
4. Select existing HTTPS binding and click **Edit Bindings**.
5. Provide a new **Port** number and **Host name** and select newly created **SSL certificate** for the Admin site.
6. Select the **Require Server Name Indication** checkbox.
7. Submit the changes by clicking **OK**.
8. Repeat the preceding steps for the remaining websites.

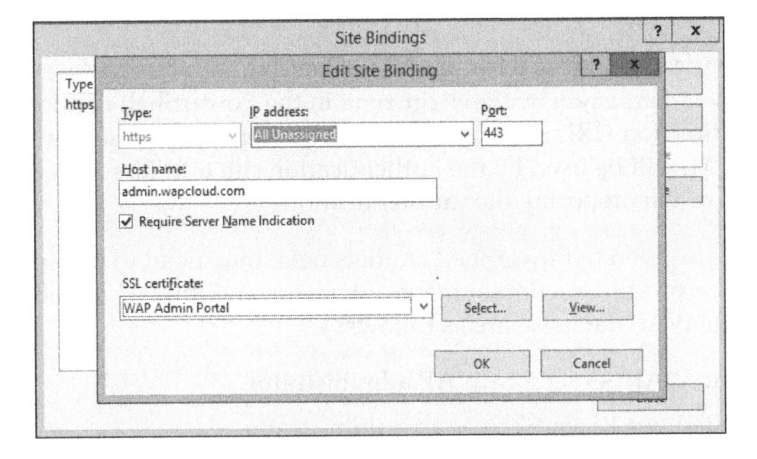

The following are the IIS website names and the corresponding WAP websites:

IIS WebSite Name	WAP component
MgmtSvc-AdminSite	Management Portal for Administrators
MgmtSvc-WindowsAuthSite	Admin Authentication Site
MgmtSvc-TenantSite	Management Portal for Administrators
MgmtSvc-AuthSite	Tenant Authentication Site

Updating changes in the Windows Azure Pack database

All changes performed in the previous steps have to be updated in the Windows Azure Pack configuration store to make them effective. Let's update the changes made in portal URLs and ports in the WAP Configuration database residing on the Management SQL Server.

Windows Azure Pack PowerShell will be used to update the changes. We need to update the value in the following three configurations in the WAP DB for both admin and tenant portals:

- **Portal FQDN**: Configured by using `Set-MgmtSvcFqdn` in the PowerShell cmdlet, this will update FQDN for websites' portals in the WAP database such as `admin.wapcloud.com`.

- **Authentication Service Relay**: Configured by using `Set-MgmtSvcRelyingPartySettings` in the PowerShell cmdlet, this will update the URL of the authentication site in the WAP database. This URL will be used by the portal to redirect when the user accesses the portal without any security token.

- **Authentication Service Redirection**: Configured by using `Set-MgmtSvcIdentityProviderSettings` in the PowerShell cmdlet, this updates the redirection URL used by the authentication site post user authentication. This URL will be used by the authentication site to redirect the user to the admin or tenant portal after authentication.

Sample URLs are given in PowerShell cmdlets next, they need to be replaced with actual names for production deployments. Steps for updating new websites' URLs and ports in the WAP database are as follows:

1. Log into WAP Server as a WAP administrator.
2. Run Windows PowerShell as an administrator.
3. Import the Windows Azure Pack PowerShell module by executing the following commands:

   `Import-Module -Name MgmtSvcConfig`

4. Update the Admin portal FQDN by issuing the following command in the PowerShell. FQDN in this cmdlet is the admin portal's FQDN:

   `Set-MgmtSvcFqdn -Namespace "AdminSite" -FullyQualifiedDomainName "admin.wapcloud.com" -Port 443 -Server "WAPMGT-SQLDB-01.wapcloud.com"`

5. Update the Admin Authentication site FQDN by issuing the following PowerShell. FQDN in this cmdlet is admin authentication site's FQDN:

   ```
   Set-MgmtSvcFqdn -Namespace "WindowsAuthSite"
   -FullyQualifiedDomainName "adminauth.wapcloud.com" -Port 443
   -Server "WAPMGT-SQLDB-01.wapcloud.com"
   ```

6. Update the Admin Authenticate site redirection changes by issuing the following PowerShell. FQDN in this cmdlet is admin authentication site's FQDN:

   ```
   Set-MgmtSvcRelyingPartySettings -Target Admin -MetadataEndpoint
   'https://adminauth.wapcloud.com:443/FederationMetadata/2007-06/
   FederationMetadata.xml' -ConnectionString "Data Source=WAPMGT-
   SQLDB-01.wapcloud.com ;User ID=sa; Password=*******"
   ```

7. Update the Authenticate Service redirection by issuing the following PowerShell. FQDN in this cmdlet is admin portal's FQDN:

   ```
   Set-MgmtSvcIdentityProviderSettings -Target Windows -
   MetadataEndpoint 'https://admin.wapcloud.com/
   FederationMetadata/2007-06/FederationMetadata.xml'
   -ConnectionString "Data Source=WAPMGT-SQLDB-01.wapcloud.com ;User
   ID=sa;Password=********"
   ```

8. Update the Tenant Admin portal FQDN by issuing the following PowerShell. FQDN in this cmdlet is the Tenant portal's FQDN:

   ```
   Set-MgmtSvcFqdn -Namespace "TenantSite" -FullyQualifiedDomainName
   "manage.wapcloud.com" -Port 443 -Server "WAPMGT-SQLDB-01.wapcloud.
   com"
   ```

9. Update the Tenant Authentication portal FQDN by issuing the following PowerShell. FQDN in this cmdlet is the tenant authentication portal's FQDN:

   ```
   Set-MgmtSvcFqdn -Namespace "AuthSite" -FullyQualifiedDomainName
   "manageauth.wapcloud.com" -Port 443 -Server "WAPMGT-SQLDB-01.
   wapcloud.com"
   ```

10. Update the Tenant Authenticate redirection site changes by issuing the following PowerShell. FQDN in this cmdlet is the tenant authentication site's FQDN:

    ```
    Set-MgmtSvcRelyingPartySettings -Target Tenant -MetadataEndpoint
    'https://manageauth.wapcloud.com:443/FederationMetadata/2007-06/
    FederationMetadata.xml' -ConnectionString "Data Source=WAPMGT-
    SQLDB-01.wapcloud.com ;User ID=sa; Password=*******"
    ```

11. Update the tenant Authenticate Service redirection by issuing the following PowerShell. FQDN in this cmdlet is the tenant admin portal's FQDN:

   ```
   Set-MgmtSvcIdentityProviderSettings -Target Membership -
   MetadataEndpoint 'https://manage.wapcloud.com/
   FederationMetadata/2007-06/FederationMetadata.xml'
   -ConnectionString "Data Source=WAPMGT-SQLDB-01.wapcloud.com ;User
   ID=sa;Password=********"
   ```

12. Successful updated configuration will give an output as follows:

```
PS C:\Windows\system32> Set-MgmtSvcFqdn -Namespace "AdminSite" -FullyQualifiedDomainName "admin.wapcloud.com" -Port 443
-Server "WAPMGT-SQLDB-01.wapcloud.com"

Scheme                         FullyQualifiedDomainName                                                          Port
------                         ------------------------                                                          ----
https                          admin.wapcloud.com                                                                 443

PS C:\Windows\system32>
```

Verifying portal customizations

The following steps can be followed to verify if customization made in the previous section is effective:

1. Verify if portal URLs and port customizations are working fine by logging into both tenant and admin portals.
2. Check SSL certificates of websites by clicking on the SSL button in the web browser for the website.
3. Verify no SSL trust related warnings are displayed during login or accessing the portal.

Registering Service Provider Foundation with WAP

Now that we have our portal ready for Admin and Tenant usage, it's time to integrate or make WAP APIs communicate with Fabric prepared in the previous chapter. In this section, we will register Service Provider Foundation with Windows Azure pack Service Management APIs.

See *Chapter 1, Know Windows Azure Pack and Its Architecture*, System Centre integration section, to learn more about integration between WAP APIs and SPF.

Before registering, verify if SPF is deployed and configured properly to ensure successful registration:

- There is network reachability on required ports between the WAP server and SPF
- SPF application pools identity are running as a domain user
- The SPF App Pool identity user has admin permissions on SCVMM and SPF DB
- The local user is created on SPF server for WAP integration. Ensure that this local user is added to the SPF Local Groups Server (`SPF_Admin`, `SPF_Provider`, `SPF_Usage`, and `SPF_VMM`)

Steps to register SPF Endpoint in WAP are as follows:

1. Log into the WAP admin portal using WAP administrator credentials.
2. Select VM clouds. Opening the VM clouds page will give the option to register SPF. If not available, click on the Quick Start() button.
3. Select **Register System Center Service Provider Foundation**.

Installing and Configuring Windows Azure Pack

4. Provide the SPF server FQDN and login credentials:

    SPF Server: `https://WAPMGT-SCSPF-01:8090/`

    Use the spflocal account created earlier in *Chapter 2, Getting the Cloud Fabric Ready*, during SPF installation. Do not provide any domain name or computer name in the login name.

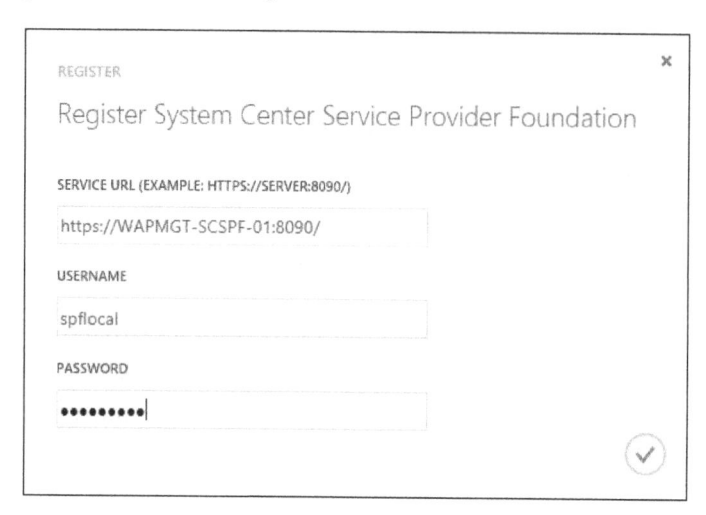

    REGISTER

    Register System Center Service Provider Foundation

    SERVICE URL (EXAMPLE: HTTPS://SERVER:8090/)

    https://WAPMGT-SCSPF-01:8090/

    USERNAME

    spflocal

    PASSWORD

    •••••••••

5. The registration task starts by clicking on the checkmark.

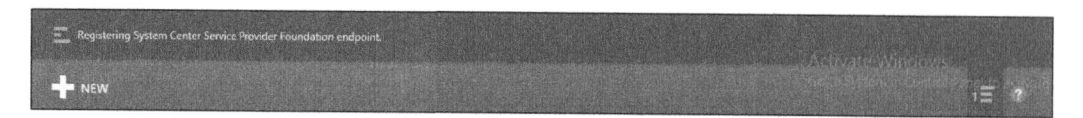

    Registering System Center Service Provider Foundation endpoint.

6. Click **OK** once registration is successfully completed:

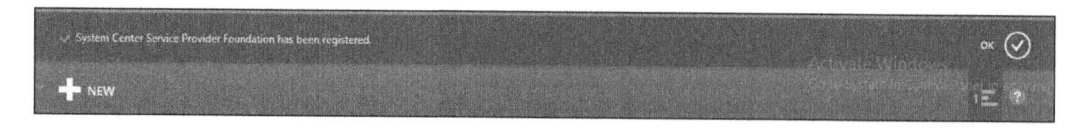

    System Center Service Provider Foundation has been registered.

7. Now, we can start integrating SCVMM and building IaaS services, which will be covered in next chapter.

Summary

In this chapter, we learned about installation and configuration of Windows Azure Pack in the Express Deployment model and Distributed Deployment model. We did an installation and configuration walkthrough of different WAP components.

We also covered customizing portals' URLs, ports, and SSL certificates to provide better user experience and to comply with organizations' and cloud providers' needs. At the end of this chapter, we customized Admin and Tenant portals accessible for users (Admin and Tenant users), waiting to offer cloud services.

In the next chapter, we shall be building IaaS cloud offering catalogues.

4
Building VM Clouds and IaaS Offerings

In the previous chapter, we installed and configured Windows Azure Pack components. The portals accessible to admins and tenants, available at this point of time, are just plain with respect to cloud services offering. In this chapter, we will build VM Clouds with the integration of Windows Azure Pack, SPF, and SCVMM. Windows Azure Pack VM Clouds are used to provide IaaS (Infrastructure as a Service) capabilities, such as virtual machines, virtual networks, and so on.

You will learn about VM Cloud's architecture, planning, and implementation. Furthermore, we will start building the cloud offerings, such as VMs and templates, gallery resources and their integration, and mapping with fabric resources in SCVMM. You will learn to use Microsoft-provided standard cloud services gallery items as well as develop custom gallery items for custom needs.

In this chapter, we will be covering the following topic:

- VM Clouds overview
- Registering SCVMM with Windows Azure Pack
- Building a SCVMM cloud for Windows Azure Pack cloud
- Preparing OS images for a cloud catalogue (Windows and Linux VMs)
- IaaS virtual machine offerings – standalone VM versus VM role
- Building standalone VM IaaS offerings
- The VM Role architecture
- Building VM Role IaaS offerings using gallery resources

- Using the **GRIT** (**Gallery Resource Import**) tool
- Developing VM Role gallery resources using VM Role Authoring Tool
- Accessing tenant's virtual machines – Windows Azure Pack Console Connect

VM Clouds overview

VM Clouds in Windows Azure Pack cloud solution is a top-level umbrella to provide IaaS services. Clouds created in **System Center Virtual Machine Manager (SCVMM)** are represented as VM Clouds in the Windows Azure Pack management portal.

VM Clouds can be used to provide IaaS services with multitenancy capabilities. In Windows Azure Pack-based cloud, cloud plans and subscriptions and cloud offering catalogues and fabric resources are provisioned, mapped, and managed on a VM Cloud level.

Windows Azure Pack uses SPF to communicate with VMM for all operations and management with respect to VM Clouds. There can be a multiple number of VM Clouds created in one or more SCVMM as per requirements; it is recommended to only single or fewer VM Clouds.

Use case for creating multiple VM Cloud includes GEO site locations, dedicated hardware services to tenants, backup/secondary/DR infrastructure, or as per the features available as per the cloud provider's strategy; but, they are not limited to these.

IaaS services include virtual machines, virtual networks, and IaaS machines with automated application deployment, and they are provided using VM Clouds. But, they are not limited to these.

VM Clouds are responsible for delivering IaaS services including virtual machines and networks along with automated application deployment inside the virtual machines.

Registering SCVMM with Windows Azure Pack

Before we start building VM Clouds and IaaS offerings, we must register our SCVMM instance with Windows Azure Pack. This is also called stamp registration.

Chapter 4

The following steps need to be carried out for registering SCVMM stamp with Windows Azure Pack:

1. Log into the Windows Azure Pack Management portal for administrators.
2. Browse the **vm clouds** workspace.

3. Click on **USE AN EXISTING VIRTUAL MACHINE CLOUD PROVIDER TO PROVISION VIRTUAL MACHINES**.
4. Provide **VIRTUAL MACHINE MANAGER SERVER FQDN** and **PORT NUMBER** (if customized). Note that it doesn't ask for credentials as Windows Azure Pack uses the service provider foundation VMM service account for accessing VMM. Enter **REMOTE DESKTOP GATEWAY FQDN**, which will be used for Azure Pack Console Connect. This can be configured later as a remote Desktop Gateway is covered later in this chapter.

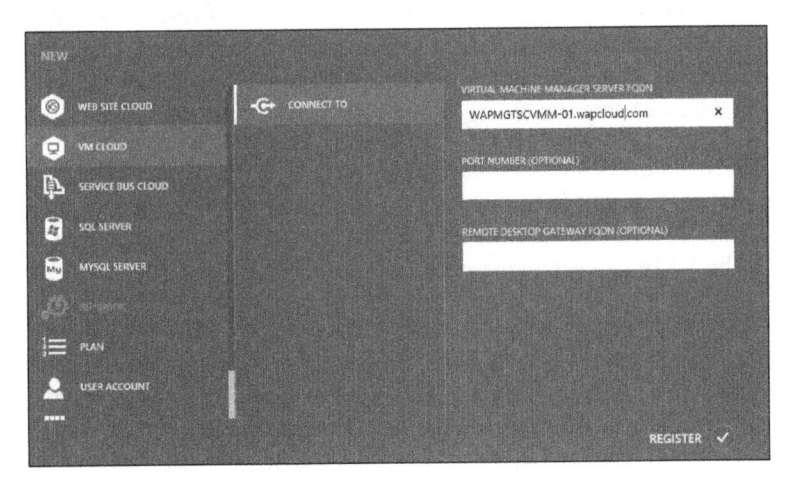

5. Upon successful registration, VMM stamps will be displayed in the **CLOUDS** workspace in the Windows Azure Pack portal.

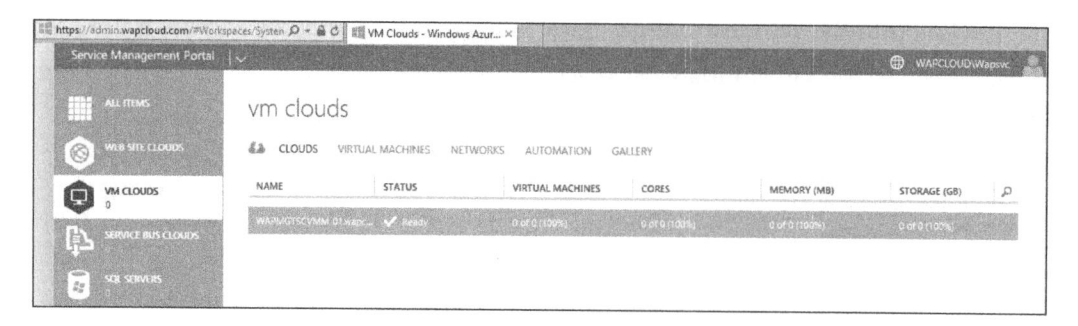

6. Review the Windows Azure Pack registration error, Windows Azure Pack, SPF, and VMM logs in case of any registration failure.

We do not see any cloud listed in the Windows Azure Pack portal at this point as we have only integrated the virtualization machine cloud provider. Now, we will start building VM Clouds.

Building a SCVMM cloud for Windows Azure Pack cloud

A cloud in **SCVMM** is an umbrella containing our VMM fabric resources, such as compute (hypervisors), networking, and storage along with resources, such as VM, services, and templates. A cloud created in SCVMM is used by Windows Azure Pack to offer IaaS services to tenants using plans and subscriptions.

A cloud in SCVMM can be created using SCVMM host groups, which may contain different hypervisors or can be created from the VMware resource pool. At the time of writing this book, Windows Azure Pack VM Cloud didn't support SCVMM cloud created using the VMware resource pool.

Note that though VMware or server resources can be added in a SCVMM Cloud, IaaS resource provisioning on these via Windows Azure Pack tenant portal isn't possible. At this point of time, only Hyper-V is the supported hypervisor for IaaS services in a WAP VM Cloud. The third-party partner solutions are available for using Windows Azure Pack with VMware-based virtualization solutions. This limitation is applicable only for tenants' IaaS workloads, VMware/Xen, and other based VMs that can be used to host Windows Azure Pack management servers, websites, DBaaS servers, and more.

Before creating a SCVMM cloud, let's have a look at the SCVMM cloud's requirements with respect to Windows Azure Pack VM Cloud support.

Requirements for Windows Azure Pack VM Clouds

While creating a SCVMM cloud, consider the following prerequisites that need to be taken care of with respect to the Windows Azure Pack VM Cloud:

- An SCVMM cloud must be created from host groups. A cloud created with VMware resource pool is not supported by Windows Azure Pack at this point of time.
- The cloud capability profile (ESX server, Hyper-V, or XenServer) must not be selected while creating the cloud.
- A cloud capacity (compute/network/storage resource) must be selected as per the available capacity. The limits of these resources will be applicable for tenants using Windows Azure Pack cloud while provisioning resources.
- Logical network planned for Windows Azure Pack must be already created and associated with the SCVMM cloud.
- The VMM library share must be already created and configured with the cloud.
- **Service Management Automation (SMA)** will be discussed in the upcoming chapters. If it is being used for automation with respect to the SCVMM cloud, then the SMA web service certificate must be trusted on the SPF server. This will be discussed in detail in *Chapter 9, Automation and Authentication – Service Management Automation and ADFS*.

Creating a cloud in SCVMM

The SCVMM management console is used to create a cloud in VMM. Before creating a cloud, verify that you have configured all the required fabric components. See *Chapter 2, Getting the Cloud Fabric Ready*, to review the fabric components requirements.

Carry out these steps to create the SCVMM cloud:

1. Log into the SCVMM server using the VMM console with administrative access.

Building VM Clouds and IaaS Offerings

2. Click on **Create Cloud** in the **Home** ribbon.

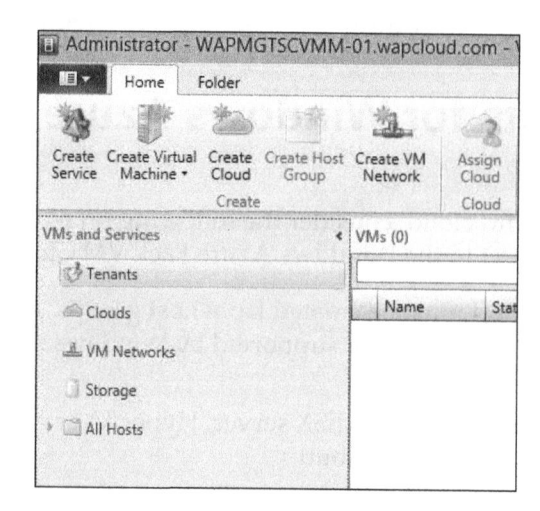

3. Provide the cloud name and description in **Create Cloud Wizard**.

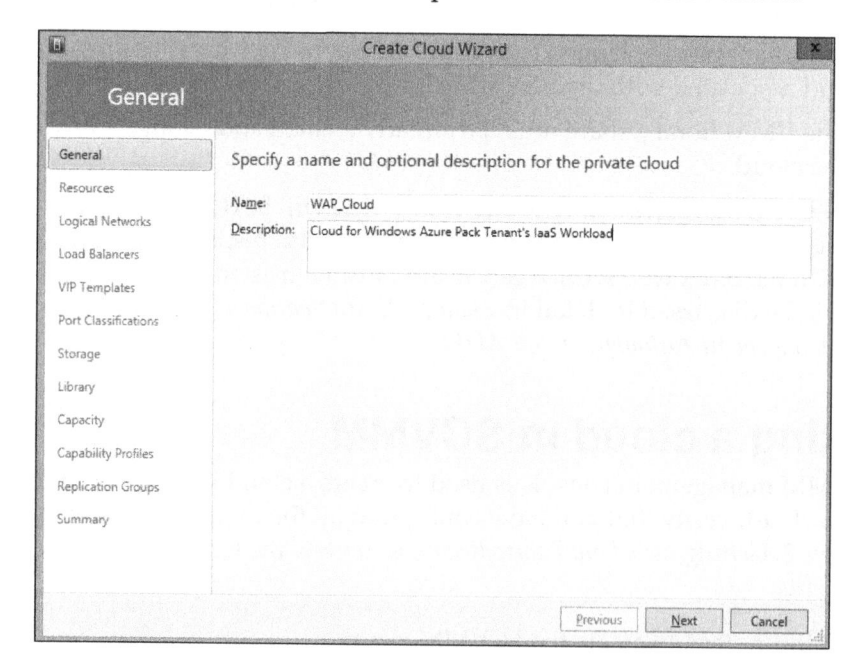

4. Select the **Host groups** cloud that is to be used for Windows Azure Pack tenant's workload in the **Select resource for this cloud** section. The wizard will also display the capacity or host groups in terms of CPU's memory and network.

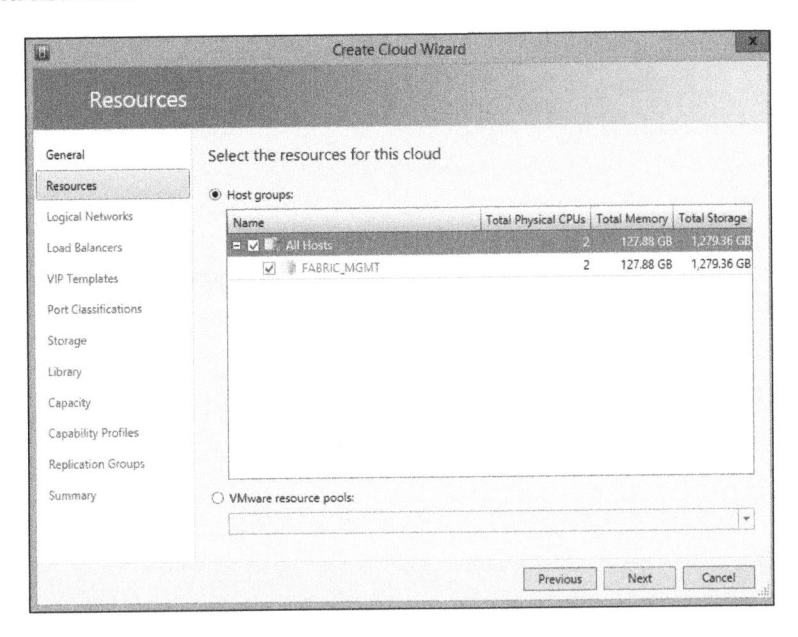

5. On the **Logical Networks** page, select logical network or networks created for the usage of Windows Azure Pack Cloud. It will be used by tenants to create and use VM networks. This will leverage network virtualization for provisioning virtual networks for tenants independent of each other. See *Chapter 2, Getting the Cloud Fabric Ready*, to learn more about network virtualization.

> Note that logical networks assigned with physical network adaptors on Hyper-V hosts will only be visible on this page.

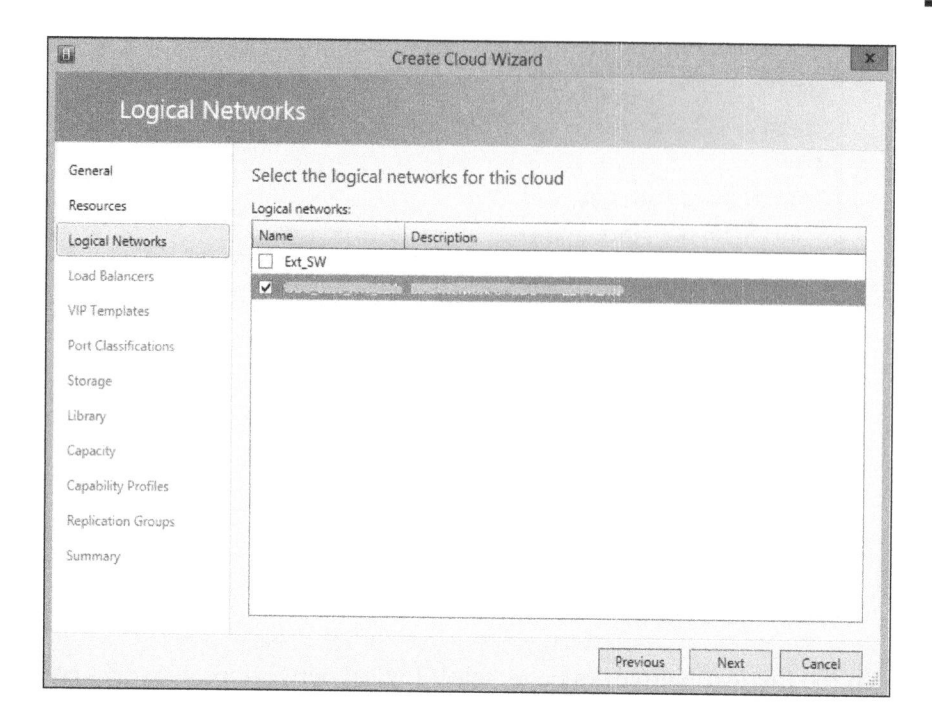

![Create Cloud Wizard - Logical Networks screen]

6. Optionally, select **Load Balancers** to be made available for access in this cloud.

7. Optionally, select **VIP Templates** for cloud usage. VIP templates are used in conjunction with load balancers for virtual IPs and other related configurations.

8. Optionally, select **Port Classifications** to be used for cloud resources. The port profile can be used to specify **QOS (Quality of Service)** at the cloud layer along with a granular control at the Windows Azure Pack plans level.

9. Optionally, select **Storage** to be used to store virtual machines for this cloud. See *Chapter 2, Getting the Cloud Fabric Ready*, to know more on storage options for the Windows Azure Pack cloud.

10. Select the stored VM path and read only library shares for cloud usage.

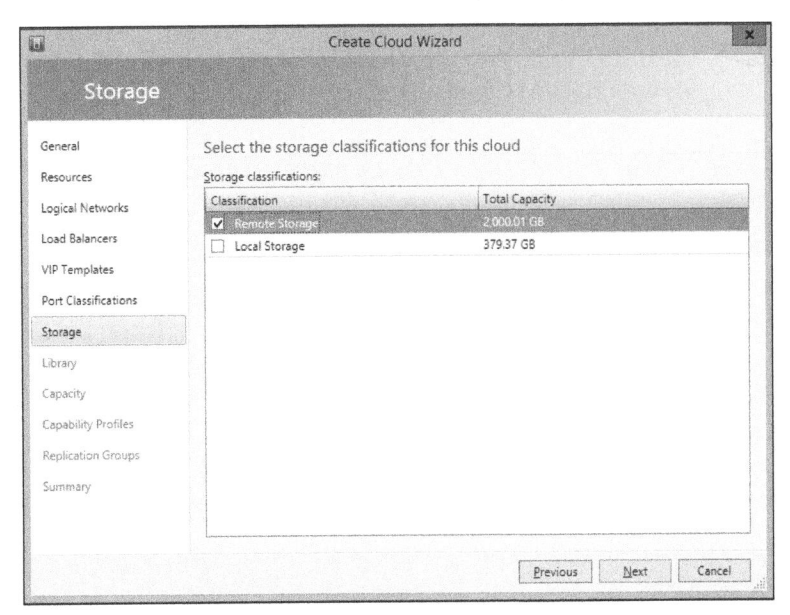

11. Select **Capacity** to know about the cloud capacity available for usage by tenants. This is one of the most important settings at the SCVMM layer for the cloud. The capacity should be wisely selected as per the availability of resources. This capacity limit will be applicable for all the tenants that the IaaS workload has hosted inside the cloud. The tenant level capacity limit shall be configured and at the Windows Azure Pack plan's level. While values such as CPU and memory are self-explanatory, custom quota values in capacity are values defined for virtual machine templates based upon parameters such as size. Later, these are used for restricting maximum resources provisioned by any self-service user in cloud.

Building VM Clouds and IaaS Offerings

> Note that custom quota points provide backward compatibility and are only applicable for self-service users created in VMM 2008 R2. These aren't applicable for Windows Azure Pack VM Clouds.

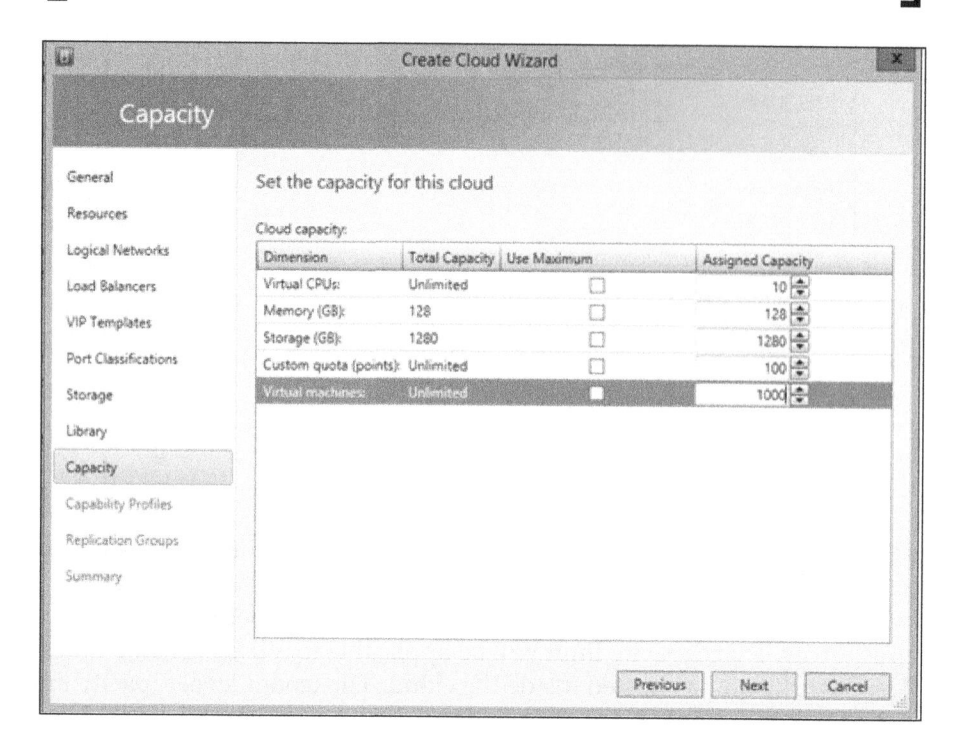

12. On the **Capability Profiles** page, do not select any of the profiles (ESX/Hyper-V/XenServer). Windows Azure Pack doesn't support using a SCVMM cloud with a capability profile for IaaS workload of tenants.
13. If applicable, add any **Cloud Disaster Recovery Solutions** on **Replication Groups** page.
14. Review the settings on the **Summary** page.
15. Click on **Finish** to create the cloud.

16. View the jobs to verify the status of cloud creation jobs. The newly created cloud will be visible in the **SCVMM VMs** and **Service Management** workspaces.

> Azure Site Recovery, Microsoft's cloud-based disaster recovery offering, can be leveraged for protecting SCVMM clouds against disasters. See https://azure.microsoft.com/en-in/services/site-recovery/ to learn more about Azure Site Recovery.

Verifying a SCVMM cloud in the Windows Azure Pack portal

We created a SCVMM cloud in the previous topic. In order to use it for building IaaS cloud offerings, it must be visible in the Windows Azure Pack Management portal for administrators under VM Clouds. Service provider foundation does the job of synchronizing the changes made at SCVMM and Windows Azure Pack level and vice versa. Let's verify that the cloud is visible in the Windows Azure Pack Management portal:

1. Log into the Windows Azure Pack Management portal for administrators.
2. Browse the **VM CLOUDS** sections.
3. Expand the currently registered SCVMM stamp.
4. The newly created cloud in the previous topic will be visible.

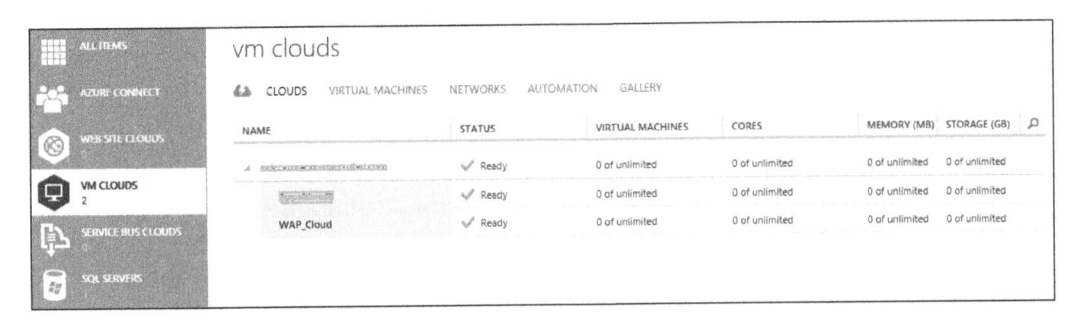

If you do not see the newly created cloud listed in the Windows Azure Pack Management portal, verify the status of **Create new Cloud** Job in VMM. Have a look at the SPF SCVMM and Windows Azure Pack Integration checklist and status.

The SCVMM **Jobs** window provides clear details, comprising events occurred to perform any particular task along with individual status. This can be handy for any troubleshooting operation.

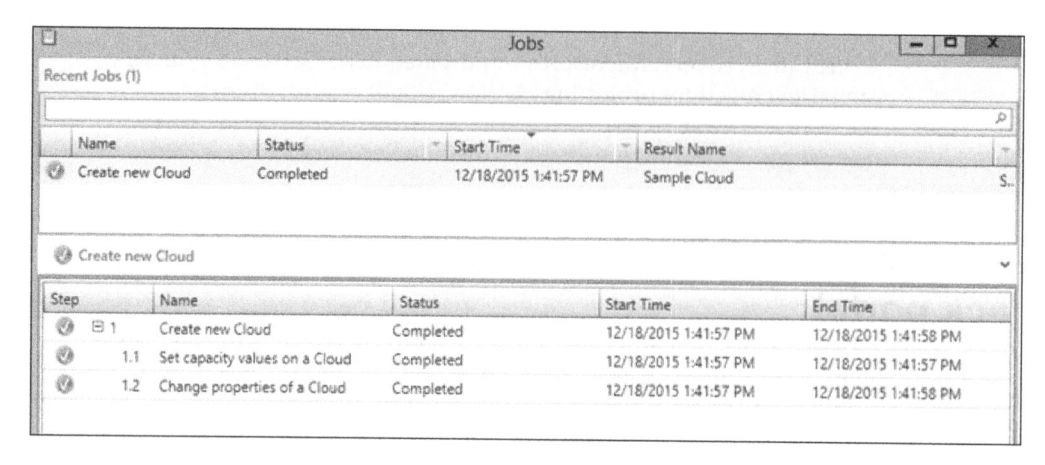

Name	Status	Start Time	Result Name
Create new Cloud	Completed	12/18/2015 1:41:57 PM	Sample Cloud

Create new Cloud

Step		Name	Status	Start Time	End Time
	1	Create new Cloud	Completed	12/18/2015 1:41:57 PM	12/18/2015 1:41:58 PM
	1.1	Set capacity values on a Cloud	Completed	12/18/2015 1:41:57 PM	12/18/2015 1:41:57 PM
	1.2	Change properties of a Cloud	Completed	12/18/2015 1:41:57 PM	12/18/2015 1:41:58 PM

With this topic, we have successfully integrated our fabric and cloud with Windows Azure Pack. Furthermore, we will start creating cloud offerings for our Windows Azure Pack cloud.

Preparing OS images for a cloud catalogue (Windows and Linux VMs)

A cloud offering catalogue can be compared with any online shopping websites items catalogue. In any online shopping website, there are different types of items available for purchase, and then each item maybe available in different sizes or versions.

Customers choose items available in the given catalogue and make a purchase. The similar purchase aspect applies in the case of cloud catalogues. If we see any public cloud provider, such as Microsoft, Amazon, and more such catalogues for virtual machines offerings, there would be a range of operating systems available in different formats, such as Vanilla OS or an OS customized for particular application or workload type, which are available in different size configurations (CPU/memory/storage capacity). There can be other characteristics as well as differentiating catalogues, such as high availability, performance, features, and so on.

In the case of Windows Azure Pack-based cloud solution, SCVMM VM templates and Windows Azure Pack gallery items are the backbone of cloud catalogues. Both VM templates and gallery items rely on preinstalled OS VHDXs for the provisioning of virtual machines and applications. This Hyper-V **Virtual Hard Disk (VHD)** or VHDXs is stored in the VMM library for usage by VM templates and gallery resources.

In this section, we will cover the planning and execution of the preparation of virtual disks for VM templates and gallery items.

Planning VM images

Preparing VM images and catalogues is a continuous process in any cloud solution since the cloud has to fulfil the daily changing needs of IT solutions. The number and types of images to be prepared for any cloud will depend on the provider's strategy and offerings portfolio.

In a generic scenario for a Windows Azure Pack-based cloud solution, the following images can be prepared for both organizations and service providers cloud solutions.

The following are based upon the operating systems supported by Hyper-V:

- Images for all the available and supported Windows operating systems are as follows:
    - Windows Server 2012 R2
    - Windows Server 2012
    - Windows Server 2008 R2 SP1
    - Windows Client Operating Systems (Win 7/8/8.1)
- Images for all available and supported Unix/Linux flavor operating systems are as follows:
    - Red Hat Enterprise Linux
    - Cent OS
    - Any other supported Unix distributions
- Any other Hyper-V supported operating system

For the size of the operating system disk, Windows Azure Pack provides the same size to the tenant's virtual machines as that of the VHD's template. Though it can be customized using Windows Azure Pack automation capabilities, it's a good idea to have OS virtual disks available in multiple size variants such as the following:

- 150 GB
- 100 GB
- 80 GB
- 40 GB
- Any other size as per the organization's or tenant's needs

In applications or workload specific OS disk Infrastructure as a Service (IaaS) Virtual machines are not just about providing plain operating systems for tenants' workloads; it can also provide servers with preconfigured applications of automated application deployment as per tenant's requirement; examples include web servers, dedicated database server dedicated for tenant, and so on. Separate OS disks can be created for applications or workload specific offerings having specific preinstalled or configuration apps or platforms for deploying applications (such as .NET framework).

Preparing a Sysprepped virtual disk for Windows OS virtual machine

Each Windows operating system has a unique identifier attached, that is, a SID (secure ID). To avoid any SID conflict, Sysprep is used for VMs deployed using template VHD.

Once planning is completed for VM images to be prepared, the following instructions can be followed to prepare a Sysprepped virtual disk.

Steps for preparing VHD for Windows operating systems templates are as follows:

1. Create a Hyper-V virtual machine.
2. Mount OS installation ISO and install the operating system.
3. Install or verify Hyper-V integration services.
4. Configure any required local hardening policies.
5. Configure the accessibility setting such as enabling RDP and configuring Windows Firewall.
6. Install required agents (Antivirus, Backup, and so on).

7. Install any required Windows Roles and features if applicable.
8. Install any other third-party applications if applicable.
9. Add any script in start-up (such as Windows activation, agents configuration, and application deployment).
10. Update OS with the latest Windows patches and services packs.
11. Perform the necessary housekeeping such as removing installation media, event viewer logs, temp files, and more.
12. Have a final look at the OS to identify any missing component or issue.
13. For generalizing the OS image using Sysprep, we can find `Sysprep.exe` in `C:\Windows\System32\Sysprep` folder. Select **Enter System Out-of-Box Experience (OOBE)** in **System Clean-up Action** with the **Generalize** option checked. Select **Shutdown** in **Shutdown Options** to power off the VM post in completion of Sysprep.

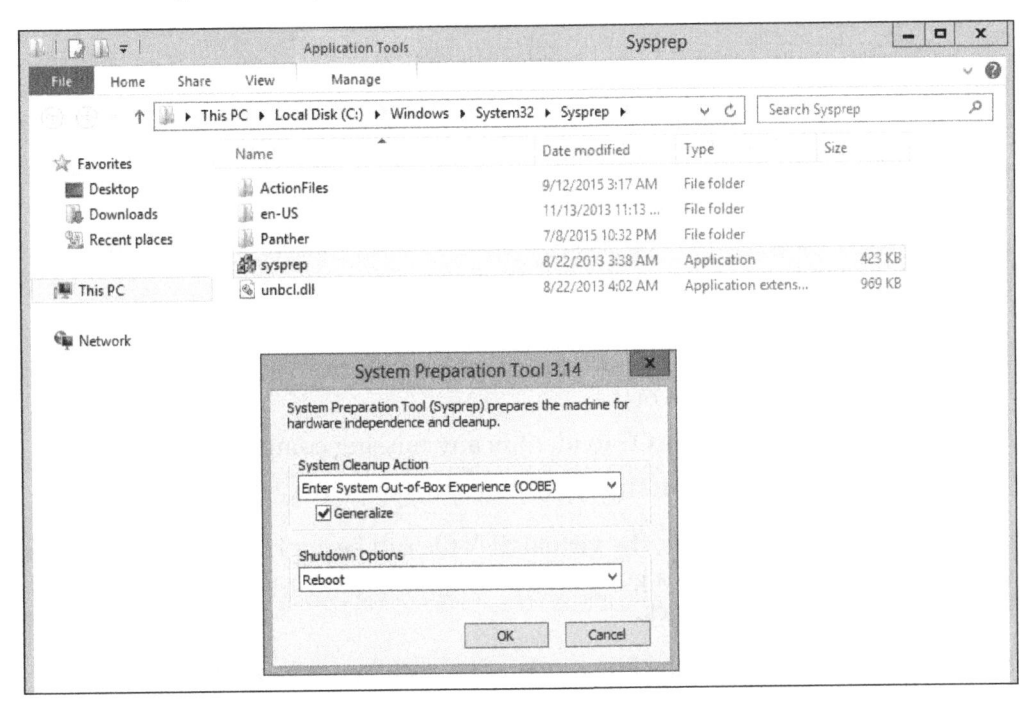

Post completion of this process, the virtual disk file can be copied to the VMM library for the usage of templates. It's a good idea to keep multiple copies of the prepared disk file for future usage and rollback.

> Product key, hostname, and other values configured in the virtual disk don't have any effect on the provisioned VM using this. These will not be used after the Sysprep process.

Preparing VHDX for a Linux OS virtual machine

Linux operating systems don't have any SID associates; hence, it does not require any Sysprep operation to be performed. However, there are additional considerations that need to be followed for generalizing OS image for the Linux workload.

Let's carry out the following steps to prepare the Linux OS image:

1. Finalize the Linux version, partitions/LVM configurations, and more.
2. Mount the OS installation ISO and install the operating system.
3. Install or verify **Linux Integration Services** (**LIS**).
4. Configure any required local hardening policies.
5. Install required agents (Antivirus, Backup, and so on).
6. Install the SCVMM guest agent.
7. Install any other third-party applications if applicable.
8. Add any script in start-up (such as agents configuration /application deployment).
9. Update the OS with the latest patches and updates.
10. Perform some necessary housekeeping, such as removing installation media, logs, temp files, and so on.
11. Have a final look at the OS to identify any missing components or issues.
12. Remove any IP configuration and shutdown the virtual machine.

Post completion of this process, the virtual disk file can be copied to the VMM library for the usage of templates. It's a good idea to keep multiple copies of prepared disk file for future usage and rollback.

The SCVMM guest agent for the Linux operating system can be found on `C:\Program Files\Microsoft System Center 2012\Virtual Machine Manager\agents\Linux` on the VMM management server. Copy the agents into the Linux VM and execute the following commands for installation:

- Run the following command:

  `chmod +x install`

- Run either of the following commands as applicable for x86 or x64:

  `./install scvmmguestagent.1.0.0.544.x64.tar`

  `./install scvmmguestagent.1.0.0.544.x86.tar`

IaaS virtual machine offerings – standalone VM versus VM Role

Windows Azure Pack-based cloud solution provides the following two options to tenants for provisioning virtual machine workloads:

- Standalone virtual machine
- Virtual machine role (VM Role)

Standalone virtual machine

Standalone virtual machine in Windows Azure Pack tenant admin portal is a direct mapping between standalone the VM offerings catalogue and the VM template created and configured in SCVMM.

For a standalone virtual machine, all the configurations are performed at the SCVMM level. The Windows Azure Pack portal is used to create virtual machine using predefined configurations in the SCVMM VM template. This does not give any flexibility to the tenant user to customize VM as per custom needs.

Cloud administrator needs to precreate multiple SCVMM VM templates for different sizes and options for providing flexibility to tenants in terms of choice. Any changes in the existing standalone VM offering has to be performed at the SCVMM end only.

Since standalone VM in Windows Azure Pack uses SCVMM VM templates directly, it is normally used to provide the vanilla operating system or OS with preinstalled or configured applications. It cannot be used to install applications as per tenants' needs in an automated fashion (which is provided by the service template engine in SCVMM).

In further topics, you will learn to create a SCVMM VM template, which can be used by standalone VM Role in Windows Azure Pack.

VM Role

VM Role in Windows Azure Pack provides a customizable self-service wizard for tenant users to request for virtual machines, which gives flexibility to tenant users to customize their virtual machines as per requirements. VM Roles can also be used to deploy automated applications at the top of virtual machines being delivered in the same self-service manner.

Unlike standalone VM Role, VM Role uses a service template engine of SCVMM for provisioning OS and apps.

VM Role in Windows Azure Pack subscription may contain multiple virtual machines of the same type or application and can be scaled easily (by just moving a sliding bar).

VM Role provides a lot of flexibilities over standalone VMs such as the following:

- Customizable self-service wizard for tenant's VM requests
- With VM Role, tenants control VM configurations and deployment with options provided by the cloud provider, which removes any dependency on the VMM administrator for any VM changes required on the standard template.
- It adds extreme automation capabilities with the integration of **SMA (Service Management Automation)**
- It deploys applications and not just virtual machines in a self-service automated manner
- It deploys and manage multiple instances of the same type under a single umbrella
- It scales out the number of instances in just one click (by moving a slider)
- It provides the flexibility of using Hyper-V differencing or dedicated disks (added in CU5) for operating systems saving ample amount of disk space and management in larger deployments
- Microsoft and third-party vendors provide a wide range of preconfigured gallery items for VM Roles for standard usage. Custom VM Roles can also be developed which makes sky the limit for VM Role offerings possibilities.

In further topics, you will learn architecture, implementation, and other aspects of VM Roles.

Building standalone VM IaaS offerings

For every standalone VM offering in Windows Azure pack cloud, there has to be a direct mapping present with VM template in the SCVMM library. The VM template in the SCVMM library can be configured using a virtual disk prepared in the earlier topics. Let's start creating VM templates in SCVMM for Windows Azure Pack usage. Multiple templates can be created using the same VHD and defined hardware/OS profile combinations to provide flexible options for tenants for deploying VM workloads.

Requirements for using VM templates for Windows Azure Pack

The following consideration must be taken care while creating VM templates to be used for a standalone VM in Windows Azure Pack:

- There must not be any cloud capability profile selected on the hardware profile page in the template creation wizard. The same case applies in case of any preconfigured hardware profile that is being used.
- The VHD that is being used to create the template must have a remote desktop enabled.
- While creating the VM template, the guest OS profile must be selected from the drop-down list. It should not be selected as none.

Creating a SCVMM virtual machine template for Windows Azure Pack standalone VM Cloud offerings

Before creating VM templates, prepare the required VHDs for templates and copy them to the VMM library.

Steps for creating a VM template for the standalone VM Role are as follows:

1. Log into SCVMM using the VMM management console with administrator privileges.

2. Navigate to the **Library** workspace and expand **Templates**.

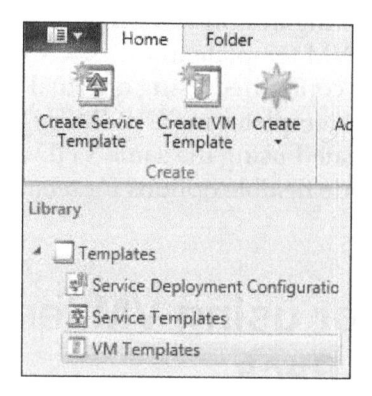

3. Click **Create VM Template** to start the VM template wizard.
4. Select **Use an Existing VM template or virtual hard disk stored in the library**. You can also choose **From an existing virtual machine that is deployed on a host** if the VHD file isn't already copied to the VMM library.

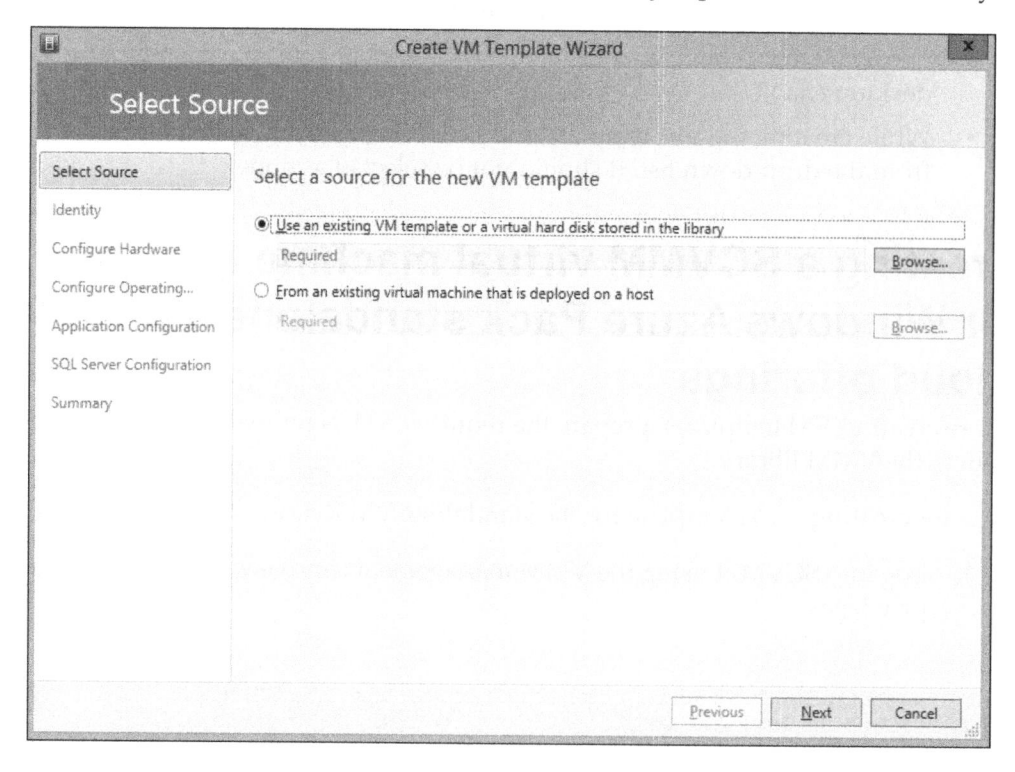

5. Click on **Browse** to select VHD from the disks available in the VMM library.
6. Provide the Template Name, Description, and Generation. Use a self-explanatory name and description that provides details about VM as this will be visible to the tenant user on the Windows Azure Pack portal. It's a good idea to include both hardware and software configurations along with the feature set available in the description.

> The generation of VM describes features and functionality available with virtual machines. Generation 2 VM introduces the Hyper-V 2012 R2; it provides support for the UEFI firmware, all synthetic devices, and more. See https://technet.microsoft.com/en-in/library/dn282285.aspx to learn more about generation 2 virtual machines.

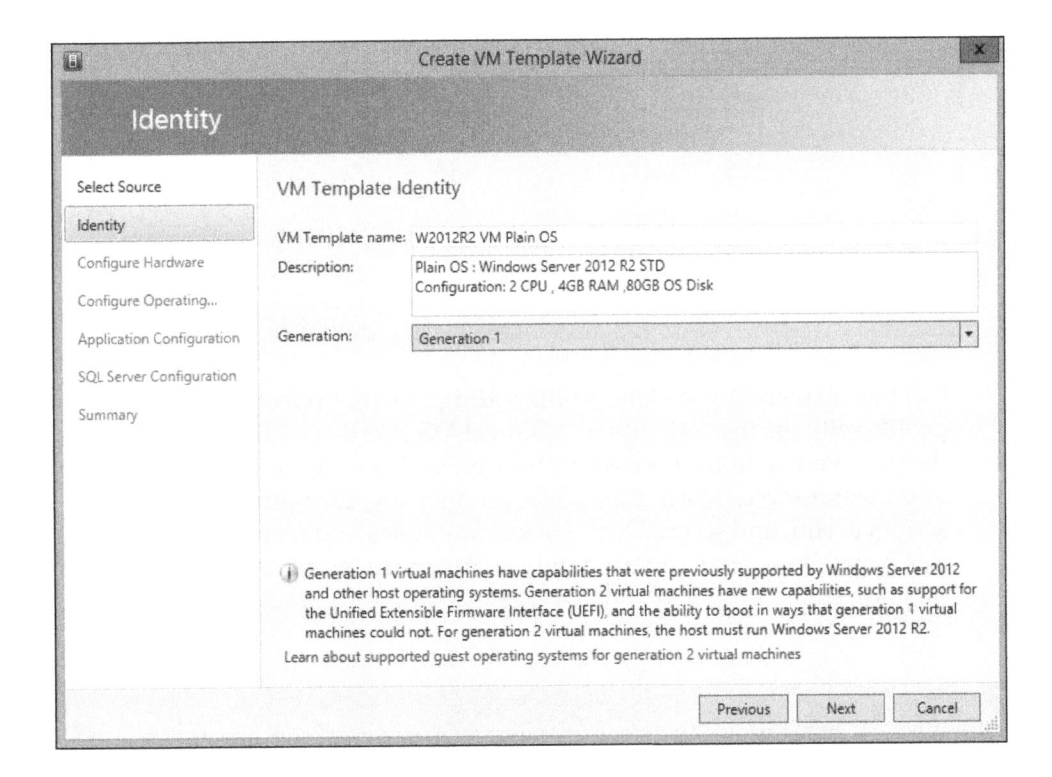

![Create VM Template Wizard - Identity screen showing VM Template name "W2012R2 VM Plain OS", Description "Plain OS : Windows Server 2012 R2 STD Configuration: 2 CPU, 4GB RAM, 80GB OS Disk", and Generation set to "Generation 1"]

7. Use a precreated hardware profile or custom settings to customize hardware for the template. Ensure that no cloud capability profile is selected. Any hardware change in the offering at later storage has to be done in the hardware profile properties of the VM template.

8. Configure a proper network configuration such as virtual switch name, IP pool, and MAC (has to be static) as per the tenant's requirement. Add any additional hardware such as data disks at this stage.

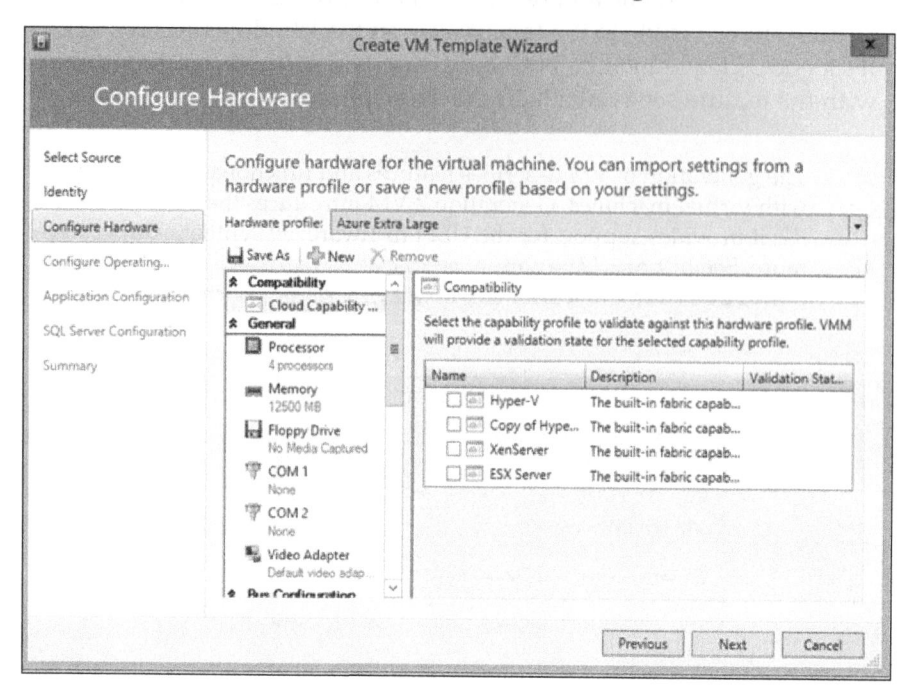

9. Configure operating system profile settings. Do not select none in the OS profile settings; instead, precreate **Guest OS profiles** and select it from the drop-down list. Make necessary changes, such as Windows OS version, administrator password, time zone, product key, Domain/Workgroup, scripts to run, and so on. Do not select any Roles and features to add in this page. These are supported only with service templates or VM Role.

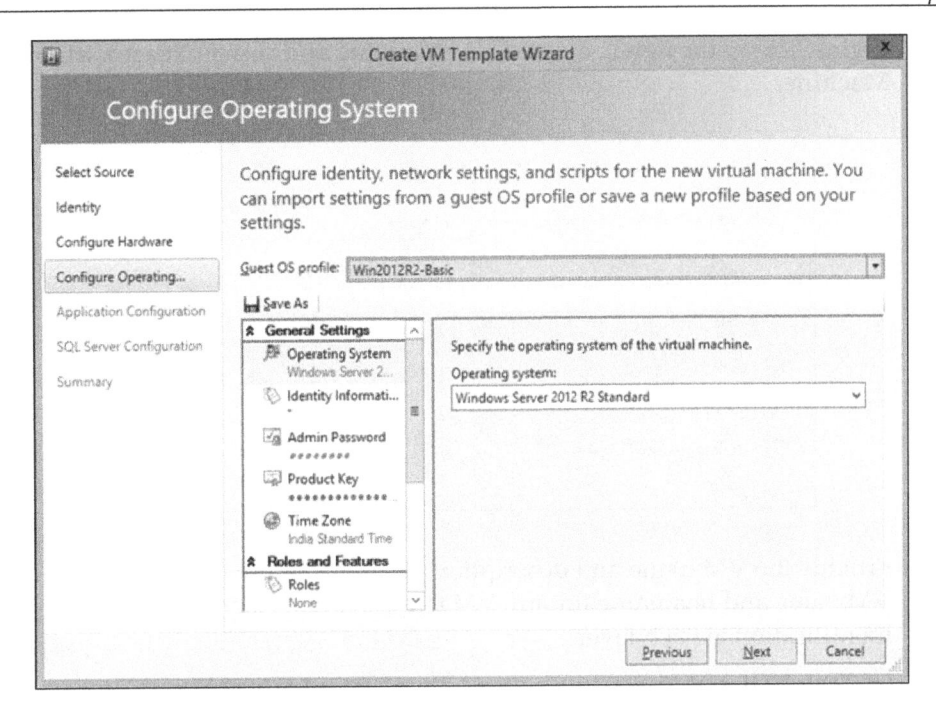

10. Select none for the application profile and SQL profile settings as these aren't supported with standalone VM.
11. Review the settings on the **Summary** page and finish the wizard for creating the VM template.
12. View job status under the **Jobs** windows in **Settings**.
13. The newly created template will be available in the VMM library workspace under the **VM Templates** section.

Testing the VM template functionality

Before assigning this standalone VM template in a Windows Azure Pack deployment, it's a good idea to test the configuration by provisioning a test virtual machine using the following steps:

1. Log into SCVMM and browse the **VM template** section under the **Library** workspace.

Building VM Clouds and IaaS Offerings

2. Right-click on the newly created VM template and select **Create Virtual Machine**.

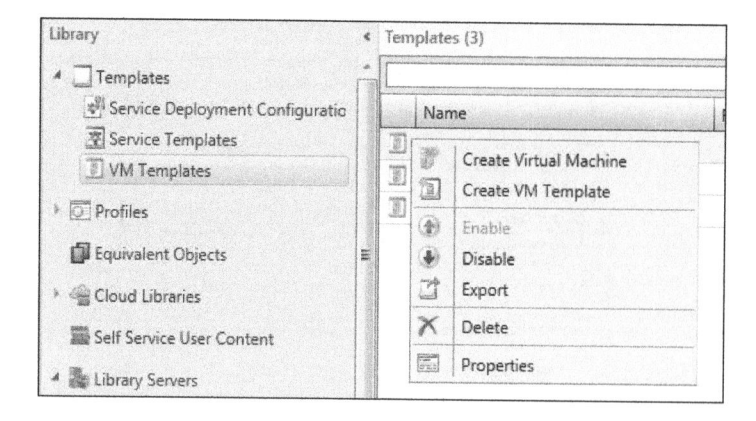

3. Provide the VM name and description. It's good to use the same the VM name and hostname for any VM to ensure consistency and easy identification at each layer.
4. Customize the hardware and guest OS profile if required.
5. Select the newly created cloud or host group as the destination for VM.

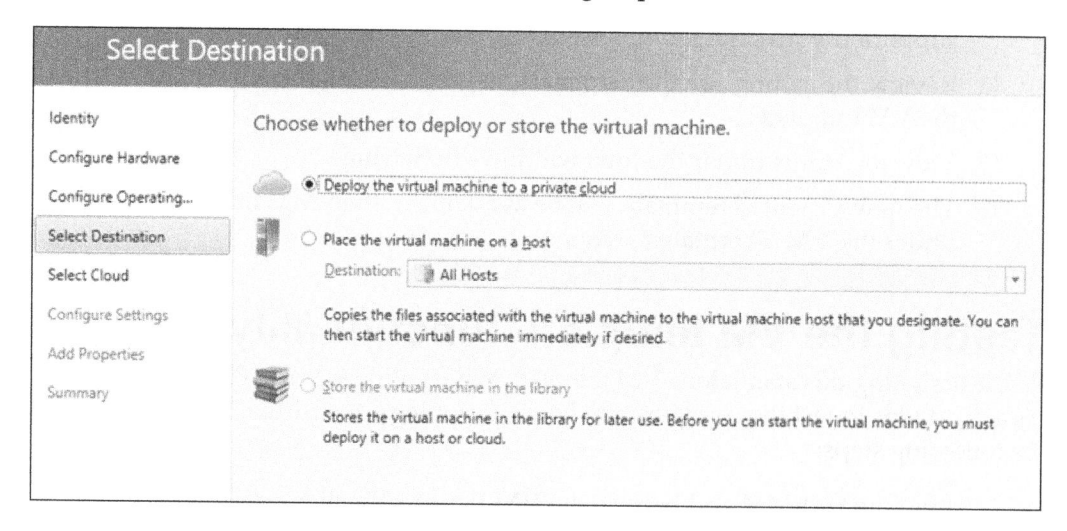

6. Configure the operating system computer name and add custom properties such as server power on/off action.
7. Review the selected values in the summary and click on **Create** to start creating this virtual machine.

8. Monitor the VM creation job for any errors; browse VMs and the service workspace in SCVMM management console post successful completion.
9. Log into the newly created virtual machine and verify the expected results as per the configuration.

The VM Role architecture

VM Role in Windows Azure Pack adds greater flexibilities and self-service capabilities in IaaS offerings. VM Role is not just about providing virtual machines for tenant's workload, it takes IaaS services to another level by offering automated applications deployment in VM in a self-service manner.

VM Role packages are developed in JSON and provide resources or values, which are used to provision virtual machines and applications. **JSON (JavaScript Object Notation)** is a lightweight format used for data interchanging.

JSON files for a VM Role along with metadata such as logos, resources, and more make a VM Role package.

A VM Role is primarily made up of two components/packages as follows:

- Resource Definition package
- Resource Extension package

Before diving into these packages, let's understand VM Role's working mechanism. In a traditional scenario without any self-service portal, VM creation requires some set of input as variables, such as hardware configuration (the number of CPUs, the amount of memory, and more) and network configurations (virtual switch), which are provided by virtualization administrators during the VM creation process. Similar things happen in a cloud-based self-service scenario where some value, such as VM name, configuration, and so on, would be provided to tenants as per their needs and some will be preconfigured by the cloud administrator, such as the hypervisor host to use, or SCVMM cloud to leverage for deploying VM.

In Windows Azure Pack-based cloud solution, a tenant user will provide tenant-specific values in Windows Azure Pack tenant portal using a self-service wizard. These values need to be passed to SCVMM where it will add up the administrator specified values and start the creation of virtual machine. In a similar manner, application deployment on IaaS services will also have to get values from the tenant user and administrator to deploy applications.

All these operations have to be done in a self-service and automated manner.

VM Role packages or gallery resource packages that were mentioned previously facilitate the preceding functionalities.

Resource definition packages

A resource definition package consists of VM configuration or values available to tenant users in a self-service wizard and their mapping with resourced resources in SCVMM, defined via a resource extension package. The definition of resource also contains a small package called `View Definition`, which includes values and graphical images visible to tenant users. If applicable, view resource definition values are mapped to the resource extension, and they are passed to VMM for VM and application deployment. Resource definition packages are stored with the `.resdefpkg` extension and gets imported in Windows Azure Pack.

Overall, the following files make up the resource definition package:

- **Resource Definition file (RESDEF File)**: It contains all parameters required by SCVMM — from VM Role to provisioning virtual machines and services
- **View Definition file (VIEWDEF File)**: It contains forms and icon mapping (Publisher icon/Resource icon) that are visible to tenant users while requesting IaaS resource using the VM Role gallery items
- **Icons**: These icons are visible to tenant users in the list of gallery items
- **Localization files**: These files are used to display the gallery item self-service deployment wizard with localized values

Resource definition package includes conditions or parameters values, which must be met at SCVMM resource level to know which hard disk to use for OS or data . These values need to be configured on resources stored in SCVMM for VM Role usage. For example, a VM Role for Windows Server 2012 R2 VM is likely to have a condition configured that uses VHD available in SCVMM with the operating system family Windows Server 2012 and so on. Only compatible resources are available to tenant users to choose in the gallery resource deployment wizard.

Resources extension packages

Resources extension packages are imported in System Center Virtual Machine Manager. Extension packages are used to provision the applications as a part of VM Role deployment. This is an optional component of VM Role and is used only while deploying VM Roles with automated applications provisioning. This can be compared to application profiles in VMM service templates. Resource extension leverages the SCVMM service template engine for executing application logic.

Parameters configured in resource extension packages are mapped to parameters in resource definition.

Along with resource extension packages, some VM Roles also contain **Application payload**.

Application payload contains resources such as installation binaries or media and scripts and other prerequisites for application deployment. This is an optional component, and its necessity varies from application to application.

Getting VM Role gallery resources

Gallery resources consist of required packages such as resource definition packages, resource extension packages, and application payloads for any VM Role. Organizations or service providers choose the following ways to get gallery resources for their Cloud VM Role offerings:

- **Use Microsoft or third party provided gallery resources**: The Microsoft web platform installer includes a wide range of ready-made gallery resources for various offering, such as Windows Server Virtual Machine, web servers, domain controllers, and more. These gallery items can be downloaded and customized as per specific environment-based requirements
- **Develop own custom gallery items**: Organizations or service providers may also choose to develop their own gallery items in JSON. This gives the flexibility of offering almost everything in the Windows Azure Pack-based cloud solution.

Dealing with gallery items – available tools

While JSON files and packages look more of developer stuff instead of IT professional, there are certain tools available that can be leveraged by IT professionals or cloud providers to deal with gallery items without any development knowledge (at least language specific). Microsoft and third-party vendors provide the following tools for dealing with gallery items in Windows Azure Pack-based deployment:

- **VM Role authoring tool**: This tool can be used to create, view, and edit gallery item packages, such as resource definition package, resource extension package, and more. It can also be used to edit Microsoft or vendor provided gallery items for custom modifications. This tool is developed by CodePlex (https://vmRoleauthor.codeplex.com/).

- **Gallery resource import tool**: This tool simplifies the process of importing resource definition package into Windows Azure Pack, resource extension package into SCVMM, and sets the properties of resources such as hard disks. This tool is completely written in PowerShell.

Building VM Role IaaS offerings using gallery resources

Microsoft and some third-party vendors have developed a wide range of standard gallery items for public usage. These gallery items can be downloaded and used by organizations or service providers for their cloud IaaS offerings. The beauty is that these can also be customized or modified to meet specific custom requirements.

The Microsoft Web Platform installer is used to download the Microsoft provided Windows Azure Pack gallery items.

Downloading gallery items using Microsoft Web PI

Windows Azure Pack gallery items aren't available in the standard WEB PI downloads list; custom feeds have to be added. Let's have a look at the steps to download these resources:

1. Log into Windows Azure Pack or any other server with Internet connectivity.
2. Launch **Microsoft Web Platform Installer** (https://www.microsoft.com/web/downloads/platform.aspx).
3. Click on the **Options** link at the bottom of Web PI.
4. Add http://www.microsoft.com/web/webpi/partners/servicemodels.xml in **Custom Feeds**.

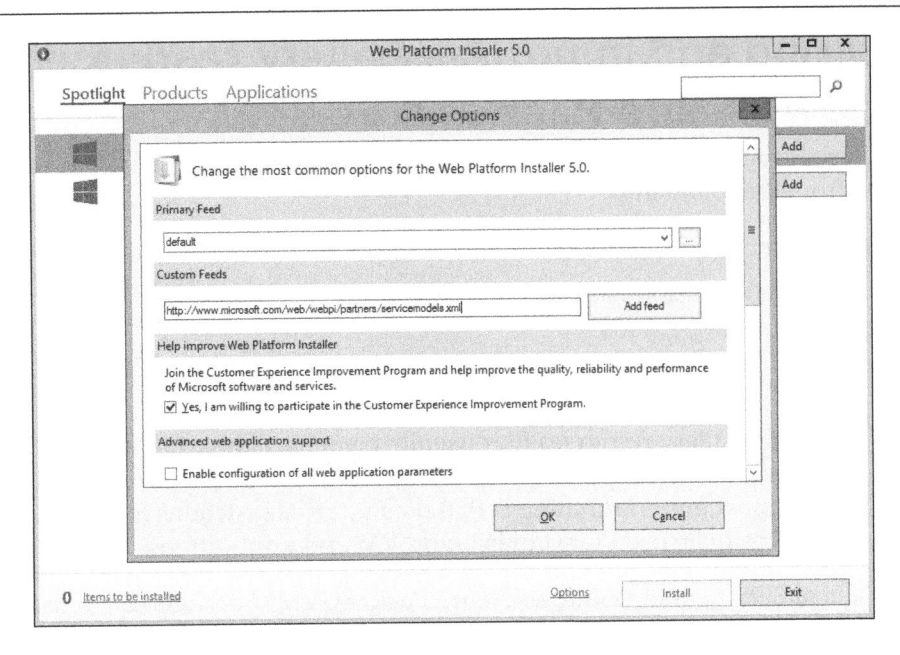

5. The new **Service Models** options will now be available in the Web PI.
6. Browse through the **Server Model** option and **Gallery Resource**. Select **Add** for gallery resources to be downloaded.
7. Clicking on **Install** will download these gallery resources on a local folder on a server where PI is running.

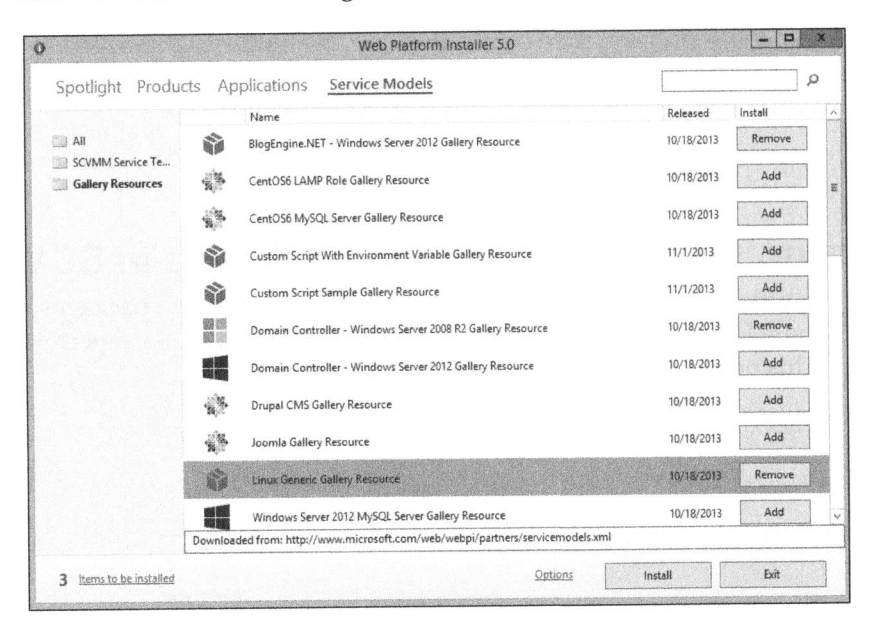

Preparing and importing gallery resources in Windows Azure Pack and SCVMM

Each gallery resource downloaded from Web PI usually contains one or more packages from the following:

- One or more Resource Definition Packages
- Resource Extension Packages
- ReadMe file
- Any other application payload files

The ReadMe file in gallery resources files usually contains a description about VM Role, package details, other application payload details, and download link if applicable. The most important thing is that it contains instructions for preparing SCVMM resources to be used for provisioning VM and applications.

Importing a gallery item in Windows Azure Pack/SCVMM and making it usable usually consists of the following operations:

1. Download gallery resources and any application payload specified in the. ReadMe file.
2. Prepare operating system or data disks as specified in ReadMe. The OS disk must be prepared with sysprep and uploaded to the VMM library.
3. Import Resource Extension Package in SCVMM.
4. Prepare virtual hard disks (OS/data disks) properties as specified in ReadMe.
5. Import Resource Definition Packages in Windows Azure Pack.
6. Perform any other additional tasks if required as per the ReadMe file.
7. Test the provisioning.

Importing resource extension packages in SCVMM

Windows PowerShell cmdlet is used to import resource extension packages in SCVMM. There is no VMM or Windows Azure Pack GUI available to perform this function at this point of time.

The following PowerShell commands can be used to import this:

1. Launch Virtual Machine Manager PowerShell Module.

2. Connect to the VMM server using admin privileges. The following PowerShell code can be used for connecting to the VMM server in a PowerShell session:

   `Get-VMMServer`

3. Enter VMM FQDN on the computer name attribute value. This will connect to the VMM service using credentials logged into Windows.

4. Execute the following PowerShell as per requirements to import the resource extension in VMM.

   The following code will import the Resource Extension named `SampleVMRole.resextpkg` stored at the `SystemDrive\GalleryResources\Sample-VMRole-Pkg\MyVMRole.resextpkg` folder in the SCVMM library named `MSSCVMMLibrary`:

   ```
   $libraryShare = Get-SCLibraryShare | Where-Object {$_.Name -eq
   'MSSCVMMLibrary'}
   $resextpkg = $Env:SystemDrive + "\GalleryResources\Sample-VMRole-
   Pkg\SampleVMRole.resextpkg"
   Import-CloudResourceExtension -ResourceExtensionPath $resextpkg
   -SharePath $libraryShare -AllowUnencryptedTransfer
   ```

5. Verify successful import by checking resource extension imported status using the following PowerShell command:

   `Get-CloudResourceExtension`

6. The results will display all the Resource Extension imported in SCVMM.

Configuring virtual hard disks properties for VM Role

Each VM Role gallery resource requires at least one OS virtual disk for VM deployment, and optionally, it requires one or more additional data disks. Since VMM usually contains lots of virtual hard disks, VHD properties such as OS name, OS family name and release, and tags are used to identify disks compatible with a specific VM Role.

Each gallery resource has its own specific values for the previously mentioned parameters, which are defined in the ReadMe file. These parameters need to be configured manually on virtual hard disks prepared for the given VMM Role. All the compatible virtual hard disks, as per required parameters, are made available to tenant users' self-service portal while requesting for resources.

For example, the following attributes are required to be configured to the virtual hard disks that are available for a given gallery resource, which provisions VMs for Windows Server 2012 operating systems:

Configuration	Install the following software: • Windows Server 2012
The Operating System property	Use one of the following: • 64-bit edition of Windows Server 2012 Datacenter • 64-bit edition of Windows Server 2012 Standard • 64-bit edition of Windows Server 2012 Essentials • Windows Server 2012 R2 Datacenter Preview • Windows Server 2012 R2 Standard Preview • Windows Server 2012 R2 Essentials Preview
The Familyname property	Consider the following values for a familyname: • Windows Server 2012 Datacenter • Windows Server 2012 Standard • Windows Server 2012 Essentials • Windows Server 2012 R2 Datacenter Preview • Windows Server 2012 R2 Standard Preview • Windows Server 2012 R2 Essentials Preview
Tags	Add all of the following tags: • Windows Server 2012 • Windows Server 2012 R2

These parameters can be configured using VMM GUI or VMM PowerShell. Tags parameter can only be configured using VMM PowerShell.

Configuring the operating system property

The operating system property specifies the operating system installed inside the virtual hard disk. This can be configured using the VMM management console or PowerShell.

In the following sample PowerShell, values can be replaced as per the gallery resource specific `Readme` file values:

```
$myVHD = Get-SCVirtualHardDisk | where {$_.Name -eq '2012R2BASE.vhd'}
$WS2012Datacenter = Get-SCOperatingSystem | where { $_.name -eq
'Windows Server 2012 R2 Datacenter Preview' }
Set-scvirtualharddisk -virtualharddisk $myVHD -OperatingSystem
$WS2012Datacenter
```

For data disks, the operating system property must be set to *None*.

Configuring family name and release property

The `familyName` and `release` properties are the configuration behind virtual disk availability in the tenant self-service provisioning wizard. All virtual disks having `familyName` and `release` properties configured, as per gallery resources requirements, are visible to a tenant user for usage.

The `familyName` usually contains OS version and VM Role specific values, such as webserver, domain controller, and so on. The `release` property usually controls multiple versions of virtual hard disks and is usually mentioned as 1.0.0.0, 1.0.0.1, 1.1.0.0 and more.

The `familyName` and `release` properties can be configured using the VMM administrator console or PowerShell. See the following sample PowerShell for configuring the `familyName` and `release` properties for virtual hard disks. The values can be replaced as per requirements provided in the gallery resource `Readme` file:

```
$myVHD = Get-SCVirtualHardDisk | where {$_.Name -eq '2012R2BASE.vhd'}
$familyName = "Windows Server 2012 R2 DataCenter Preview"
$release = "1.0.0.0"
Set-scvirtualharddisk -virtualharddisk $myVHD -FamilyName $familyName
-Release $release
```

Data disks may have values, such as SQL DB disk, larger disks, smaller disks, and so on.

Configuring the tags property

The `tags` property must be configured properly as per gallery resource requirements to make it available for provisioning. While it is a must for operating systems disks to have `tags` configured, data disks may or may not have `tags` specific requirement. Tags may be words defining Roles or features that VM Roles provides.

Tags can be configured only using VMM PowerShell. There is no VMM GUI option available at this point of time for configuring `tags` on virtual hard disks.

See the following sample PowerShell for configuring the `tags` property for virtual hard disks. Values can be replaced as per requirements provided in the gallery resource `Readme` file:

```
$myVHD = Get-SCVirtualHardDisk | where {$_.Name -eq '2012R2BASE.vhd'}
$tags = $myVHD.Tag
if ( $tags -cnotcontains "WindowsServer2012R1" ) { $tags += @("
WindowsServer2012") }
Set-scvirtualharddisk -virtualharddisk $myVHD -Tag $tags
```

> PowerShell for configuring virtual disk properties must be executed on VMM PowerShell or Windows PowerShell, loaded with VMM modules, connected with the SCVMM instance.

Importing the Resource Definition package in Windows Azure Pack

The Windows Azure Pack management or administrator portal or Windows Azure Pack PowerShell can be used to import gallery Resource Definition package in Windows Azure Pack.

The following are the steps for importing gallery resource definition package in Windows Azure Pack:

1. Log into the Windows Azure Pack management portal for administrators.
2. Navigate to the **vm clouds** workspace.
3. Click on the **GALLERY** tab.
4. Click the **IMPORT** button from the tasks pane.

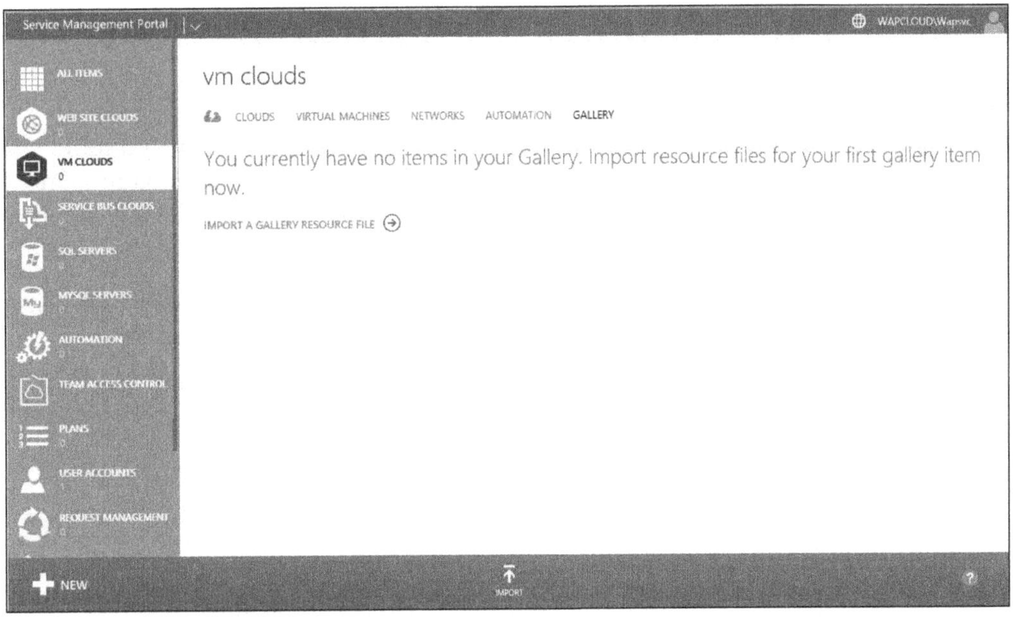
Service Management Portal
WAPCLOUD\Wapsvc
ALL ITEMS
WEB SITE CLOUDS
VM CLOUDS
0
SERVICE BUS CLOUDS
SQL SERVERS
MYSQL SERVERS
AUTOMATION
TEAM ACCESS CONTROL
PLANS
USER ACCOUNTS
REQUEST MANAGEMENT
vm clouds
CLOUDS
VIRTUAL MACHINES
NETWORKS
AUTOMATION
GALLERY
You currently have no items in your Gallery. Import resource files for your first gallery item now.
IMPORT A GALLERY RESOURCE FILE
NEW
IMPORT

5. Select the resource definition file (`RESDEFPKG`) to be imported.
6. Items will be listed in the gallery upon successful import.

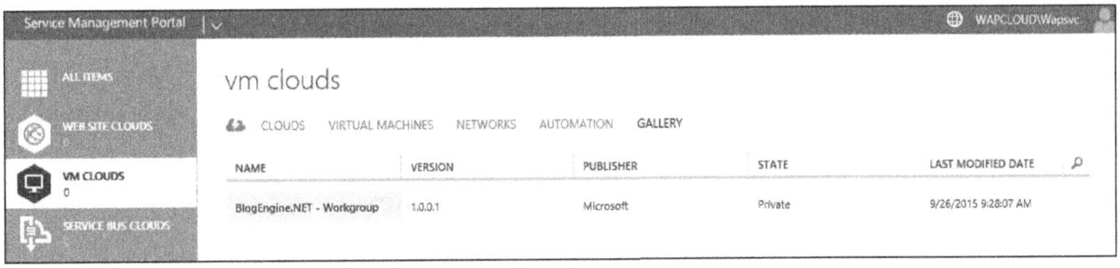
Service Management Portal
WAPCLOUD\Wapsvc
ALL ITEMS
WEB SITE CLOUDS
VM CLOUDS
0
SERVICE BUS CLOUDS
vm clouds
CLOUDS
VIRTUAL MACHINES
NETWORKS
AUTOMATION
GALLERY
NAME
VERSION
PUBLISHER
STATE
LAST MODIFIED DATE
BlogEngine.NET - Workgroup
1.0.0.1
Microsoft
Private
9/26/2015 9:28:07 AM

Imported gallery items can now be tested for deployment using Windows Azure Pack tenant portal. This will be covered in detail in the next chapter.

Using GRIT (Gallery Resource Import) tool

GRIT, also known as Gallery Resource Import tool, is a Microsoft provided tool written in PowerShell. It can be used to ease the gallery resource downloading and installing process covered in the previous topic. The GRIT tool provides a graphical user interface for the lifecycle of gallery resource installation or import.

It is recommended to use the GRIT tool while dealing with gallery resources for ease administrator and to avoid any human errors in PowerShell scripts.

GRIT functionalities

GRIT provides the following capabilities in an easy-to-use graphical user interface:

- It can be used with both Microsoft provided gallery resources as well as custom developed resources
- It can download gallery resources directly from Microsoft (no need for a web PI)
- Importing of Resource Extension files
- Importing of Resource Definition files
- It can compare and configure virtual disk properties (for both OS and data disks) required for gallery resource with disks available in the VMM library
- It makes gallery items private and public (this is discussed in detail in the next chapter)
- Removal of Resource Definition or Extension files

Using GRIT for dealing with gallery resource

The latest version of the GRIT tool is 1.2, which can be download from https://gallery.technet.microsoft.com/Gallery-Resource-Import-2273ce71. The GRIT tool needs to have access to SCVMM, SPF, and Windows Azure Pack; hence, the SPF server is the best place to run the tool.

We need to carry out the following steps to use GRIT:

1. Download the GRIT tool and log into Windows with an account having permission on SCVMM, SPF, and Windows Azure Pack.
2. Execute the downloaded `GalleryResourceImportTool.ps1` PowerShell script with elevated access.

3. The PowerShell script execution will start with check parameters and prerequisites.
4. It will launch a GUI console similar to the following, depending upon Internet access.

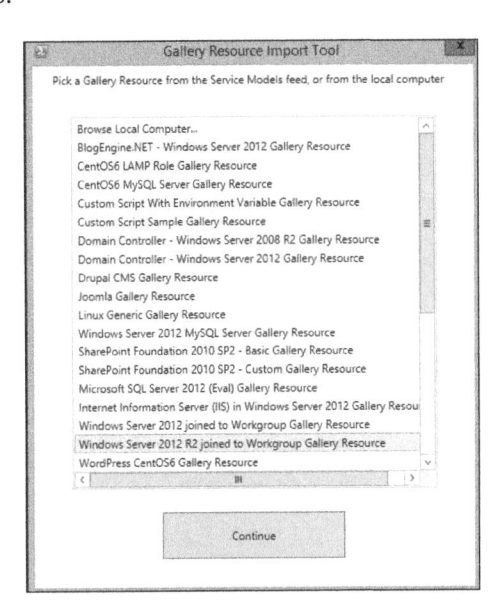

5. Browse your local computer for gallery resource files or select any online available gallery resource to download and import the files.

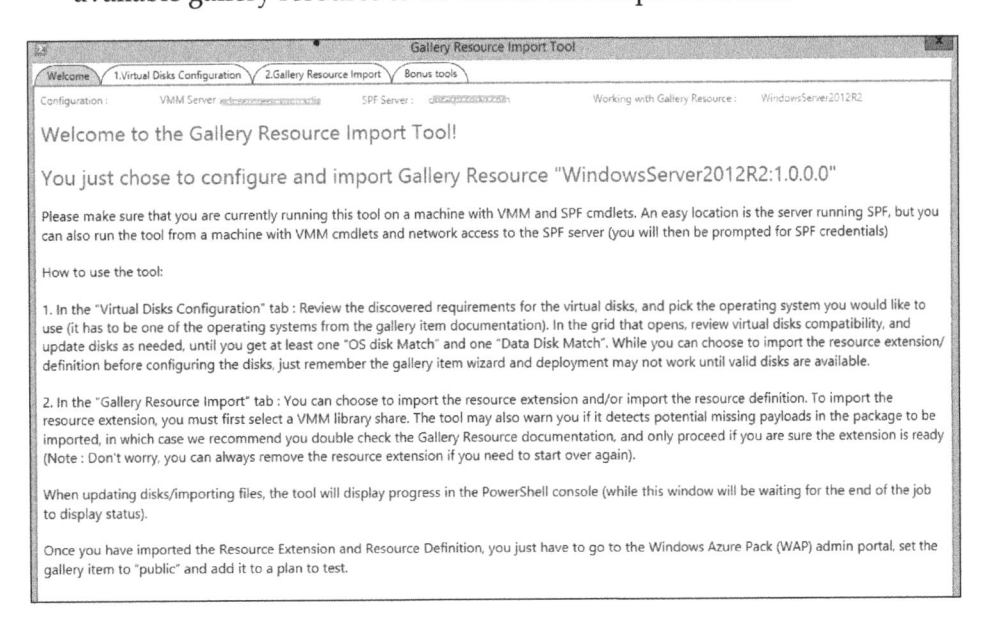

6. Select the **Virtual Disks Configuration** page to set VHD properties.
7. Choose an operating system version from the drop-down list as applicable.
8. Choosing the OS version will automatically display the available VHD and its status (matching with requirement specified in VM Role packages). Select VHD to use this particular gallery items, and hit **Apply These OS Disk Settings to Selected Disks(s) and Refresh List** to apply OS disk parameters and **Apply These Data Disk Settings to Selected Disks(s) and Refresh List** to apply data disk parameters. The refreshing list will display disks configured with status as green, which means configured.

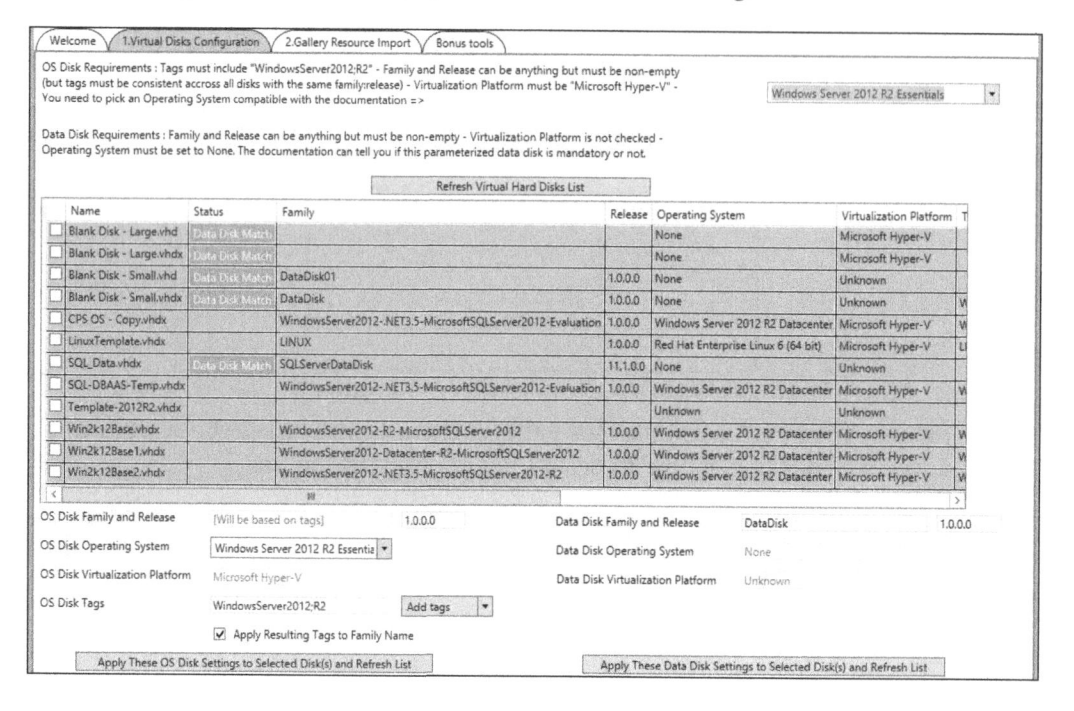

9. Select the **Gallery Resource Import** page to import Resource Extension and Definition packages in SCVMM and Windows Azure Pack respectively.
10. Choose **VMM Library Share** from the drop down list.
11. Select **Import Resource Extension**, **Import Resource Definition**, or both as applicable.
12. Select **Make Gallery Item Public** if required (this is discussed in detail in the next chapter).

13. Clicking on import will import the resource Extension and Definition packages in SCVMM and Windows Azure Pack respectively.

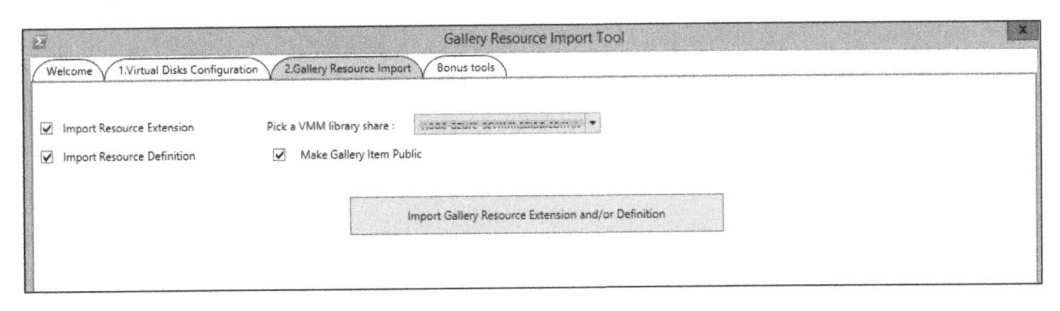

14. The **Bonus tools** page can be used to access additional features such as removing extension and definition packages or making any definition package private.

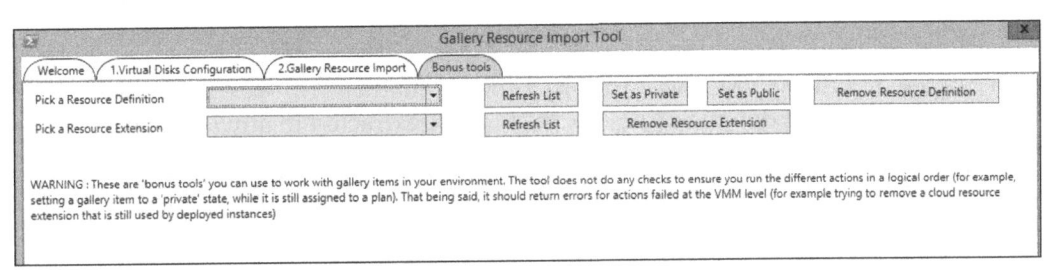

Developing VM Role gallery resource using VM Role Authoring tool

VM Role Authoring tool is published as an open source project on CodePlex. It provides an easy-to use-GUI for developing custom gallery resources for Windows Azure Pack VM Role.

With VM Role Authoring tool, the components of VM Role such as Resource Definition package and Resource Extension package can be developed from scratch, and it can also be used to modify the available gallery items at Microsoft for environmental specific requirements.

VM Role Authoring tool can be used for VM Roles developing and modifications operations, including:

- A Resource Definition package
- View Definition packages and localized resource files
- Resource Extension packages for Windows and Linux machines
- The mapping of parameters and values of Resource Definition to Resource Extension

Getting the VM Role Authoring tool

This tool is available on the CodePlex site. The latest, stable version available at the point of writing this book was 1.1.

Any supported Windows system can be used for developing VM Roles using this tool.

You can the download VM Role Authoring tool from https://vmroleauthor.codeplex.com/. Post downloading, the tool can be extracted to any location in the system.

Developing sample gallery resource – VM Role

VM Roles are written in JSON language. The VM Role Authoring tool adds a basic graphic user interface to it. Using VM Role Authoring tool, IT professionals can develop custom gallery resources without the knowledge of JSON (it's good to have it though).

The VM Role Authoring tool displays each configuration and bindings in two ways:

- Editor View: This provide GUI.
- JSON View: This is the configuration view in the advanced JSON language. It can be modified for any deep custom modifications.

Let's create a sample VM Role gallery resource for a Windows machine IaaS VM Role to learn more about using VM Role Authoring tool and developing custom VM Roles.

Chapter 4

The following are the steps to create VM Role:

1. Execute `VM Role Authoring Tool.exe`.

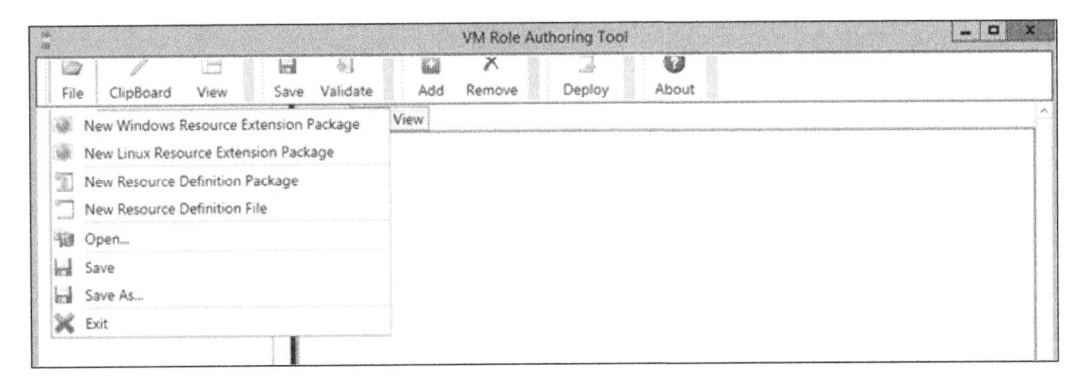

2. Provide the package name and directory to store the gallery resources.

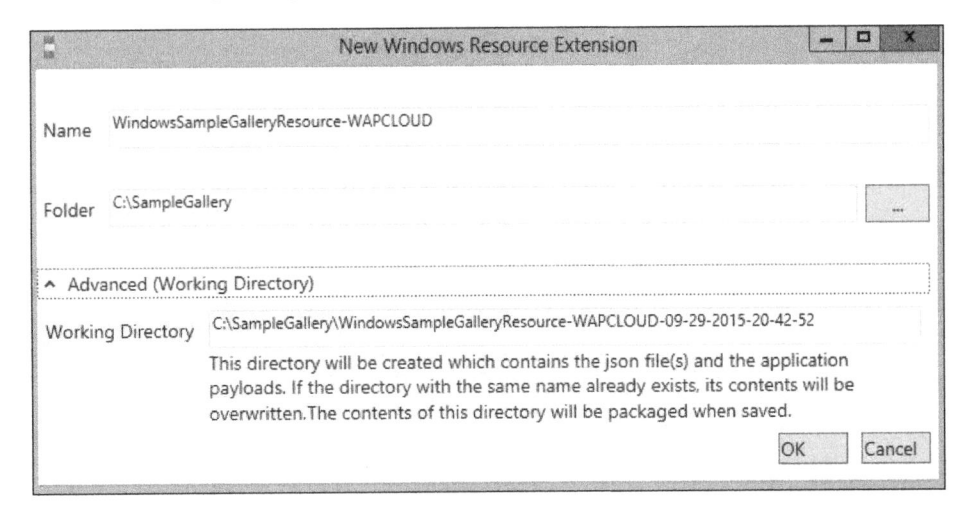

Building VM Clouds and IaaS Offerings

3. Provide gallery resources called **Version** and **Publisher**.

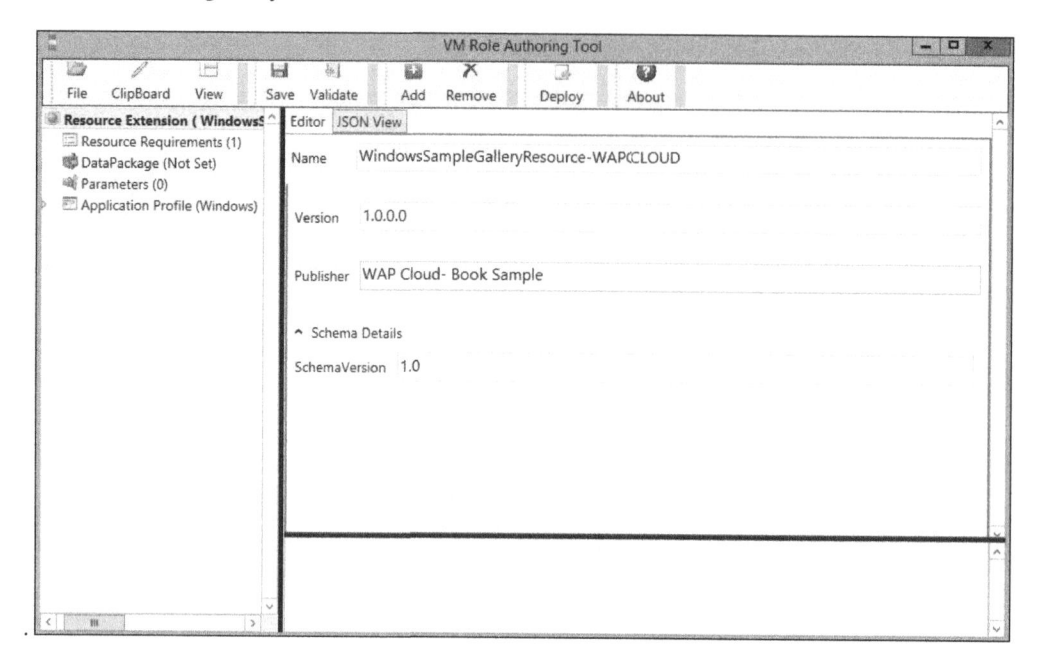

4. **Resource Requirements** contains parameters that are required to be set on virtual hard disks to be used for provisioning of this VM Role. Enter parameters such as Tags.

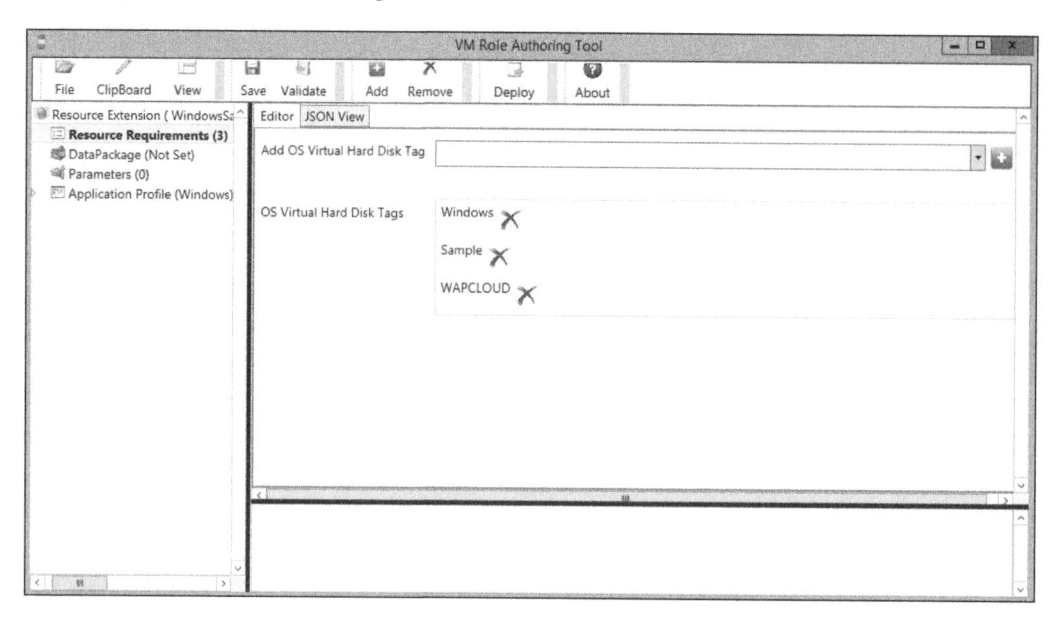

Chapter 4

5. Expand **Application Profile (Windows)** and select **Roles & Features**. This option can be used to enable Windows Roles and features in VM Role post deployment in an automated fashion. Select the compatible OS and required Roles and features.

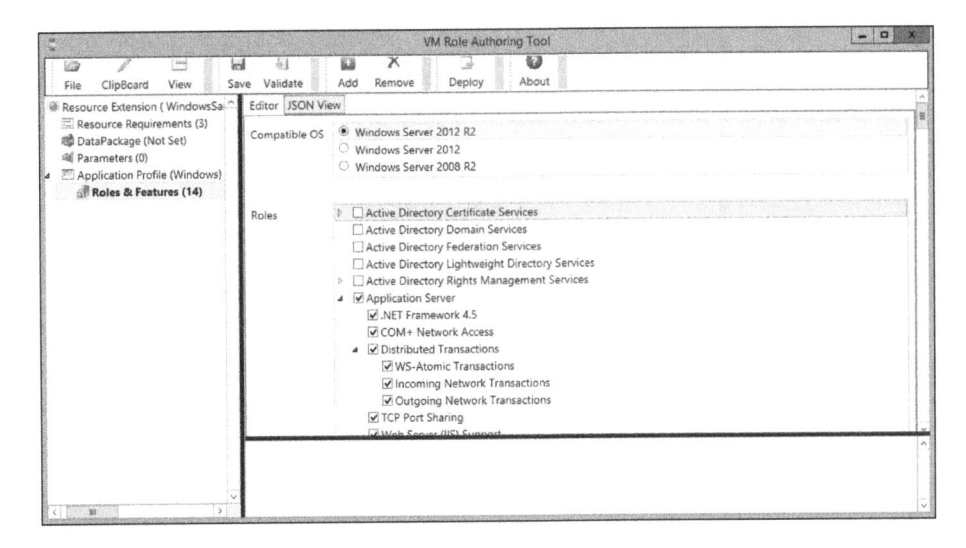

6. Click on **Add** and select **Web Application / SQL DAC Application / Script Application** or anything else, as applicable for automated application installation. This feature enables cloud providers to deliver more than IaaS: automated web, applications, and database provisioning at the top of Vanilla IaaS services.

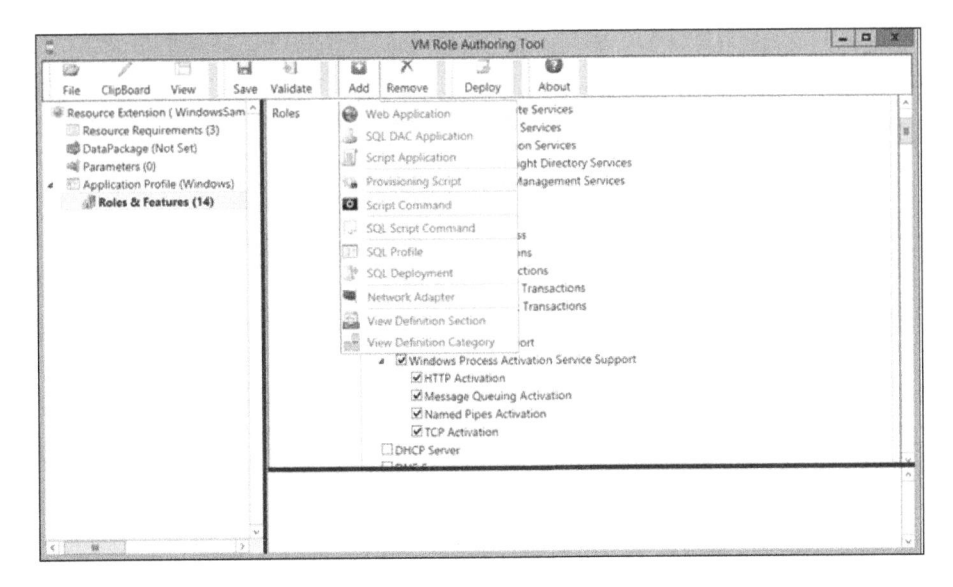

Building VM Clouds and IaaS Offerings

7. Select **File** and select the new **Resource Definition** file. Provide the Resource Definition file name and location. Add **Version** and **Publisher** properties.

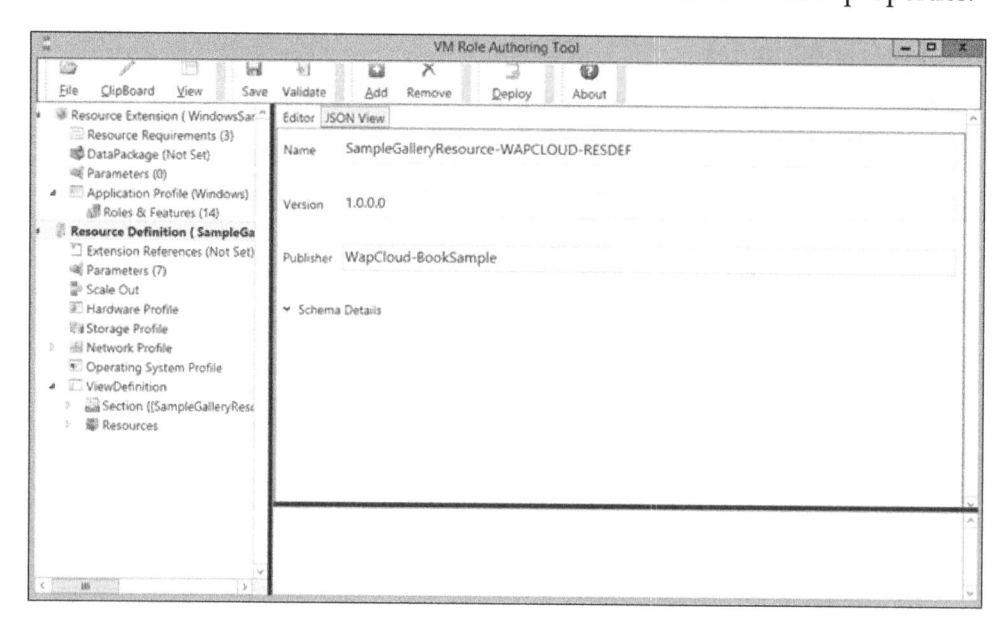

8. In the **Extension Reference** page, binding or mapping between Resource Definition and Resource Extension parameters is performed. Select the available Resource Extension package. It will populate **Name** and **Publisher** details and more automatically.

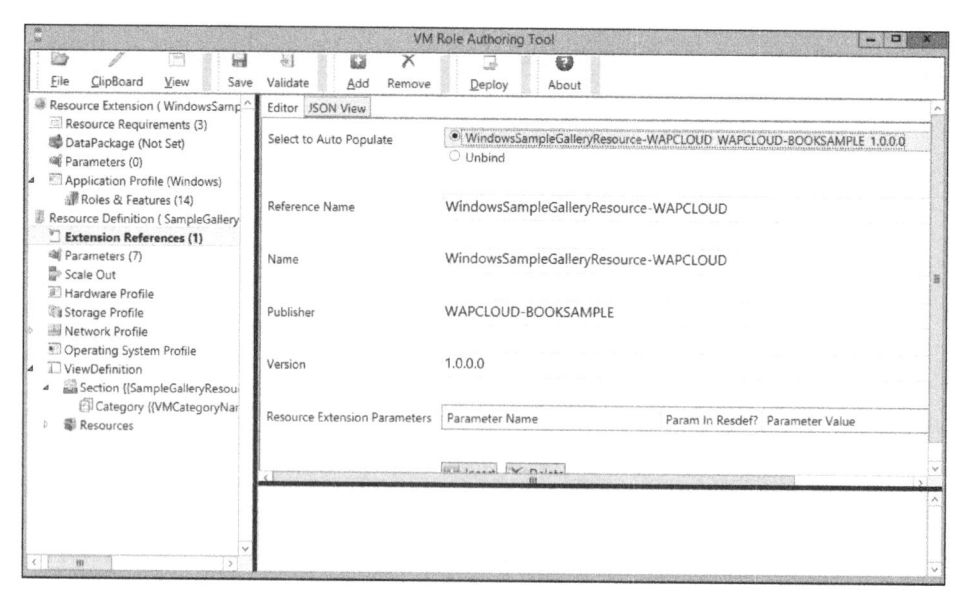

Chapter 4

9. In the **Parameters** tab, add values to be provided by tenant users in self-service form.

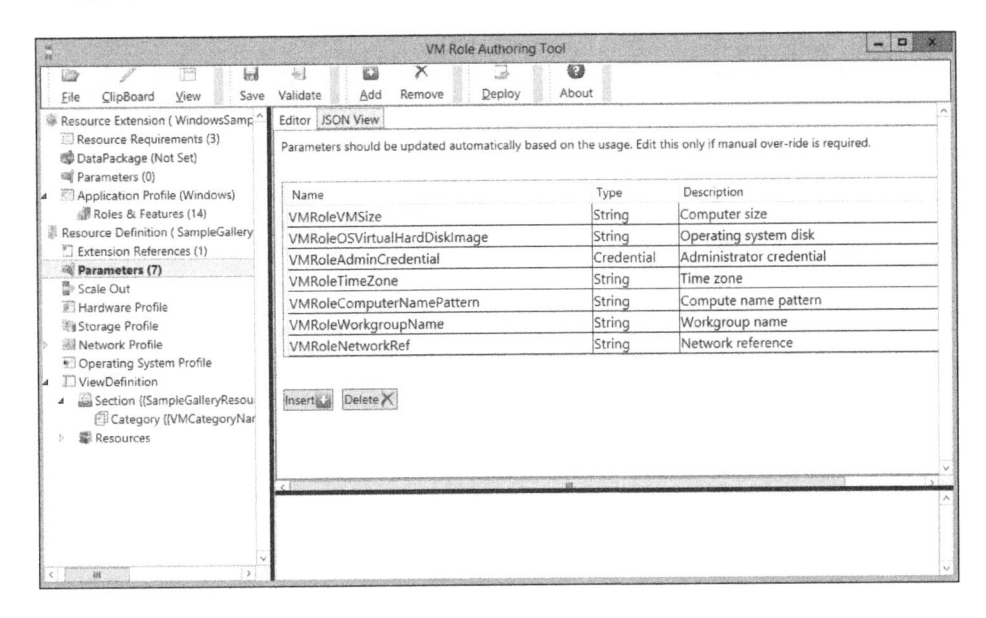

   ![VM Role Authoring Tool - Parameters tab showing Name, Type, and Description columns with entries for VMRoleVMSize (String, Computer size), VMRoleOSVirtualHardDiskImage (String, Operating system disk), VMRoleAdminCredential (Credential, Administrator credential), VMRoleTimeZone (String, Time zone), VMRoleComputerNamePattern (String, Compute name pattern), VMRoleWorkgroupName (String, Workgroup name), and VMRoleNetworkRef (String, Network reference).]

10. The **Scale Out** configuration adds easy (by just moving a slider) scale in and scale out features for this VM Role. Minimum, initial, and maximum instance counts can be provided.

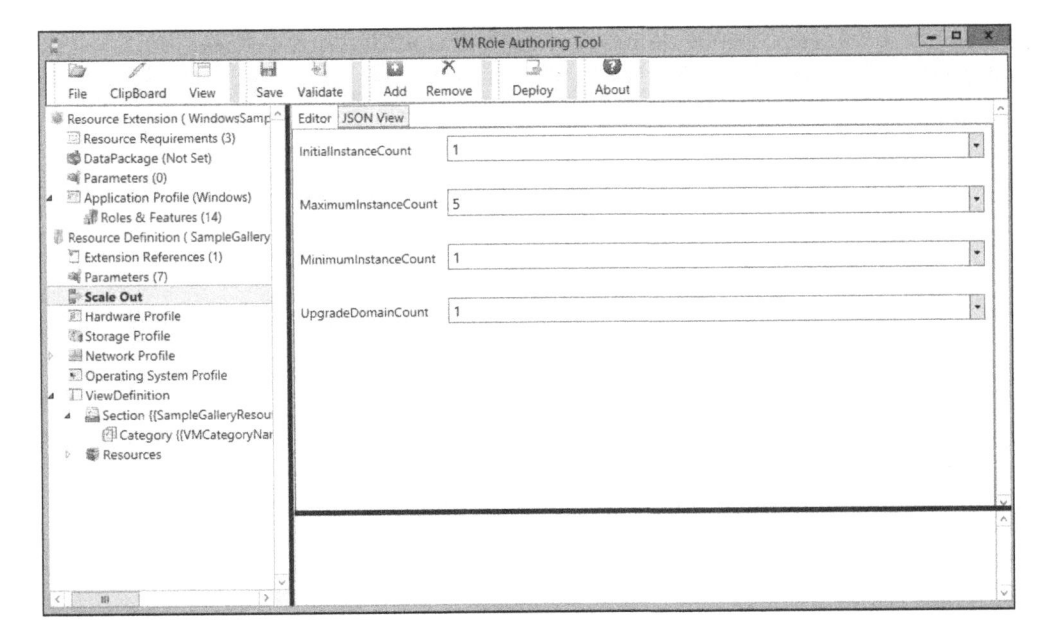

    ![VM Role Authoring Tool - Scale Out configuration showing InitialInstanceCount: 1, MaximumInstanceCount: 5, MinimumInstanceCount: 1, UpgradeDomainCount: 1.]

[157]

Building VM Clouds and IaaS Offerings

11. **Hardware Profile** provides options to tenant users with respect to the size of VM in terms of compute (CPU and memory). **Param.VMRoleVMSize** provides standard Azure size available to tenant users, such as extra small, small, and so on.

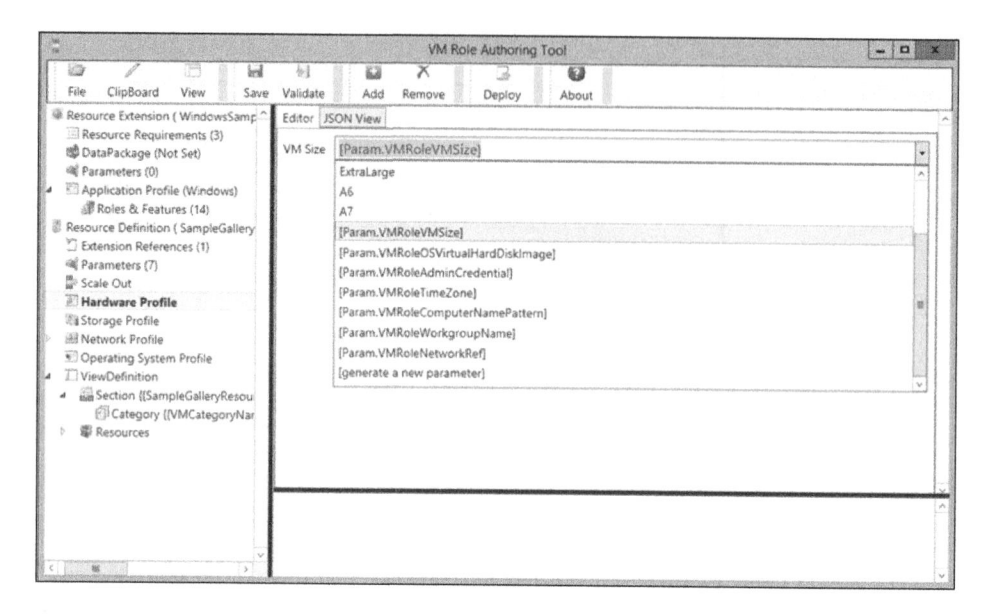

[Screenshot: VM Role Authoring Tool – Hardware Profile view showing VM Size dropdown with options ExtraLarge, A6, A7, [Param.VMRoleVMSize], [Param.VMRoleOSVirtualHardDiskImage], [Param.VMRoleAdminCredential], [Param.VMRoleTimeZone], [Param.VMRoleComputerNamePattern], [Param.VMRoleWorkgroupName], [Param.VMRoleNetworkRef], [generate a new parameter]]

12. In **Storage Profile**, cloud administrators can add additional VDHXs to VM Role such as data disks and DB disks as applicable. Parameters such as tags and others need to be defined for each disk added in VM Role.

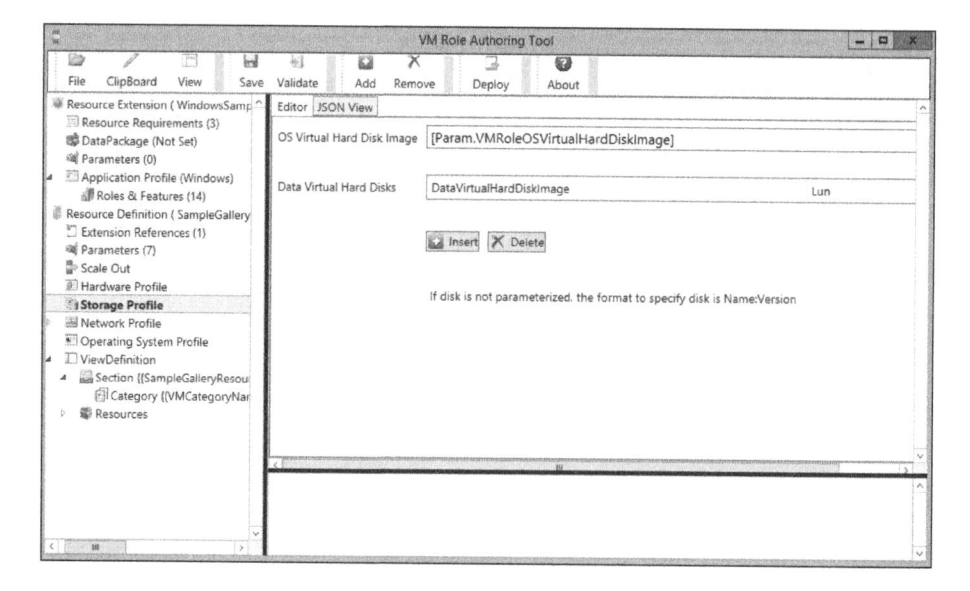

[Screenshot: VM Role Authoring Tool – Storage Profile view showing OS Virtual Hard Disk Image [Param.VMRoleOSVirtualHardDiskImage] and Data Virtual Hard Disks DataVirtualHardDiskImage with Lun, Insert/Delete buttons. Note: "If disk is not parameterized, the format to specify disk is Name:Version"]

[158]

13. **Network Profile** provides options to configure networking options for a VM Role such as NIC connectivity, load balancers, and more. Additional network adaptors can be used using the **Add** button.

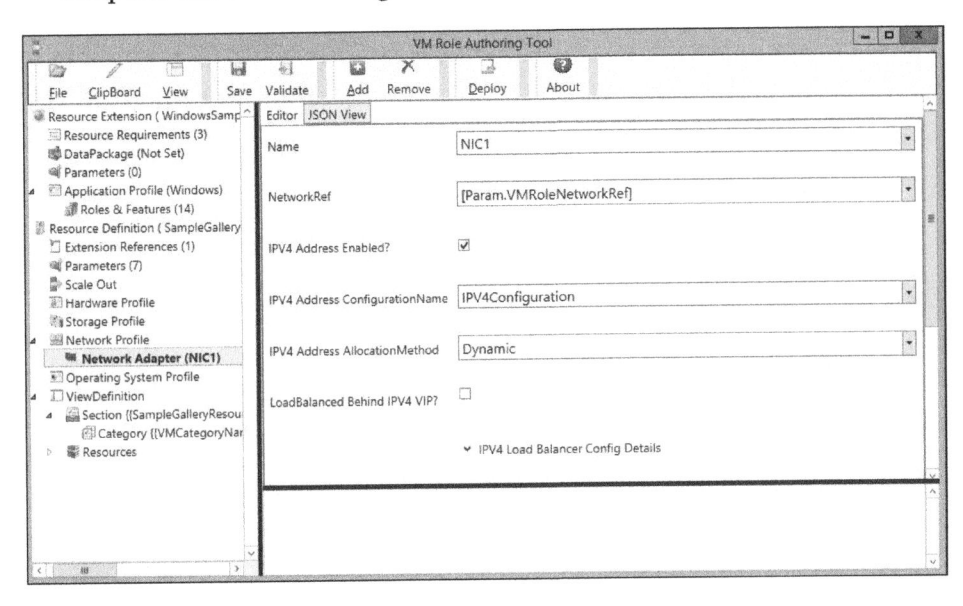

14. **Operating System Profile** provides OS options to configure such as local administrator password, machine to join domain, or workgroup. Tenant specific settings can be entered by user in a self-service wizard. Map values to the self-service wizard using generate new parameter in the drop-down list.

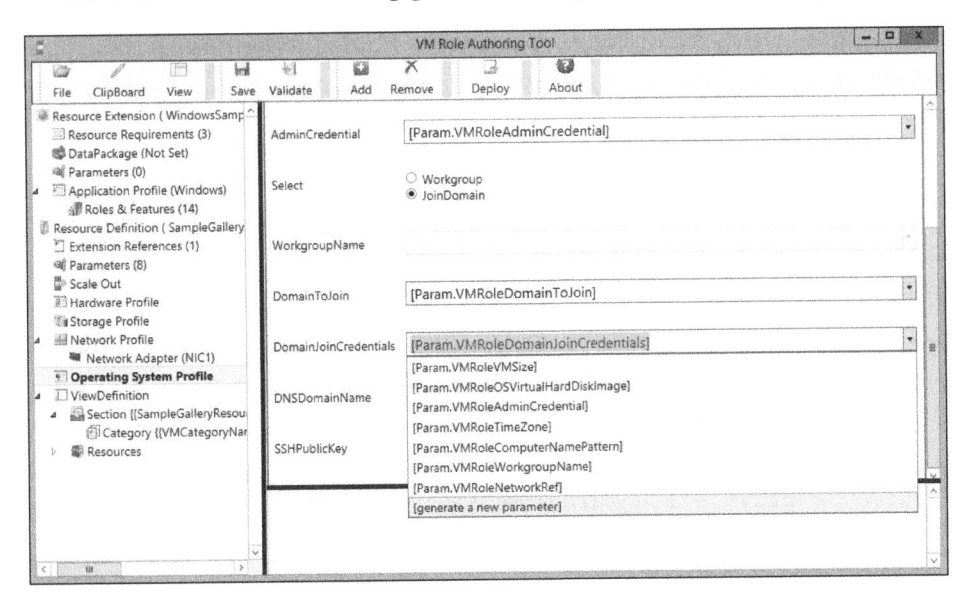

15. In the **ViewDefinition** section, graphical icons such as **Label**, **PublisherLabel**, and **Description** that are available to tenant users in the gallery catalogue can be added.

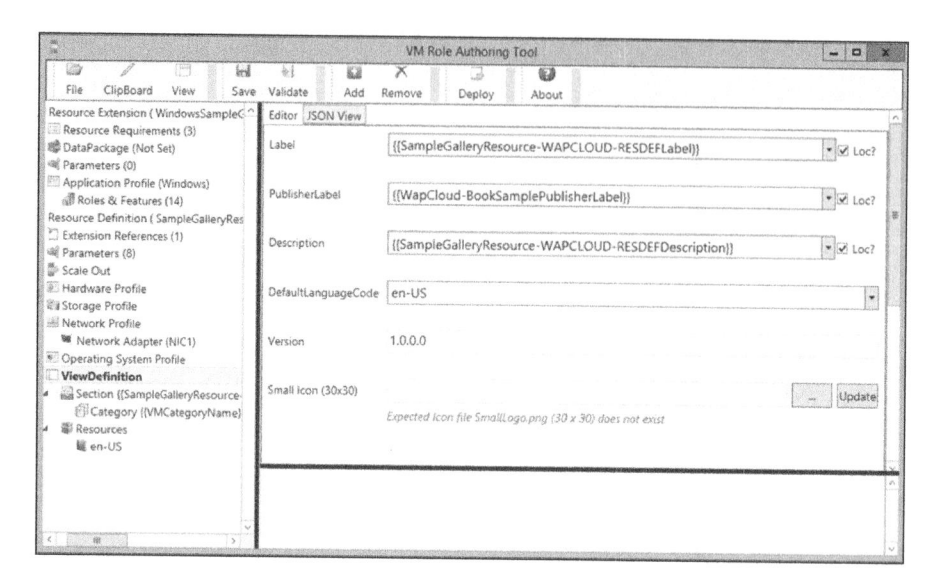

16. Click on **Validate** to verify all configurations and mapping.
17. Click on **Save** to save packages and other components.

These packages can now be imported to Windows Azure Pack and SCVMM respectively. See the previous topic to see how to import gallery resources.

With VM Role Authoring tool, JSON language scripting capabilities, and **Service Management Automation** (**SMA**), service providers may configure XaaS (anything as a service) cloud service offerings.

The virtual machine Role example kit

Microsoft provides a virtual machine Role example kit, which can be used as a reference for developing custom VM Role using VM Role Authoring tool.

The example kit contains example configurations of Resource Extension packages, Resource Definition packages, payload, custom scripts, and a lot more. This can help cloud providers in developing customer VM Role gallery resources.

The virtual machine Role example kit can be downloaded from http://blogs.technet.com/b/privatecloud/archive/2013/12/11/virtual-machine-Role-example-kit.aspx.

Accessing tenant virtual machines – Windows Azure Pack Console Connect

Windows Azure Pack provides two ways of connecting to virtual machine for tenants:

- Remote desktop connection
- Windows Azure Pack Console Connect

Remote desktop connection in a Windows Azure Pack Cloud works in the traditional RDP mechanism, requiring network connectivity to VM guest OS, RDP to be enabled, firewall rules to allow RDP communications, and lots more. If machines need to be accessed on Internet (service provider cloud scenarios), public IP would also be required.

The other option, Windows Azure Pack Console Connect, solves the challenges of RDP method. It provides access to VM guest OS through Hypervisor host using remote desktop gateways. Console Connect does not require any network reachability to the guest OS.

The Console Connect gives access to tenant users of their VM in similar way as of VM connect for Hyper-V manager over SSL using remote desktop gateway.

Console Connect doesn't have any dependency on the state of the operating system inside virtual machine (powered off, crashed, or something else). Since Console Connect works in a different way from RDP, few RDP features such as clipboard redirection, drives mapping, sound and printer redirection, and more aren't available.

Windows Azure Pack Console Connect architecture

Windows Azure Pack Console Connect leverages the Remote Desktop Gateway services of Windows Server 2012 R2 for establishing Console Connect to VM via an underlying hypervisor on SSL.

Console Connect doesn't use any guest OS (inside VM) level authentication. It works upon SSL certificate token claim-based authentication. This requires Windows Azure Pack, SPF, remote desktop gateway server, VMM, and Hyper-V hosts to trust each other.

Windows Azure Pack along with the remote desktop gateway, SPF, and SCVMM authenticates users and authorizes access to virtual machine and generate token assigned to tenants for accessing this particular VM. This token is used by Hyper-V host to ensure that tenant users get access to only authorized virtual machine.

This process isn't visible to tenant users. When a tenant user connects to any VM using Console Connect on the Azure Pack portal, it downloads a RDM file containing all required connectivity details. Running this RDP file connects user to the VM's console.

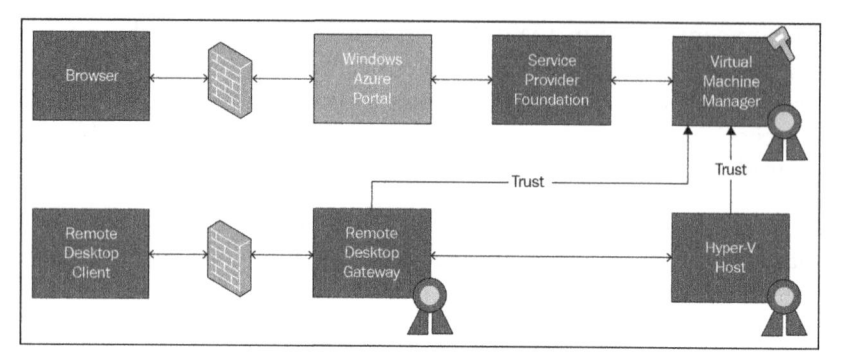

Diagram Source: TechNet

> All servers participating in the Console Connect architecture must run Windows Server 2012 R2.
>
> Minimum RDP version for Console Connect at the client end is 8.1.

Preparing certificates for Console Connect deployment

A trust relationship needs to be configured between remote the Desktop Gateway Server, SPF, SCVMM, and Hyper-V hosts to support claim token-based authentication. Single or multiple SSL certificates can be used to establish this trust relationship.

The SSL certificate used for Console Connect must meet the following requirements:

- The certificate must be valid, which is not expired
- The key usage field must contain a digital signature
- The enhanced key usage field must contain the following client authentication object identifier: (1.3.6.1.5.5.7.3.2)

- Root certificates for the **certification authority (CA)** that issued the certificate must be installed in the Trusted Root Certification Authorities certificate store
- The cryptographic service provider for the certificate must support SHA256

SSL certificates can be self-signed as well as issued from any internal enterprise or public certificate authority. It is recommended to use CA provided SSL for better management and easy renewals.

Deploying Console Connect

Deploying Windows Azure Pack Console Connect requires multiple operations to be performed, such as importing the Console Connect certificate, configuring RDS Gateway, and adding RDS Gateway in Windows Azure Pack.

Importing trusted certificates (Console Connect) to management servers

Instead of importing a Console Connect certificate to each Hyper-V hosts individually, it can first be imported in the VMM database, and then be distributed to Hyper-V hosts. For this, the following steps are carried out:

1. Execute VMM PowerShell on as an administrator.
2. Connect to the SCVMM server using the `Set-SCVMMServer` PowerShell cmdlet.
3. Use the following script to import the certificate in the VMM DB. Update highlighted values as per environmental specific details:

   ```
   PS C:\> $mypwd = ConvertTo-SecureString "password" -AsPlainText -Force

   PS C:\> $cert = Get-ChildItem .\RemoteConsoleConnect.pfx

   PS C:\> $VMMServer = WAPCLOUD-SCVMM01.wapcloud.com

   PS C:\> Set-SCVMMServer -VMConnectGatewayCertificatePassword $mypwd -   VMConnectGatewayCertificatePath $cert -VMConnectHostIdentificationMode FQDN -VMConnectHyperVCertificatePassword $mypwd -VMConnectHyperVCertificatePath $cert -VMConnectTimeToLiveInMinutes 2 -VMMServer $VMMServer
   ```

4. Wait for all Hyper-V hosts to refresh in SCVMM, or manual refresh it by logging into the VMM management console.

5. If you use a self-signed certificate, import the public key of the certificate to the trusted root certification authorities certificate store for the Hyper-V hosts. Restart the Hyper-V management service post import:

   ```
   Import-Certificate -CertStoreLocation cert:\LocalMachine\Root
   -Filepath "<certificate path>.cer"
   ```

6. Import a certificate to the SPF server; here, PowerShell can be used:

   ```
   Import-PfxCertificate -CertStoreLocation Cert:LocalMachineMy
   -Filepath "<certificate path>.pfx"-Password <Secure String>
   ```

7. Configure the service provider foundation to use this certificate to create claim tokens using the following PowerShell cmdlet. Replace thumbprint values as applicable:

   ```
   import-module spfadmin


   Set-SCSPFVmConnectGlobalSettings -AccessTokenLifetimeInMinutes 5
   -CertificateThumbprint 4D92EF6B88AA2A76A1BA28834A42E599C917A9C2-
   HostIdentityType IPv4
   ```

8. Define token lifetime in minutes from 1 to 60. Thumbprint value of SSL certificate can be found using the following PowerShell cmdlet:

   ```
   $thumbprints = @(dir cert:localmachineMy | Where-Object {
   $_.subject -eq "CN=Remote Console Connect" } ).thumbprint
   ```

Setting up Remote Desktop Services Gateway

To set up Remote Desktop Services Gateway, the following steps are carried out:

1. Log into the VM designated for RDS Gateway Role.
2. Install the Remote Desktop Gateway component using **Add Roles and Features** in Server Manager.
3. Install the Microsoft System Center Virtual Machine Manager Console Connect Gateway component on the Remote Desktop Gateway server. The MSI installer for SCVMM Console Connect Gateway can be found in the SCVMM installation media location `CDLayout.EVAL\amd64\Setup\msi\RDGatewayFedAuth`.
4. Import the public key of the certificate into the personal certificate store:

   ```
   Import-Certificate -CertStoreLocation cert:\LocalMachine\My
   -Filepath "<certificate path>.cer"
   ```

5. Configure the RDS Gateway server to accept tokens using Console Connect SSL and hash algorithms.

    This is configured using the `TrustedIssuerCertificateHashes` and `AllowedHashAlgorithms` properties in the **Windows Management Instrumentation (WMI)** `FedAuthSettings` class. Use the following PowerShell to configure the RDS Gateway server:

    Replace the server as thumbprint values with environment-specific values:

    ```
    $Server = "WAPMGT-RDSG.wapcloud.com"
    $Thumbprint = "4D92EF6B88AA2A76A1BA28834A42E599C917A9C2"
    $TSData = Get-WmiObject -computername $Server -NameSpace "root\TSGatewayFedAuth2" -Class "FedAuthSettings"
    $TSData.TrustedIssuerCertificates = $Thumbprint
    $TSData.Put()
    ```

6. Configure the SSL certificate for RDS Gateway server. This certificate will be used to identify RDS server by clients. Use the RDS Gateway manager to create a self-signed SSL or use the existing trusted SSL.

7. Verify the configuration at SCVMM, Hyper-V hosts, SPF, and RDS Gateway server.

Registering RDS Gateway server in Windows Azure Pack

Windows Azure Pack provides the option to register Remote Desktop Gateway server while registering the SCVMM stamp. The RDS Gateway server must be registered with mapping to the VMM server to function.

Any existing registered SCVMM connection can also be modified to add RDS Gateway at a later stage.

Let's see the following steps for registering RDS Gateway:

1. Log into the Windows Azure Pack management portal and browse to the VM Clouds.
2. Select an existing SCVMM registration and click on **Edit**.

3. Provide RDS Gateway FQDN and click on **Finish** to complete the configuration.

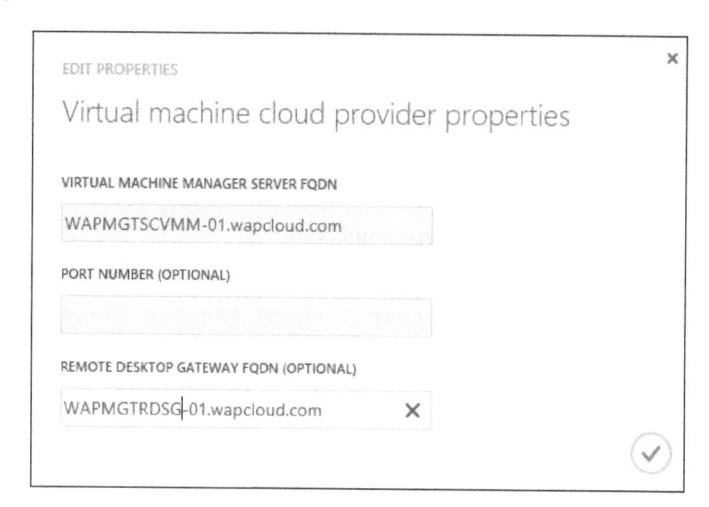

EDIT PROPERTIES

Virtual machine cloud provider properties

VIRTUAL MACHINE MANAGER SERVER FQDN

WAPMGTSCVMM-01.wapcloud.com

PORT NUMBER (OPTIONAL)

REMOTE DESKTOP GATEWAY FQDN (OPTIONAL)

WAPMGTRDSG-01.wapcloud.com

Securing the Console Connect deployment

Windows Azure Pack Console Connect uses SSL token-based claim authentication. It is recommended to consider the following security recommendations while deploying the Console Connect environment:

- Token Lifetime: RDP File downloaded by the tenant user for accessing VM console contains the `EndpointFedAuth` token to verify user's authenticity. It is recommended to configure token lifetime to small values such as 1 or 2 minutes to eliminate the security risk of losing or leaking this file.
- Configure strong firewall and security policies on the RDS Gateway server to protect it from malicious users or attacks. For example, it's a good idea to block the RDP (3389) port.
- Access to the certificate store on the SCVMM server generating token should be restricted.
- It is recommend to use a CA-provided certificate with a valid chain for the Hyper-V host. This will prevent the RDP connection warning related to the identification of the computer's identity.
- The RDP file downloaded by tenant user contains hostname/network details of Hyper-V server hosting that machine. This allows tenant users to see hypervisor host network details. It is recommended to secure Hyper-V hosts and prevent Internet access to avoid the misuse of these details.

Summary

With this chapter, we are ready with a Windows Azure Pack-based cloud solution having IaaS services ready for tenants. You learned about Windows Azure Pack VM Clouds architecture and steps for building SCVMM cloud for Windows Azure Pack. You learned about building IaaS offerings, also known as catalogues, for Windows and Linux operating systems. We also covered creating custom offerings using the VM Role authoring tool as well as using GRIT for easy import of gallery resources in Windows Azure Pack and SCVMM.

Accessing virtual machines using RDP and Console Connect along with Console Connect architecture and deployment was also covered.

In the next chapter, we will be assigning these services to tenants using Windows Azure Pack plans and subscriptions.

5
Assigning Cloud Services – Plans, Add-Ons, Tenant Accounts, and Subscriptions

In the previous chapter, we built VM Clouds and IaaS services for our WAP-based cloud. In this chapter, we will move ahead toward completing a ready-to-use cloud solution by learning about methods of assigning these services to tenants. We will cover planning and the implementation of cloud plans to which tenants need to be subscribed to use services. We will also cover add-ons, the tenant's subscriptions, and the tenant's user account management.

We will be covering the following topics in this chapter:

- Windows Azure Pack plans and add-ons – overview and planning
- Creating and managing Windows Azure Pack Cloud plans and add-ons
- Creating and managing tenants' user accounts
- Tenant subscriptions – an overview and management

Windows Azure Pack plans and add-ons – overview and planning

Windows Azure Pack plan, also known as hosting plan, is a mechanism of assigning cloud service offerings to tenants as per their deal or contract agreement considerations, such as a variety of services, quota, the amount of resources available, the quality of service, and so on. The cloud provider creates and configures the plan as per the deal or cloud offering strategy; tenants subscribe to the plan to get access to configured cloud service offerings. A plan usually contains a collection of services to be made available along with defined restrictions or limits.

A single plan can be subscribed by multiple tenants having the same requirements. A plan may consist of multiple resource provider services, such as **VM Clouds (IaaS)**, websites and **Service Bus (PaaS)**, **Databases (DBaaS)**, or other custom offerings.

Tenants cannot access cloud services without subscribing to at least one plan. They may subscribe to multiple plans as per requirements. When a tenant user subscribes to WAP plans, a new subscription is generated and is dedicated for that particular tenant. This subscription is used to identify and access tenants' resources across the cloud.

Normally, plans are also mapped with the pricing of services. Multiple plans with different pricing schemes and services can be created. There are multiple billing adaptors or solutions available that can be used along with WAP plans for offering cloud services as per the pricing defined by cloud providers.

Add-ons are used to provide additional capabilities and limits over a plan, such as additional quotas for using any additional number of virtual machines or compute resources. Add-ons are linked to plans and can only be subscribed if the tenant has an active subscription to the plan.

One add-on can be linked to multiple plans.

Planning Windows Azure Pack Cloud plans

Windows Azure Pack plan, offering IaaS services, using VM Clouds can be configured with only one SCVMM server and SCVMM cloud. That is, if a cloud provider is having multiple SCVMM stamps or clouds, there has to be separate plans for these. This is also one of the reasons behind keeping single or fewer number of SCVMM cloud's recommendation in the previous chapter.

Before talking about planning WAP plans, let's have a look at all the options or configurations that we can add up in the plan offering IaaS services using VM Clouds resource providers:

- **Services or resource provider offerings**: A plan can consists of one or multiple resource providers' cloud services, such as IaaS (VM Clouds), DBaaS (SQL/MySQL), websites, or any custom resource providers.
- **VMM Management server and VM Cloud**: WAP plans, offering IaaS services, using VM Clouds are mapped to VMM management server and VMM Cloud. Separate plans need to be created for other management servers or VM Clouds.

- **Usage limit**: A WAP plan may contain limits of using resources such as the following:
    - Number of virtual machines
    - CPU cores
    - RAM(MB)
    - Storage (GB)
    - Number of virtual networks
    - MB per second network in and out
    - Site to site VPN per network
    - Storage IOPS

    These limits must be in line with limits configured at cloud level in SCVMM.

- **Networks**: Network here refers to the logical network created in SCVMM. This can be used to restrict tenants in a plan to a specific network depending upon performance and features, such as isolation, virtualized networks, and so on. All the networks are created and configured in the SCVMM fabric.

- **Hardware profiles**: Hardware profiles contain virtual machines' hardware configuration options, such as the amount of CPU/RAM, and more. Hardware profiles in WAP plans directly refer to the hardware profiles created in SCVMM. These hardware profiles are available to tenants while provisioning a standalone VM. A plan may contain multiple hardware profiles as per business decision to provide flexibility to tenants in terms of the VM size.

- **Templates**: Templates here directly refer to VM templates created in SCVMM for WAP standalone VM offerings. A plan may contain multiple templates as per the business decision to provide flexibility to tenants in terms of the variety of virtual machines. See the previous chapter to learn more about the planning of VM templates.

- **Gallery**: In gallery, cloud providers can choose which gallery VM role resources are to be provided for tenants. A plan may contain multiple galleries as per the business decision to provide flexibility to tenants in terms of the variety of virtual machines and applications. See *Chapter 4, Building VM Clouds and IaaS Offerings* to learn more about the planning of gallery resources.

- **Additional settings**: This allows cloud providers to configure if certain operations mentioned here are to be made available to tenants.
    - Create, view, and restore Virtual Machine Checkpoints (also known as Hyper-V VM Checkpoints or snapshots)
    - Save the virtual machine state
    - Store VM to the library and deploy it from there
    - Connect to the console of the virtual machine (Azure Pack Console Connect)
- **Custom settings**: This allows cloud providers to configure custom settings given here for tenants and their resources:
    - Disable built-in network extension for tenants
    - Use templates to define computer names
    - Enable protection for all virtual machines

> WAP plans configuration for other resource providers, such as websites and databases, which will be covered in the coming chapter along with their building services.

Planning Windows Azure Pack plans

The number of plans and their configurations in a cloud solution depends upon cloud providers' business decisions or strategy, offerings, and capability in terms of the variety of cloud services and resources availability. Usually, multiple plans can be created having different service offerings and resources capability. For example, strategically, plans can be designed in multiple ways such as the following:

- **Standard packs plans or public plans**: These type of plans are pre-configured including specific service offerings and limits with defined pricing models. Multiple plans can be created targeting different industries, business sizes, or use cases. For example, a plan designed for hosting small website services may include IaaS resources of up to 5 VMs, 2 DB, and more where a plan dedicated for a hosting application server may include up to 50 Windows or Linux VMs.
- **Customized plans**: When standard plans don't suit the needs for any specific organization, customized plans can also be created and dedicated for particular organizations having services and limits configured as per the business deal.

- **Plans with special services or features**: Separate plans can be created for special features or offerings, such as some custom application services or capabilities including backup or DR.
- **Financials**: All plans created as per any of the previous strategies can be mapped to pricing; thus, multiple plans are created in each type of plan for different pricing as per business decisions.

Planning Windows Azure Pack Cloud add-ons

Add-ons are linked to plans and provide additional capability at the top of the services configured in plans. Add-ons are optional and can be subscribed by tenants as per requirements. Add-ons only increase quota or start services in a plan; they cannot be used to provide additional services that aren't included in a plan. Quotas provide limits for services offered in a plan.

Multiple add-ons can be created and linked to plans. Add-ons can be planned in a similar manner as plans including standard packages available for public usage, customized add-ons for customized tenants' needs, and specialized add-ons for particular features.

Creating and managing Windows Azure Pack plans and add-ons

Windows Azure Pack cloud administrators can create and manage plans or add-ons using the WAP management portal. Before creating a plan or an add-on, a cloud provider must plan and decide the number of plans and add-ons for their configuration.

Creating a WAP plan

Let's carry out the following steps to create a WAP plan:

1. Log into the WAP management portal for administrators.
2. Navigate to the **plans** workspace.

Assigning Cloud Services – Plans, Add-Ons, Tenant Accounts, and Subscriptions

3. Click on **CREATE A NEW HOSTING PLAN**.

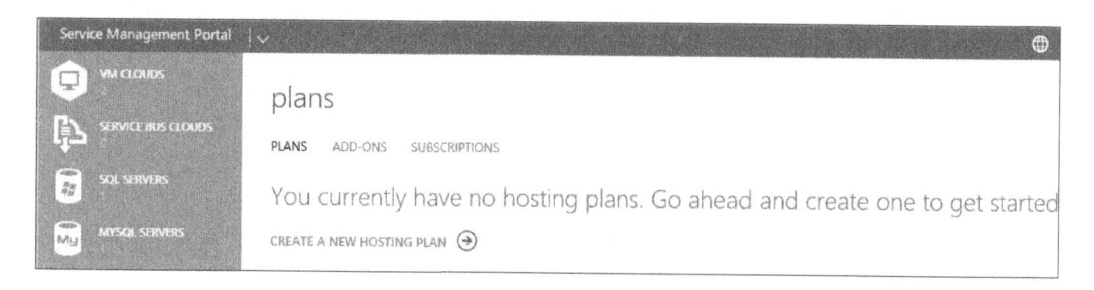

4. Provide a friendly name for the hosting plan; by default, this name will be visible to tenants while signing up.

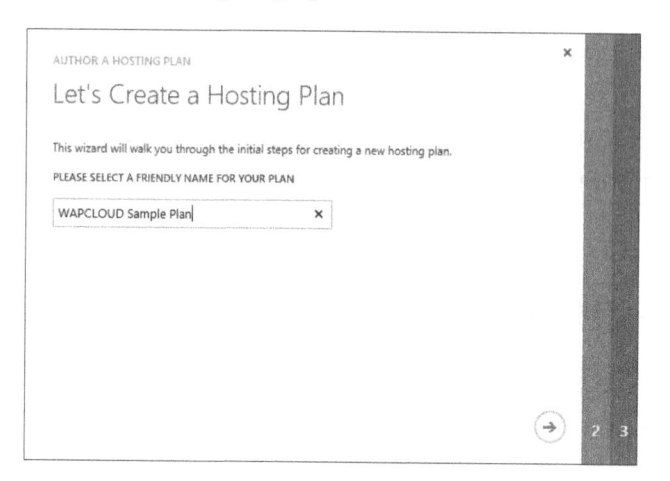

5. Select the services or the type of resource providers to be made available in the plan.

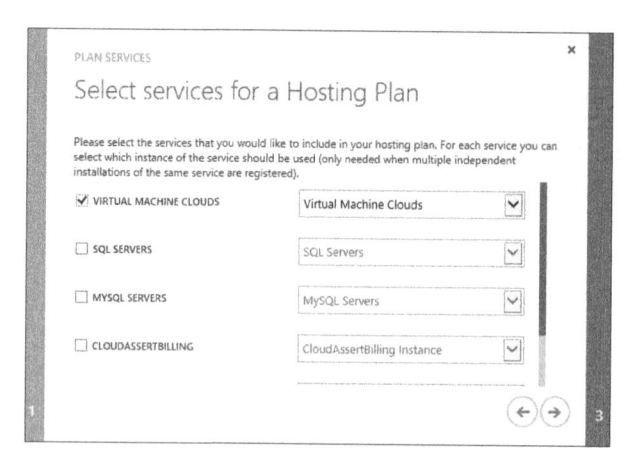

6. Select any **add-on** to be linked to the plan. This can also be configured later.
7. Click on the checkmark to create the plan.
8. By default, any plan gets created in a private state. It has to be changed to **Public** manually to make it available for tenants.
9. Click on the **NAME** plan to start configuring the plan for selected services.

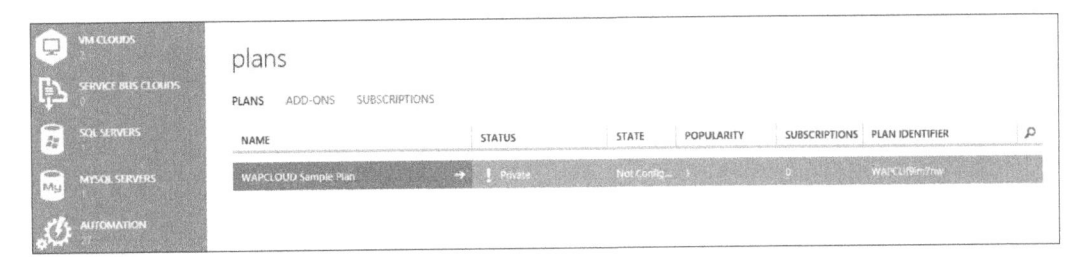

10. The WAP portal will display the plan dashboard stating that it's not configured. Click on **Virtual Machine Clouds** at the bottom of the screen to start the configuration. Additional services can also be added using the **ADD SERVICE** button.

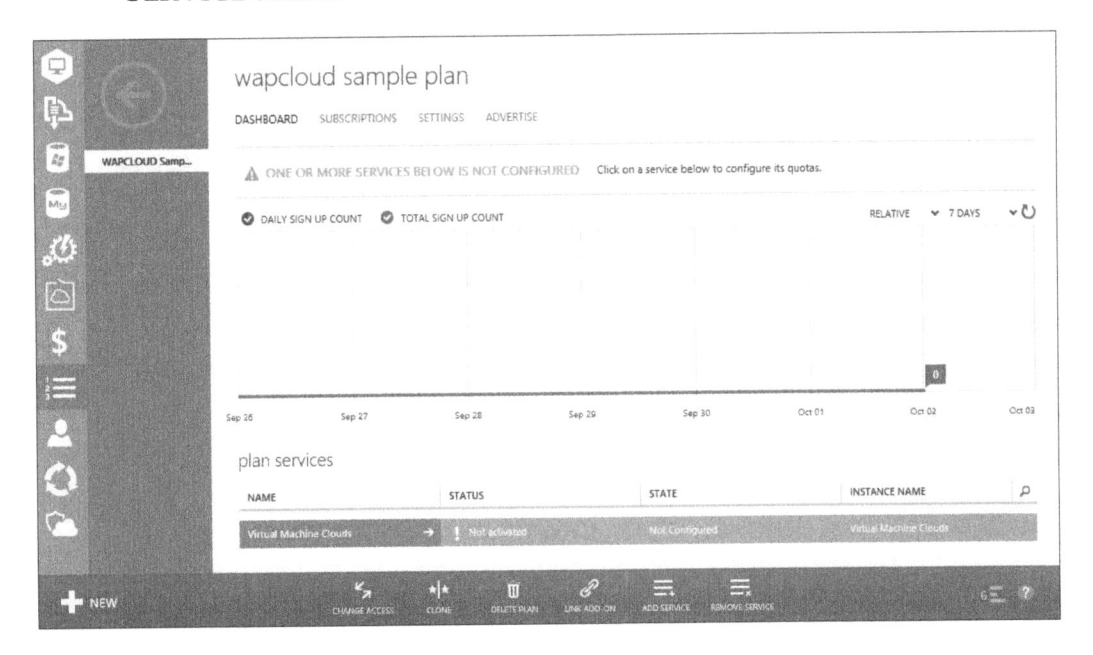

11. Select **VMM MANAGEMENT SERVER** and **VIRTUAL MACHINE CLOUD** that is to be associated with plan.

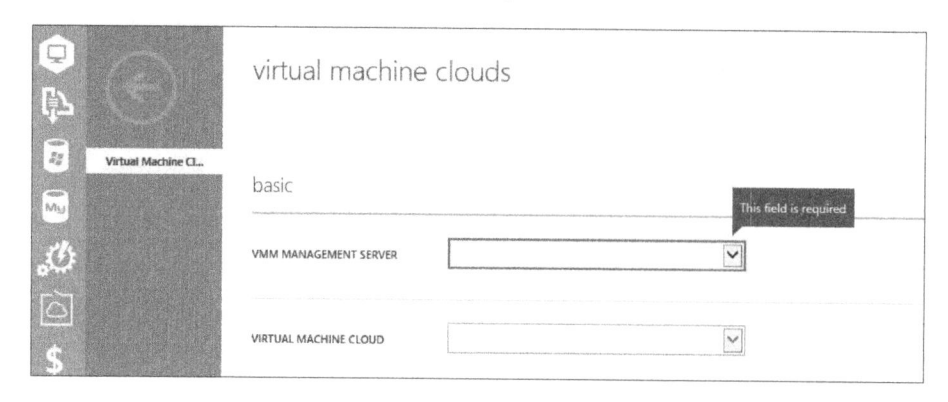

12. Select **USAGE LIMIT** as applicable. Keep VMM cloud level limits in consideration while configuring these settings. The portal will display the available configuration as per the limits configured at the SCVMM cloud level.

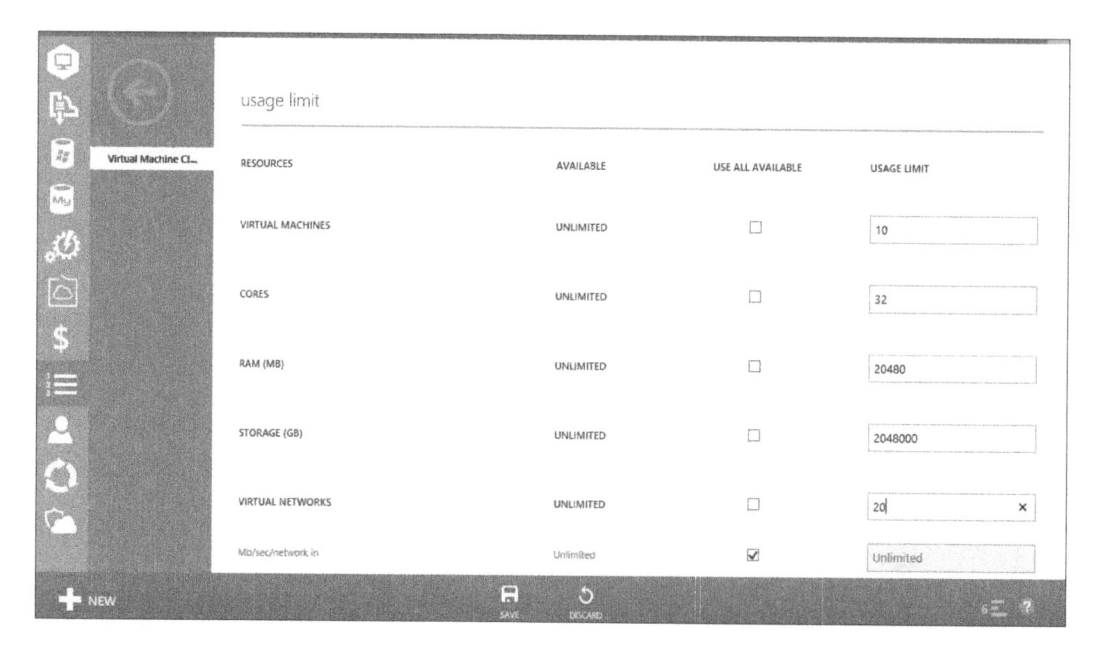

13. Add logical networks created in SCVMM to be made available to the tenants subscribing to this plan.
14. Add hardware profiles to be added to the plan. These hardware profiles will be available for tenants to choose from while requesting a standalone VM.

15. Add VM templates profiles to the plan. These VM templates will be available for tenants as a standalone VM to choose from while requesting a standalone VM.
16. Add gallery items to the plan. These gallery items will be available for tenants to choose from while requesting the VM Role resources.
17. Configure the additional setting to allow tenants-specific operations and custom settings for additional features.
18. Click on **Save** to finish configuring the plan.
19. Additional plans can be created in a similar manner.

Publishing, configuring, advertising, and cloning a WAP plan

Now, we already have a plan configured for offering cloud services to tenants. Before starting to assign plans to tenants; let's review a few management operations on the plans.

For publishing a plan by default, newly created plans are in private mode, that is, not visible to tenants for subscriptions. In order to make plans visible to tenants, they must be published first:

- **Publishing a plan**: Select **Plan** and click on **CHANGE ACCESS** to make the plan public. The plan can also be decommissioned or made private in a similar manner.

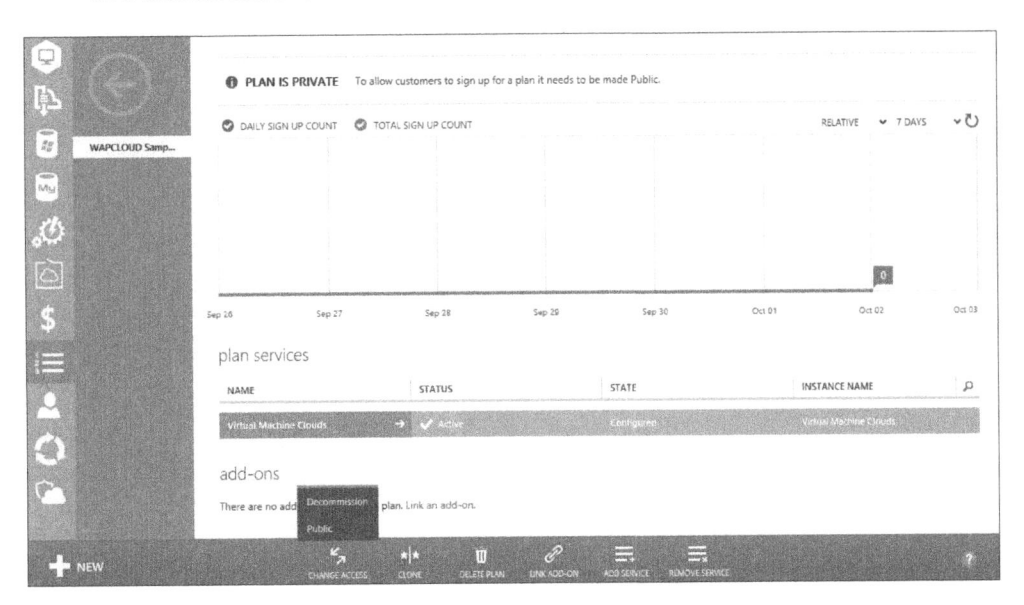

- **SETTINGS**: This page contains additional configurations such as:
    - **INVITATION CODE**: This can be used to verify the authenticity of tenants while signing up for the plan. A cloud provider can create invite codes and share them with tenants. Tenants will not be able to subscribe to the plan without this code.
    - **MAXIMUM ALLOWED SUBSCRIPTIONS PER ACCOUNT**: This defines the maximum number of subscriptions one account can have using this. This allows users to sign up for the plan more than once.

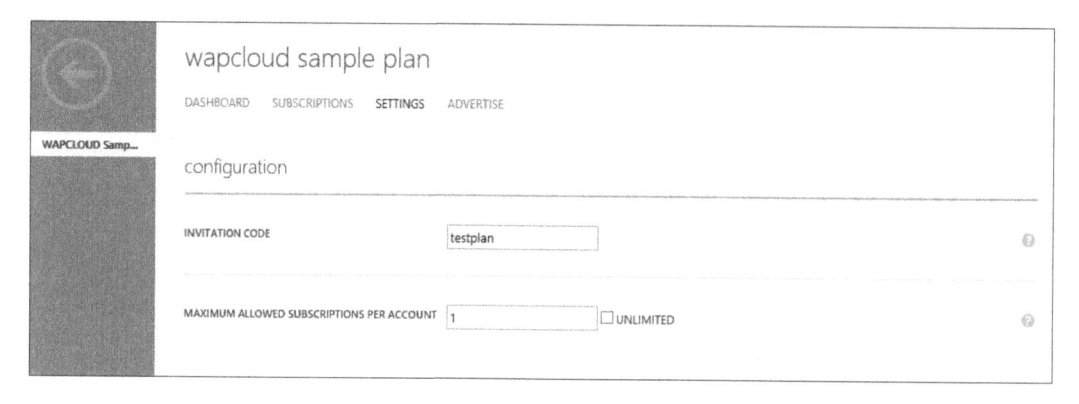

- **ADVERTISE**: Localized plan advertisements can be configured using this page. The plan display name and description visible to tenants can be modified using this page:
    - By default, WAP uses the plan name as the display name, which can be modified using the edit advertisement button.
    - Additional localized advertisements can be created using the **ADD ADVERTISEMENT** button, and then providing a locale, display name, and description.

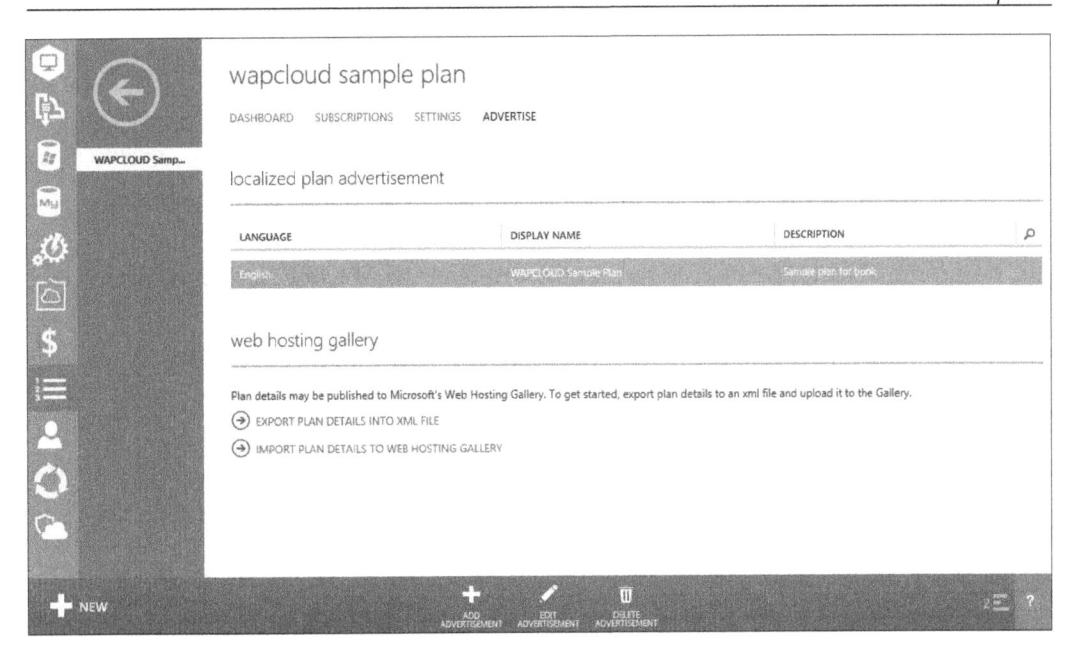

- Plans can be published on the Microsoft web hosting gallery directly from the WAP portal or by exporting plans into XML and uploading this XML manually.

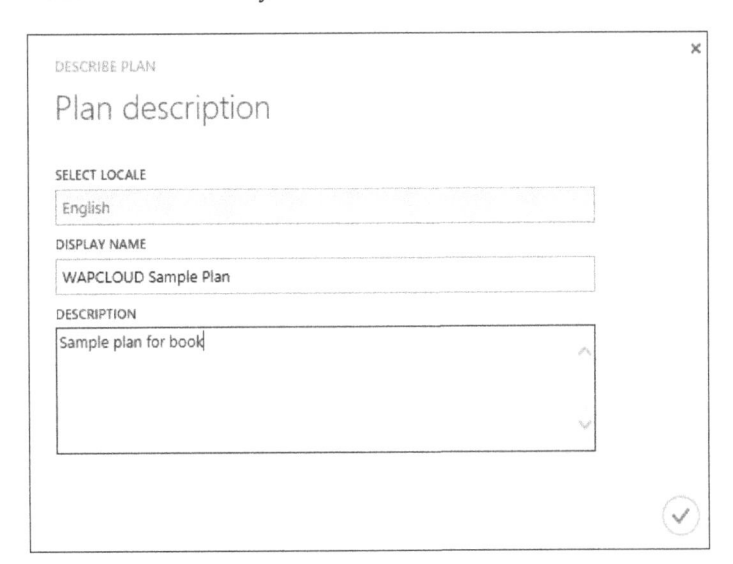

- **Cloning a plan**: Windows Azure Pack plans can be cloned to create new plans having existing plans settings preconfigured. Cloned plans will have all the settings preconfigured as per the original plan including advertisements and so on. The following steps are carried out to clone a plan:
    1. Log into the WAP management portal and browse to the **plans** workspace.
    2. Select the plan to be cloned and click on **CLONE**, which is in the bottom pane.
    3. Provide a new plan name and click on **Finish** to clone the plan. The cloned plan will be visible in the **plans** workspace.

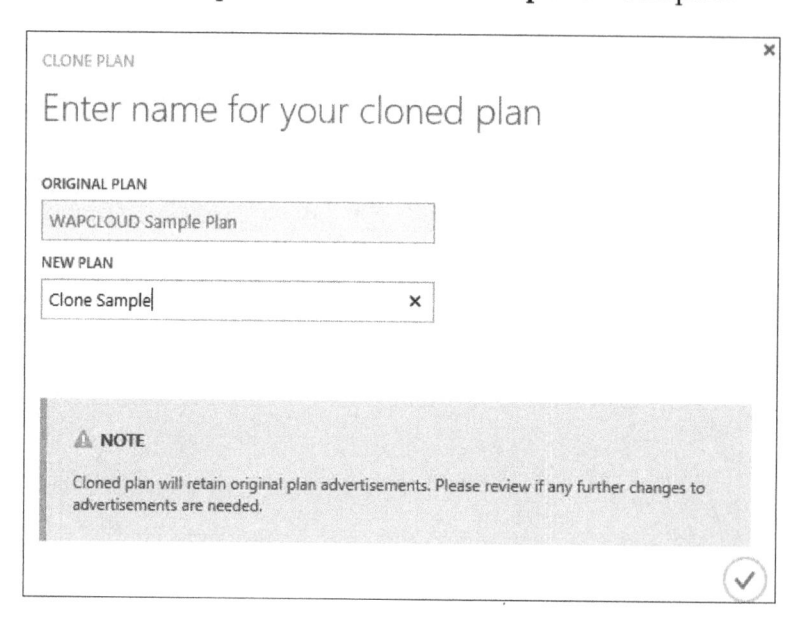

Creating and managing add-ons

Follow these steps to create an add-on:

1. Log into the WAP administration portal and browse to the **plans** workspace.
2. Go to the **ADD-ONS** tab.

3. Click on **CREATE A NEW ADD-ON** to provision add-ons.

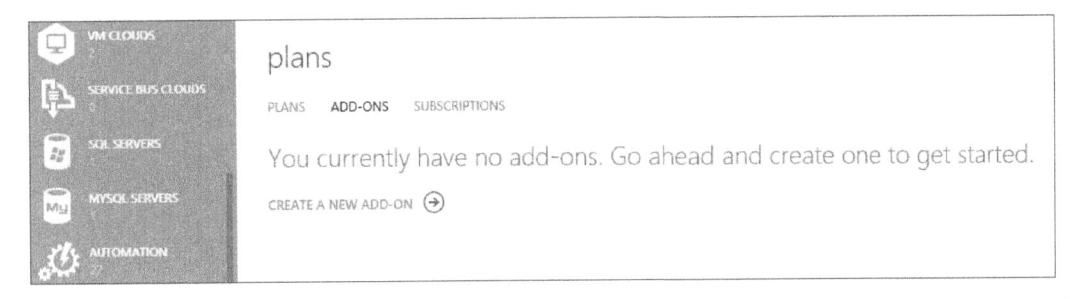

4. Provide a friendly name for the add-on. This name will be visible to the tenants.
5. Select **Services** and the add-on will extend. Note that the plan with which this add-on will be linked must provide these services.
6. Click on the add-on name to start configuring the settings.
7. For IaaS using VM Clouds add-on, select **VMM Management Server** and **VMM Cloud** as per the original plan of configuration.
8. Configure the usage limit that the add-on will provide.
9. Add additional networks, hardware profiles, templates, and gallery items that this add-on will provide.
10. Select additional and custom settings as applicable.
11. Click on **SAVE** to configure the add-on with defined settings.
12. Additional add-ons can be created in a similar manner.

The following add-on management operations can be performed in a similar manner as per the plans, operations:

- Making an add-on public or private
- Adding or removing services
- Cloning an add-on to create new add-on
- Maximum times an add-on can be subscribed on the top of specific plan
- Advertisement configuration

Linking an add-on to a plan

Let's follow these steps to link an add-on to a plan:

1. Log into the WAP administration portal and browse to the **plans** workspace.
2. Go to the **Add-Ons** tab.
3. Select the add-on and click on the **Link a plan** button on the bottom pane.
4. Select the plan to which the add-on needs to be linked.

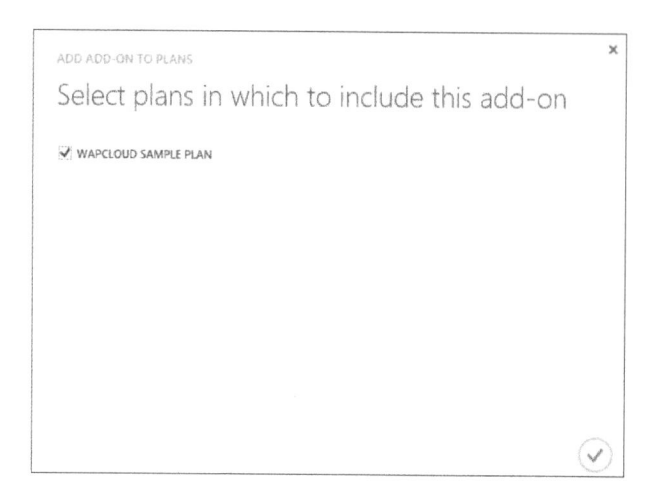

ADD ADD-ON TO PLANS

Select plans in which to include this add-on

☑ WAPCLOUD SAMPLE PLAN

- Click on **Finish** to link the add-on to the plan.

Creating and managing tenants' user accounts

While signing up on Windows Azure Pack tenant portal, tenants must provide an email address and password. This creates an account for tenants in Windows Azure Pack directory (ASP .Net or ADFS as applicable).

Tenant user accounts can be created in Windows Azure Pack in two ways:

- They can be created by a tenant's self-sign up operation
- They can be created by a cloud administrator

Creating user accounts for tenants

The following steps are to be carried out for creating user accounts for tenants:

1. Log into the WAP management portal for administrators.
2. Browse the **user accounts** workspace.
3. Click on **CREATE A NEW USER**.

4. Provide user details including email address, password, and a plan to subscribe. Note that a plan made public will only be available here.

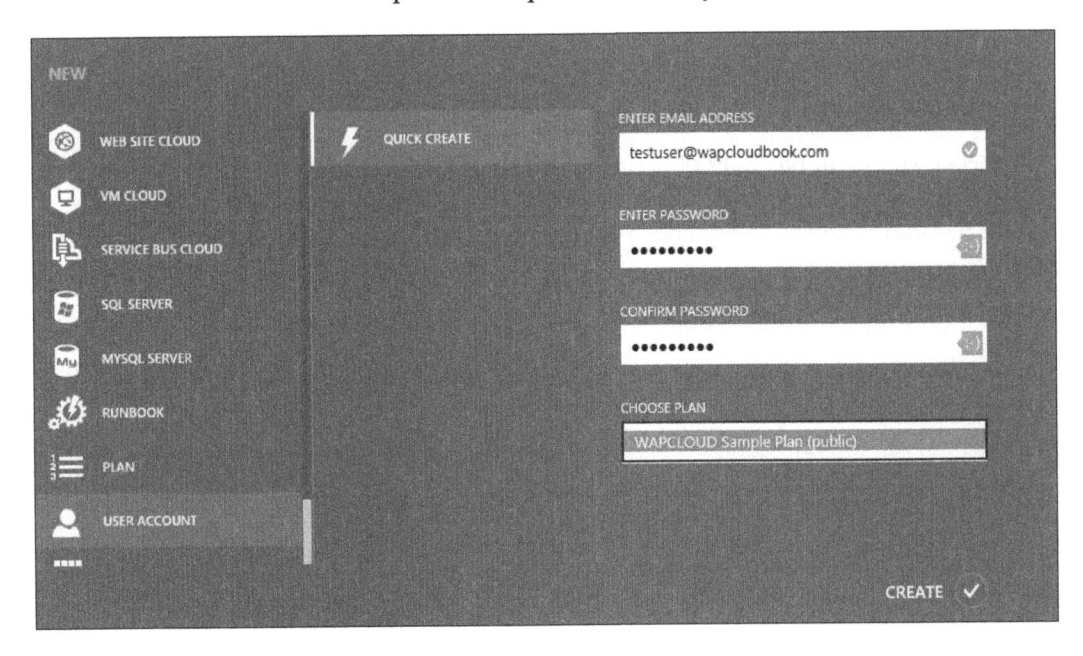

5. Tenants can use this account now for logging into the tenant portal and using services under the selected plan.

An administrator can perform additional operations on user accounts such as:

- Suspend account
- Reset password
- Delete account

> Note that all tenant user account-related operations aren't applicable when any other authentication and federation services are used, such as ADFS. These are applicable only with WAP built-in ASP .Net provider user accounts.

Configuring notification settings and rules

Windows Azure Pack provides notification features for standard user account management operations such as the following:

- Verifying user email account by sending a verification link on the users' email addresses
- Sending a new password to users
- Sending users a link to reset the password

Additional rules can be created as per requirement. Activating any rule requires SMTP settings to be configured first as notifications require a mail server to send emails to tenants' users. Let's have a look at the steps for configuring SMTP settings and notification rules:

1. Log into the WAP management portal for administrators.
2. Browse through the **user accounts** workspace and then the **SETTINGS** tab.

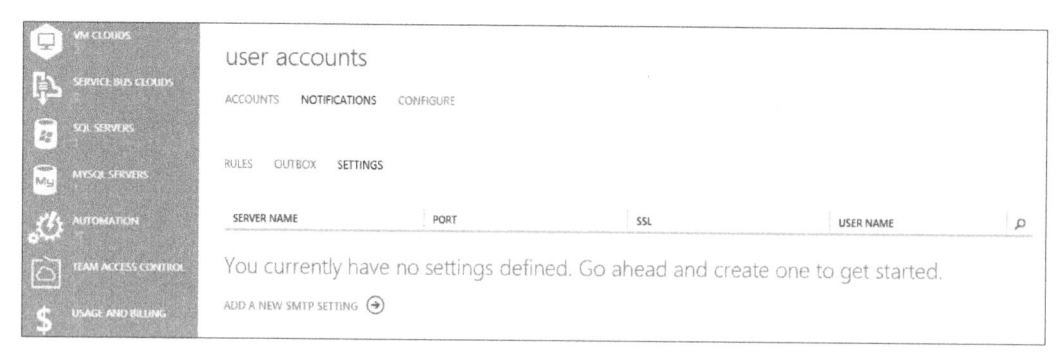

SERVER NAME	PORT	SSL	USER NAME

You currently have no settings defined. Go ahead and create one to get started.

ADD A NEW SMTP SETTING →

Chapter 5

3. Click on **ADD A NEW SMTP SETTING**.
4. Add the server address and port number.
5. Select the **Authentication** type (basic or anonymous).
6. If applicable, provide a username and password to be used to connect to the SMTP server.

To configure notification rules, perform the following steps:

1. Log into the WAP management portal for administrators.
2. Browse the **user accounts** workspace and the **RULES** tab.

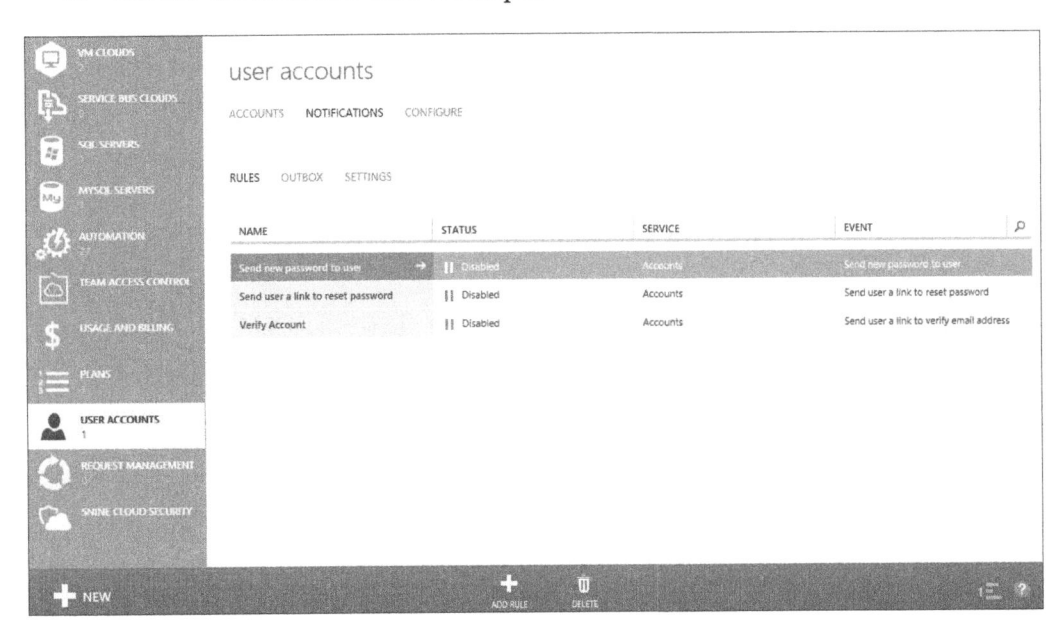

[185]

3. Click on any existing rule to configure settings or add rules to create a new rule.
4. Configure email setting for the rule, such as the following:
    - Enabled status: yes or no
    - Reply to the email address: This will be used if tenants wish to reply to autogenerated emails
    - Email subject: Email subject for notifications messages
    - Email body: Cloud providers can modify existing templates as per requirements
    - SMTP account to use

Additional rules for notifications can be created and configured in a similar manner. The outbox tab can be used by the administrator to see all the notifications sent to users.

Configuring additional accounts management settings

The **CONFIGURE** tab on the user account workspace in the WAP portal allows cloud providers to select a generic control over user accounts as per their choice:

- **Required Password Strength**: Weak/Fair/Strong
- **Tenant Self Service Subscription Management**: Enable or Disable

    This allows cloud administrators to choose if tenants can subscribe to plans in a self-service manner (using invite code), or whether it has to be through cloud administrator only

- **Account Validation Required**: Yes/No

    This setting requires corresponding notification rules and SMTP settings to configure

- **Forgot Password Enabled**: Yes/No

    This setting requires corresponding notification rules and SMTP settings to configure

Tenant subscriptions – an overview and management

A subscription is an object that defines a tenant's access to a plan and is used to identify the tenant's resources and access across the cloud. A subscription is created when tenants sign up for any plan or add-on.

A subscription is one-to-one mapping between tenant user and plan access. One subscription can be attached to only one plan, whereas single tenants can have multiple subscriptions. Windows Azure Pack provides self-services access to tenants for creating and managing subscriptions as defined by cloud administrators. In this topic, you will learn about subscription management from a cloud administrator's point of view; the tenant's point of view will be covered in the next chapter.

Subscription management operations – administrators

The Windows Azure Pack administration portal allows management operations on subscription, which can be performed by a cloud administrator. The following management operations can be performed:

- Viewing a list of all the subscriptions per plan or throughout a cloud
- Dashboard showing resource usage in a subscription
- Suspending or deleting a subscription
- Migrating a subscription from one plan to another plan
- Adding a co-administrator (tenant) to any subscription
- Linking any add-on to a subscription

The following steps are to be carried out for subscription management operations:

1. Log into the WAP management portal for administrators.
2. Browse the **plans** workspace and the **SUBSCRIPTIONS** tab.

3. All **SUBSCRIPTION** under the WAP cloud will be visible.

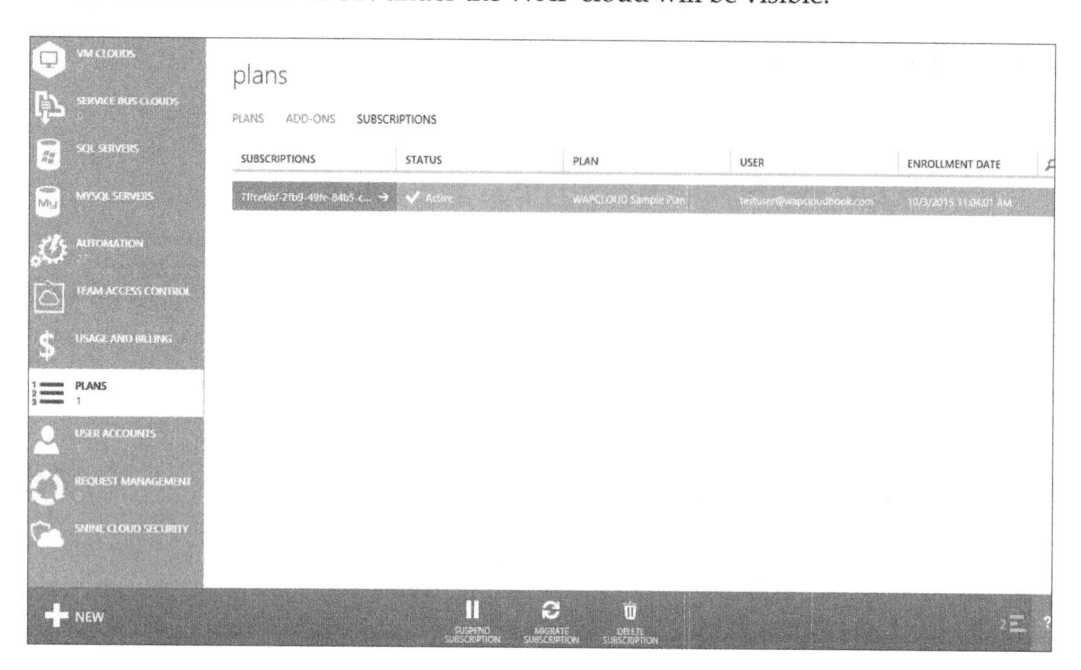

4. Subscriptions management operations can be performed using buttons in the bottom pane. Operations include the following:
    - **SUSPEND SUBSCRIPTION**
    - **MIGRATE SUBSCRIPTION TO A DIFFERENT PLAN**
    - **DELETE SUBSCRIPTION**
5. Click on the subscription name to get a dashboard of the subscription usage.
6. Additional co-administrators can be created using the **ADMINISTRATORS** tab.
7. Add-ons can be mapped using the **Add-Ons** tab.

Adding a new subscription to the tenant's user account

Usually, subscriptions are automatically created when any tenant signs up for any plan or add-on. Cloud administrators can also create additional subscription, for the existing or new tenant users as per requirement.

Carry out the following steps for adding a new subscription for the existing tenant account:

1. Log into the WAP management portal for administrators.
2. Browse the **User Accounts** workspace.
3. Click on the user account to add a new subscription to the existing account. A new user can be created using the **Add User** button.
4. Clicking on the user account will display subscriptions associated with that tenant user.
5. Additional subscriptions can be created using the **Add Subscription** button.

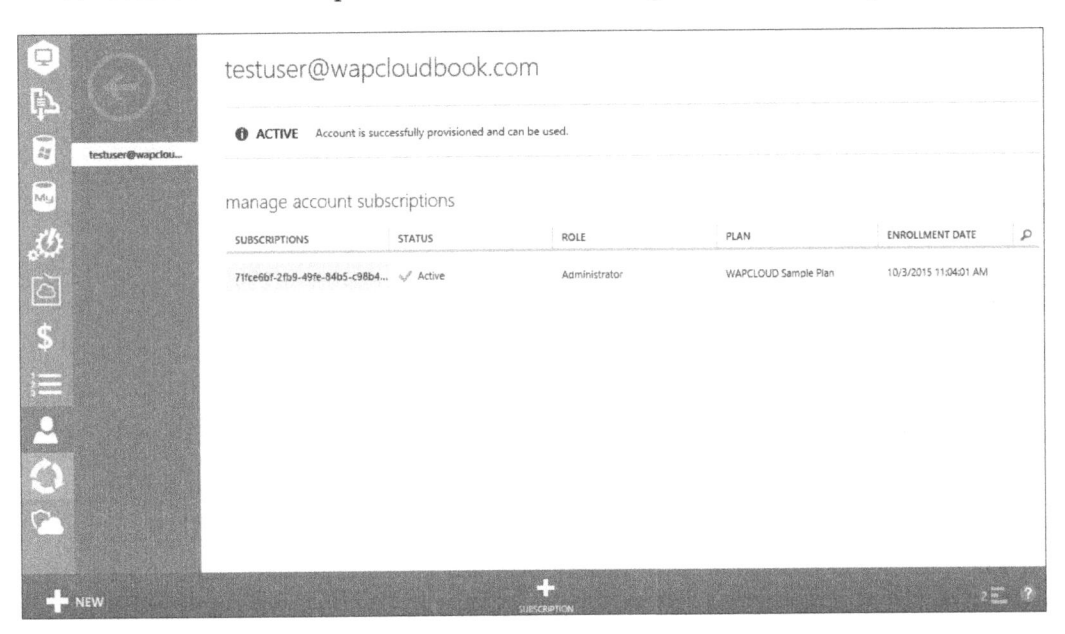

Summary

In this chapter, you learned the ways of delivering cloud services to tenants created in the previous chapters. We covered the planning of Windows Azure Pack hosting plans and add-ons along with their implementation. You also learned about user account management for tenant's accounts and subscriptions.

At the end of this chapter, we have our cloud solution ready with IaaS services configured with plans for the tenants' usage. In the next chapter, we will access this solution as a cloud tenant, which is also known as a customer. We will experience the cloud services provisioning and management operations.

6
Experiencing the Cloud Services – the Tenant's Point of View

After five hard-core technical chapters, this chapter will be relaxed and rewarding. In this chapter, we will look at our cloud set up that we deployed earlier from a customer or tenant's point of view. We will register a new tenant in the cloud by subscribing to a plan that we created earlier. We will then request and manage cloud services available in the subscribed plan.

We will be covering the following topics:

- Tenant's registration and accounts management
- Creating and managing virtual networks
- Standalone VMs – provisioning and management
- Virtual machine Role – provisioning and management

Tenant registrations and account management

As briefly covered in the previous chapter, there are two ways for tenants to get registered for using cloud services in Windows Azure Pack. One is self-signup and subscription by the tenant, the other is pre-registering by the cloud provider.

We have already covered the second method in the previous chapter. Let's experience the first one in this chapter.

Sign up and plan subscription

The steps mentioned here should be followed to sign up a tenant and plan or add-on subscriptions:

1. Log into the Windows Azure Pack tenant portal.
2. Click on **Signup**.
3. Provide an e-mail address and password, and click on **Signup**. This will create an account in the Azure Pack cloud directory (ASP.NET provider).

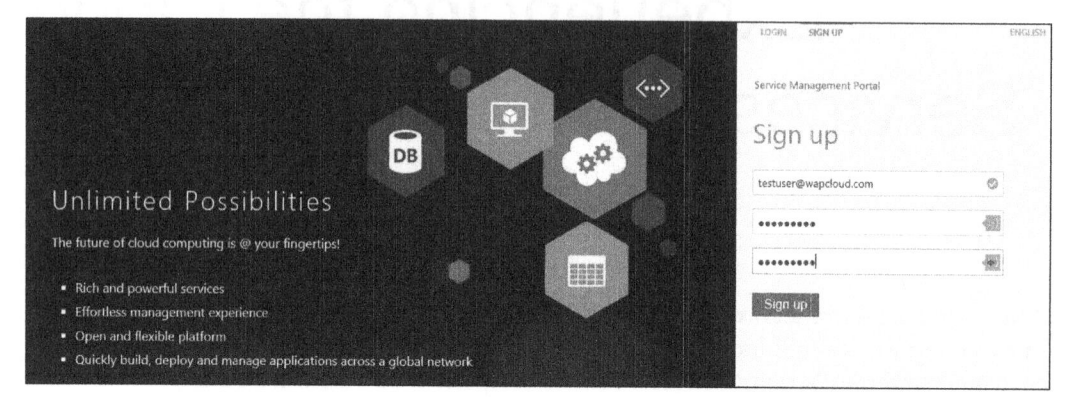

4. Upon successful registration, the portal will display the management portal tour.
5. To use any cloud services, a tenant must subscribe to a plan first. Click on the **New** button at the bottom of the **my account** page to subscribe to a plan.
6. Public plans published by cloud providers will be displayed here. Select **plan** to subscribe and provide **INVITATION CODE** to verify its authenticity.

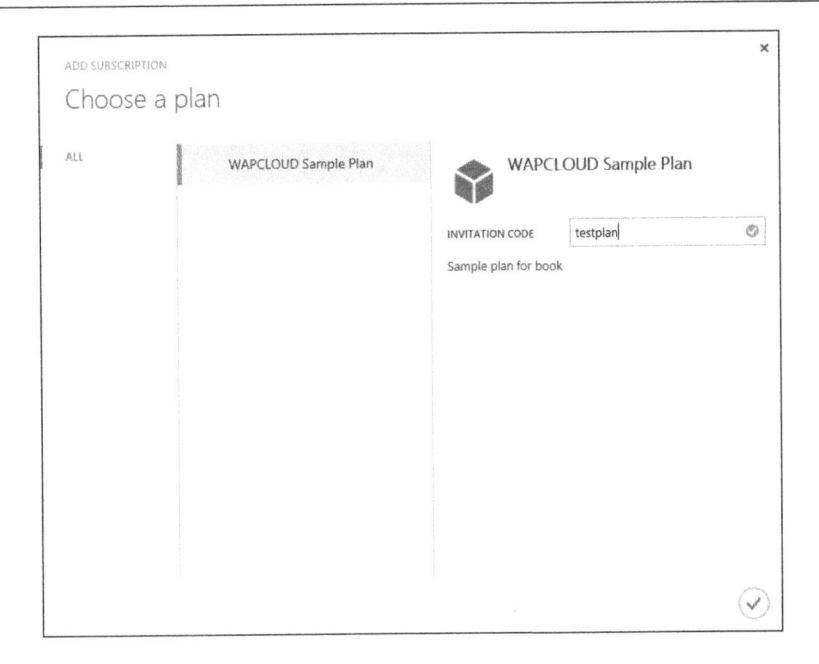

The subscription will start getting created; it may take a few minutes for it to finish.

7. After the subscription creation, tenants will be able to see additional options and workspaces as per services configured in the plan.
8. A subscription ID can be found in the **my account** workspace under the **SUBSCRIPTIONS** tab.

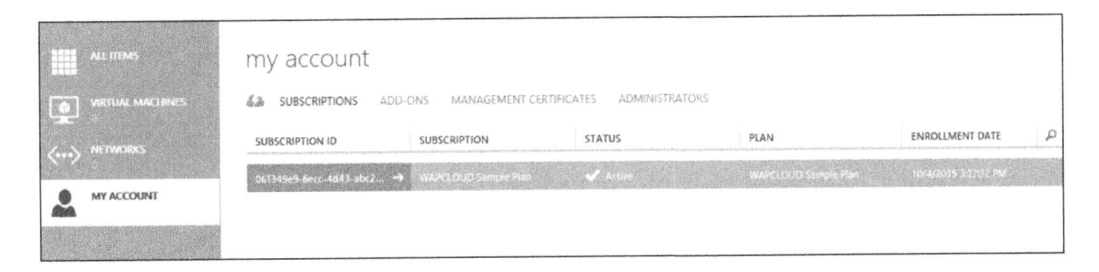

9. A friendly name can be assigned to the subscription using the **change name** button in the bottom pane.
10. Navigate to **New** | **My Account** | **add Add-on** to subscribe to an additional add-on available with the plan.

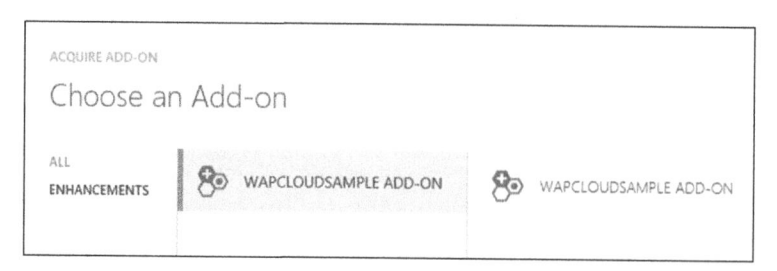

Tenant account and subscriptions management operations

A tenant's administrator can perform the following management operations on accounts and subscriptions in a self-service manner through a tenant portal:

- It can view a list and status of active subscriptions
- It can view the current usage and the usage limit of resources under subscriptions and add-ons
- It can upload a management certificate to use a certificate-based authentication for accessing the assigned cloud services
- It can assign one or more co-administrators to a subscription
- It can subscribe to additional plans or add-ons
- It can delete a subscription
- It can delete an account

Now, we will see the previously mentioned management operations in detail:

- View list, status, usage, delete an active subscriptions, and add-on:
  Carry out the following steps to perform these kind of operations:
    1. Log into the tenant portal using the tenant admin account.
    2. Browse the **MY ACCOUNT** workspace and click on subscriptions.

3. All subscriptions associated with the account will be displayed along with a subscription ID, name, status, plan, and enrolment date.
4. Click on the **delete** button to delete any existing subscription.
5. Click on **subscription ID** to get uses and limits associated with the certificate.
6. Click on the **Add-ons** tab to perform similar operations on add-ons.

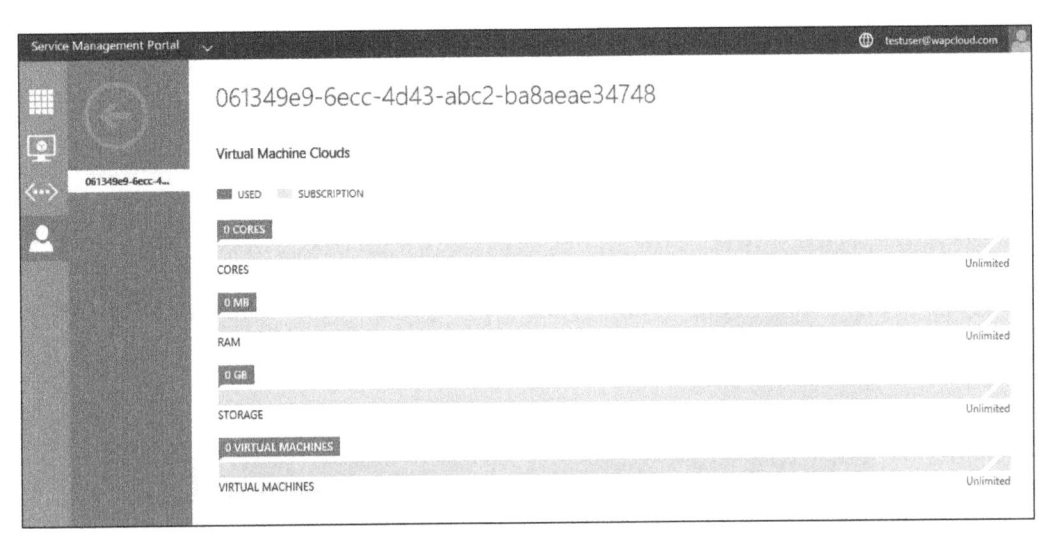

- **Uploading a management certificate**: Tenants can upload management certificates to WAP tenant portals, which can be used by tenants to verify their authenticity while logging in using the tenant PowerShell or the APIs.
- Management certificates can be uploaded using the **UPLOAD A CERTIFICATE** button in the **my account** workspace on the tenant portal.

Experiencing the Cloud Services – the Tenant's Point of View

- **Adding co-admins**: Additional administrators can be added using WAP tenant portals for any subscription. This allows multiple users to login and request/manage cloud services assigned to a tenant:
    - Additional administrators can be added on a tenant portal in the **ADMINISTRATORS** tab under the **my account** workspace.

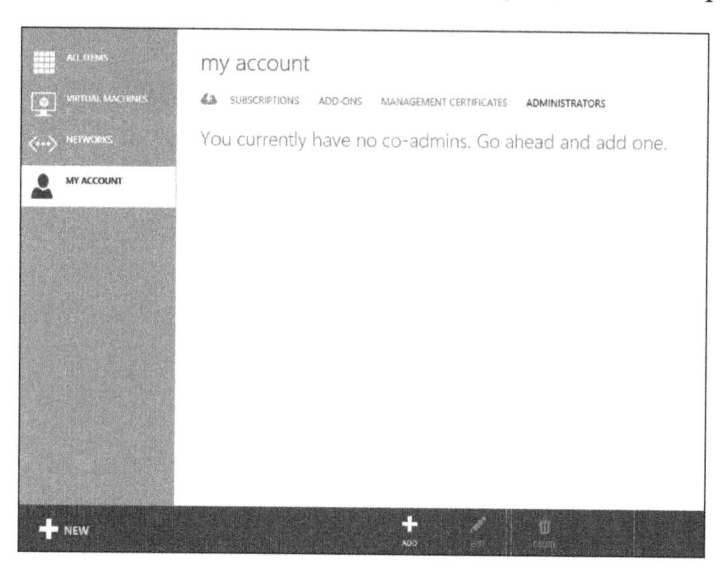

    - Click on the **ADD** button to add new co-admins. Provide the user's ID and select subscriptions to associate with it.

- ○ The same page can be used to add more co-admins or edit or delete the existing ones.
- **Deleting an account**: Deleting an account deletes all the associated subscriptions. Browse the **my account** workspace on a portal to get the option to delete the account.

Creating and managing virtual networks

Tenants can create virtual networks as per their custom needs. A virtual network may have any IP range as per the tenant's choice and can also be used to set up a site-to-site VPN connectivity between the tenant's existing datacentres and Windows Azure Pack cloud networks. VNet also allows the usage of **Network Address Translation (NAT)** for virtual machines. The IP's tenants can create multiple virtual networks isolated with each other.

Windows Azure Pack virtual networks are powered by the Hyper-V network virtualization with SCVMM.

Creating a virtual network

Follow these steps to create a virtual network:

1. Log into the tenant portal using the tenant's admin account.
2. Browse the **network** workspace.
3. Click on **CREATE A VIRTUAL NETWORK**.

4. Click on **QUICK CREATE** or **CUSTOM CREATE**.

Experiencing the Cloud Services – the Tenant's Point of View

5. Provide a virtual network name and protocol (IPv4 or IPv6).

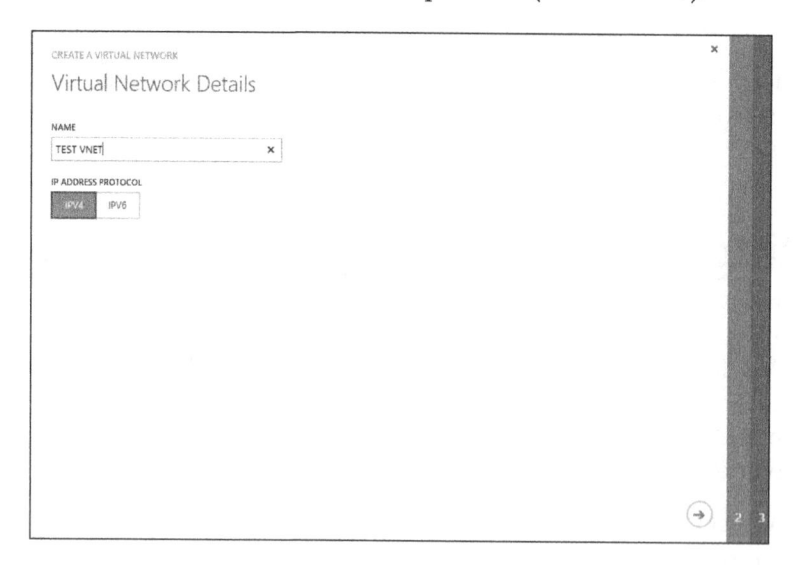

6. Provide the DNS server's IP that is to be used in VNET. Providing a DNS will automatically assign the DNS's IP to the VM under this virtual network. This can be configured later as well.

7. Select additional options such as **Enable direct internet access using NAT** or **Configure site to site VPN** as applicable.

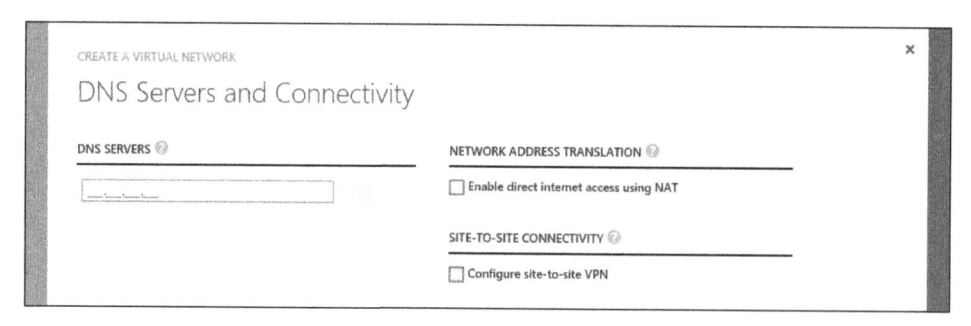

Chapter 6

8. Select **ADDRESS SPACE** and subnet it as per the tenants' choice.

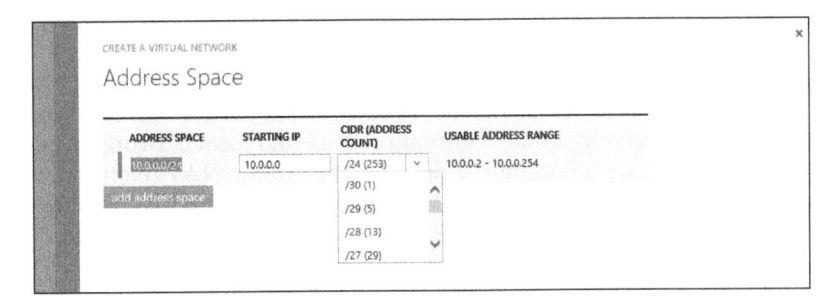

9. The newly created virtual network will now be visible under the **networks** workspace, and it is ready for the virtual machine's usage.

> While requesting for any resource in the Windows Azure Pack tenant portal, two options **QUICK CREATE** and **CUSTOM CREATE** or **FROM GALLERY** will be available. While **QUICK CREATE** will create the resource request with some default values without asking details from a tenant user, **CUSTOM CREATE** will allow tenants to customize the request as much as possible.

Managing and extending a virtual network

A tenant's administrators can perform the following management and extensibility's operations using a tenant portal on a precreated virtual network:

- It can virtual network the IP usage
- It can add an additional address space
- It can configure the DNS server IP
- It can enable or disable NAT or a site-to-site VPN
- NAT rules
- It can configure a site-to-site VPN
- It can download an on-site VPN configuration script

[199]

Experiencing the Cloud Services – the Tenant's Point of View

> Configuring a DNS Server IP will allow a DNS name translation between virtual machines inside and outside of the virtual network. Any virtual machine provisioned with connectivity to a VNet will have DNS server IP configured automatically as provided in the VNet configuration. A site-to-site VPN will allow a hybrid cloud networking set up between the cloud's virtual network and local network on an on-premises datacenter of the tenant. Enabling **NAT (Network Address Translation)** for any VM allows the VM's private IP to be NATed with the public IP for access from the Internet. See http://blogs.technet.com/b/privatecloud/archive/2013/11/20/hyper-v-network-virtualization-architecture-and-key-concepts.aspx to learn more about hybrid cloud networking for Windows Azure Pack.

The steps mentioned here should be followed to perform management operations:

1. Log into the tenant portal using the tenant's admin account.
2. Browse the **network** workspace, and click on network to manage.
3. **DASHBOARD** will display VNet details such as status, network ID, external IP, and gateway IP along with the virtual IP usage.

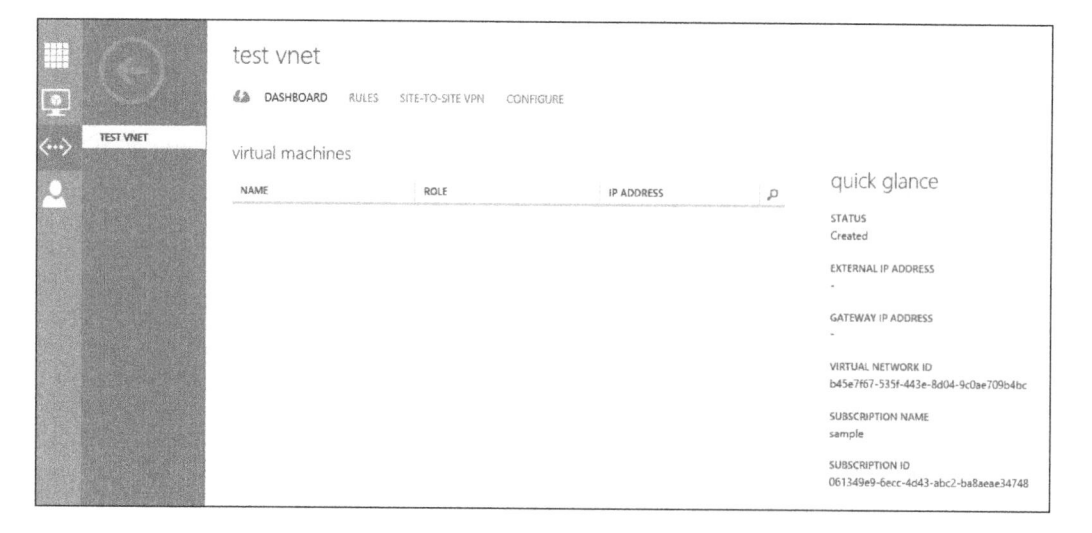

4. The **RULES** page allows tenants to create and manage all NAT rules for public Internet facing virtual machines.
5. **SITE-TO-SITE VPN** allows tenants to configure and manage a site-to-site VPN connectivity between Cloud VNET and a tenant's on-premises network.

6. The **CONFIGURE** page allows tenants to add or modify the address space and DNS server. It also allows a site-to-site VPN or NAT.

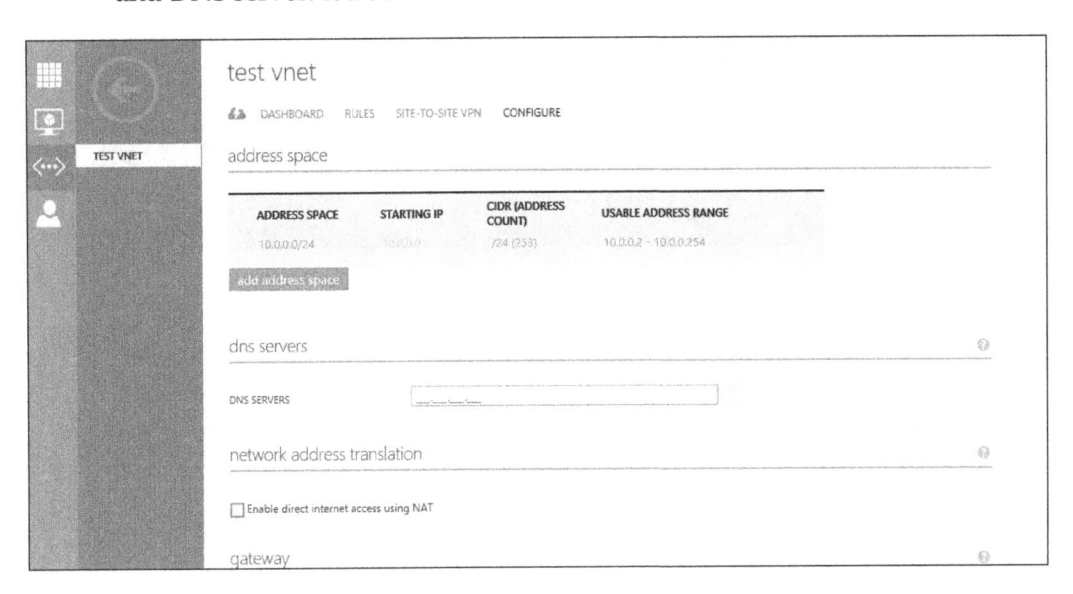

7. The on-site VPN configuration script can be downloaded from the **networks** workspace quick start menu.

Standalone VM – provisioning and management

Standalone virtual machines allow the tenant's administrator to create and manage virtual Vanilla OS virtual machines as configured by the cloud provider in the plan. All the added VM templates in the plan by the cloud provider will be visible to tenants in the create standalone VM menu.

Creating a standalone virtual machine

To create a standalone virtual machine, we will have to follow these steps:

1. Log into the tenant portal using the tenant's admin account.

2. Click on the **NEW** button in the bottom pane and select **STANDALONE VIRTUAL MACHINE**.

3. Click on **QUICK CREATE** or **FROM GALLERY** as applicable.
4. Select the templates or disks available to tenants. Clicking on the object will display its descriptions configured by the cloud administrator.
5. Provide the VM name, password, and product key if applicable.

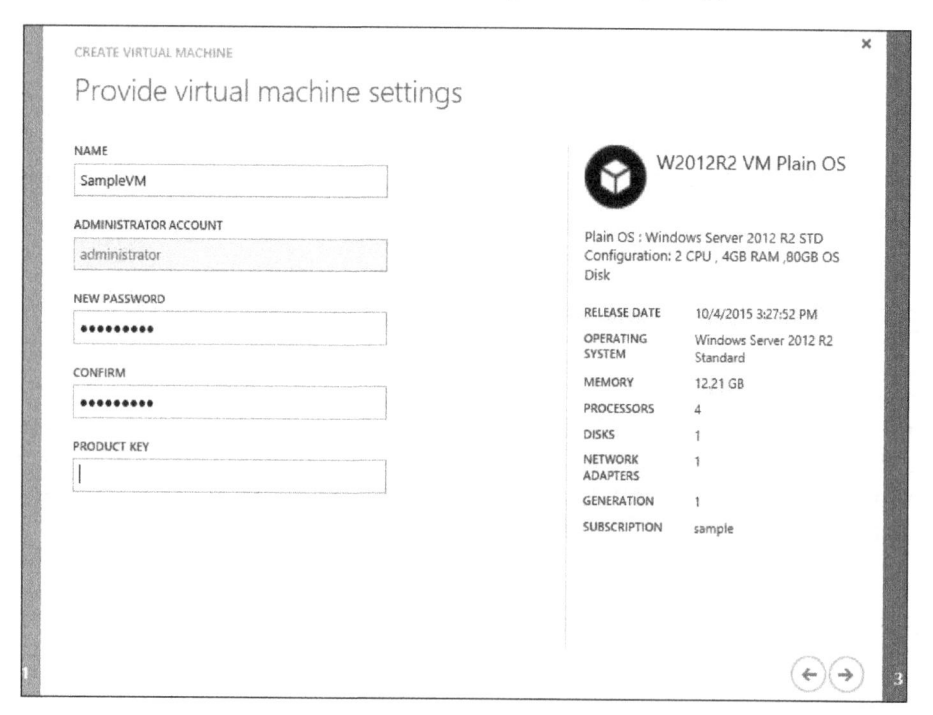

6. Select the network to which this VM needs to be attached. The newly created VNet will be visible in the drop-down list.
7. Now the **CREATE VIRTUAL MACHINE** operation will start. VM will be listed under the virtual machines workspace in portal post completion.

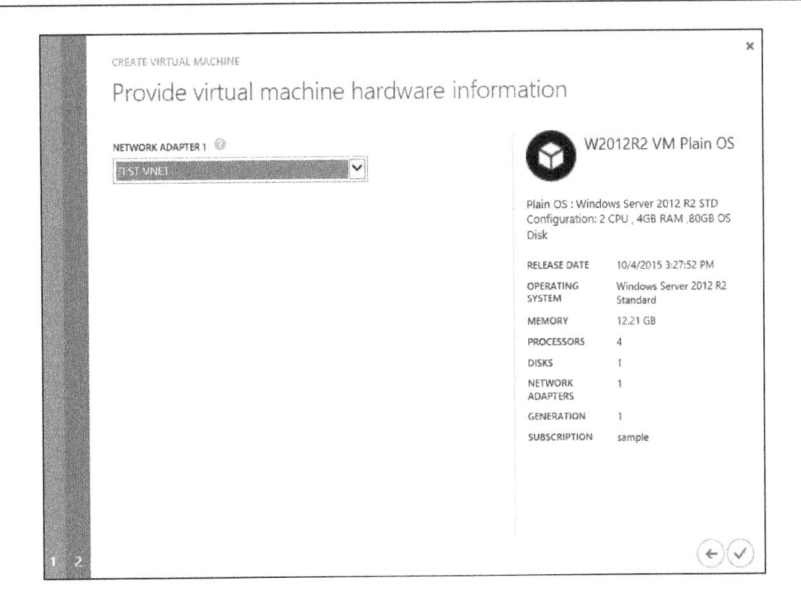

Management operations – standalone virtual machine

The tenant's administrators can perform the following management operations using the tenant portal on a standalone virtual machine:

- View status and resource the usage of the virtual machine
- Connect to the virtual machine using the console or RDP
- Pause, restart, shutdown, start, stop, and delete the virtual machine
- Create, view, and restore checkpoints
- Modify the virtual machine size
- Attach additional devices to the VM such as network adaptor, disk, and DVD

Basic operations given next can be accessed by selecting virtual machines in the VM workspace.

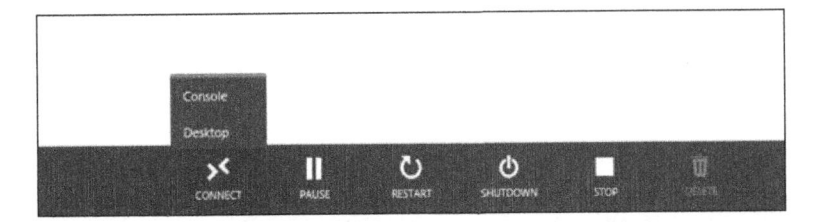

Experiencing the Cloud Services – the Tenant's Point of View

Additional operations such as dashboard of VM resource usage and additional advanced operations can be performed under **samplevm | DASHBOARD**.

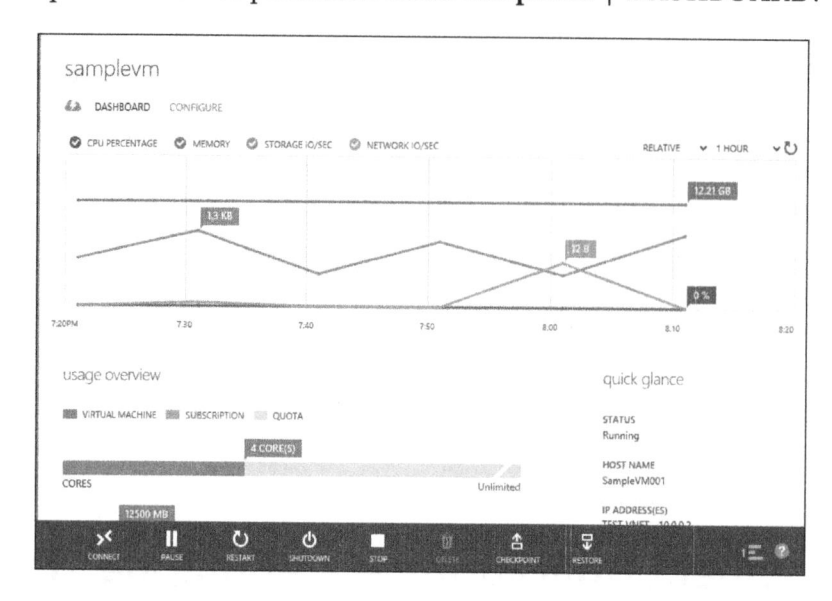

The **CONFIGURE** page allows tenants to modify VM configuration such as **VIRTUAL MACHINE SIZE**, attaching devices to VMs such as network, DVD, and disk.

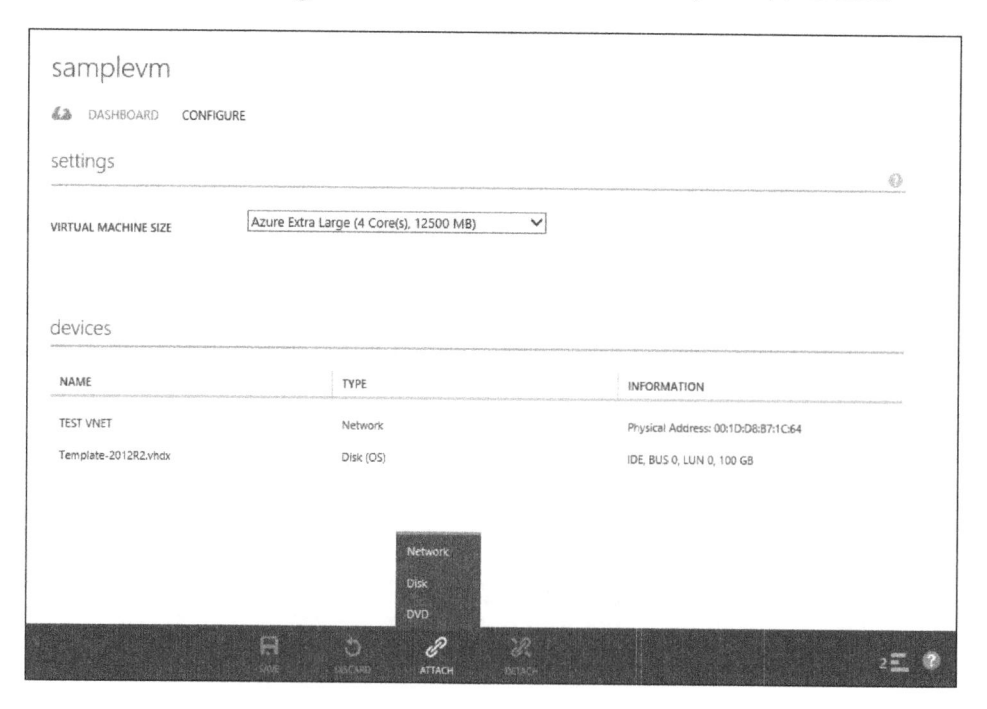

Virtual machine Role – provisioning and management

Virtual machine Role enables tenants to deploy virtual machines along with applications in an easy scale in and out manner. A VM Role may contain one or more virtual machines of the same type. See *Chapter 4*, *Building VM Clouds and IaaS Offerings* to know more about VM Role.

Creating a VM Role

For creating a VM Role, steps are required to be followed:

1. Log into the tenant portal using the tenant admin account.
2. Click on the **NEW** button in bottom pane, and click on **VIRTUAL MACHINE ROLE**.

3. Click on **QUICK CREATE** or **FROM GALLERY** as applicable.
4. Choose the gallery item to deploy VM Role.

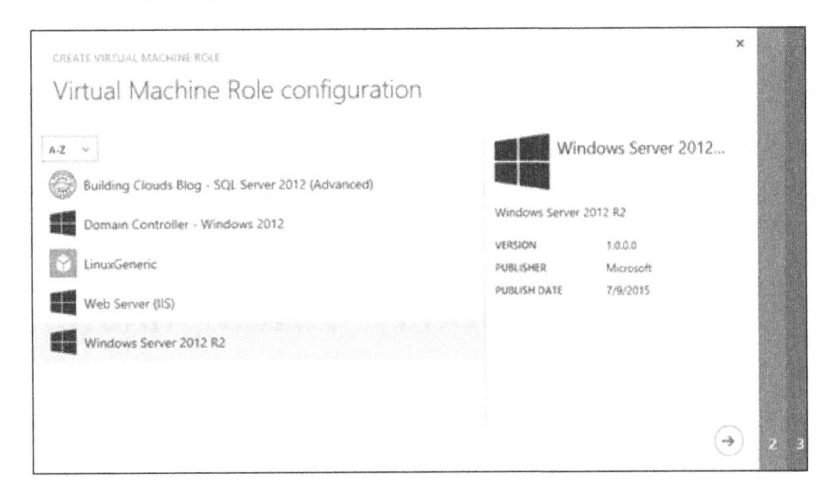

Experiencing the Cloud Services – the Tenant's Point of View

5. Provide the VM Role name and select its version. Note that this is not the VM's name or hostname. All VM instances will be available under this VM Role name.
6. Provide the virtual machine configuration such as VM size, disk, IP address type, network, hostname pattern, domain, or workgroup settings as applicable.
7. Provide scaling settings such as **INITIAL INSTANCE COUNT**, **MINIMUM INSTANCE COUNT**, and **MAXIMUM INSTANCE COUNT**.

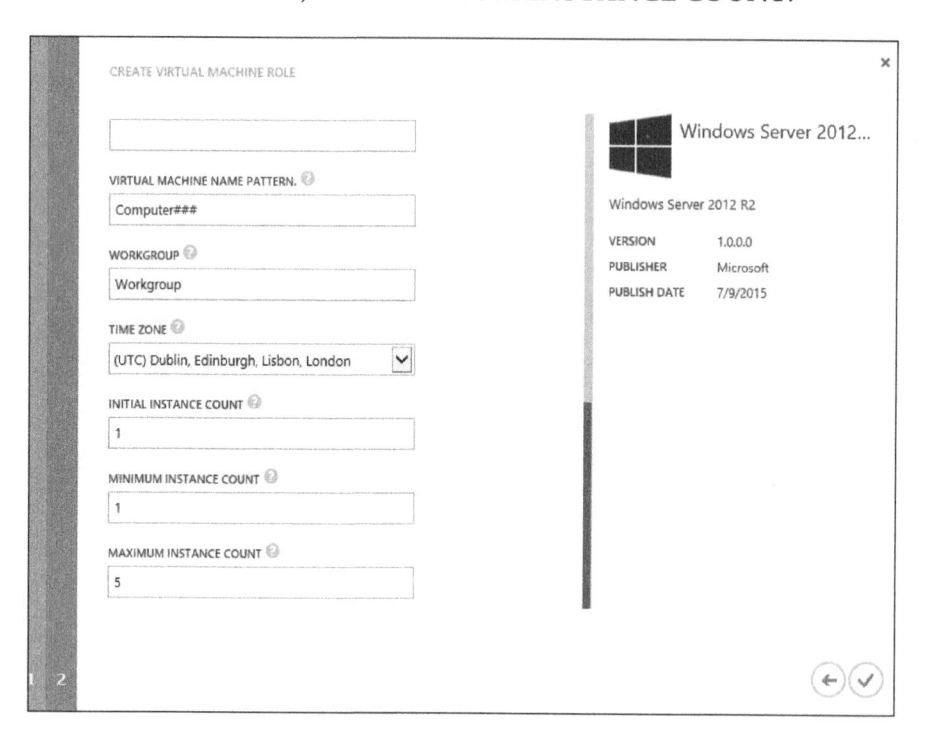

8. **CREATE VIRTUAL MACHINE ROLE** operation will be start. VM Role will be listed under virtual machines workspace in the portal post successful provisioning.

Management operations – virtual machine Role

The tenant's administrators can perform the following management operations using the tenant portal on virtual machine Roles:

- It can view status and resource the usage of virtual machine Role
- It can view the list of virtual machine instances under VM Role
- It can connect to virtual machines using a console or RDP
- It can pause, restart, shutdown, start, stop, and delete virtual machines
- It can view status and resource usage of individual VM instances
- It can scale in and out VM Role
- It can create, view, and restore checkpoints
- It can modify the virtual machine Role configuration (this impacts all MV instanced under VM Role)
- It can attach additional devices to a VM such as network adaptor, disk, and DVD
- It can delete virtual machine Role

VM Role management operations are spread across four pages or categories as follows:

- **VM Role Dashboard**: The **DASHBOARD** page can be used to get a quick glance at VM Role and resources usage as follows:

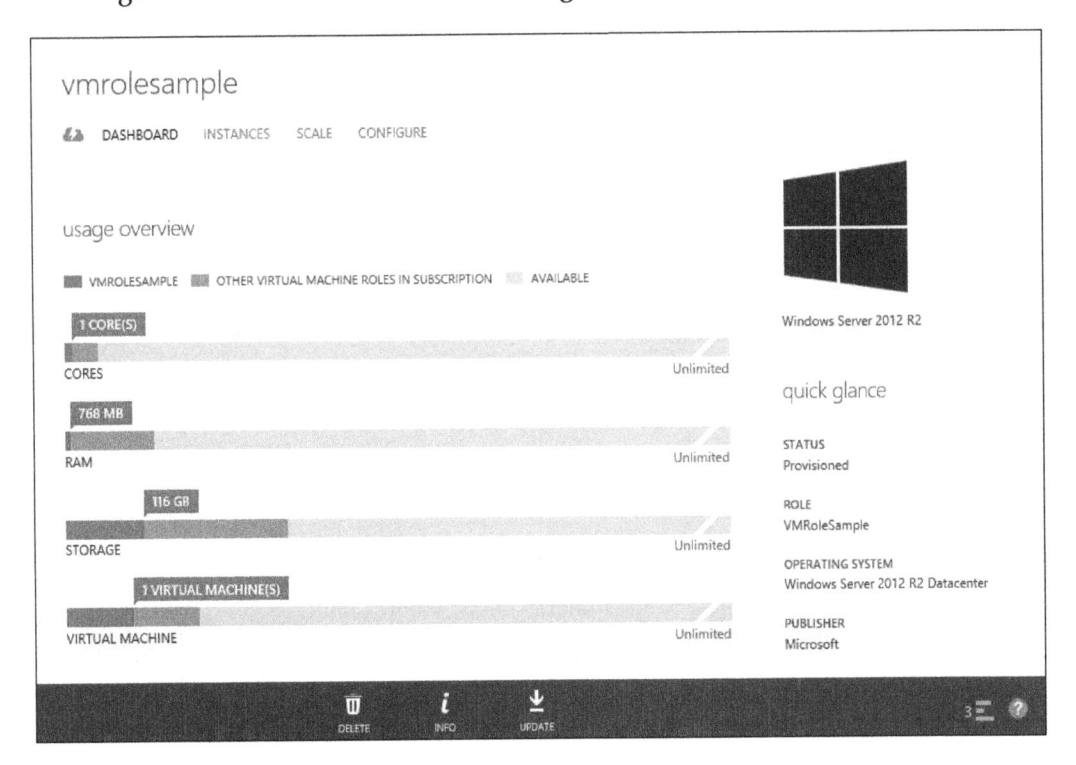

Experiencing the Cloud Services – the Tenant's Point of View

- **Instances**: The **INSTANCES** page gives a list of all VM instances under selected VM Role. Each VM instance can be selected for VM-specific operations in the same standalone VM Role.

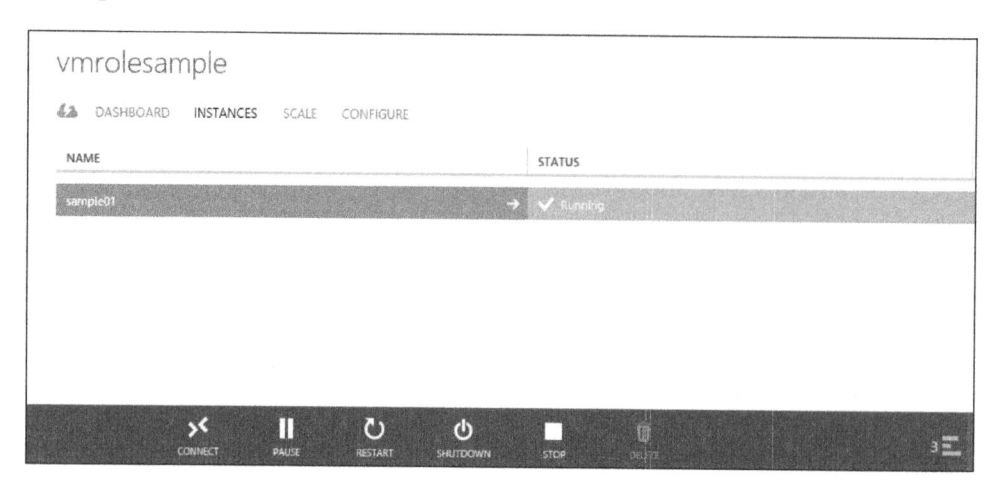

![vmrolesample INSTANCES page showing a VM named sample01 with Running status, and toolbar options: CONNECT, PAUSE, RESTART, SHUTDOWN, STOP, DELETE]

- **Scale**: The **SCALE** page can be used to scale in and out VM Role as per defined settings by the cloud provider or the tenant administrator during the VM Role creation. Scaling out a VM Role will deploy additional VMs using VM Role settings. Scaling in and out can be performed by just moving the slider from left or right.

    Move the scaling slider left or right, and click on save to perform scaling in or out a VM Role.

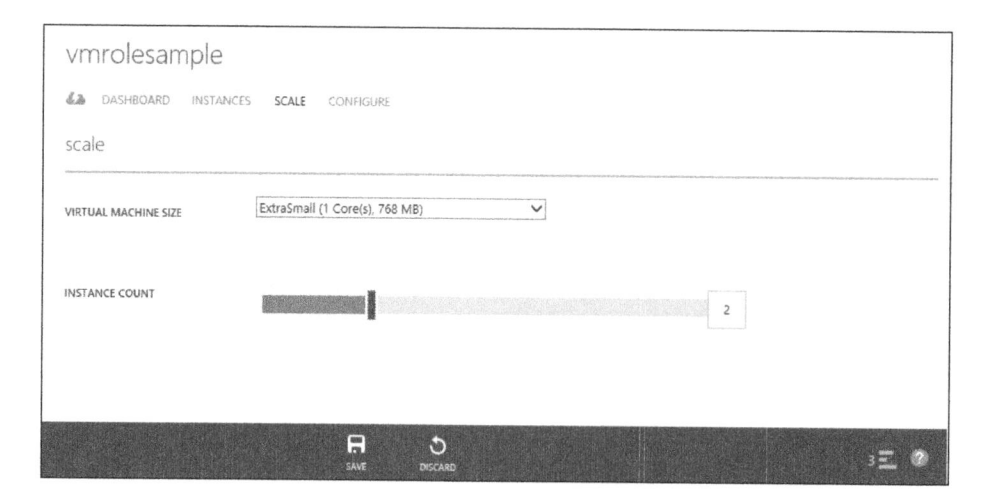

![vmrolesample SCALE page showing VIRTUAL MACHINE SIZE set to ExtraSmall (1 Core(s), 768 MB) and INSTANCE COUNT slider set to 2, with SAVE and DISCARD buttons]

[208]

- **Configure**: The **CONFIGURE** page can be used to modify VM Role settings selected during the VM Role provisioning. Note that only the new VMs that are being deployed in VM Role will be configured with new settings. Any existing VM has to be recreated to have an effect of new settings unless it is manually modified.

Summary

In this chapter, we experienced provisioning and management of IaaS cloud services from a tenant's point of view. We registered a new tenant using WAP's self-service portal and subscribed to a plan created earlier. We created virtual networks, standalone virtual machines, and VM Role. You also learned about management operations on networks and virtual machines such as modifying a network and scaling in and out a VM Role.

In the next chapter, we will move forward to building **PaaS** (**Platform as a Services**) cloud offerings including websites and service bus services.

7
Delivering PaaS – WebSites Cloud and Service Bus

In this chapter, we will be focusing on delivering the **PaaS (Platform as a Service)** cloud offerings of Windows Azure Pack. PaaS enables tenants and organizations to develop, run, and manage their applications on the cloud provider's platform without worrying about the infrastructure layer, such as hardware or the operating system.

In this chapter, we will be talking about two major PaaS offerings available in Windows Azure Pack, which includes WebSites and Service Bus. The WAP WebSite cloud can be used by organizations and cloud providers to deliver website hosting services to internal business lines and tenants. The WAP website cloud supports multiple programming languages, such as ASP.NET, PHP, and Node.js.

WAP websites work in a consistent manner with Azure WebSites. Tenants are responsible for their website's development and management, whereas platform responsibility lies with the cloud service provider.

Though it looks more of like IT developers' stuff, this chapter is for IT professionals only. We will be focusing upon building a reliable platform, which is capable of hosting thousands of high density websites in a multi-tenant fashion. Any website development or programming will work in the same traditional web development service mechanism and won't be a part of the Windows Azure Pack Websites cloud.

Another PaaS offering of WAP is Service Bus, which provides a reliable and scalable messaging service. This can be used by applications to pass messages or information.

In this chapter, we will be covering the following topics:

- Overview and capabilities of the WebSites cloud
- Planning the WebSites cloud platform
- Preparing the installation of Windows Azure Pack WebSites cloud
- Installing and configuring the WebSites cloud
- WebSites cloud – management operations
- WebSites cloud – a tenant's experience
- Windows Azure Pack Service Bus
- Installing and configuring the Service Bus cloud farm

Overview and capabilities of the WebSites cloud

The WebSites cloud in Windows Azure Pack enables organizations and service providers to offer high-density web hosting services to their internal or external tenants. The WAP Websites cloud provides a platform to tenants to develop and run their websites.

WAP websites are designed to provide services at a web scale, hosting thousands of websites with flexibilities and capabilities in terms of scalability, granular control, and metering. The WebSites cloud platform is made up by combining capabilities and features of Windows server, IIS, SQL database, and many third-party and open source technologies.

WAP websites capabilities from the service provider's point of view

Windows Azure Pack websites provide a similar experience to that of Microsoft Azure's website, which is one of the largest website hosting service providers. The Websites service works on a distributed architecture that offers scalability and eliminates any single point of failure. Let's have a look at the capabilities and features that the WAP websites cloud offers for service providers:

- **High density and scalability**: WAP websites are designed to run tens of thousands and more websites in a single farm with flexible scaling decisions. Service providers can start with a small farm and add more resources at a later stage as per requirement without any interruption to the services.

- **Multi tenancy**: WAP websites services are multi tenant in nature and provide isolated services with granular control and self-service to tenants on shared platforms. Reserved, also known as dedicated servers, can also be provided to tenants.

- **Simple and faster deployment and management**: Simplicity is one of the key requirements from IT solutions in today's world. WAP websites are easy, fast, and hassle free to deploy, manage, and scale.

- **Automatic and self service**: WAP websites provide automated platform and websites deployment in a self-service manner for both cloud administrators and tenants.

- **Application and framework support**: WAP websites support a wide range of frameworks and programming languages without any extra administrative burden. This includes both Microsoft and third-party frameworks along with open source technologies. WAP websites support frameworks and technologies, such as ASP.NET, classic ASP, PHP, Node.js, and more with source control using GitHub, Bitbucket, Dropbox, and Team Foundation Server. Along with applications and programming language support, it also provides a Web App Gallery having preconfigured website templates and application templates.

- **Flexible service levels**: By default, Windows Azure Pack Websites provide multiple service levels, such as shared or dedicated servers for tenants. Customers can choose their website scale between shared and reserved mode as per requirements.

- **Granual QOS and metering**: Windows Azure Pack plans for websites provide a granular level of quality of service control. This ensures that tenants get their required resources as per contract even if it's running in shared mode. All these service levels are delivered with a strong metering mechanism for chargeback.

- **Resilient distributed architecture**: WAP websites work in a distributed architecture spread across multiple roles and servers with full resiliency eliminating any single point of failure.

- **Hypervisor agnostic**: Websites cloud services require Windows Server 2012 or 2012 R2 operating to run, which can be hosted on any supported hypervisors or physical servers.

> Although, Windows Server 2012 is supported for hosting WAP websites servers, it is recommended to use Windows Server 2012 R2 with the latest Windows updates.

WAP websites overview and capabilities from a tenant's point of view

Apart from typical cloud computing benefits, WAP websites service offers the following capabilities and benefits for tenants:

- **Simple and faster website provisioning and management**: In a traditional IT delivery mechanism, a website platform deployment is likely to take days to get the web up and running. This platform deployment includes infrastructure level readiness, an operating system, and middleware or web server deployment. With WAP websites, tenants can have the website up and running in just a few clicks. This enables tenants to focus more on web development pieces instead of platforms.

- **Scalability**: Scalability in traditional deployment models is the most challenging aspect. Windows Azure Pack eliminates this by providing easy scale in and out with just a few clicks. Tenants may choose to have more servers during peak hours or days only in a very easy and cost-effective manner.

- **Self service**: Windows Azure Pack websites service operations, such as provisioning and administration, which are available through an easy-to-use, self-service portal, eliminating any possible errors and delay due to human interaction.

- **A wide range of frameworks and programming options**: Tenants are free to choose a development framework as per their necessity and choice. WAP supports multiple application frameworks, such as ASP .NET, PHP, Node.js, and more.

- **Flexible development and deployment tools**: WAP supports a wide range of development and deployment tools including Visual Studio, FTP, WebDeploy, GIT, Bitbucket, Dropbox, Team Foundation Server, and more.

- **The web app gallery**: The web app gallery available in Windows Azure Pack has a wide range of preconfigured website templates and popular web applications from Microsoft, third-party vendors, and open source. Tenants can leverage these to develop websites faster and in an efficient manner.

WAP WebSites – architecture

The WebSites cloud solution consists of multiple roles and runs on multiple servers. All servers are based on Windows Server 2012 R2 (2012 is also supported). The overall solution makes use of Windows server capabilities, such as the dynamic **Windows Process Activation Service**, resource throttling, IIS, and more along with SQL database and website roles. Let's dive deeper into the architectural components of WebSites cloud solution.

WebSites cloud service roles

Windows Azure Pack-based websites cloud service consist of a minimum of six server roles:

- **WebSites controller**: This role deploys and manages other roles. This is the first role to install, and it contains all media, setup, and configurations used for deploying and configuring other roles.

- **WebSites management server**: This role communicates with Windows Azure Pack management portals and APIs. It exposes a **Representational State Transfer (REST)** endpoint that is used by WAP to connect and communicate with Website cloud platforms. All website provisioning operations are performed via this management server.

- **Web worker**: This role hosts and runs tenants' websites. Client requests for websites are processed by web workers only. Web worker servers can work in shared or reserved mode. In shared mode, one web worker role handles website requites for multiple tenants, whereas in the case of reserved, it's dedicated to a single tenant.

- **The front end role**: This role accepts the client's requests, routes to the worker role for processing, and returns the response to the client. One front end server can route requests to multiple web worker roles along with load balancing capabilities. Front end servers are also responsible for SSL termination.

- **File server**: A file server is a Windows-based file server role and is used to store files for hosting website content. Files include application and data content for all the websites hosted in the website's cloud. Websites leverage the File Server Resource Manager feature of Windows file servers for managing files for websites' hosting.

- **Publisher role**: This role publishes content to the website's farm via FTP clients, Visual Studio, and WebMatrix. Publisher role uses FTP and Web Deploy protocols. Tenants use the publish server to upload and publish their website's content.

WAP Websites – database roles

Just as any other Microsoft product, WAP websites cloud leverages the Microsoft SQL Server for its database necessities. The WAP website's database requirements can be alienated in three categories:

- **The website's run time database**: This database hosts the run time database and configuration for the tenant's websites. This must be a Microsoft SQL Server based database.

- **Application database or tenants DB**: This database is used by tenants to host websites' data. This isn't a mandatory requirement and depends upon the tenant's website architecture and requirement. Tenant must subscribe to database services of WAP to use this. This can be a MS SQL or MySQL based database as per web application support.

- **Service management API database**: This database is used by the WAP service management API to store configuration data. It is the same database that we used while configuring Windows Azure Pack installation in *Chapter 3, Installing and Configuring Windows Azure Pack*. This must be a Microsoft SQL Server-based database.

Planning the WebSites cloud platform

In this topic, we will discuss about planning factors and best practices for the website's cloud platform in terms of capacity, resiliency, and more.

Planning for resiliency

Windows Azure Pack Websites cloud solution can be protected against failures by adding redundant servers at each role or layer. Adding additional server for redundancy is quite an easy and simple process.

Following are the resiliency recommendations for each role:

- **WebSites roles**: This role can be protected against failure by deploying additional servers for redundancy:
    - **Controller servers**: A maximum of two controller servers can be provisioned in a WAP website's deployment. This provides high availability at the controller layer.
    - **Management and publisher**: For the management and publisher role, it is recommended to have a minimum of two servers hosting this to provide resiliency. Additional servers can also be added as per scalability requirements.

- **Front end**: Two front end servers can be deployed for providing high availability; however, more than two front end deployments are also supported for capacity and load balancing. Load balancers should be configured for client access requests load balancing to front end servers.
- **Web worker role**: It is recommended to have a minimum of four web worker roles—two for shared hosting and two for reserved. Additional worker roles can be deployed as per scalability requirements.

- **File servers**: It is recommended to use a preconfigured Windows-based File Server Cluster for the WAP websites cloud usage for production environments. Note that the Sale-out File Server cluster isn't supported for the website's cloud usage as it requires the File Server Resource Manager to function.
- **SQL servers**: For production environments, it is recommended to use a database server that is configured with SQL level cluster technologies such as SQL server cluster or SQL Server Always On.

It is also recommended to host the website's cloud role in virtual machines to take advantage of high-level, hypervisor availability techniques.

Planning for capacity

Windows Azure Pack websites cloud solution can be easily scaled in and out as per capability requirements. The following guidelines provide basic design consideration while planning for capacity:

- **WebSites Roles**:
    - **Controller servers**: A controller server does not require much compute, network, or storage resources since it is used only for provisioning other roles. Standard sizing includes two virtual CPUs and four or eight Gig RAM with decent storage space to host OS. The controller should suffice these requirements.
    - **Management**: This role handles communication between WAP and WebSites cloud. This server doesn't require much resources unless multiple simultaneous provisioning operations are initiated.

- **Front end**: The front end server routes all the website's access requests to worker rules. For a better load sharing, it is recommended to deploy multiple front end servers. As per Microsoft guidelines, one core can handle 100 requests per second. Compute power for the front end can be sized using this value, considering peak hours as one additional factor.
- **Publisher server**: Publisher server usually experiences high compute utilization only when multiple publishing operations are initiated by tenants.
- **Web worker role**: This role is the most resource-intensive role in WebSites cloud since all websites are hosted on these servers. It is recommended to deploy multiple servers for a web worker role. Memory for web worker roles needs to be planned as per the number of active websites at a single point of time. As per Microsoft recommendations, average memory footprint in a production environment for one website is 70 MB. It's a good idea to plan memory considering the number of regular active websites along with peak hours or day values.
- **File server**: A file server hosts all the content and applications of websites running in farm and is disk IO intensive. It is recommended to use disks with a higher number of IOPS for file servers.
- **SQL Server**: As per Microsoft's guidelines, SQL memory should be sized as four GB per 30,000 provisioned websites. It is recommended to take extra memory, and the SQL performance is mostly dependent on the available memory. Four GB of disk space per 10 K websites is required.

Domain versus workgroup for WebSites server roles

Windows Azure Pack websites roles can be deployed in both domain and workgroup environments. It is recommended to use domain-joined servers in production deployments to take advantage of AD capabilities, such as secure authentication with Kerberos and simple user management along with better control with Group policies. Work group servers can be used for test and development environments.

Preparing the installation of Windows Azure Pack WebSites cloud

Before starting the installation and configuration of WAP websites cloud, there are multiple prerequisites that need to be fulfilled. Let's have a look at them.

Preparing Windows servers

All servers designated to host websites cloud components must be running Windows Server 2012 or 2012 R2 operating system. It is recommended to patch the server with latest updates. It is advised to use a clean installation of the operating system.

Enable Windows Remote Management on all servers. Create inbound an access firewall rule for the following services for publisher and front end servers:

- File and printer sharing (SMB-In)
- Windows Management Instrumentation (WMI-In)

On all the server's user account control must be disabled for remote operations. This can be performed by adding the following registry key. Server must be restarted post adding the following registry key:

```
reg add HKLM\SOFTWARE\Microsoft\Windows\CurrentVersion\Policies\system /v LocalAccountTokenFilterPolicy /t REG_DWORD /d 1 /f
```

> Adding the previous registry key does not affect the local UAC configuration.

Preparing DNS records

Windows Azure Pack websites requires DNS records to do the following:

- **Access websites**: By Default, each website hosted in Windows Azure Pack websites contains a DNS suffix configured by the service provider. This DNS suffix needs to point to front end servers for the website's name resolution. For example, FQDN for a website named 'abc' in a website cloud having a DNS suffice 'xyz.com' would be 'abc.xyz.com'. The service provider needs to plan and decide the DNS suffix and create necessary zones in internal or public DNS server.

- **Develop/Publish**: This record is used by tenants to upload and publish the website's content. Two 'CNAME' records are required for this, and they point to the publisher server.

Overall, the following DNS records need to be created in DNS Server for websites cloud to function:

Name	IP Address	Usage
*	Front End Server(s)	For accessing websites
*.scm	Front End Server(s)	For Content publishing via Git
ftp	Publisher Server(s)	For publishing content via Web Deploy or FTP
publisher	Publisher Server(s)	For publishing content via Web Deploy or FTP

Preparing a SQL server for the WebSites cloud database

The following database configuration needs must be met while using the SQL Server for the WebSite's cloud:

- The SQL version must be SQL Server 2012 SP1 or later. The Express edition can be used for evaluation; the full edition is required for production. The database server must be reachable from all nodes.
- The necessary clustering technologies must be configured as per the design such as SQL Cluster or Always On.
- Mixed mode authentication must be enabled.
- If using the names instance, the SQL browser service needs to be started manually along with opening the 1434 port.

Preparing SSL certificates

By default, Windows Azure Pack Websites generate and install self-signed certificates for websites cloud. It is not recommended to use self-signed certificates in a production environment. You can use internal CA to issues the following certificates for an internal private cloud. For service providers, it is recommend to get the SSL issued by the public trusted CA.

The following two SSL certificates are required in a WAP solution:

- **Default Domain certificate**: These are used while accessing websites and source control. Since this certificate is used by all tenants' websites, it needs to be a wildcard and must be in the .pfx format. This certificate is placed at the front end servers. The following subject names need to be configured as per the service provider's naming convention:
    - `*.dnssuffix.com`
    - `*.scm.dnssuffix.com`

- **Publishing certificate**: Publishing SSL certificates is used to provide secure communication to developers for uploading or publishing the website's content via FTP or Web Deploy. This certificate needs to be placed at the publishing server and should contain the following SAN names as per the service provider's naming convention:
    - `Publish.dnssuffix.com`
    - `ftp.dnssuffix.com`

> Wild certificates used for default domain certificates can also be used for publishing since it contains the same parent domain name.

Preparing file servers

Windows Azure Pack websites support both the standalone and preconfigured File Server Cluster or NAS device. It is recommended to use a File Server Cluster or a NAS device in a production deployment to achieve high availability and better performance. The following steps are required to configure a File Server Cluster for WAP websites:

1. Configure the File Server Cluster or the NAS device.
2. Create user accounts and groups (for file share owners and users).
3. Enable **WinRM (Windows Remote Management)** and **FSRM (File Server Resource Manager)**.
4. Provision Content Shares and Certificate Store Shares using standard file server operations.
5. Add the `FileShareOwners` group to the local Administrators group of the file server to enable WinRM.
6. Configure the access control to share as per the provisioned user account and group.

Installing and configuring the WebSite cloud

Microsoft Web Platform Installer is used to download and install websites cloud components. See *Chapter 3, Installing and Configuring Windows Azure Pack* to know more on the Web Platform Installer.

Before starting installation, verify that all the design decisions and planning is made and prerequisites are completed.

First, the controller server is installed, and later, it is used to install and configure other roles. The installation of the controller server also installs one management console for Windows Azure Pack websites, which can be used to install and configure other server roles in conjunction with the WAP service management portal.

Installing and configuring controller and management servers

The following steps outline the installation and configuration process for the controller and management servers:

1. Log into the server designated for the WebSites controller.
2. Run the Microsoft Web PI.
3. Search for Windows Azure Pack WebSites.
4. Select **Windows Azure Pack: WebSiteVersion2 Update 7** (the latest version available at the time of writing this book).

> Installing controller servers includes downloading all media required for deploying and configuring other roles.

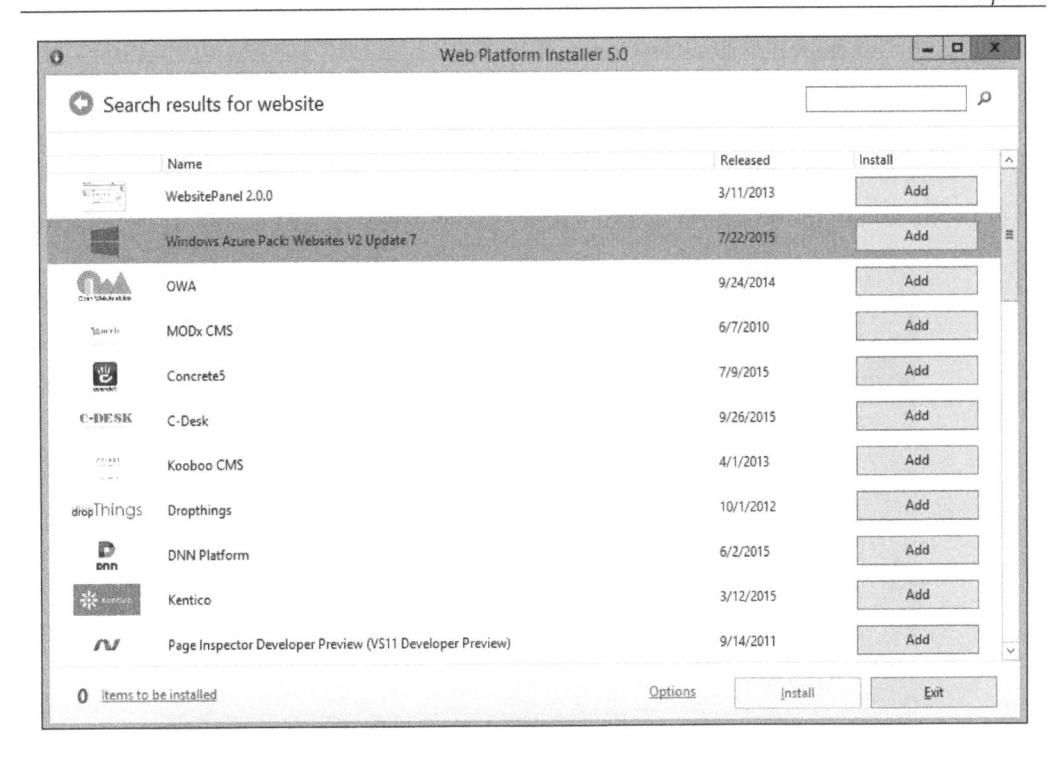

5. Click on **Install** to proceed.
6. The WebSites installer will be downloaded, installed, and launched automatically.

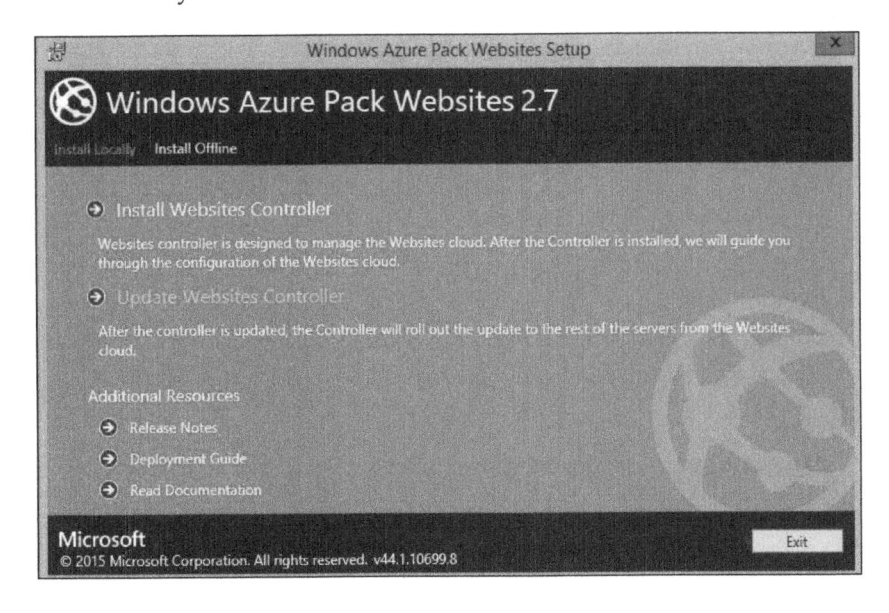

Delivering PaaS – WebSites Cloud and Service Bus

7. Click on **Install Websites Controller**.
8. Accept the agreement and proceed further.
9. Verify all the Microsoft and third-party components to be installed. You can choose to install locally or download them for installation on another server.
10. The installation will proceed; wait for the download and installation to finish.

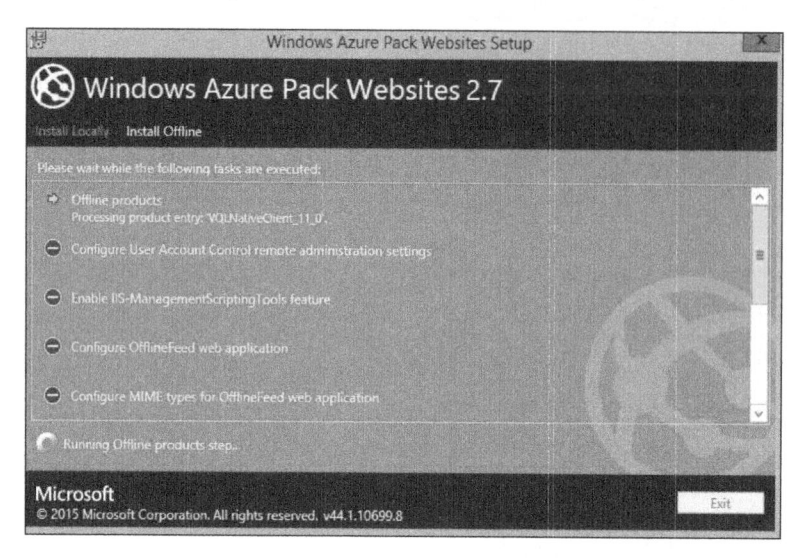

11. Click on **Configure** to start configuring the controller deployment.

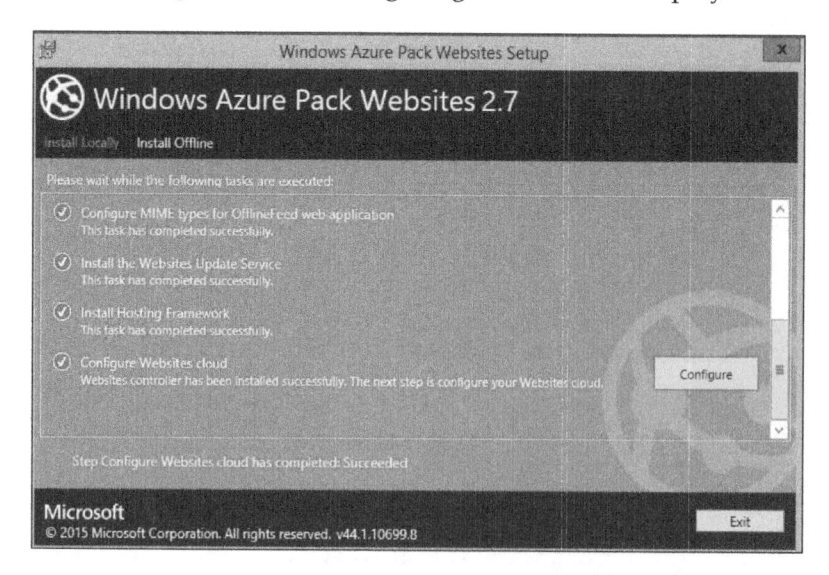

12. Clicking on **Configure** will launch the Windows Azure Pack WebSites Management console. All the other website's roles can be installed and configured using this wizard or the WAP management portal.

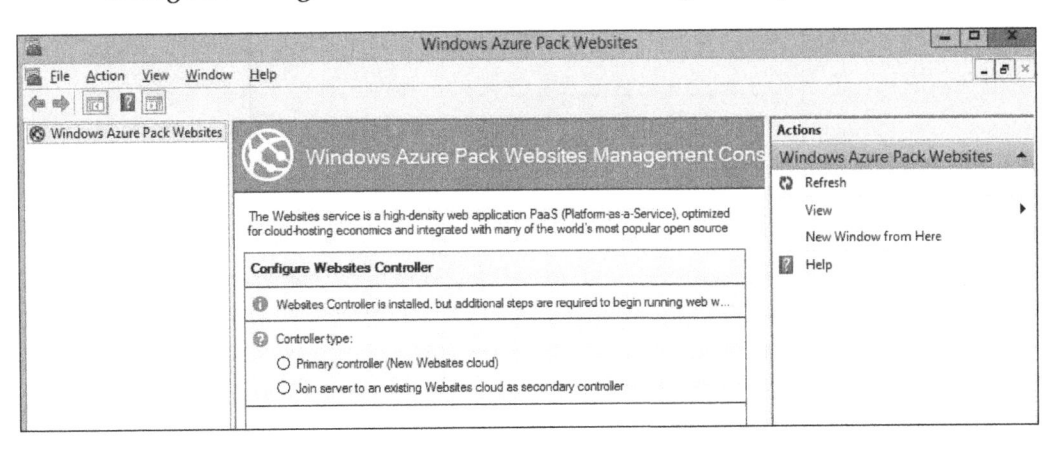

13. Select **Controller type**; since we are deploying the first controller server, it will be the primary controller in our case.

14. Select **File server type**. Selecting the file server will display additional options including hosting database configuration and other system setting, such as DNS suffix, credentials, and more.

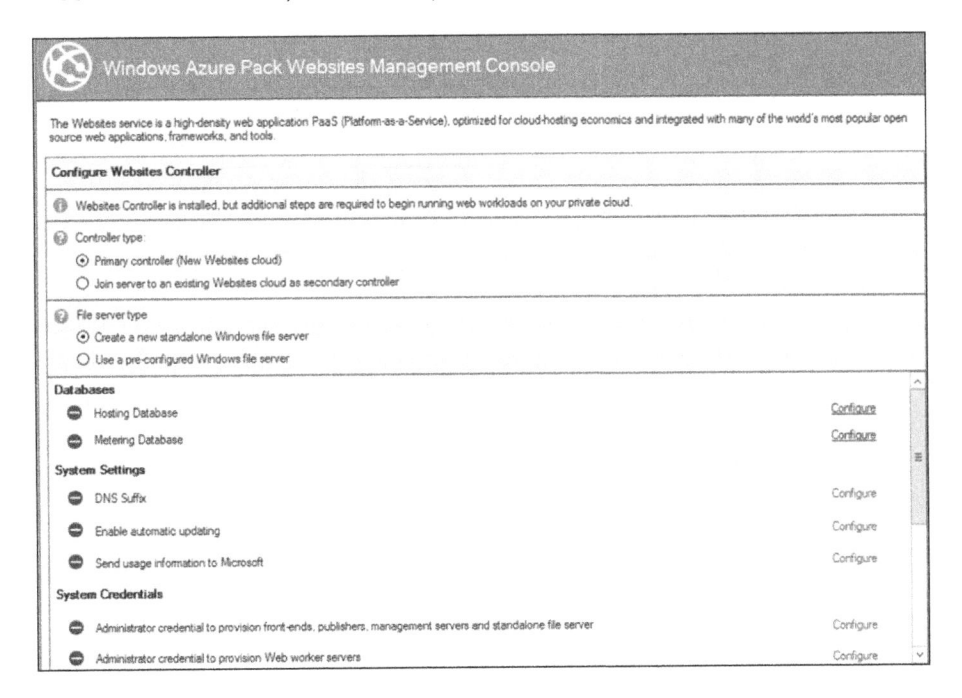

15. Enter the database configuration for both hosting and metering databases.

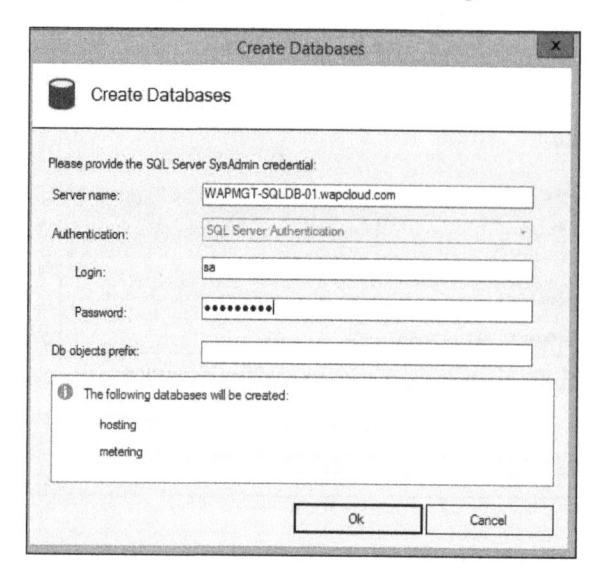

16. Provide the DNS suffix and automatic updates for websites, and send the usage information to Microsoft settings.

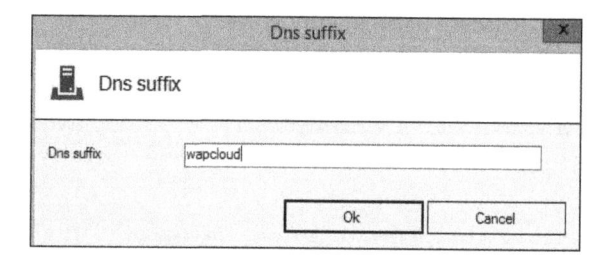

17. Provide system credentials for the following:
    - Administrator credentials for provisioning the website's cloud roles including front end, publisher, file server, and management servers
    - Administrator credentials for provisioning the web worker role
    - File share owner credentials
    - File share user credentials
    - Service endpoint credentials (used by WAP)

      These user accounts must be a member of the local administrator group on the target servers

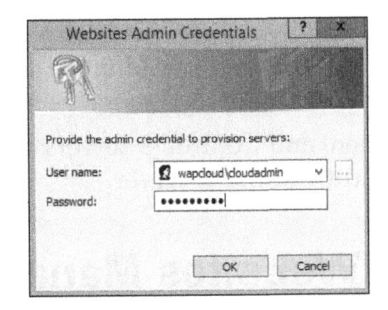

18. Enter the standalone or preconfigured file server details.
19. At last, enter server details to configure the management role.

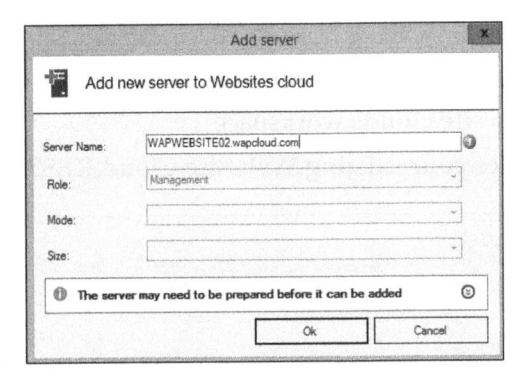

20. The Website cloud farm is now configured. The controller service status will be displayed in the **Windows Azure Pack Websites Management Console**.

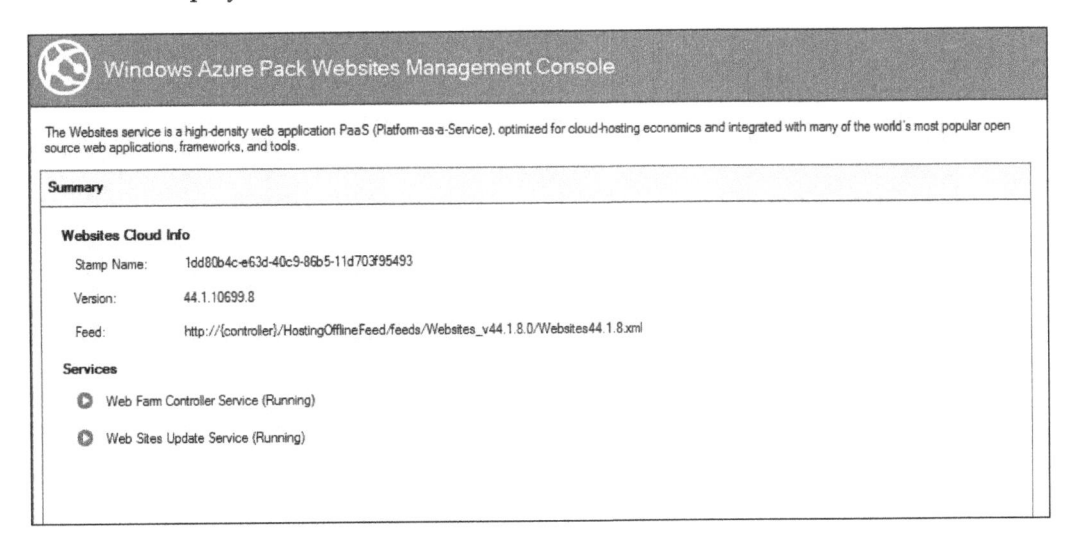

21. **Windows Azure Websites Management Console** can now be used to modify any existing configuration or deploy additional servers. Verify the server's status in the server's console. Review error logs in case of any issue.
22. Additional Management and Controller servers can be deployed in a similar fashion by selecting add additional server.

Registering the Websites Management Server with Windows Azure Pack

Windows Azure Pack uses the REST endpoint of WebSites Management Server to register the website's cloud resource providers and operations. Perform the following steps to register a websites cloud with Windows Azure Pack:

1. Log into the Windows Azure Pack Management portal for administrators.
2. Browse the **web site clouds** workspace.
3. Click on **Register your existing Web Site Cloud REST Endpoint.**

4. Provide cloud connection details including display name, management server address, and credentials (the service endpoint credentials).

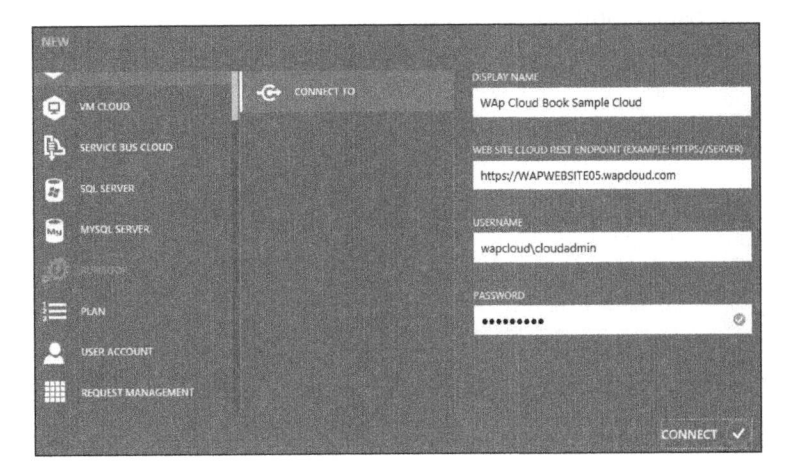

5. The registered website cloud will now be visible under the **web site clouds** workspace in the WAP portal.

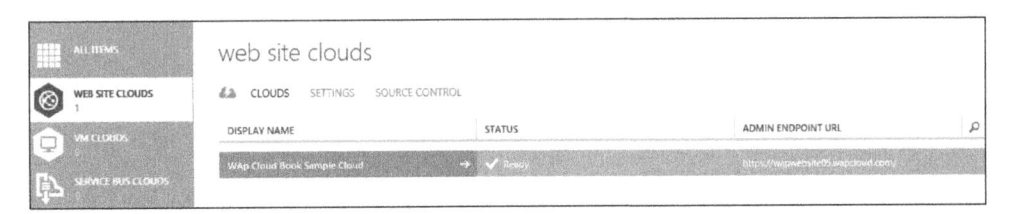

6. The Windows Azure Pack portal can now be used to provision other roles and management tasks.

Installing and configuring frontend, web worker and publisher roles

The remaining websites cloud roles including front end, web worker, and publisher can be installed and configured using the Windows Azure Pack Service Management portal or WebSites Management Console installed on the controller server. For the purpose of demonstration in this book, we will be using the WAP Service Management portal. The following steps outline the process of deploying the remaining website's cloud components:

1. Log into the Windows Azure Pack Management portal for administrators.
2. Browse the **WEBSITES** workspace.

Delivering PaaS – WebSites Cloud and Service Bus

3. Open the newly registered website cloud endpoint.
4. Open the **ROLES** workspace; this will list all the website roles configured in the website cloud farm currently.

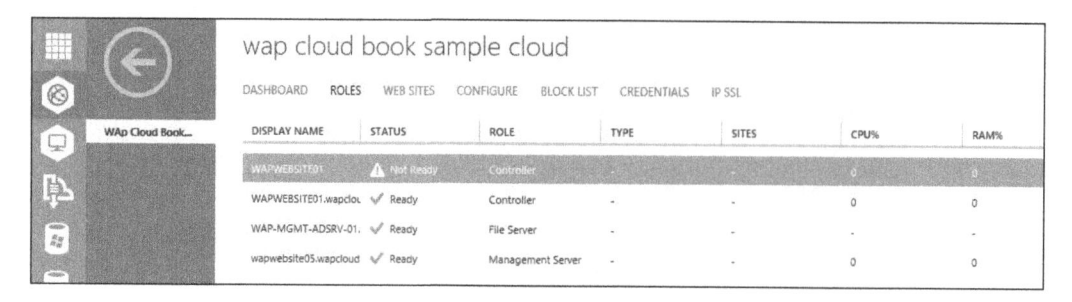

DISPLAY NAME	STATUS	ROLE	TYPE	SITES	CPU%	RAM%
WAPWEBSITE01	Not Ready	Controller	-	-	0	0
WAPWEBSITE01.wapclou	Ready	Controller	-	-	0	0
WAP-MGMT-ADSRV-01.	Ready	File Server	-	-	-	-
wapwebsite05.wapcloud	Ready	Management Server	-	-	0	0

5. Click on **Add role** to provision the website's roles.

ADD SERVER

Add Cloud Server

Which cloud server role would you like to install?

→ ADD NEW WEB WORKER
→ ADD NEW FRONTEND
→ ADD NEW PUBLISHER

6. Select **ADD NEW WEB WORKER** to add a new worker role.
7. Provide a worker role server name and configuration including the work type. **WORKER TYPE** includes the following:
    - **Shared**
    - **Reserved - Small**
    - **Reserved - Medium**
    - **Reserved- Large**

ADD WEB WORKER
Setup a new Web Worker

The web worker is responsible for running all the web sites in the cloud. Each additional worker increases the number of web sites that can be run simultaneously in the cloud. It also increases the elasticity potential for each web site.

ENTER THE HOSTNAME OR IP ADDRESS OF YOUR MACHINE

WAPWEBSITE04.wapcloud.com

WORKER TYPE

- Shared
- Reserved - Small
- Reserved - Medium
- Reserved - Large

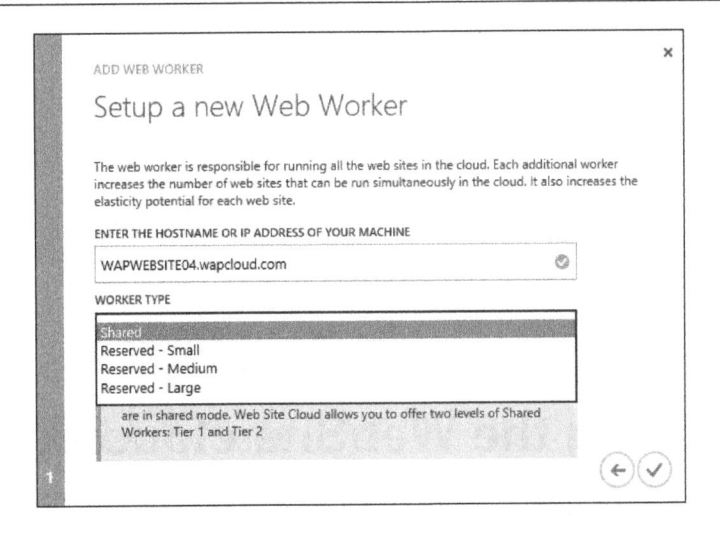

...are in shared mode. Web Site Cloud allows you to offer two levels of Shared Workers: Tier 1 and Tier 2

8. The worker role installation will now start. The WAP portal displays the status of the installation.

9. Add a new front end by just providing the hostname or IP for the server designated to host the front end role.

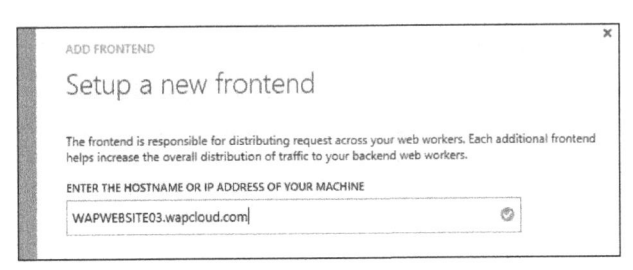

ADD FRONTEND
Setup a new frontend

The frontend is responsible for distributing request across your web workers. Each additional frontend helps increase the overall distribution of traffic to your backend web workers.

ENTER THE HOSTNAME OR IP ADDRESS OF YOUR MACHINE

WAPWEBSITE03.wapcloud.com

10. Add a new Publisher server by just providing the hostname or IP for the server designated to host the front end role.

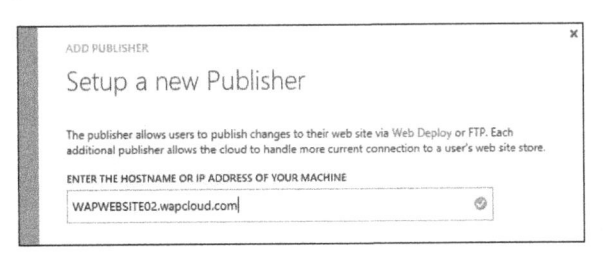

ADD PUBLISHER
Setup a new Publisher

The publisher allows users to publish changes to their web site via Web Deploy or FTP. Each additional publisher allows the cloud to handle more current connection to a user's web site store.

ENTER THE HOSTNAME OR IP ADDRESS OF YOUR MACHINE

WAPWEBSITE02.wapcloud.com

11. Additional servers can be configured for achieving high availability and capabilities in a similar manner.

12. Post installation, all the server roles available can be listed in the **ROLES** tab under the **website clouds** workspace.

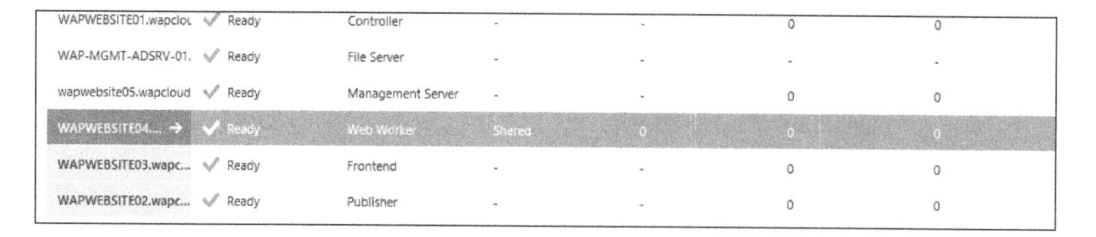

WAPWEBSITE01.wapclou	✓ Ready	Controller	-	-	0	0
WAP-MGMT-ADSRV-01.	✓ Ready	File Server	-	-	-	-
wapwebsite05.wapcloud	✓ Ready	Management Server	-	-	0	0
WAPWEBSITE04... →	✓ Ready	Web Worker	Shared	0	0	0
WAPWEBSITE03.wapc...	✓ Ready	Frontend	-	-	0	0
WAPWEBSITE02.wapc...	✓ Ready	Publisher	-	-	0	0

Customizing the WebSite cloud source control and the web gallery feed settings

The source control and the WebApp gallery feed settings are global to the WAP site cloud. All websites and websites cloud farms can take advantage of source control mechanisms configured at the WAP level. The same goes for the Web App gallery feed as well.

Configuring source control

Windows Azure Pack supports multiple repositories for the source control of websites. These can be utilized for tenants to affect the content management and publishing of their websites.

This setting is configured on the WebSite cloud globally.

Service providers need to register on a respective source control website first to allow tenants to use these. The following source control repositories are supported:

- Bitbucket
- GitHub
- CodePlex
- Dropbox

To configure source control settings, we need to follow these steps:

1. Log into the Windows Azure Pack Management portal for administrators.
2. Browse the **web sites clouds** workspace.
3. Click on **SOURCE CONTROL**.

4. Enter the source control website's specific settings such as client ID, credentials, and more.

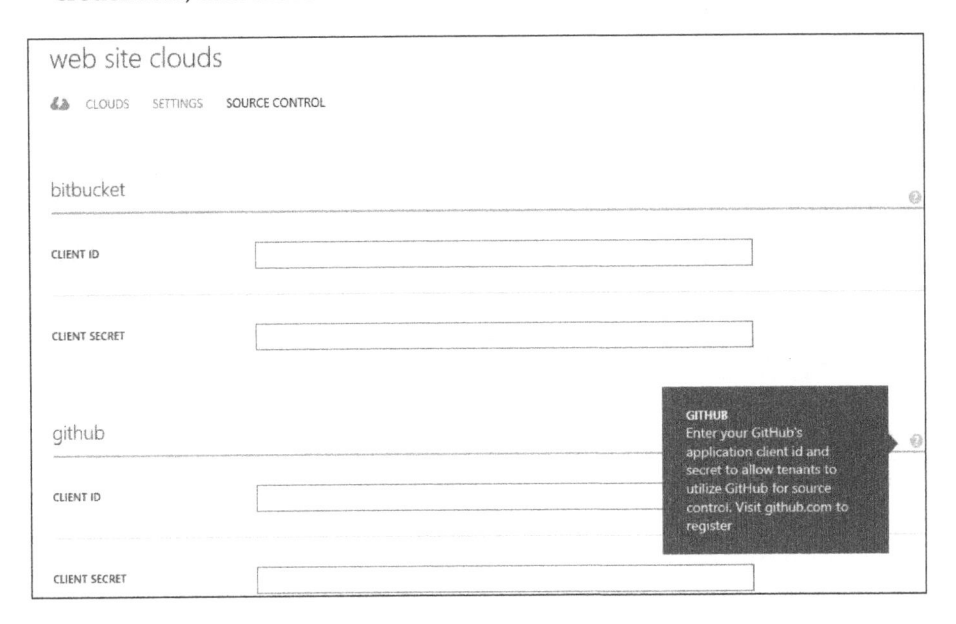

Web Gallery feed settings

Windows Azure Pack fully integrates with the Web App Gallery, which contains many preconfigured website templates and web applications. This enables customers to deploy top web applications faster and in an efficient manner. By default, Windows Azure Pack websites cloud is configured to the Microsoft standard Web App Gallery. Cloud providers can also choose to create custom the Web App Gallery. The following steps are required to change the Web App Gallery URL for a WAP deployment:

1. Log into the Windows Azure Pack Management portal for administrators.
2. Browse the **websites cloud** workspace.
3. Click on **SETTINGS**.

4. By default, the Microsoft Web App Gallery URL is configured; any custom gallery feed URL can be configured using this setting.

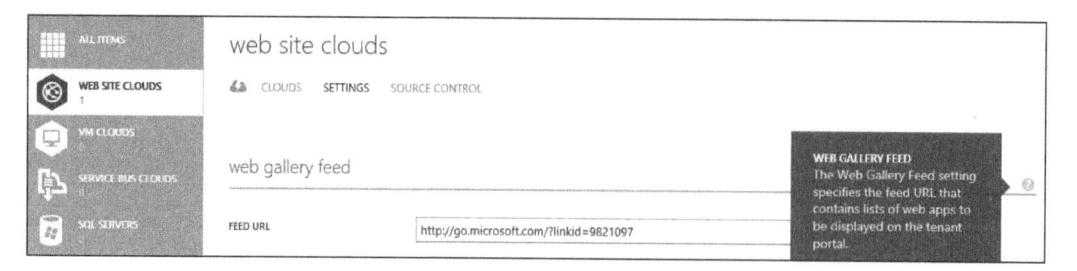

WebSites cloud – management operations

The Windows Azure Pack management portal offers a self-service experience not only for tenant users but also for cloud administrators. The WAP management portal can be used to perform monitoring and management operations on a websites cloud farm such as the following:

- Monitoring the utilization and availability status of the cloud farm and the tenants' websites
- Provisioning, monitoring, and starting or stopping websites roles
- Customizing WebSites settings such as SSL and DNS records
- Configuring and managing block lists, IP SSL, and platform credentials

The utilization dashboard

The **DASHBOARD** page of the WebSites cloud provides graphs for the CPU and memory utilization of a complete website cloud farm. Along with utilization, event logs for website cloud can also be viewed using the **DASHBOARD** page.

Roles – configuration and management

The **ROLES** page enables administrators to perform the following operations:

- Provision and remove any websites server roles
- Reboot, repair, and make any server role offline
- View the list of server roles along with their status

The following steps outline the process to access the roles page:

1. Log into the Windows Azure Pack Management portal for administrators.
2. Browse the **website clouds** workspace.
3. Select the websites cloud to manage and access the **ROLES** tab.

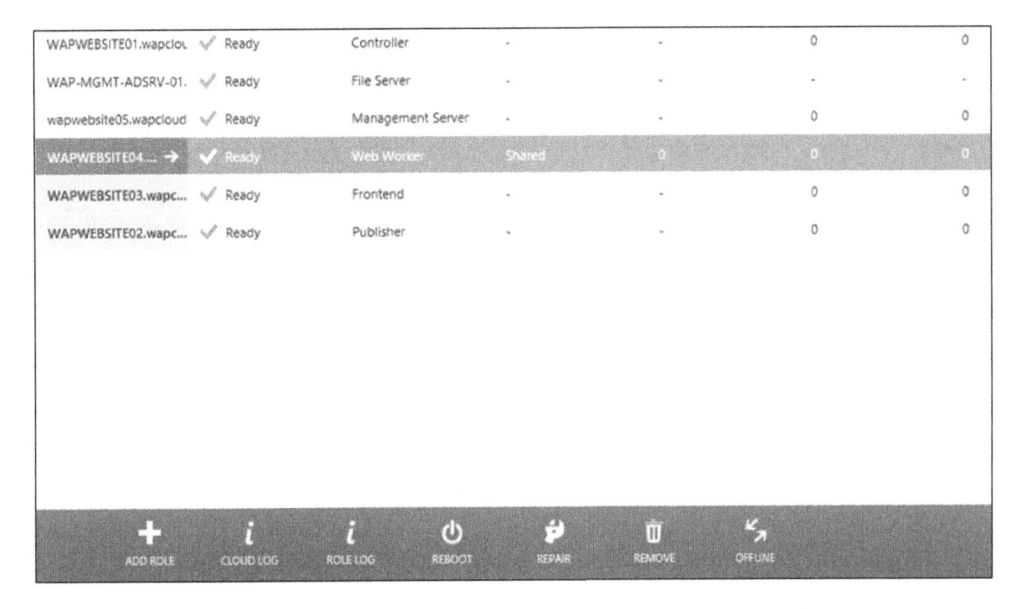

WebSites – monitoring and operations

The websites page enables the following operations to be performed on the websites created by tenants:

- Viewing and monitoring all websites created by tenants
- Performing tenant operations on websites such as modifying the .NET framework version on behalf of tenants

The following steps outline the process to access the **ROLES** page:

1. Log into the Windows Azure Pack Management portal for administrators.
2. Browse the **websites cloud** workspace.

3. Select the website's cloud to manage and access the **WEB SITES** tab.

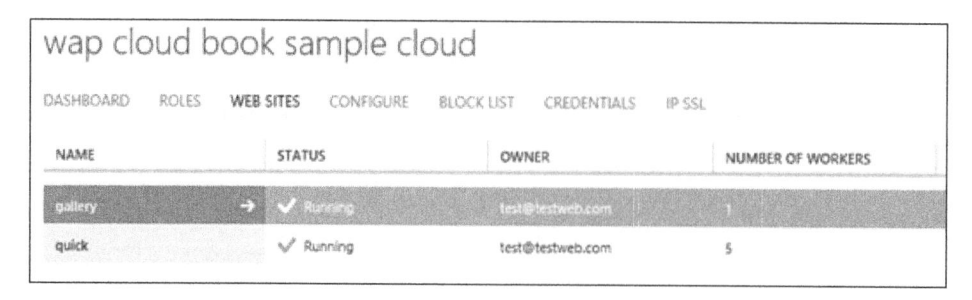

Configuring WebSites cloud settings

This page can be used to modify website cloud setting such as SSL certificate and DNS names.

The following settings can be customized using this page:

- Upload a new WebSites default certificate. By default, all WAP websites are configured with the self-signed SSL, which is a potential security issue. Using this option, cloud providers can upload the publicly trusted CA issued SSL for the website's usage. Normally, it would be the wildcard certificate consisting of the DNS suffix for websites as domain name.
- It can enable, disable, or force websites Windows authentication.
- It can allow or disallow **CUSTOM APPLICATION POOL IDENTITY**.

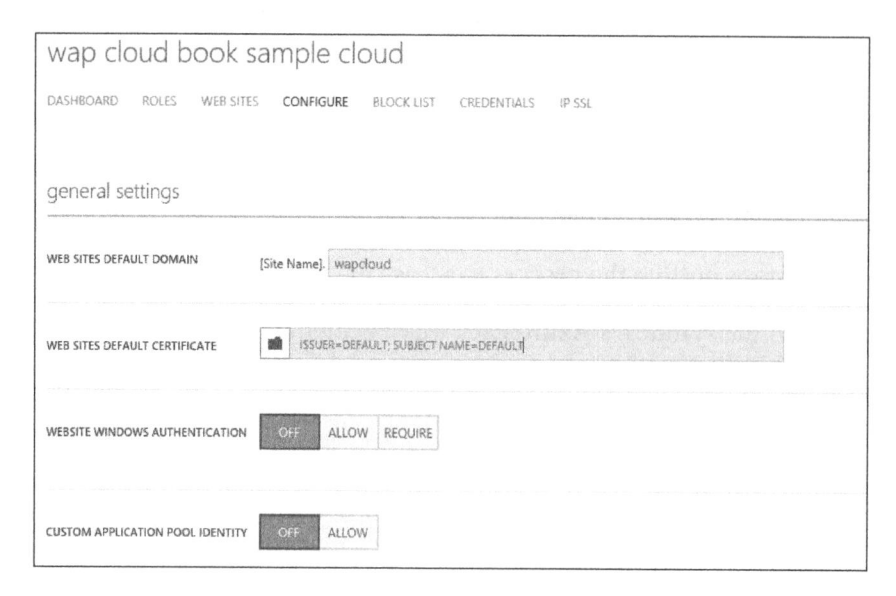

Chapter 7

- Configuring **publishing settings** includes the following:
    - Web Deploy DNS Record
    - FTP Deploy DNS Records
    - Publishing a certificate

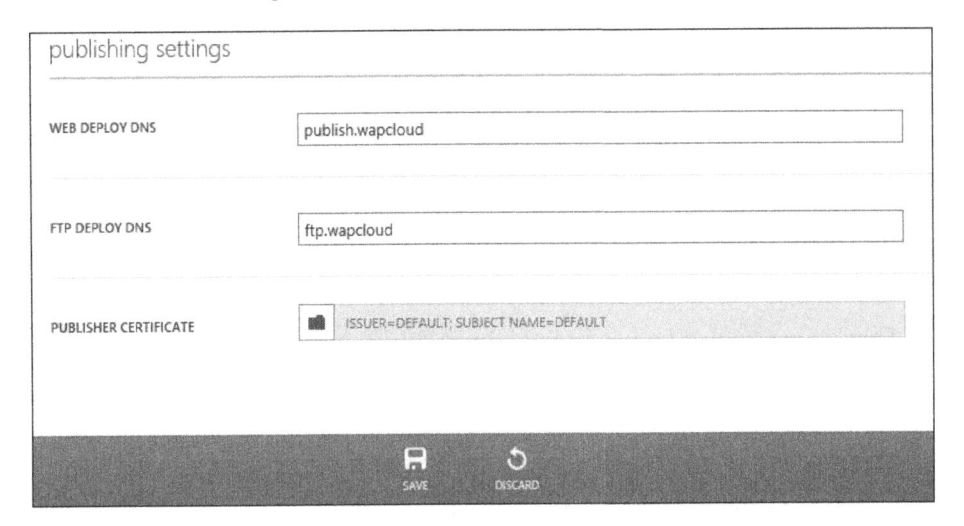

The block list – IP filtering

Windows Azure Pack provides a strong IP filtering mechanism, which can be used to prevent and a **DOS (Denial of Service)** attack. A block list can be used to block a selected IP or a range of IP addresses to access websites. This can be automated to prevent any attack in conjunction with a firewall device.

The following steps outline the process to block any given IP range to access websites:

1. Browse the **BLOCK LIST** tab.

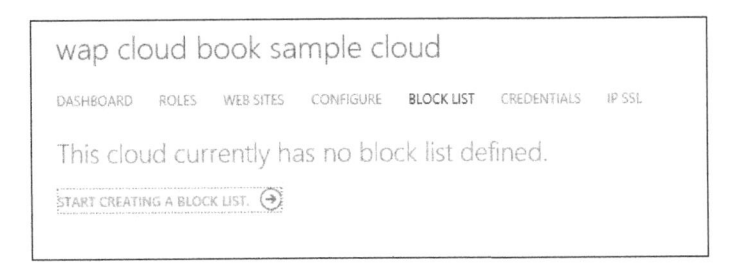

2. Click on **START CREATING A BLOCK LIST**.
3. Enter the required IP range to block:

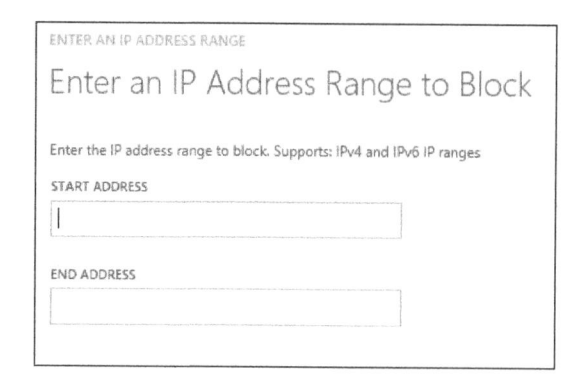

ENTER AN IP ADDRESS RANGE

Enter an IP Address Range to Block

Enter the IP address range to block. Supports: IPv4 and IPv6 IP ranges

START ADDRESS

END ADDRESS

4. This page can also be used to create an additional block list, delete any existing block list and upload a CSV file for blocking access.

Websites cloud platform credentials

The **CREDENTIALS** tab displays all credentials configured for authentication and authorization between websites cloud components. These credentials are defined while deploying the first website controller role. Any of these can be easily edited by selecting the credential's name and hitting **edit** at the bottom pane. Browse the **CREDENTIALS** tab under website cloud settings to modify any credential.

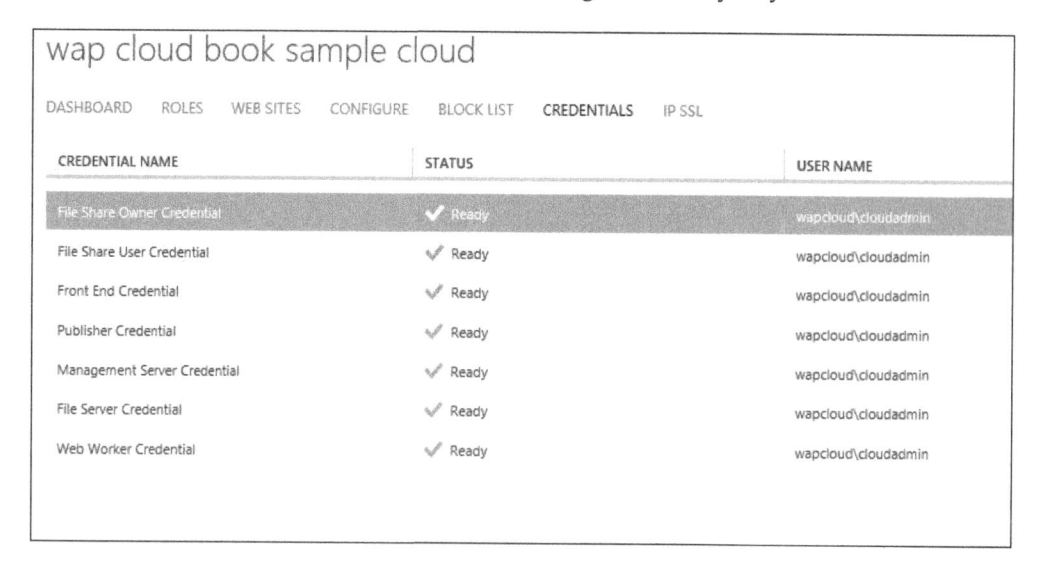

wap cloud book sample cloud

DASHBOARD   ROLES   WEB SITES   CONFIGURE   BLOCK LIST   CREDENTIALS   IP SSL

CREDENTIAL NAME	STATUS	USER NAME
File Share Owner Credential	Ready	wapcloud\cloudadmin
File Share User Credential	Ready	wapcloud\cloudadmin
Front End Credential	Ready	wapcloud\cloudadmin
Publisher Credential	Ready	wapcloud\cloudadmin
Management Server Credential	Ready	wapcloud\cloudadmin
File Server Credential	Ready	wapcloud\cloudadmin
Web Worker Credential	Ready	wapcloud\cloudadmin

Websites IP SSL

Tenants' websites can be configured to use the IP-based SSL certificate, providing more secure mechanisms of the website's access. In this case, a service provider must configure all website-specific IP addresses on all front end servers.

The IP SSL page under websites cloud settings can be used to configure the VIP and local address between VIP. VIP settings and their port mapping must also be configured on load balancer devices for the IP SSL to function.

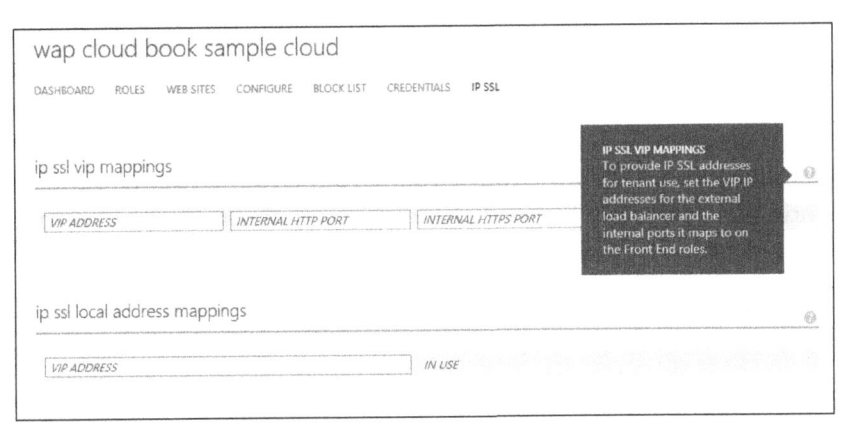

Authoring WebSite cloud plans

Windows Azure Pack plans for websites allows administrators to offer websites cloud services to tenants with granular control on services and resources, such as CPU or memory. Multiple plans can be created from a single cloud farm with different limits and capabilities. See *Chapter 5, Assigning Cloud Services – Plans, Add-Ons, Tenant Accounts, and Subscriptions* to know more about Windows Azure Pack plans.

Websites cloud plans overview and service models

WAP plans for websites are configured to provide three service models:

- Intro
- Basic
- Reserved

For each plan, 17 quota settings can be configured, which include QOS such as subscription CPU time, maximum memory working set, and more.

- **The Intro mode**: This is also known as the free mode. It provides a shared platform for hosting a tenant's websites. This is an entry level offering and should be used for test and development purposes. A tenant website in the Intro mode can be upgraded to basic and reserved as per requirement. This mode does not include any scaling capabilities.
- **The Basic mode**: This mode also works in a shared model, but it provides better performance than free mode websites. This provides a low-cost websites hosting for tenants' websites with production-ready features, such as easy scaling, custom DNS names, and more.
- **The Reserved mode**: In the Reserved mode, a tenant's websites can be provisioned to run on dedicated resources such as CPU core, memory, or bandwidth. This mode provides the highest performance in comparison to the other two models.

Service providers can create multiple plans as per available platform capabilities and business strategies. Basically, plans can be configured in two manners:

- **Standard plans**: These are publicly available plans for standard websites requirements
- **Customized plans**: These are dedicated for a particular tenant as per customized requirements and contracts

Creating a plan for WebSites cloud offerings

The following steps outline the steps to create and configure a WAP plan for offering WebSites cloud services to tenants:

1. Log into the management portal.
2. Browse the **plans** workspace.
3. Click on **Let's Create a Hosting Plan**.
4. Enter a friendly name for the plan.

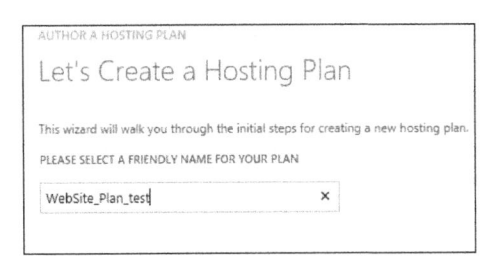

5. Select the **WEB SITES CLOUD** on **PLAN SERVICES** page.

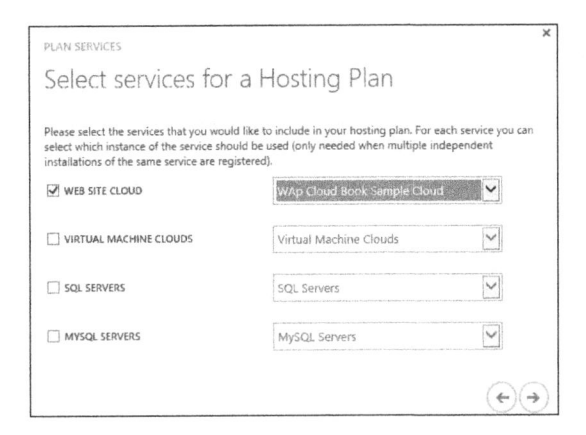

6. Select Add-Ons if applicable.
7. Click on the newly created plan to start the configuration.

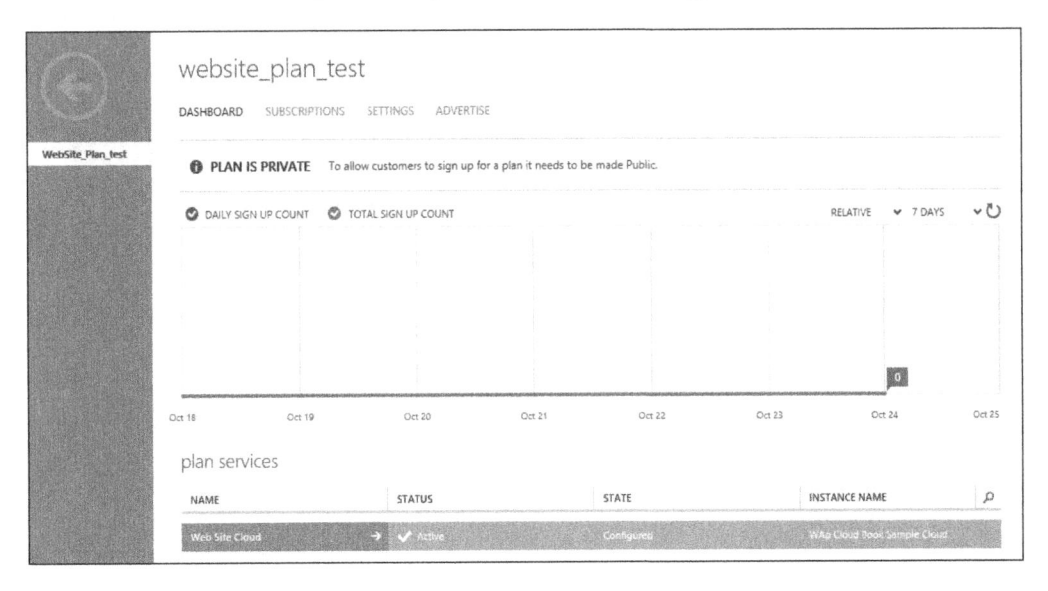

8. Click on the plan name under the **PLAN SERVICES** workspace to start customizing.

9. Configure additional QOS and capabilities settings as per requirements and business strategies.

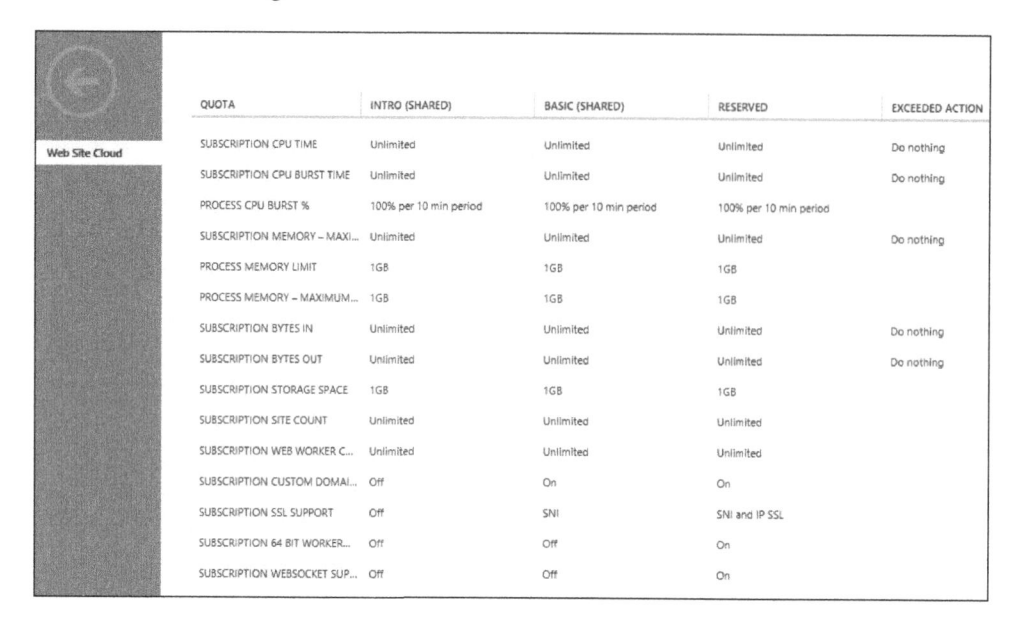

	QUOTA	INTRO (SHARED)	BASIC (SHARED)	RESERVED	EXCEEDED ACTION
Web Site Cloud	SUBSCRIPTION CPU TIME	Unlimited	Unlimited	Unlimited	Do nothing
	SUBSCRIPTION CPU BURST TIME	Unlimited	Unlimited	Unlimited	Do nothing
	PROCESS CPU BURST %	100% per 10 min period	100% per 10 min period	100% per 10 min period	
	SUBSCRIPTION MEMORY – MAXI...	Unlimited	Unlimited	Unlimited	Do nothing
	PROCESS MEMORY LIMIT	1GB	1GB	1GB	
	PROCESS MEMORY – MAXIMUM...	1GB	1GB	1GB	
	SUBSCRIPTION BYTES IN	Unlimited	Unlimited	Unlimited	Do nothing
	SUBSCRIPTION BYTES OUT	Unlimited	Unlimited	Unlimited	Do nothing
	SUBSCRIPTION STORAGE SPACE	1GB	1GB	1GB	
	SUBSCRIPTION SITE COUNT	Unlimited	Unlimited	Unlimited	
	SUBSCRIPTION WEB WORKER C...	Unlimited	Unlimited	Unlimited	
	SUBSCRIPTION CUSTOM DOMAI...	Off	On	On	
	SUBSCRIPTION SSL SUPPORT	Off	SNI	SNI and IP SSL	
	SUBSCRIPTION 64 BIT WORKER...	Off	Off	On	
	SUBSCRIPTION WEBSOCKET SUP...	Off	Off	On	

10. Save the changes and configure the additional plan setting such as invite code, advertisement, changing access to public, and more. See *Chapter 5, Assigning Cloud Services – Plans, Add-Ons, Tenant Accounts, and Subscriptions*, to know more on performing these operations on WAP plans.

WebSites cloud – a tenant's experience

Using the tenant portal, tenants can provision and manage their websites on the Windows Azure pack Websites cloud in a self-service and automated manner. In this topic, we will walk through the tenant's experience for WAP websites provisioning and management operations.

Creating Websites – Quick Create and the Web App Gallery

The following steps outline the process followed by tenants to provision websites:

1. Log into the Windows Azure Pack tenant portal.
2. Subscribe to the websites plans using the configured invite code.
3. The **WEB SITES** workspace will not be visible in the management portal.

4. Click on **CREATE A WEB SITE** to start; select **QUICK CREATE** or **FROM GALLERY** as per choices and requirements. Note that the preconfigured DNS suffix by cloud provider is already added to the URL.

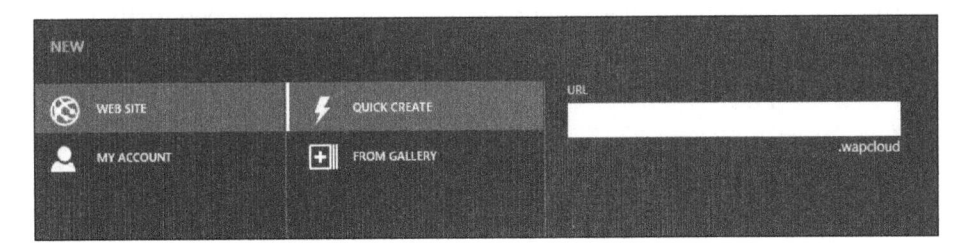

5. Websites will be created in a moment and will be available for access and further development.

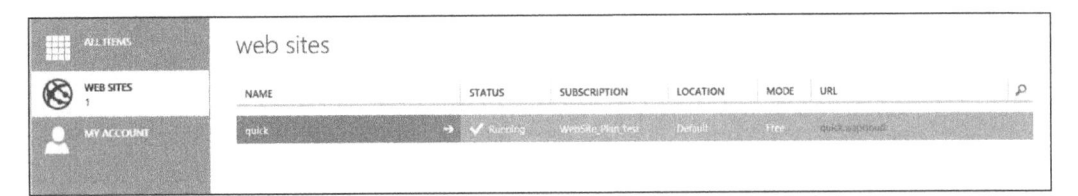

6. Clicking on **FROM GALLERY** will display the Web App Gallery to choose preconfigured website templates and other web applications.

7. Tenants can choose gallery items of their choice and proceed further.
8. Enter gallery item-specific values including URL; then, click on the check mark to deploy a website.

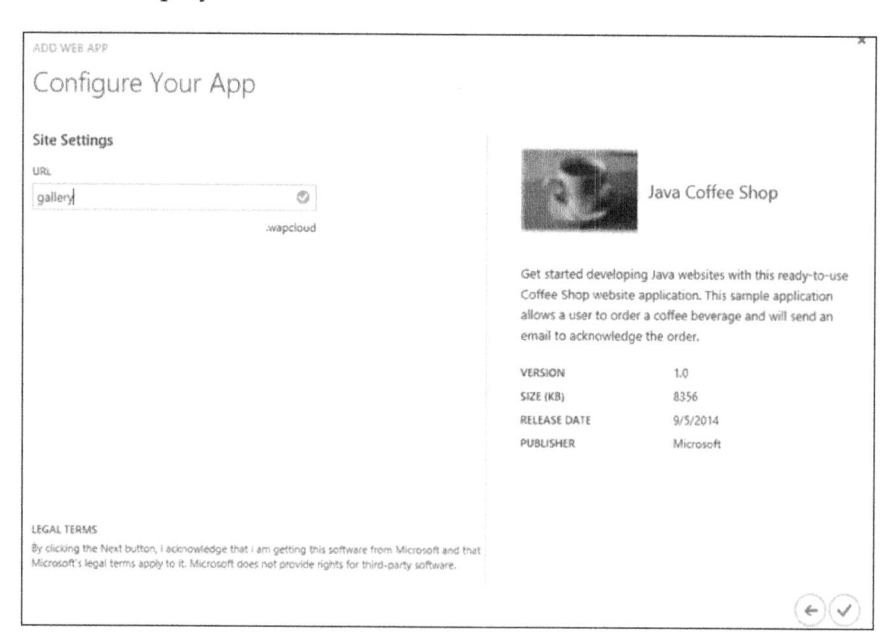

9. Now, let's try to open one of the newly created websites called `quick.wapcloud`.

Tenants can now publish content to the newly created website using traditional publishing tools, such as FTP and WebDeploy, or they can also do so using source control mechanisms such as Git.

Management operations – tenants' websites

Windows Azure pack provides self-service portal capabilities to tenants for performing, monitoring, and administrating on their websites. Let's have a look at the management and monitoring operations available for tenants.

Using the **WEB SITES** workspace on the tenant's portal, tenants can do the following:

- Browse the website
- Stop the website
- Restart the website
- Delete the website

Lets have a look at other management and administration operations available for tenants:

- The **quick settings**: Using a quick setting button under a website, tenants can learn and perform the following configurations:
    - Getting tools such as WebMatrix

Delivering PaaS – WebSites Cloud and Service Bus

- ○ Publishing the application
- ○ Setting up the deployment from the source control

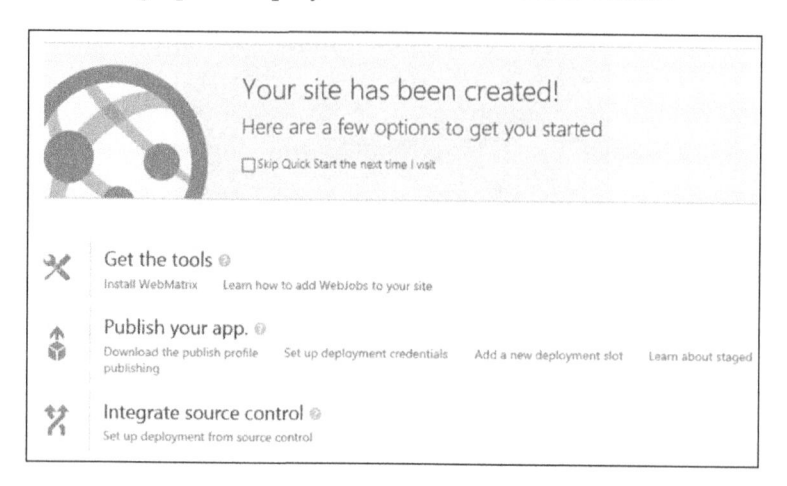

- **DASHBOARD**: This displays the websites statics data, such as CPU, memory utilization, data utilization, and additional settings, such as VIP. Adding new deployment slots can be performed on this page.. This page can also be used to manage linked resources such as database or storage.
- **MONITOR**: This displays the website usage statics. Additional statics counters can be also added, such as the count of HTTP errors or success.

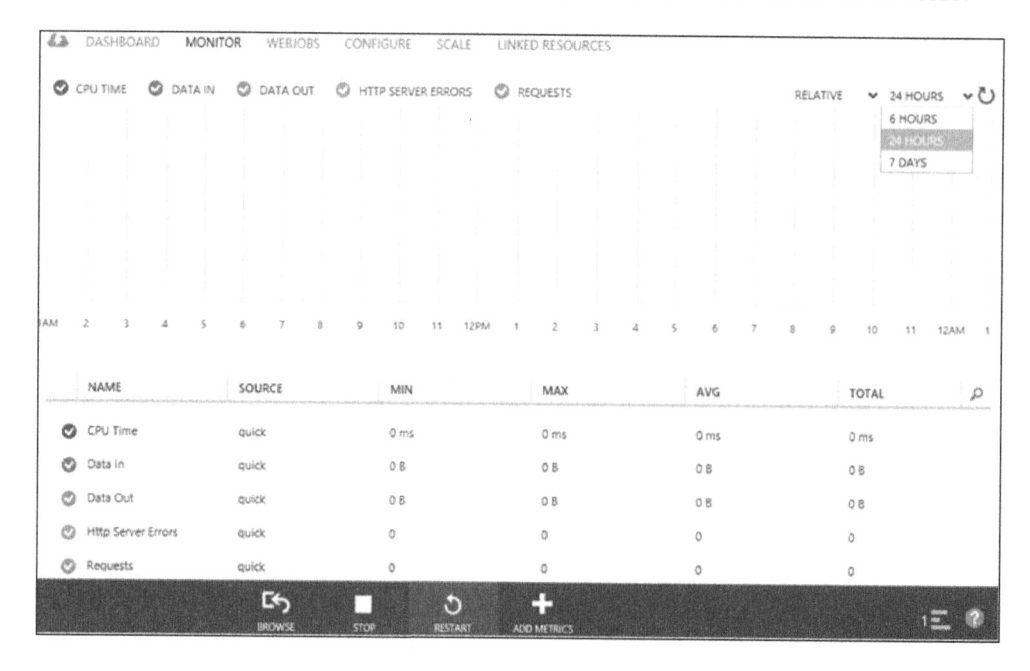

- **WEBJOBS**: This enables tenants to run continuously or on-demand scripts for any web application deployed in the WAP websites cloud.

    WAP supports the following types of files to be uploaded in webjobs:

    - cmd, .bat, .exe (Windows)
    - .ps1 (Windows PowerShell)
    - .sh (Bash)
    - .php (PHP: Hypertext Preprocessor)
    - .py (Python)
    - .js (JavaScript)

The following steps outline the process to configure and manage WebJobs:

1. Browse the **WEBJOBS** tab under the website's settings in the tenant portal.
2. Click on **ADD A JOB** to add a new WebJob.
3. Enter the **NAME** WebJob, upload the script file, and configure the execution type (continuously or on demand).

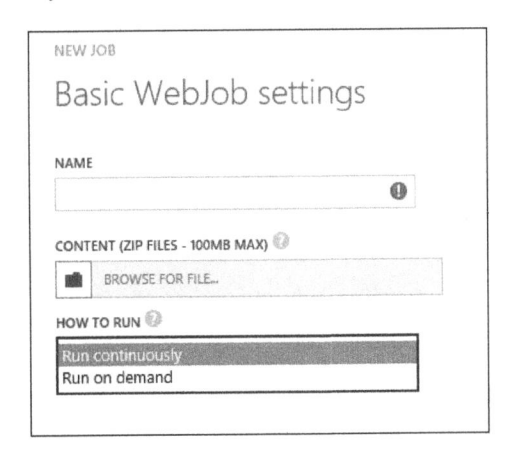

NEW JOB

Basic WebJob settings

NAME

CONTENT (ZIP FILES - 100MB MAX)

BROWSE FOR FILE...

HOW TO RUN

Run continuously
Run on demand

The **CONFIGURE** tab allows tenants to choose platforms and versions for their websites. Configuration of these items are directly dependent on the web application platform and architecture and may vary from deployment to deployment. This includes settings as follows:

- The .NET framework version
- The PHP version
- The managed pipeline mode (classic or integrated)
- Windows authentication

- Custom identity pool
- Web sockets
- SSL certificates
- Domain names
- SSL bindings
- Application diagnostics
- Site diagnostics
- Additional app settings such as virtual directories

The **SCALE** tab under the website's setting allows tenants to perform the following operations:

- Upgrade the website mode between three service models (intro, basic, and reserved)
- Scale in and out of a number of instances

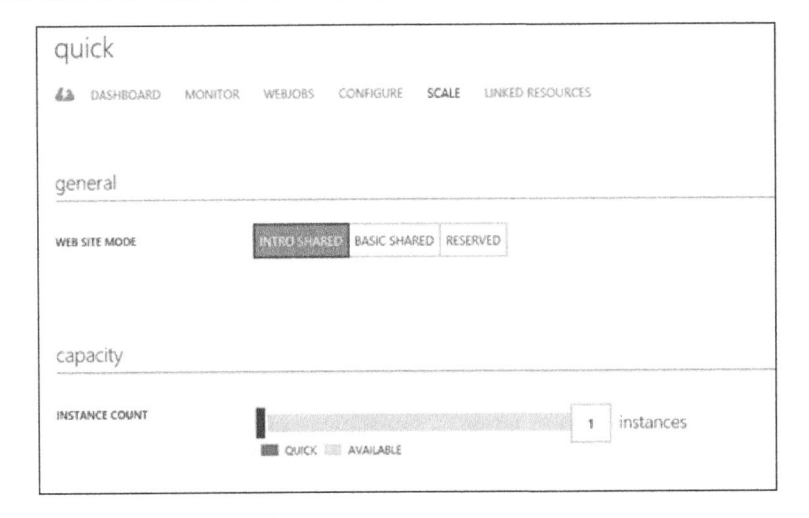

Websites and web applications deployed by tenants may need additional resources such as database or storage. The **LINKED RESOURCES** tabs allows tenants to link these resources with websites.

Windows Azure Pack Service Bus

Windows Azure Pack Service Bus provides a reliable messaging service, which can be used by a tenant's applications to pass information or messages. This service is consistent to Microsoft's public cloud offering Azure Service Bus. Applications can be hosted anywhere; that is, they can be hosted on the provider's cloud, inside the tenant's datacenter, or anywhere else.

Windows Azure Pack Service Bus can be leveraged by the organization's internal developers for passing messages between applications in an efficient manner. This can be offered as a service by service providers to external tenants enabling cloud-driven applications' messaging.

Service Bus in Windows Azure Pack provides two solutions:

- Service Bus queues
- Service Bus topics

Understanding Service Bus queues

Service Bus queues offer load leveling by adding a Service Bus namespace in between both applications, which allows message receivers to receive messages as per their own pace and resource availabilities. This enables efficient and reliable message transfer between loosely coupled applications.

There can be additional receivers as well that can receive messages from the same Service Bus name space. The following diagram explains the working mechanism of Service Bus queues.

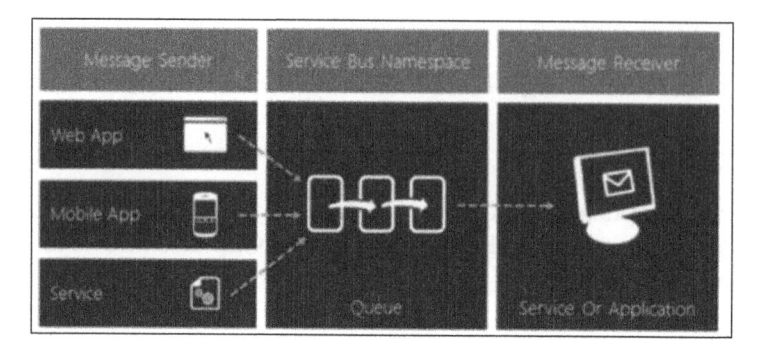

Understanding Service Bus topics

Service Bus topics provide publishing and subscribing capabilities that can be utilized by multiple subscribers and receivers to receive messages independently to each other simultaneously. Subscribers can also be configured to receive only filtered messages.

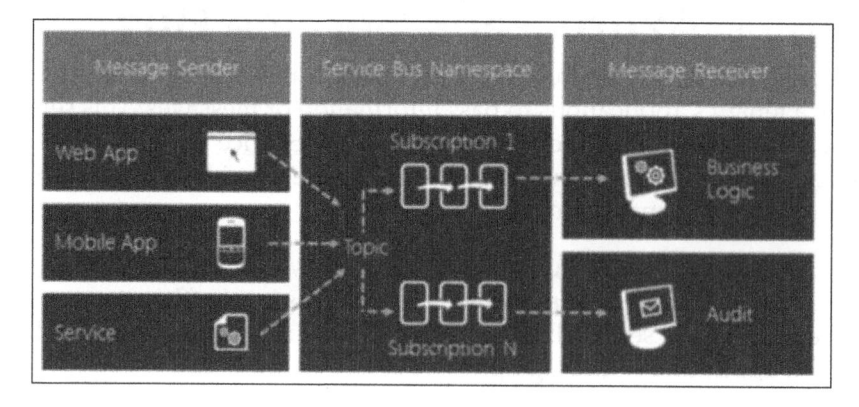

In topics, instead of using a direct communication model, a separate model of communication, *Publish and subscribe,* is used. In this model, communication is established via an intermediate, which is a topic. Service Bus topics provides additional capabilities such as one to many communication while comparing with queues. Topics allow tenants to perform large-scale message transportation, which comprises of a large number of users, applications, and devices.

The Service Bus architecture

The Windows Azure Pack Service Bus architecture contains the following components:

- Windows Server 2012 or 2012 R2 operating system
- SQL Server database
- Windows Azure Pack Service Bus 1.1
- Microsoft Windows Fabric

It is recommended to deploy multiple Service Bus servers with a SQL database in a highly available mode to eliminate any single point of failure. This architecture works in a farm model; multiple servers can be deployed under a single farm providing resiliency and load balancing

Installing and configuring the Service Bus cloud farm

The following steps are required to perform the installation and configuration of a Service Bus farm:

1. Log into the server designated for installing Service Bus.
2. Download and run Microsoft Web PI.

Delivering PaaS – WebSites Cloud and Service Bus

3. Search for Service Bus and select **Windows Azure Pack Service Bus 1.1** to install it.

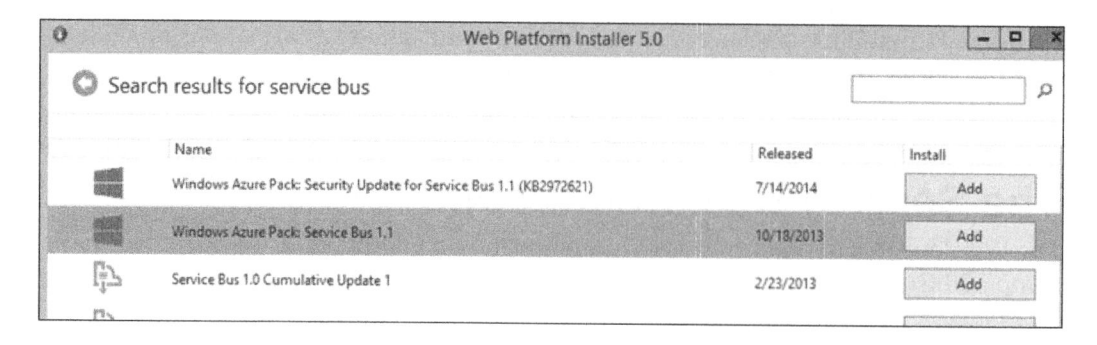

	Name	Released	Install
	Windows Azure Pack: Security Update for Service Bus 1.1 (KB2972621)	7/14/2014	Add
	Windows Azure Pack: Service Bus 1.1	10/18/2013	Add
	Service Bus 1.0 Cumulative Update 1	2/23/2013	Add

4. Install Service Bus components by the following Web PI instructions. Exit post the successful installation.

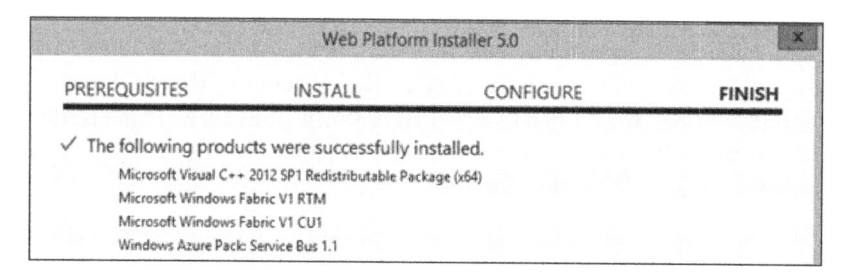

PREREQUISITES   INSTALL   CONFIGURE   **FINISH**

✓ The following products were successfully installed.
   Microsoft Visual C++ 2012 SP1 Redistributable Package (x64)
   Microsoft Windows Fabric V1 RTM
   Microsoft Windows Fabric V1 CU1
   Windows Azure Pack: Service Bus 1.1

5. Launch the Service Bus configuration app via the start menu.
6. Click on **Create a New Farm** with default or custom settings as per requirements. Choosing default settings is suitable for most of the deployment models.

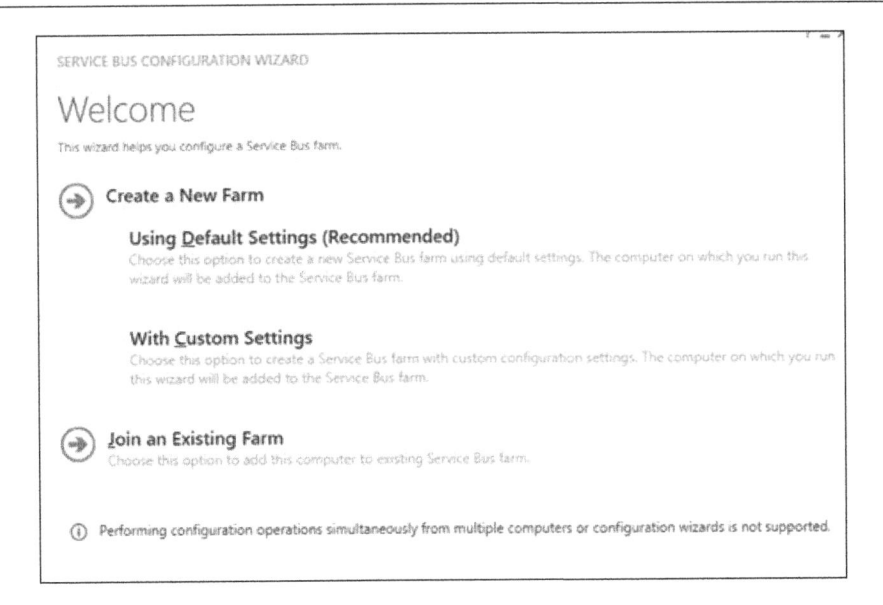

7. Enter the database server name and credentials; click on **Test Connection** to test the connectivity.

Delivering PaaS – WebSites Cloud and Service Bus

8. Enter service account details, certification, and generation key (this is used to add new servers to the existing Service Bus farm).

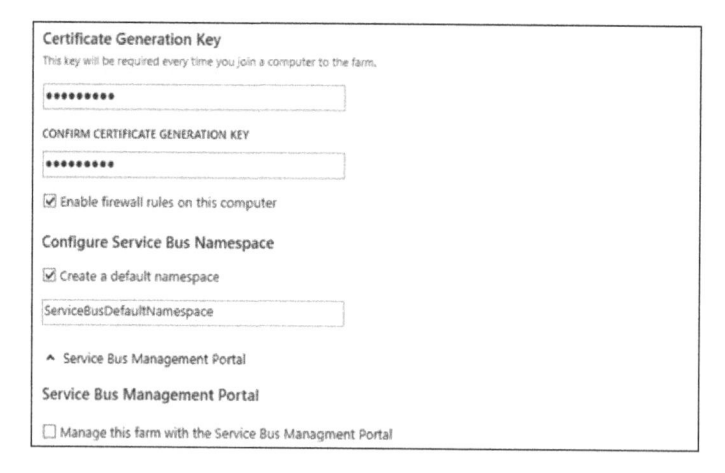

   Certificate Generation Key
   This key will be required every time you join a computer to the farm.

   `•••••••••`

   CONFIRM CERTIFICATE GENERATION KEY

   `•••••••••`

   ☑ Enable firewall rules on this computer

   Configure Service Bus Namespace
   ☑ Create a default namespace

   `ServiceBusDefaultNamespace`

   ▲ Service Bus Management Portal
   Service Bus Management Portal
   ☐ Manage this farm with the Service Bus Managment Portal

9. Provide the default namespace for the Service Bus configuration.
10. Enter service management portal access credentials; these will be used by Windows Azure Pack to communicate with Service Bus.

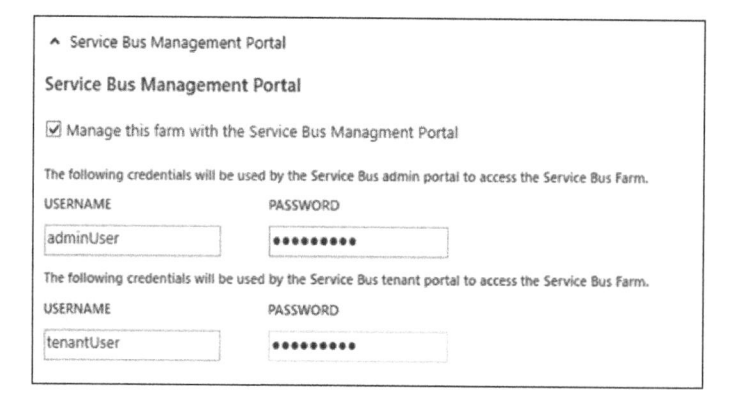

    ▲ Service Bus Management Portal
    Service Bus Management Portal
    ☑ Manage this farm with the Service Bus Managment Portal

    The following credentials will be used by the Service Bus admin portal to access the Service Bus Farm.

USERNAME	PASSWORD
adminUser	•••••••••

    The following credentials will be used by the Service Bus tenant portal to access the Service Bus Farm.

USERNAME	PASSWORD
tenantUser	•••••••••

11. Review the settings in summary and click on the checkmark to start the deployment.
12. The configuration process will start; monitor the logs in case of any errors. Click on the checkmark once this is completed.

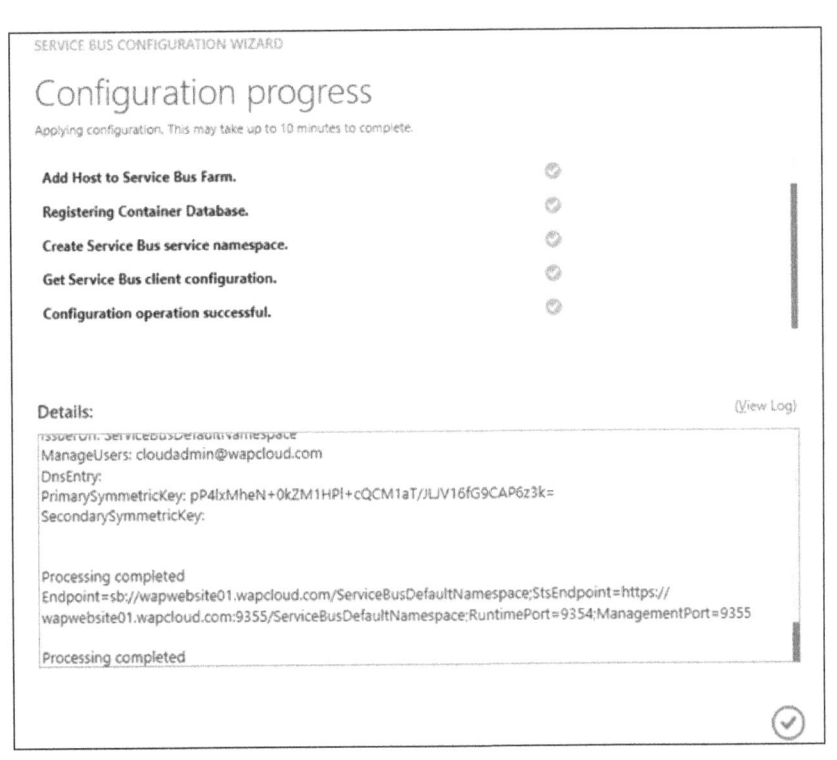

Registering the Service Bus cloud with Windows Azure Pack

The following steps outline the process to register Windows Azure Pack with a Service Bus cloud farm:

1. Log into the Windows Azure Pack Management portal.

2. Browse the **service bus clouds** workspace.

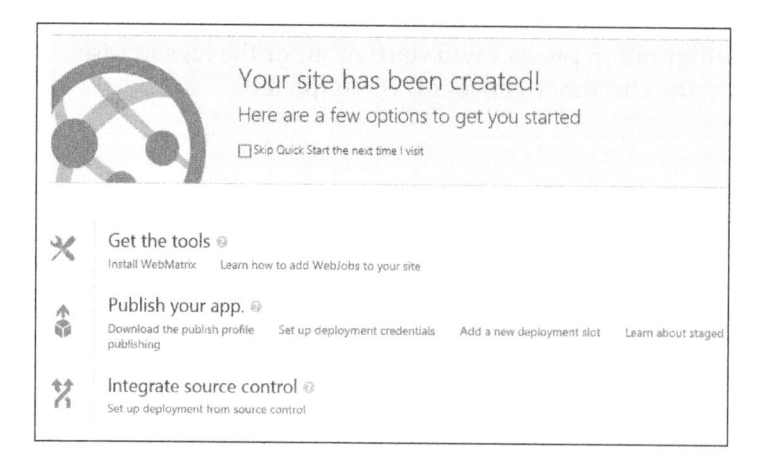

3. Click on **Connect to an existing Service Bus Cloud**.
4. Enter the **SERVICE BUS CLOUD** endpoint and credentials for admin and tenant operations while configuring the Service Bus cloud configuration.
5. Post successful registration, the newly registered Service Bus cloud will be visible under the **service bus clouds** workspace.

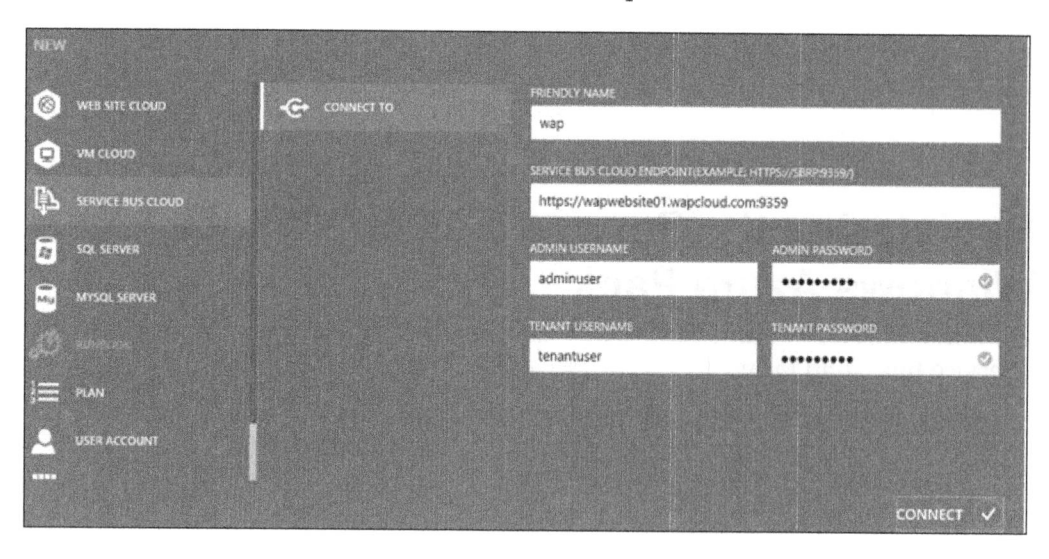

Authoring a Service Bus plan

Like any other Windows Azure Pack cloud service offering, Service Bus can also be used by tenants via subscribing to relevant plans configured by service providers. See *Chapter 5, Assigning Cloud Services – Plans, Add-Ons, Tenant Accounts, and Subscriptions* to know more about Windows Azure Pack plans. The following steps outline the process to author a Service Bus plan:

1. Log into the management portal.
2. Browse the **plans** workspace and click on **CREATE A NEW HOSTING PLAN**.
3. Enter a friendly name for the plan.
4. Select **SERVICE BUS** and the newly registered Service Bus cloud in **PLAN SERVICES**.

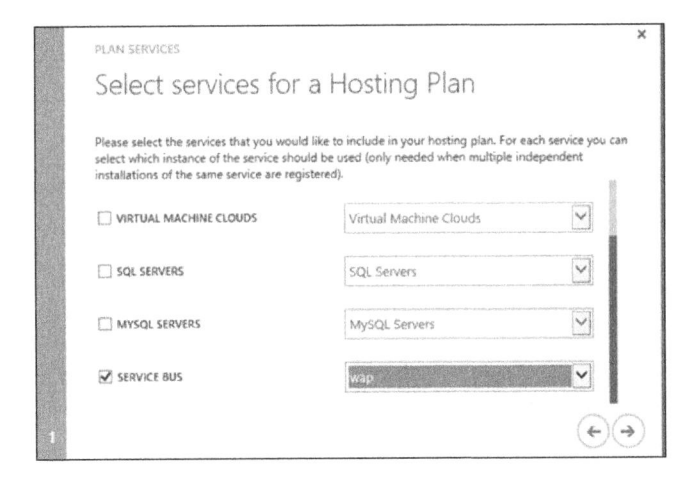

5. Configure additional plan settings. Note that there are no quotas or any other settings available to configure. Service Bus cloud works on a shared model for all users without any per user quota or limitations.

Service Bus – a tenant's experience

This topics discusses a tenant's experience for provisioning and using Service Bus operations from a tenant's point of view. A tenant must be subscribed to a WAP plan, which is configured to provide Service Bus offerings.

Provisioning and accessing a Service Bus namespace and features

The following steps are to be performed by tenants for provisioning, using, and managing a Service Bus namespace:

1. Log into the Windows Azure Pack portal for tenants.
2. Subscribe to WAP plans configured for Service Bus offerings.
3. Browse the **service bus** workspace.

4. Click on **CREATE A NAMESPACE** to start creating a namespace.

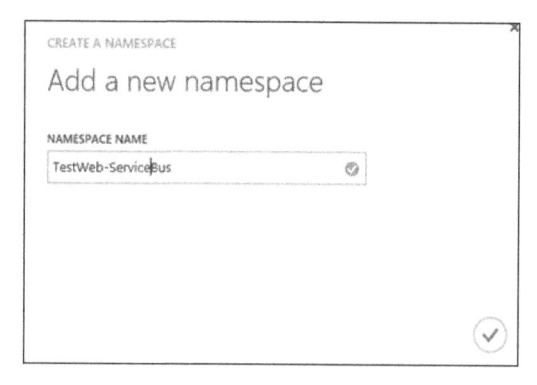

5. Post successful creation, the namespace will be available in a portal.
6. Click on **Connection Info** to know connectivity mechanisms regarding the namespace.

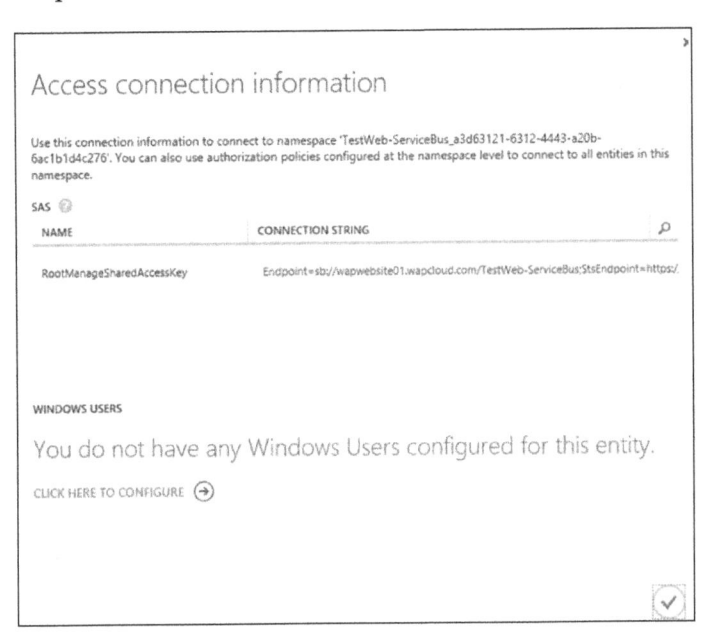

7. The **CONFIGURE** tab of the namespace allows tenants to configure and manage accessing policies and primary and secondary keys for authorization.

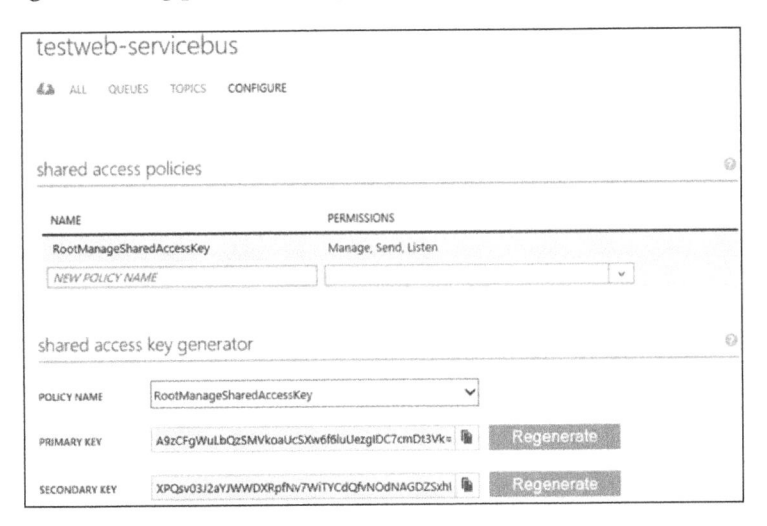

Creating topics and queues

The **New Items** workspace of the WAP portal is used to create new queues or topics. The following steps can be used for creating and managing topics and queues:

1. Click on the **NEW** button at the bottom of the WAP tenant portal.
2. Select **SERVICE BUS**.
3. Select the **QUEUE** service or **TOPIC** as per your choice and requirement.
4. Provide a name and namespace for creating the required item.

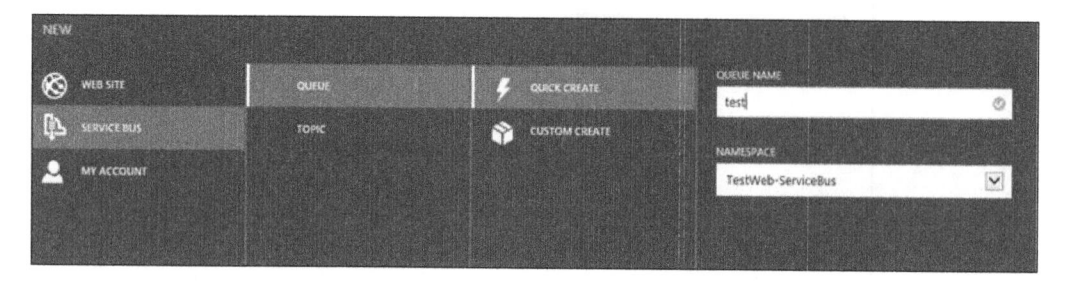

5. Post successful provisioning, the newly created queue or topic will be visible in its respective tab under the selected namespace. Select any provisioned topic to queue to view its dashboard, which includes the utilization status and connectivity related information.

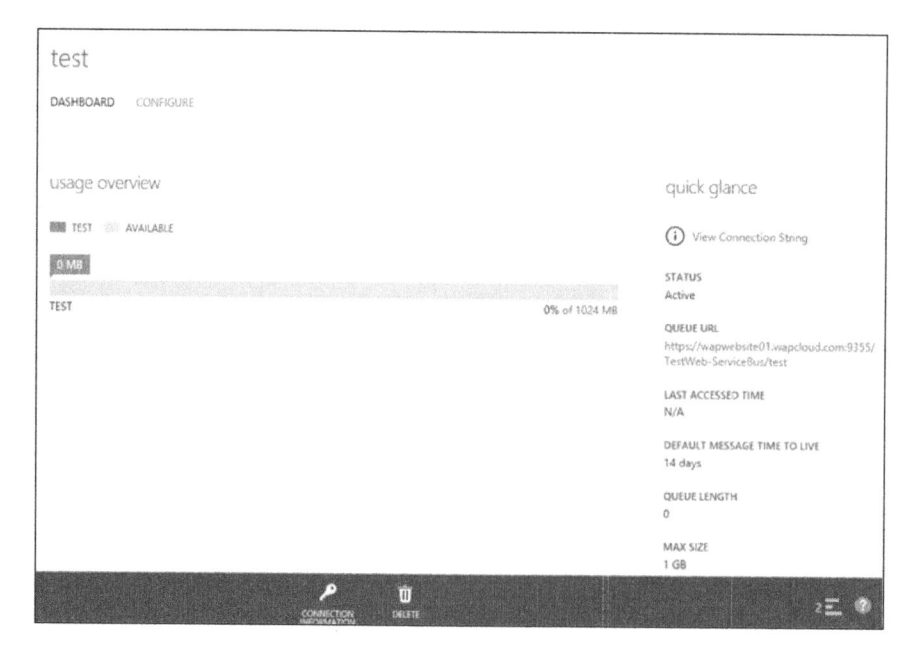

Summary

In this chapter, we covered two major PaaS cloud offerings that are WebSites and Service Bus. You learned about planning, deployment, and tenant experience for these services.

In the next chapter, we move ahead and learn about the planning and deployment of another cloud offering of Windows Azure Pack that is DBaaS.

8
Delivering Database as a Service

The Database as a Service in cloud computing service models, delivers relational databases for applications and websites without worrying about its infrastructure and middleware layer. Developers or application owners are only required to create their databases in a self-service manner. This reduces the delivery time drastically and allows organizations to focus more on applications.

Windows Azure Pack supports a variety of databases servers and versions including Microsoft SQL Server and MySQL in an integrated and self-service manner. With a little more effort, almost every database supported on Hyper-V can be delivered.

In this chapter, we will be covering the following topics:

- Windows Azure Pack DBaaS offerings overview
- Planning the DBaaS platform fabric
- Implementing SQL DBaaS
- Implementing the MySQL resource provider fabric
- SQL and MySQL DBaaS management operations – service providers
- Enabling DB QoS – the SQL resource governor
- Authoring DBaaS plans
- DBaaS – tenant experience
- Dedicating DBaaS offerings

Windows Azure Pack DBaaS offerings overview and capabilities

Windows Azure Pack Express natively includes APIs for DBaaS resource providers for SQL and MySQL. In addition, these two APIs are the only supported DBaaS resource providers available by default with WAP.

WAP DBaaS offerings provide the following features and capabilities on both private and service provider's cloud solutions:

- High density and resilient DBaaS services
- Default support for SQL and MySQL with extension capabilities for other databases offerings
- Multitenants and shared models
- The quality of service with granual control
- Self-service and automation
- Multiple service models including shared and dedicated services with IaaS and PaaS
- Usage and metering
- Supports multiple HA technologies such as Always On

Looking from a tenant's perspective, WAP DBaaS services offer the following features:

- It provides a simple, faster database provisioning and management in a self-service manner
- It runs on invisible infrastructure and platform; that is, there is no need to worry about hardware/OS/DB server layer provisioning, management, or updates
- It provides a variety of options with respect to database versions, sizing, and features

Shared and dedicated database services

Depending upon business-to-business needs and compliance, there can be both shared and dedicated databases required by tenants. In shared service models, a single database server usually hosts databases from multiple tenants. Tenants share the same computing power and other resources along with databases engines. The shared service model is common in public cloud solutions and is widely used.

In the case of dedicated services, a single server or a set of resources including hardware and software host the databases of a single tenant only. Use cases for dedicated services usually include the following:

- Customized requirements by tenants in terms of infrastructure and software that isn't available or possible in a shared mode
- Security or compliance related requirements
- Customized QoS requirements and many more

While shared database services are natively available in Windows Azure Pack, dedicated services can be achieved using VM Roles and dedicated fabric. We will be covering these in detail in the upcoming topics.

The architectural components of WAP DBaaS

Windows Azure Pack DBaaS solution in shared mode usually includes the following components:

- SQL or MySQL database servers and clusters
- Windows Azure Pack server SQL and MySQL extension API servers
- WAP SQL/MySQL groups, plans, and the tenant's subscription
- Any other database services related monitoring, management, or automation solutions such as SCOM

WAP resource provider's API is responsible for communicating with the DB server's fabric for management and tenant-related provisioning operations. All databases are created and managed by the resource provider's API.

The communication from the tenant's application to DB servers is direct; that is, it does not involve any WAP component.

Planning the DBaaS platform fabric

In this topic, we will be discussing the planning of the shared DBaaS platform fabric for both SQL and MySQL database services.

Planning the database server's groups

In Windows Azure Pack, both SQL and MySQL DB servers are categorized under groups. A group may contain multiple, standalone, or clustered database servers that can be either virtual or physical. WAP plans are configured to provide cloud database offerings services to tenants using groups. Both SQL and MySQL groups work independently; that is, a group cannot have a mix of both SQL and MySQL databases.

DB server groups work in a shared mode; that is, they host databases for multiple users or tenants in a shared instance.

Organizations or service providers can plan to create multiple groups depending upon requirements and strategies, such as one group is for high-end database hosting in terms of size and performance, whereas another can be a non-HA group.

Organizations utilizing Windows Azure Pack database services for private cloud requirements may plan to create multiple groups for SQL resource providers for different business units depending upon the type or workload, such as production and **T&D** (**test and development**) environments. A few examples are as follows:

- Categorizing on the basis of business units or departments
- Categorizing on the basis of criticality, which directly relates to the performance and availability capabilities of the fabric
- Separate groups for T&D applications or any other separate exclusive database needs
- Separate groups for different versions or features' availability, such as DR, backups, and so on
- Separate groups for different geo locations or datacenters

While most of the previous examples are applicable for service providers, service providers may choose to have groups based on the following:

- Separate groups for shared and dedicated database services for tenants
- Separate groups for standalone and clustered servers that provide high availability

- Separate groups depending upon performance and additional features such as backups
- As per database sizes; that is, separate groups for hosting large-sized databases and small-sized databases

Planning the SQL Server's fabric deployment

Windows Azure Pack SQL resource provider supports the following SQL database servers' versions:

- SQL Server 2014
- SQL Server 2012 SP1
- SQL Server 2008 R2 SP2 and SP3

While almost all planning and best practices followed for a Microsoft SQL Server deployment are applicable, the following guidelines can be followed for a Windows Azure Pack DBaaS SQL fabric group. See Microsoft's official documentation at https://msdn.microsoft.com/en-us/library/bb545450.aspx to learn more about MS SQL:

- **Using SQL availability techniques**: Windows Azure Pack SQL Resource provider can be deployed with the following types of SQL database servers. It is recommended to use SQL high availability technologies for SQL Server groups as design decisions:
    - Standalone SQL Server
    - SQL Always ON
- **Utilizing the SQL resource governor**: WAP supports the utilizing resource governor feature of SQL Server 2014 for enabling QOS control for the tenant's databases
- **Using virtual machines for SQL Servers**: It's a good idea to use virtual machines to host SQL Server virtual machines to take advantage of the hypervisor level availability and other technologies such as mobility
- **Additional requirements**: WAP requires SQL authentication to be enabled in SQL Servers

Planning the MySQL Server's fabric deployment

Windows Azure Pack MySQL Resource provider supports the following versions of MySQL Server for tenants' databases:

- MySQL 5.1 for Windows
- MySQL 5.5 for Windows

Refer to the MySQL documentation (https://dev.mysql.com/doc/) to know more about planning and sizing for MySQL databases servers. Normally, MySQL Servers can be deployed in two manners for WAP DBaaS services:

- Standalone MySQL Servers are installed using the WEB PI
- Highly available MySQL Servers are installed with Windows Cluster and MySQL Enterprise

Implementing SQL DBaaS

Implementing SQL Server DBaaS services involves the following steps:

- Planning SQL Server fabric groups
- Installing and configuring SQL Server Standalone or Always On Servers
- Creating SQL Server groups
- Adding SQL Servers to the groups
- Creating plans and assigning services

The installation and configuration of SQL Standalone or Always On isn't covered in this book. It is recommended to follow Microsoft's standard guidelines and best practices for installing and configuring SQL Servers. The SQL Server installation guides can be found at https://msdn.microsoft.com/en-us/library/bb500442.aspx.

Creating SQL groups

The following steps outline the process to create SQL groups:

1. Log into the Windows Azure Pack management portal for administrators.
2. Browse the **sql servers** workspace.
3. Click on **Create a SQL Server Group**.

4. Provide **GROUP NAME**, choose the type that is **Standalone servers** or **High availability (Always on enabled)** and select the checkbox to enable the SQL resource governance (this will be discussed in the upcoming topics).

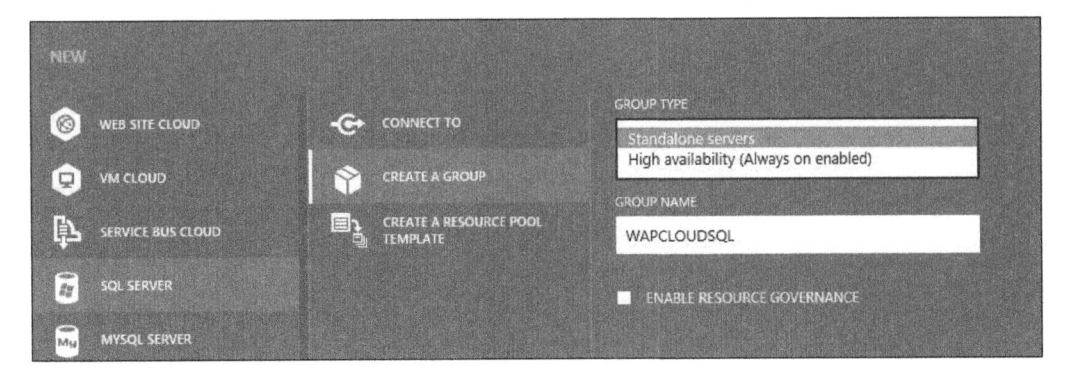

5. The newly created group will now be listed under the **GROUPS** tab in the **sql servers** workspace.

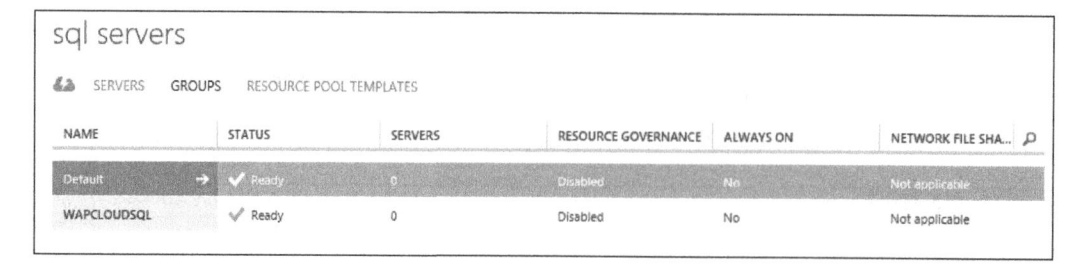

NAME	STATUS	SERVERS	RESOURCE GOVERNANCE	ALWAYS ON	NETWORK FILE SHA...
Default	Ready	0	Disabled	No	Not applicable
WAPCLOUDSQL	Ready	0	Disabled	No	Not applicable

Adding SQL Servers to groups

The following steps outline the process to add SQL Servers to a group:

1. Log into the Windows Azure Pack management portal for administrators
2. Browse the **sql servers** workspace.

> sql servers
>
> SERVERS   GROUPS   RESOURCE POOL TEMPLATES
>
> You currently have no SQL Server. Go ahead and add one to get started.
>
> ADD A NEW SQL SERVER →

3. Click on the **ADDA NEW SQL SERVER** option.
4. Enter the server name and credentials (SQL authentication and total database size of DB hosting capacity).

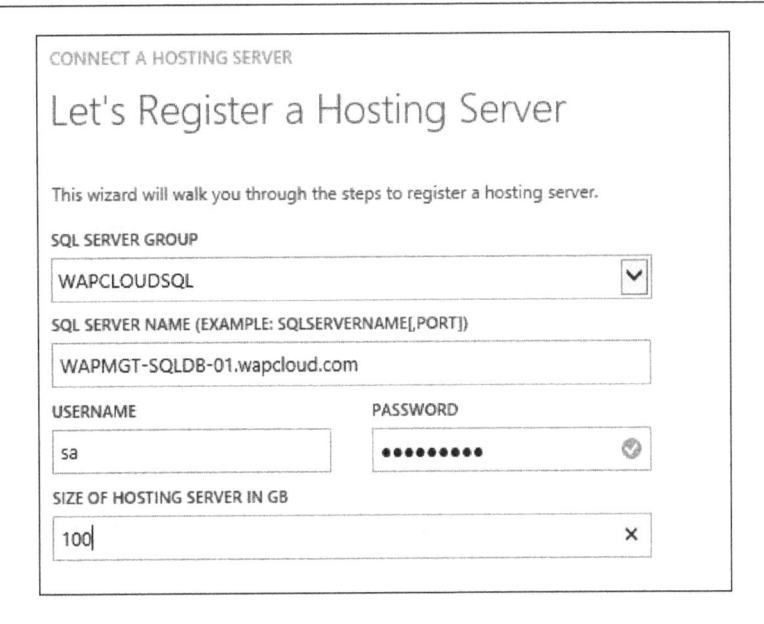

5. The newly added SQL Server will now be available in the **SERVERS** tab.

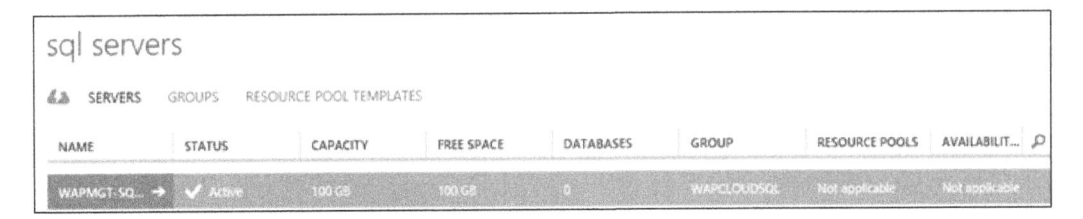

Implementing the MySQL resource provider fabric

MySQL database engines for Windows Azure Pack can be installed in two ways:

- Using the traditional MySQL mechanism
- Using the Microsoft Web Platform installer

The Microsoft Web Platform installer contains both MySQL 5.1 and 5.5 versions in the community edition. It is installed in the standalone mode. Post installation, a remote access to MySQL Servers must be enabled manually to allow the WAP communication.

Refer to the MySQL documentation to know more on production MySQL deployments. The MySQL documentation can be found at https://dev.mysql.com/doc/.

Installing and configuring MySQL servers

The following steps outline the MySQL installation using Microsoft Web Platform Installer:

1. Log into the server designated for hosting the MySQL Server database with administrative credentials.
2. Download and install the Microsoft Web Platform Installer.
3. Search for MySQL 5.5.

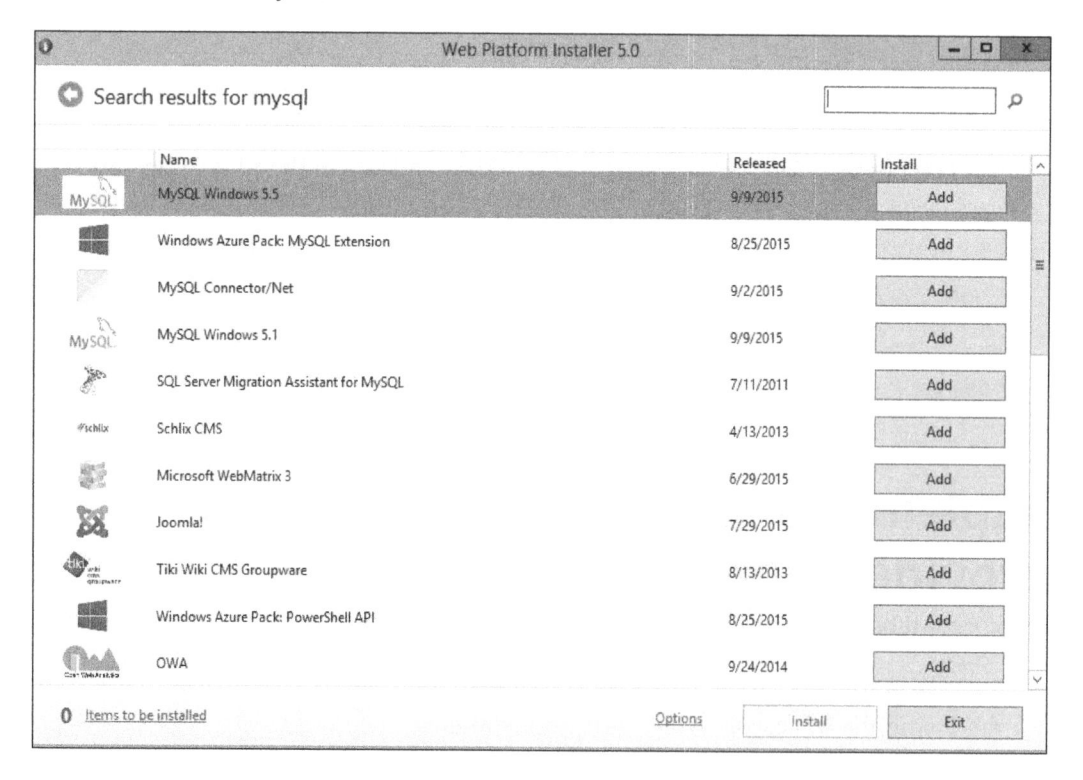

4. Select **MySQL Windows 5.5** and click on **Add**.
5. Click on **Install** to proceed further.
6. Enter the root password for MySQL DB. This will be used while communicating with MySQL Server post installation.

Chapter 8

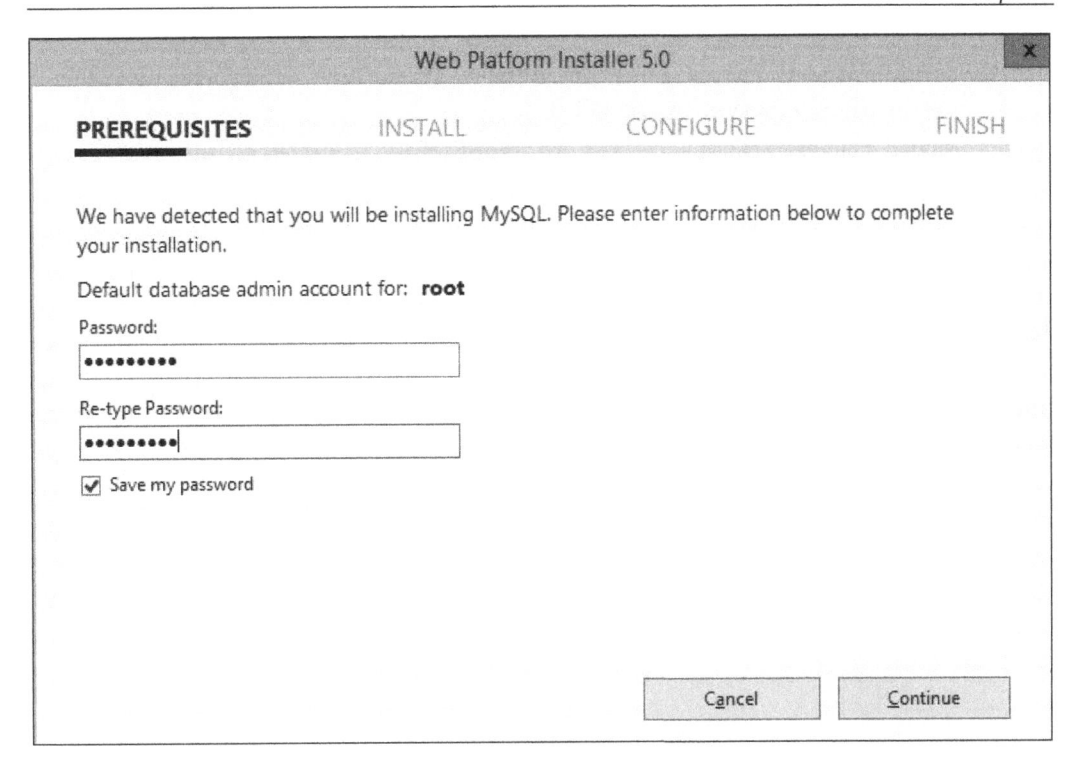

[Screenshot: Web Platform Installer 5.0 — Prerequisites step showing MySQL password entry with "Default database admin account for: root", Password and Re-type Password fields, "Save my password" checkbox, and Cancel/Continue buttons.]

7. Accept the agreement and proceed further.
8. Now, the downloading and the installation procedure will start.
9. Exit the wizard after a successful installation.

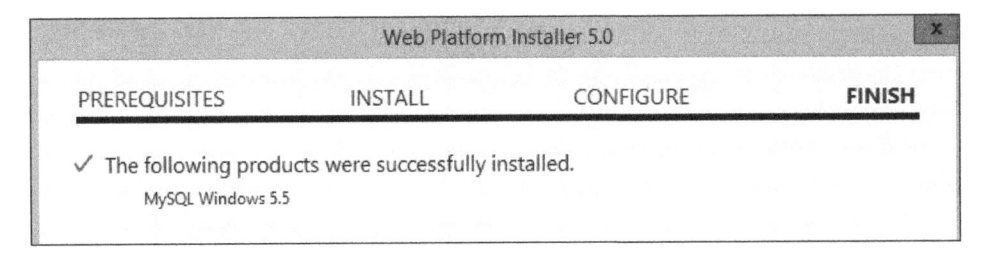

[Screenshot: Web Platform Installer 5.0 — Finish step showing "The following products were successfully installed. MySQL Windows 5.5".]

10. Launch the MySQL command-line client from the **Start** menu.
11. Enter the password for the root user that was configured during the installation.

[273]

12. Enable the remote access to remote the server by issuing the following command on the MySQL Server utility command line, which was installed on the MySQL Server by the WEB PI:

    ```
    GRANT ALL PRIVILEGES ON *.* TO 'root'@'%' IDENTIFIED BY 'password' WITH GRANT OPTION
    ```

13. This MySQL Server is now ready for integration with Windows Azure Pack.

Creating MySQL groups

Creating Windows Azure Pack groups for MySQL Servers is fairly simple and similar to SQL Server groups. The following steps outline the requirements to create MySQL Servers:

1. Log into the Windows Azure Pack management portal for administrators.
2. Browse the **MYSQL SERVERS** workspace.

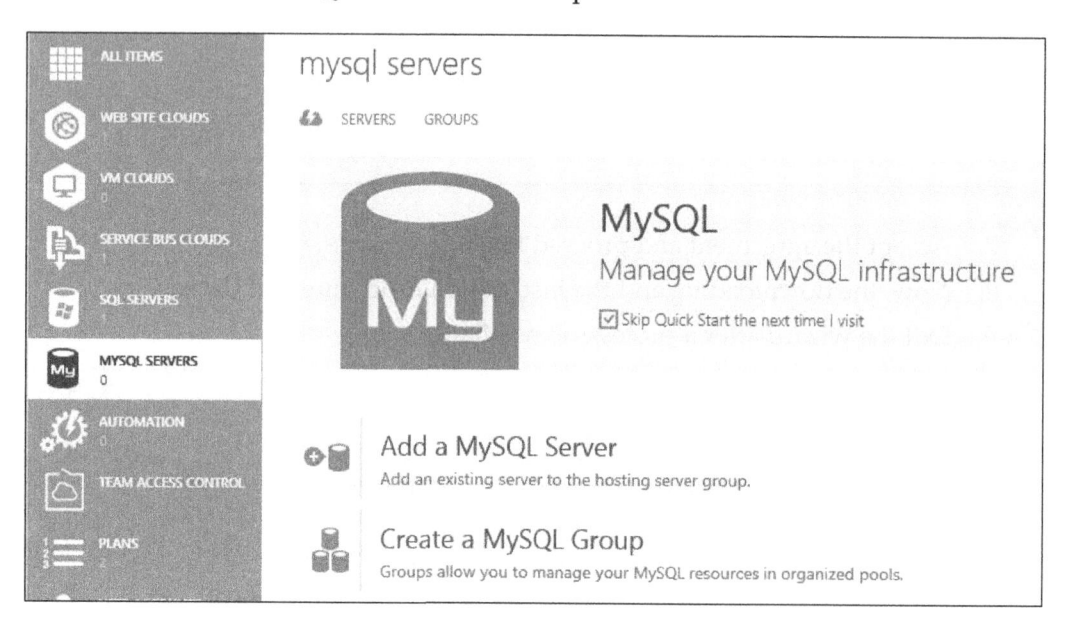

3. Click on **CREATE A GROUP**.

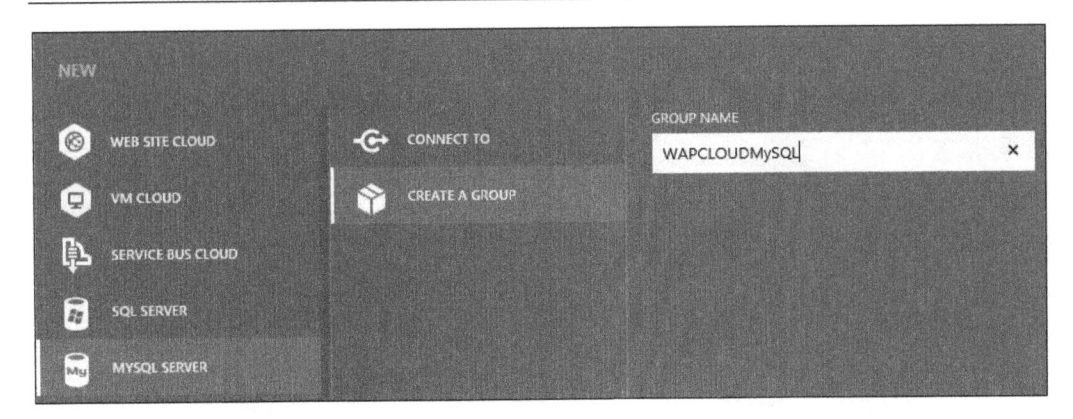

4. The newly created group will now be visible under MySQL groups.

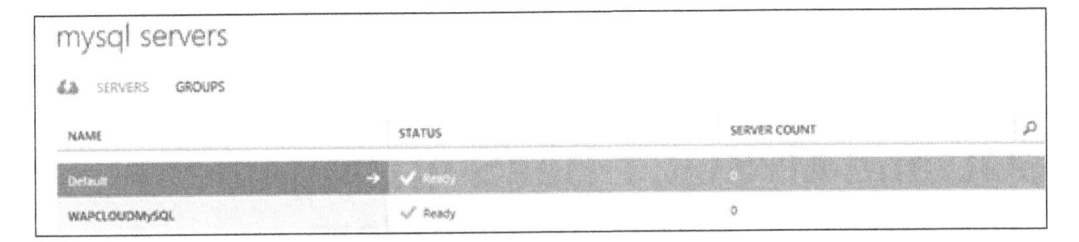

Adding MySQL Servers to groups

The following steps outline the requirements to add MySQL Server in Windows Azure Pack MySQL Server groups:

1. Log into the Windows Azure Pack management portal for administrators and browse the **mysql servers** workspace.

2. Click on **ADD A NEW MYSQL SERVER**.

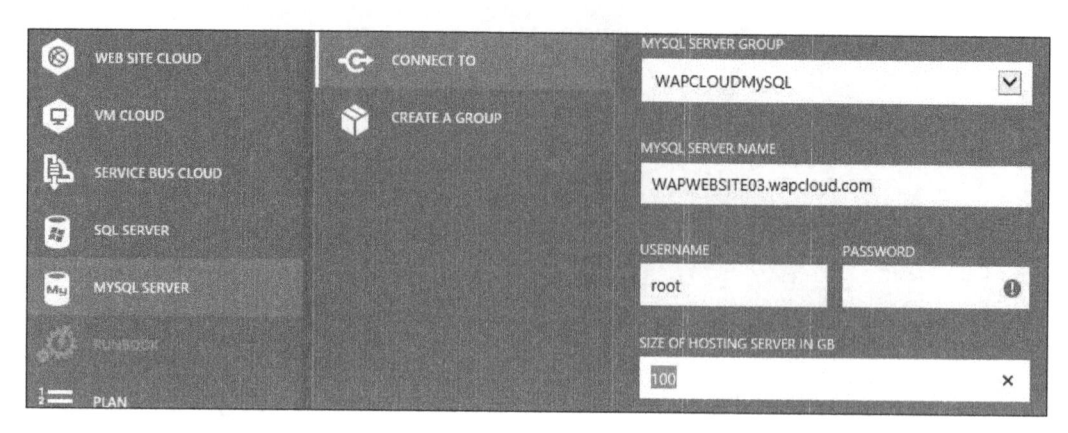

3. Upon successful completion, MySQL Server will be listed under the **SERVERS** tab in the **mysql servers** workspace.

SQL and MySQL DBaaS management operations – service providers

Windows Azure Pack provides a self-service portal for administrators for normal DBaaS management service operations. The following operations can be performed using the WAP portal for SQL and MySQL resource providers' groups and servers:

- Groups management operations are as follows:
    - Add group
    - Delete group

- Database server management operations can be performed as follows:
    1. View the utilization and count of the SQL database on the SQL Server.
    2. List all the databases created.
    3. Change the DB servers group and the hosting capacity (only for SQL Servers and not MySQL).

EDIT A HOSTING SERVER

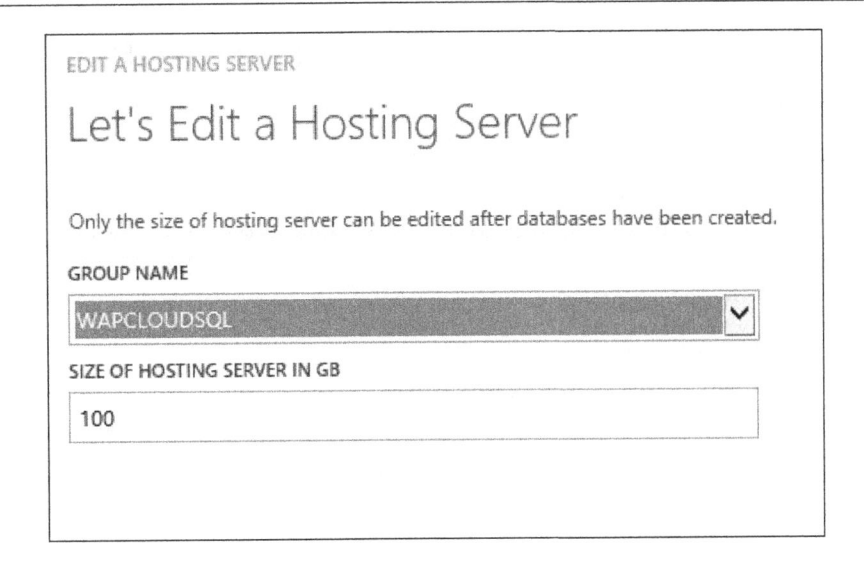

Let's Edit a Hosting Server

Only the size of hosting server can be edited after databases have been created.

GROUP NAME

WAPCLOUDSQL

SIZE OF HOSTING SERVER IN GB

100

4. Repair the connection with the existing database servers:

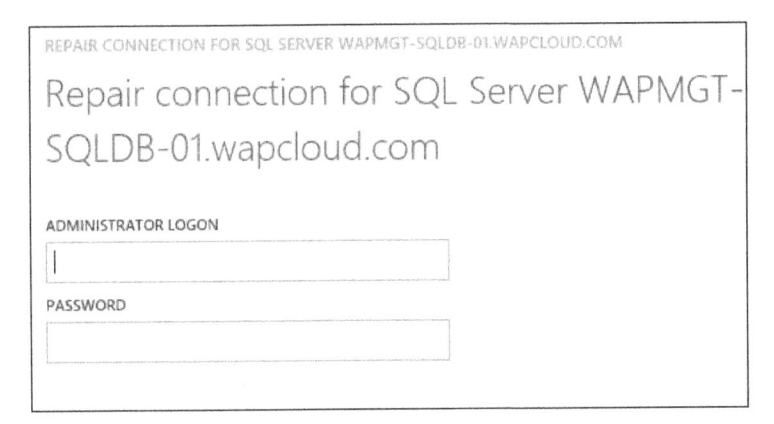

REPAIR CONNECTION FOR SQL SERVER WAPMGT-SQLDB-01.WAPCLOUD.COM

Repair connection for SQL Server WAPMGT-SQLDB-01.wapcloud.com

ADMINISTRATOR LOGON

PASSWORD

5. Remove Server.

Enabling DB QoS – the SQL resource governor

As you learned, Windows Azure Pack database as a service offering works in a sharing mode; that is, multiple tenants can access databases hosted on the same servers. Assuring the quality of the service in a shared multitenant shared cloud is necessary. The SQL resource governor feature of SQL 2014 Enterprise edition enables Windows Azure Pack to provide the quality of service control on the tenant's database.

The resource governor avoids scenarios where one tenant may consume more or all the resources that may affect the performance of other tenants' databases. This ensures that each tenant gets an equal share of resources as per the subscription.

Windows Azure Pack with SQL resource governors provides flexibilities to cloud providers to apply limits on the following parameters:

- CPU
- Memory
- IOPS

The following are the architectural components of a SQL resource governor deployment for Windows Azure Pack DBaaS services:

- SQL Server 2014 Enterprise edition servers
- SQL governance enabled SQL Server groups created in WAP
- Configured resource pool templates with limits and settings
- Windows Azure Pack plans associated with SQL Servers and resource pool template
- Resource governor is a feature provided by SQL Server 2014 Enterprise edition only; this states that WAP DBaaS Service with QoS control can only be used with SQL Enterprise 2014 databases

Implementing SQL resource governor for WAP

The following steps outline the processes required to deploy a Windows Azure Pack SQL DBaaS server with SQL governor.

Creating SQL groups and adding SQL Servers

To create SQL groups and adding SQL servers in groups perform the following steps:

1. Install and configure SQL Server 2014 Enterprise edition servers.
2. Create an SQL Server group in Windows Azure Pack with the **Enable Resource Governance** checked.
3. Add SQL Servers to the group. While adding SQL Servers, provide the number of CPU cores, installed memory, IOPs per volume, and the maximum number of resource pools to be created on the servers.

The newly created SQL Server group and SQL Servers will be displayed in the WAP portal.

> Maximum 18 pools can be created on a SQL Server.

Resource templates

Resource templates are used to configure limits and values. They are associated with plans. These values are also passed to SQL Servers for creating and configuring a resource pool.

The following steps outline the requirement for creating resource templates:

1. Log into the WAP management portal and browse the **mysql servers** workspace.
2. Select the newly created **SQL SERVER** group and browse the resource template tab.
3. Click on the **new item** workspace and select the **CREATE A RESOURCE** template under SQL Server.

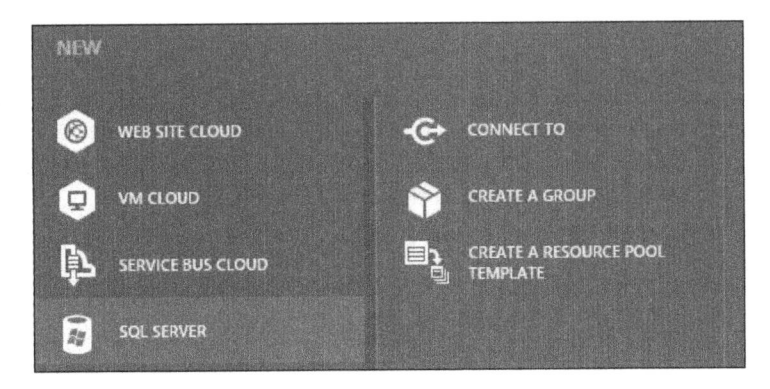

Delivering Database as a Service

4. Enter a name to identify the template.
5. Enter limit values for the following:
    - **MINIMUM CPU CORES**
    - **MAXIMUM CPU CORES (SOFT CAP)**
    - **MAXIMUM CPU CORES (HARD CAP)**
    - **MINIMUM MEMORY (MB)**
    - **MAXIMUM MEMORY (MB)**
    - **MINIMUM IOPS PER VOLUME**
    - **MAXIMUM IOPS PER VOLUME**
    - **MAXIMUM SUBSCRIPTIONS PER POOL**

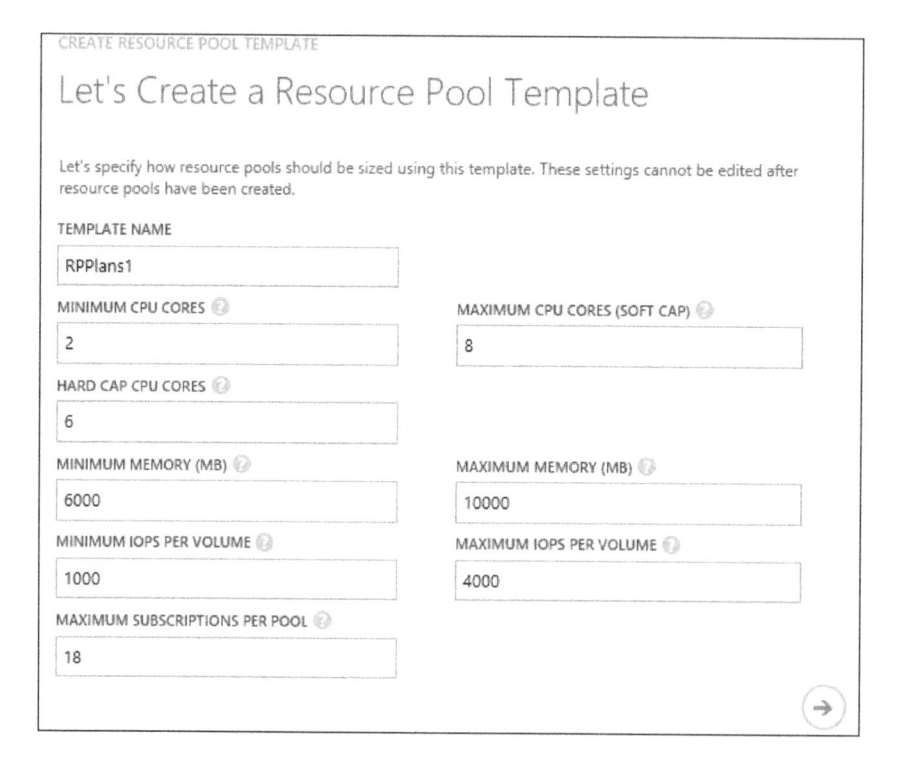

CREATE RESOURCE POOL TEMPLATE

Let's Create a Resource Pool Template

Let's specify how resource pools should be sized using this template. These settings cannot be edited after resource pools have been created.

TEMPLATE NAME
RPPlans1

MINIMUM CPU CORES	MAXIMUM CPU CORES (SOFT CAP)
2	8

HARD CAP CPU CORES
6

MINIMUM MEMORY (MB)	MAXIMUM MEMORY (MB)
6000	10000

MINIMUM IOPS PER VOLUME	MAXIMUM IOPS PER VOLUME
1000	4000

MAXIMUM SUBSCRIPTIONS PER POOL
18

6. Next provide a value for the following limits. These setting are applicable for workload groups created in the resource pool:
    - **MAXIMUM MEMORY PER REQUEST (MB)**
    - **MAXIMUM CPU TIME IN SECONDS PER REQUEST**

- MEMORY GRANT TIMEOUT IN SECONDS PER QUERY
- MAXIMUM SIMULTANEOUS REQUESTS
- MAXIMUM DEGREE OF PARALLELISM

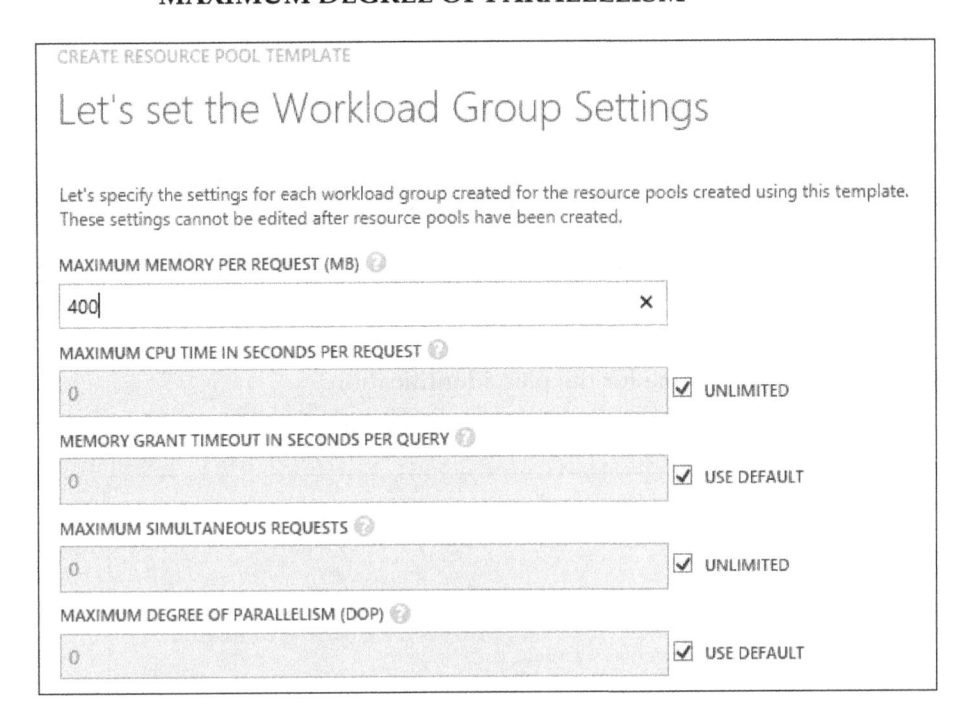

7. Finish the wizard; the resource pool template will now be available under the **mysql servers** workspace.

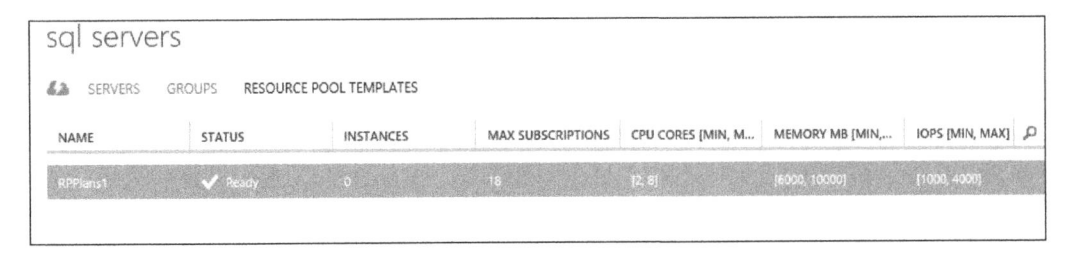

This resource template can now be associated with a WAP plan to assign QoS a control over tenants.

Authoring DBaaS plans

Like all other Windows Azure Pack cloud services, DBaaS offerings are also assigned to tenants via Windows Azure Pack plans and add-ons. See *Chapter 5, Assigning Cloud Services – Plans, Add-Ons, Tenant Accounts, and Subscriptions*, to learn more about the planning of plans and add-ons.

Creating plans for SQL and MySQL DBaaS

The following steps outline the requirement to create WAP plans for SQL and MySQL databases:

1. Log into the WAP management portal and browse the new item workspace.
2. Select **Plans** to start creating a plan.
3. Enter a friendly name for the plan identification.
4. Select **SQL Servers**, **MySQL Servers**, or both as applicable.

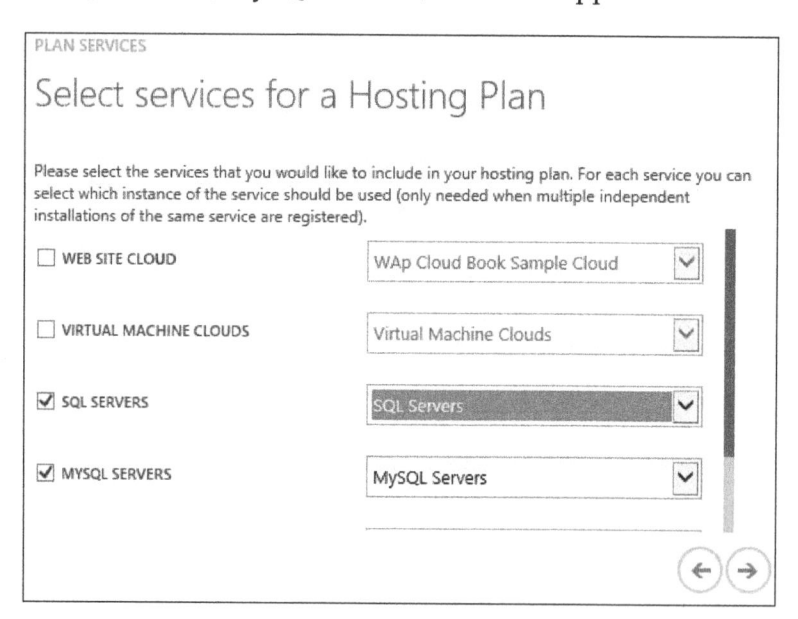

![Plan Services - Select services for a Hosting Plan dialog showing WEB SITE CLOUD, VIRTUAL MACHINE CLOUDS unchecked, and SQL SERVERS, MYSQL SERVERS checked]

5. The newly created plan will now be visible under **plans** workspace as not configured.

6. Click on the plan name to start the configuration.

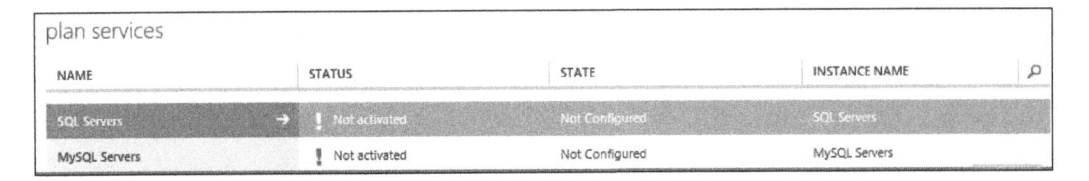

plan services				
NAME	STATUS	STATE	INSTANCE NAME	
SQL Servers	→ Not activated	Not Configured	SQL Servers	
MySQL Servers	Not activated	Not Configured	MySQL Servers	

7. Click on SQL and MySQL Servers to start adding groups to the plans. Enter the database server information including group, template, and other settings, such as edition display name of the tenants, maximum number of databases, and database size in normal subscriptions along with add-ons.

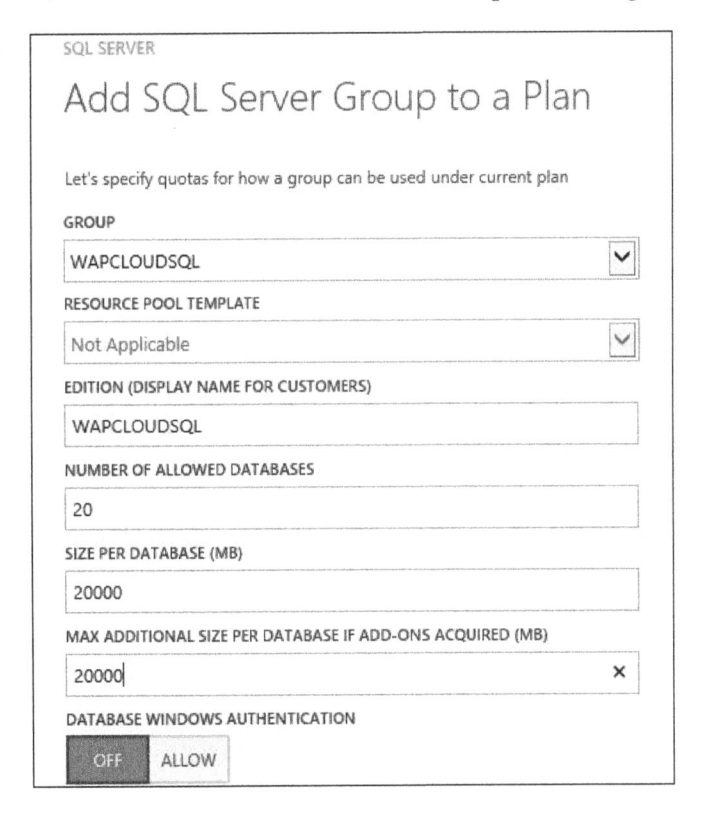

SQL SERVER

Add SQL Server Group to a Plan

Let's specify quotas for how a group can be used under current plan

GROUP

WAPCLOUDSQL

RESOURCE POOL TEMPLATE

Not Applicable

EDITION (DISPLAY NAME FOR CUSTOMERS)

WAPCLOUDSQL

NUMBER OF ALLOWED DATABASES

20

SIZE PER DATABASE (MB)

20000

MAX ADDITIONAL SIZE PER DATABASE IF ADD-ONS ACQUIRED (MB)

20000

DATABASE WINDOWS AUTHENTICATION

OFF ALLOW

For MySQL Servers, provide database group, edition name displayed to tenants, maximum number of databases, and database size. Resizing isn't available for tenants' MySQL databases, removing the option of max addition size.

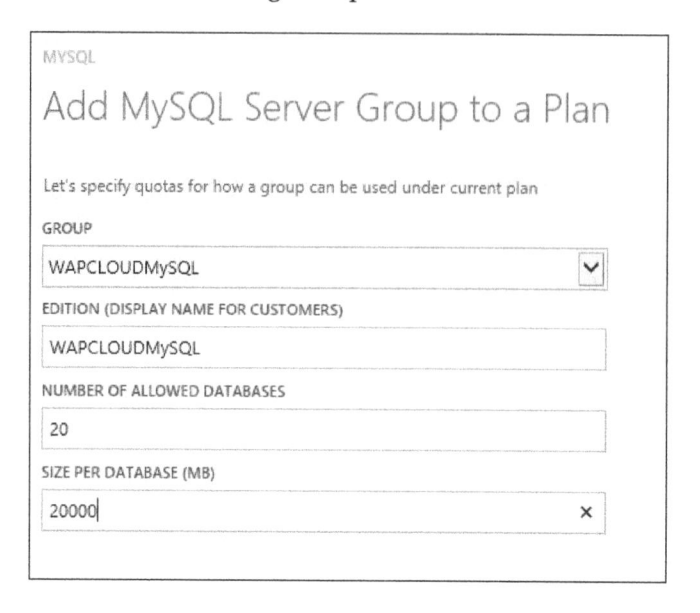

MYSQL

Add MySQL Server Group to a Plan

Let's specify quotas for how a group can be used under current plan

GROUP

WAPCLOUDMySQL

EDITION (DISPLAY NAME FOR CUSTOMERS)

WAPCLOUDMySQL

NUMBER OF ALLOWED DATABASES

20

SIZE PER DATABASE (MB)

20000

1. Save the changes and configure the additional plan setting, such as invite code, advertisement, changing access to public, and so on. See *Chapter 5, Assigning Cloud Services – Plans, Add-Ons, Tenant Accounts, and Subscriptions*, to know more on performing these operations on WAP plans.

Add-ons for SQL and MySQL DBaaS plans

Add-ons can be created and associated with plans for WAP DBaaS services for the following increase in quotas and services:

- For SQL Servers, we have the following:
    - The number of additional databases allowed
    - Total additional capacity allowed (MB)

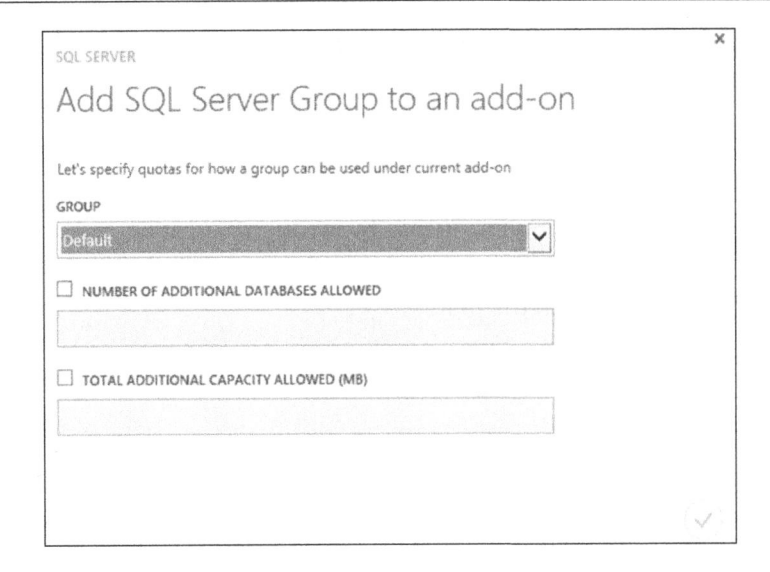

- For MySQL Servers, we have the following:
    - The number of additional databases allowed

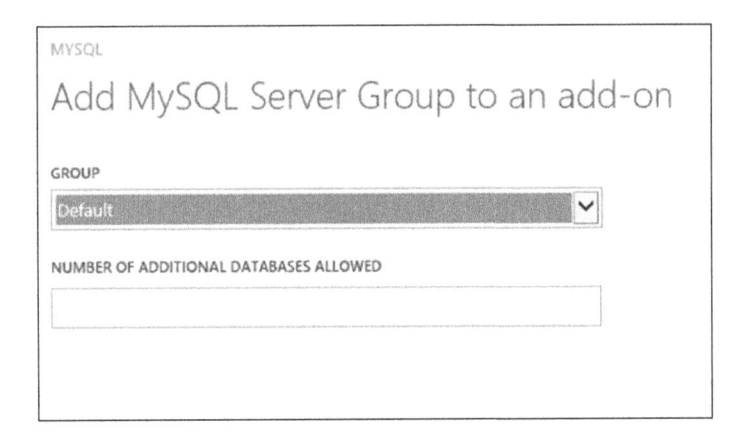

DBaaS – tenant experience

Using the tenant portal, tenants can provision and manage their databases on Windows Azure Pack website's cloud in a self-service and automated manner. In this topic, we will walkthrough the tenant experience for MySQL and SQL databases provisioning and management operations.

Database provisioning and access

The following steps outline the process followed by tenants to provision and access databases:

1. Log into the Windows Azure pack tenant portal.
2. Subscribe to the DBaaS plans using the configured invite code.
3. The SQL and MySQL workspaces will not be visible in the management portal as configured in the plan.

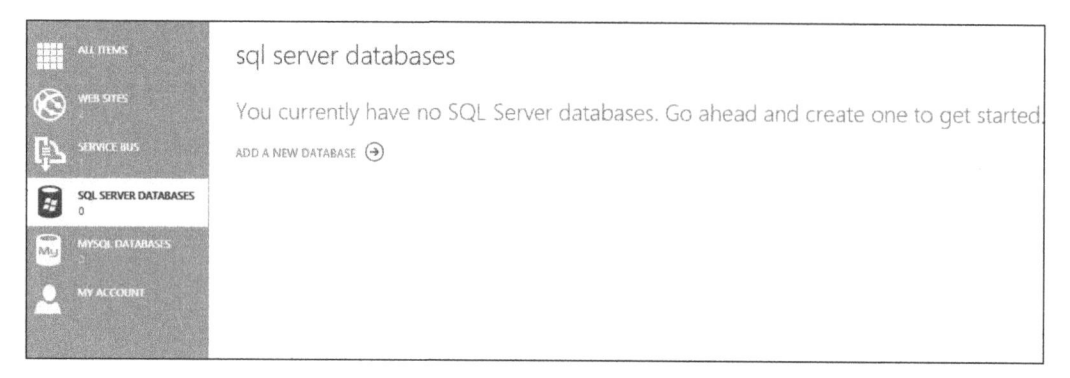

4. Click on **ADD A NEW DATABASE** to start creating a SQL DB. Provide the database **NAME** and select **EDITION** as configured by the provider in the plan settings:

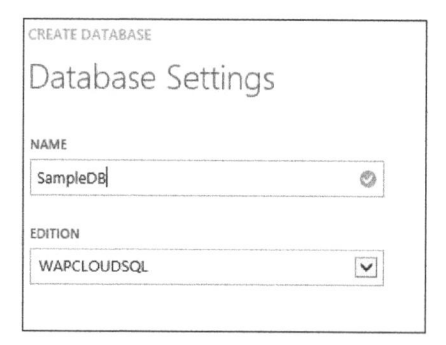

5. Enter the database admin username and credentials. A corresponding SQL and MySQL account will get created with this.

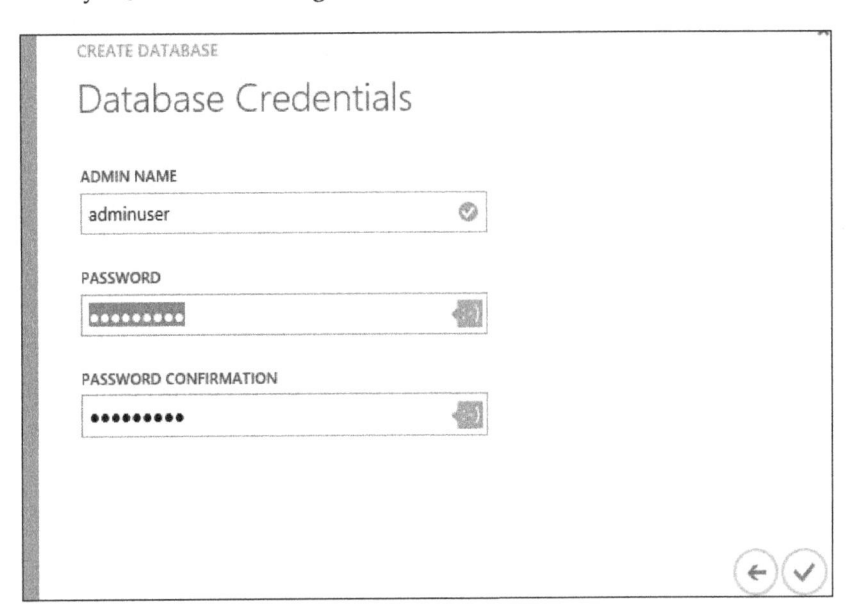

6. The newly created databases will now be visible under databases and **all items** workspace.

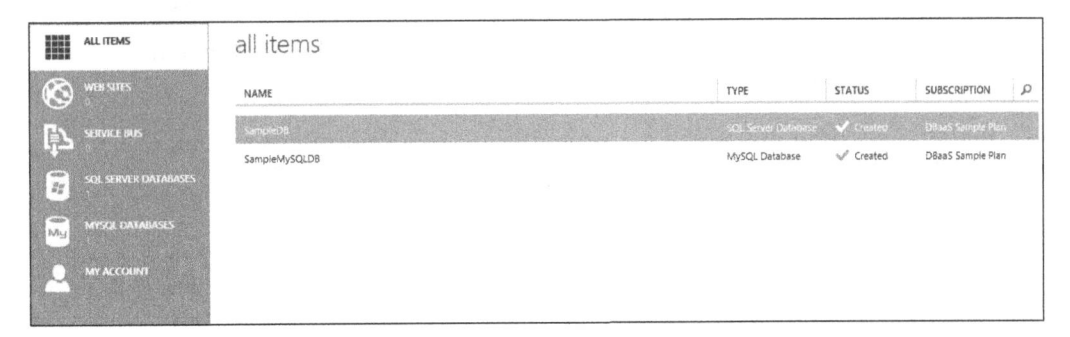

7. Select the database and click on **View info** at the bottom pane to view the connection info to integrate it into applications. Note that network connectivity must be available between the DB connectivity client and DB servers hosted inside the cloud. This can be via the Internet or VPN, depending upon architecture to architecture.

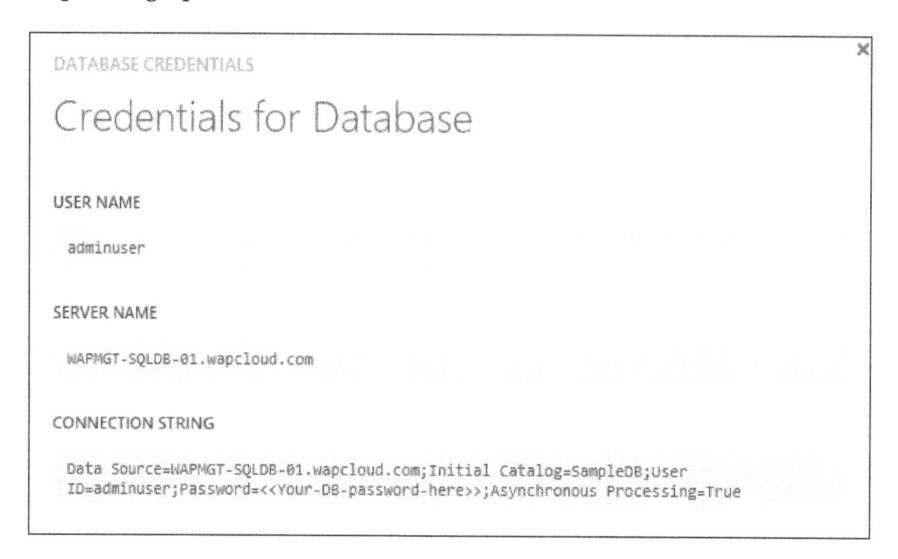

```
DATABASE CREDENTIALS
Credentials for Database

USER NAME
adminuser

SERVER NAME
WAPMGT-SQLDB-01.wapcloud.com

CONNECTION STRING
Data Source=WAPMGT-SQLDB-01.wapcloud.com;Initial Catalog=SampleDB;User
ID=adminuser;Password=<<Your-DB-password-here>>;Asynchronous Processing=True
```

Database management operations – tenants

Windows Azure Pack provides a self-service portal that can be used by tenants to perform basic management operations on created databases.

The following operations can be performed using WAP portal for SQL and MySQL databases.

The SQL and MySQL database management operations are as follows:

- **VIEW INFO**: This views the connection info and includes an admin user created by the tenant
- **DELETE**: This deletes a database
- **CHANGE PASSWORD**: This changes the admin user password

- **RESIZE**: This resizes the database size (only for SQL databases and not MySQL)

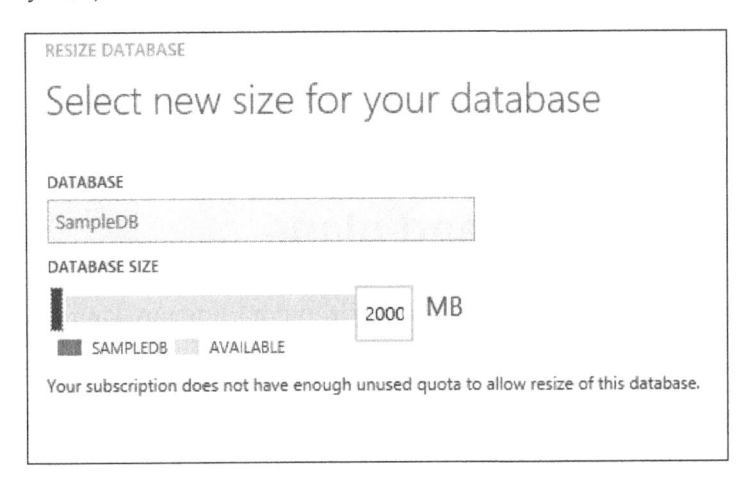

RESIZE DATABASE

Select new size for your database

DATABASE

SampleDB

DATABASE SIZE

2000 MB

SAMPLEDB AVAILABLE

Your subscription does not have enough unused quota to allow resize of this database.

Dedicating DBaaS offerings

Dedicating or reserving database server(s) for a single tenant usage, in terms of infrastructure and software, comes under a dedicated database as a service offering.

Natively, neither SQL nor MySQL resource providers have capabilities to reserve database servers for a single tenant. The following options can be leveraged for providing dedicated DBaaS services by organizations and service providers:

- VM Role gallery item (IaaS and DBaaS)
- Dedicated groups and plans (this is not recommended in large deployments)

DBaaS VM Role gallery items (IaaS and database software)

VM Role gallery items providing database services include a combination of both IaaS and DBaaS service models. Service providers can have gallery items, which include automated OS and DB Servers deployment and configurations as per the parameters provided by tenants in a self-service portal. In this scenario, both OS and DB layers have to managed by tenants only.

A supported database list is also increased in this option; that is, it can support all the databases that are supported to run on Hyper-V virtual machines.

Delivering Database as a Service

There are multiple gallery items available on Web PI, including a few for DB Servers comprising SQL and oracle databases. Custom gallery items can be developed for any other customized needs. See *Chapter 4, Building VM Clouds and IaaS Offerings*, to know more on VM Role gallery items.

While this provides dedicated servers for a tenant's database hosting, this isn't a true PaaS offering as it has infrastructure service visible to the tenant.

Dedicated groups and plans

Service providers may also choose to provide dedicated databases as a service using SQL and MySQL resource providers without adding any IaaS complexity.

Service providers can achieve this by creating the following:

- Dedicated servers groups per tenant
- Dedicated WAP plans and add-ons per tenant, corresponding to their server groups

Though this looks a simple, straightforward solution, it is not a good idea to choose in large-scale deployments. This adds complexity and management overheads for cloud providers in terms of managing the fabric along with billing and usage solutions.

Summary

In this chapter, you learned about Database as the Service offerings of Windows Azure Pack. We completed planning, deployment of groups, and fabric for both SQL and MySQL database servers along with management operations in Windows Azure Pack.

You also learned about SQL resource governor and its use cases. Later, we covered authoring plans and add-ons along with tenant experience of DBaaS services.

In the next chapter, we will cover automation and authentication solutions for Window Azure Pack, that is, **SMA** (**Service Management Automation**) and **ADFS** (**Active Directory Federation Services**).

9
Automation and Authentication – Service Management Automation and ADFS

In this chapter, we will be focusing on automating our Windows Azure Pack-based cloud solution. You will learn the installation and configuration of **SMA (Service Management Automation)**. You will also learn to create, author, and manage runbooks and assets.

Along with automation, you will also learn about the authentication, which is using ADFS to authenticate for both management and tenant portal. The following topics are covered in this chapter:

- SMA – overview and architecture
- Planning the SMA infrastructure
- Installing and configuring SMA
- Dealing with SMA assets
- Dealing with SMA runbooks
- Enabling ADFS authentication for WAP portals

SMA – overview and architecture

SMA, a part of the system center product family, adds automation capabilities to the Windows Azure Pack cloud. SMA enables a cloud provider to automate provisioning, monitoring, and managing all resources in a WAP cloud.

Let's take an example. In a large-scale cloud provider scenario, tenants create and delete virtual machines in real time on a large scale, that is, hundreds of operations everyday. This cloud provider provides multiple capabilities and features on VMs hosted on the cloud as a value added to it; such capabilities include the following:

- Backup and disaster recovery
- Real-time monitoring
- Antivirus and anti-malware protection
- Automatic point in time state snapshots

Each VM provisioned by tenants needs to be configured in respective tools to enable the previous capabilities. And after each deletion of VMs by tenants, their respective configuration needs to be removed from backup, monitoring, and so on. Assume achieving this in a cloud having hundreds or more VM provisioning operations daily using traditional methods.

SMA can drastically simplify and automate these operations. Service providers can create SMA runbooks for the provisioning and removal of configurations. Runbooks can then be linked with VM create and delete operations which will automatically initiate execution of respective runbooks with specific VM parameters.

An overview of SMA

SMA was introduced with the System Center 2012 R2 product family and is included in the System Center Orchestrator installation media. It can be used as a standalone product as well as along with Windows Azure Pack.

SMA provides the automation engine for Microsoft's on-premises cloud infrastructure. It relies on Windows PowerShell workflows; that is, almost any tasks that can be performed via Windows PowerShell can be automated using SMA.

PowerShell workflows were introduced with the release of Windows PowerShell 3.0, and they contain traditional PowerShell cmdlets to execute tasks. Runbooks in SMA are authored in PowerShell workflows adding the following capabilities of PowerShell workflows:

- Checkpoint or suspend a workflow that is a runbook
- The parallel execution of PowerShell tasks on multiple systems

Natively, SMA does not provide any GUI to create, manage, or execute runbooks. Unlike System Center Orchestrator, all runbooks in SMA must be written in PowerShell workflows manually.

The Windows Azure Pack administrator portal integrates well with SMA and provides GUI for scheduling, executing, and performing other management operations on runbooks.

It must be noted that SMA functionality isn't available for tenants to create and manage their own runbooks.

> Microsoft Azure automation works on the same architecture as SMA and provides similar automation capabilities for customers using Microsoft Azure for hosting their IT resources.

The architecture of SMA

Similar to all other WAP cloud components, SMA is distributed across multiple components and provides the flexible architecture to achieve performance and eliminate a single point of failure. SMA involves the following components to function:

- The SMA web service
- The SMA runbook worker
- The database server
- The SMA PowerShell module (optional)

The SMA web service: The web service is the interface to SMA for all other administrative mediums. Windows Azure Pack uses the SMA web service to communicate with SMA and for other SMA tasks, such as executing a runbook or getting the status of a runbook.

It exposes a REST endpoint and OData API, which can be leveraged by WAP or any other custom developed portal for integration with SMA.

Automation and Authentication – Service Management Automation and ADFS

It is also responsible for authorization and distribution of runbook execution tasks to worker roles.

The SMA runbook worker: SMA runbooks' jobs are executed or processed by worker servers. A runbook worker server executes multiple runbooks in isolated environments, which are also known as sandboxes. This ensures that activities performed by one runbook don't affect the other runbook that is being executed by the same worker server.

The SMA database: SMA leverages the Microsoft SQL server database to store its configuration and runtime data. SMA database stores SMA runbooks, jobs, and other SMA-related objects' configurations and runtime data.

The SMA PowerShell module: This can be used to automate the automation; that is, it provides 40+ PowerShell cmdlet, which can be used by admins to automate the process of executing and managing runbooks. The PowerShell module also interacts with the SMA web service to perform SMA operations. This can be installed on the administrator's endpoint and can be used as an alternative to the WAP portal for SMA operations.

The following diagram illustrates the role and flow of SMA components with Windows Azure Pack:

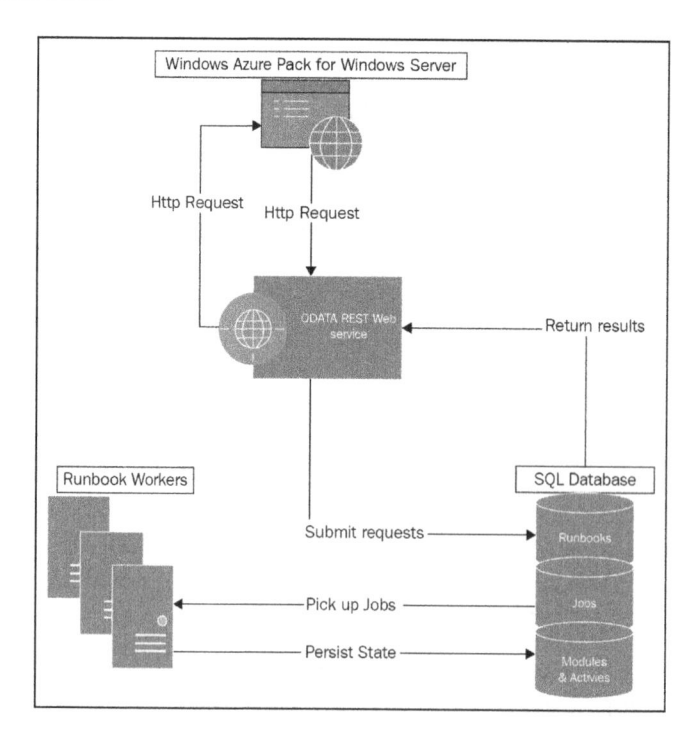

Planning the SMA infrastructure

SMA works on the distributed architecture to allow an easy and non-disruptive scale in and out of the operations. The following aspects must be taken into consideration while planning the infrastructure for SMA deployment:

- Planning for availability
- Planning for performance/capacity

Planning for availability

All the components of the SMA solution can be protected against a single point of failure by adding redundant servers. The following guidelines include the recommended configuration with respect to the availability of each role:

- **The SMA web service role**: This is recommended to deploy multiple web service roles (the minimum recommendation is two for high availability) and configure with a load balancer. Any administrative endpoint such as the WAP portal must point to the load balancer to communicate with the SMA web service.
- **The SMA worker role**: It is recommended to deploy multiple SMA worker roles (the minimum recommendation is two for high availability) to avoid any single point of failure. The SMA web service automatically distributes job tasks to different workers ensuring load balancing.
- **The SMA database**: It is recommended to protect SMA SQL database against any single point of failure using SQL availability techniques. SMA database is supported to run on the following:
    - Standalone SQL server
    - SQL server cluster
    - SQL Always on
- **Virtual machines for SMA servers**: Using virtual machines or hosting SMA servers adds another layer of protection against any hardware failure.

Planning for performance and capacity

The following factors should be taken into consideration while planning the SMA infrastructure sizing:

- The number of runbooks
- The size of runbooks (activities, variables, connections, and so on)
- The average run time of runbooks
- Remote calls being executed

There is no direct formula to calculate the sizing based on the previous factors. The following guidelines can be helpful in sizing SMA servers:

- **The SMA web service**: SMA web service is stateless; that is, it can be scaled in and out easily with increased compute and additional servers along with a load balancer. Web services are responsible for communicating with administrative consoles, such as WAP, and worker roles to assign runbook jobs. High resource utilization and requirements are unlikely for the SMA web service unless a large number of users start initiating the SMA execution process simultaneously. Two CPU cores and 4 GB of RAM (minimum), 8 GB (recommended) are good compute configurations to start with.

- **The SMA worker**: SMA worker hosts a sandbox to execute runbook jobs that aren't stateless as web services. Each sandbox can handle 30 concurrent jobs, and a worker can host a maximum of four sandboxes by default. This comes as 120 concurrent jobs per worker server. The standard SMA server's hardware recommends two CPU cores and 4 GB of RAM (minimum), but 8 GB is recommended. This can likely handle these efficiently. Worker roles can then be scaled out as per usage and requirement.

- **The SMA database**: There can only be one database as per the SMA deployment; hence, it is recommended to use a dedicated instance for the SMA database in the production environment, ensuring that it gets the required compute resources. Microsoft recommends using SQL servers for SMA databases with a minimum 8 GB of RAM and 8 cores in terms of compute. For storage as per Microsoft guidelines, 1 month of data with 12 jobs per minute requires 20 GB of disk space. Along with this, it is recommended to follow standard Microsoft SQL Server performance and capacity guidelines. See `https://technet.microsoft.com/en-us/sqlserver/bb671430.aspx` to learn about SQL server best practices.

Installing and configuring SMA

SMA installation binaries are located inside System Center Orchestrator Media and follows similar installation instructions as per other system center products.

SMA installation prerequisites

The SMA installation prerequisites can be divided in three categories:

- Software components prerequisites
- AD accounts prerequisites
- SSL certificate prerequisites

Windows Server 2012 R2 is the minimum OS version supported for SMA installation. Apart from this, the following software components must be installed before starting the SMA installation as SMA installer doesn't automatically install prerequisite components.

Software prerequisite for installing the SMA web service are as follows:

- **Internet Information Services (IIS)** 7.5 or higher
- IIS basic authentication
- IIS Windows authentication
- IIS URL authorization
- ASP.NET 4.5
- .NET Framework 3.5 (for the setup program)
- .NET Framework 4.5
- WCF HTTP activation
- SQL Server 2012 DB connectivity

> To install .NET 3.5 on Windows Server 2012/R2 using Server Manager's **Add Feature** wizard, alternate source locations must be specified during the installation, and it needs to be pointed to the `sxs` folder under sources in the Windows installation media.

Software prerequisites to install the SMA worker role—Windows PowerShell 4.0 (this is included by default with Windows Server 2012 R2):

- **Active Directory Accounts**: It is recommended to create separate dedicated accounts and groups for running following services in SMA deployment. The following table lists the accounts required for deploying SMA components:

Sample account/group name	Account usage	Remarks
SMA pool	SMA Application Pool Admin Group	A member of Local Administrators
SMA poolsvc	SMA Pool Web Service Account	A member of Local Administrators
SMA workersvc	SMA Worker Service Account	A member of Local Administrators

- **SSL certificate**: It is recommended to use an internal CA issued SSL certificate for the SMA web service instead of the automatically generated self-signed certificate. This certificate must be trusted by the SPF server.

Installing the SMA web service, runbook worker, and PowerShell module

For the purpose of evaluation in this book, we will be installing all three components on a single server. The following steps are required to install the SMA web service:

1. Log into the server designated for installing the SMA web service.
2. Start `SetupOrchestrator.exe` from System Center Orchestrator Media.
3. Click on **Web Service** on the **Install** page under **Service Management**.

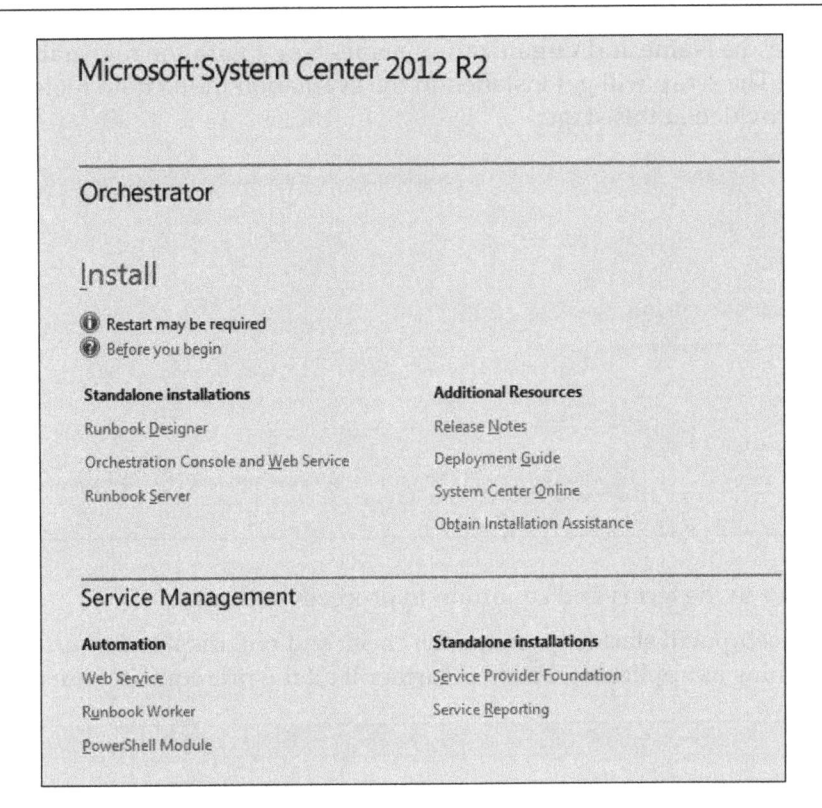

4. Click on **Install** to proceed.

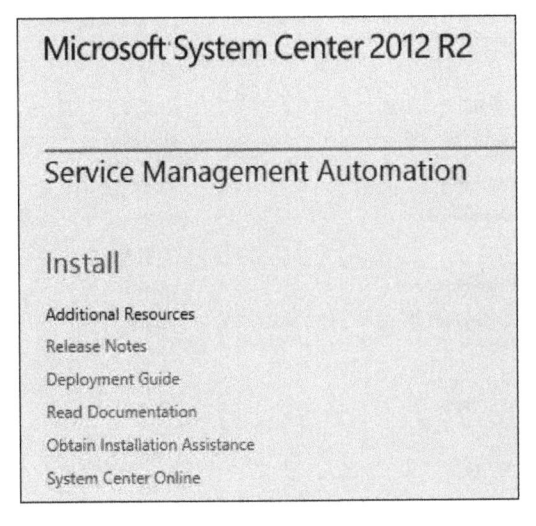

5. Enter the **Name** and **Organization** names along with the registration key if any. The setup will get installed in the evaluation mode if no registration key is provided at this stage:

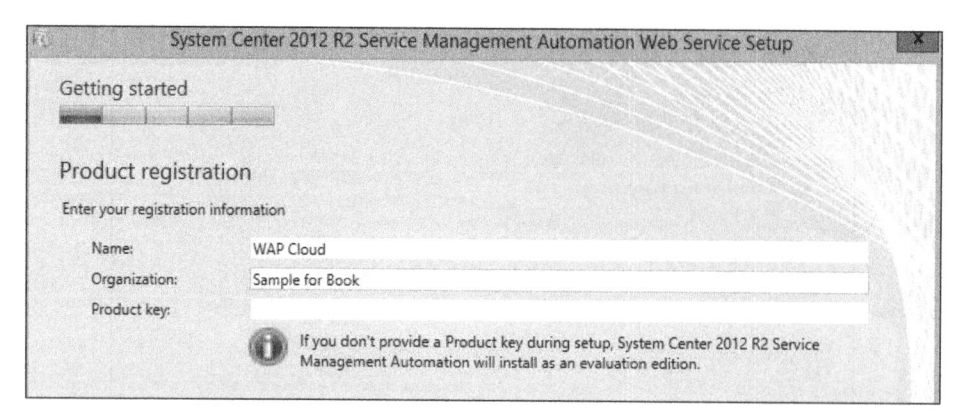

6. Agree to the terms and condition to proceed further.
7. The setup will start its prerequisite check and will display any error or warning as applicable. Proceed further if all the prerequisites are met:

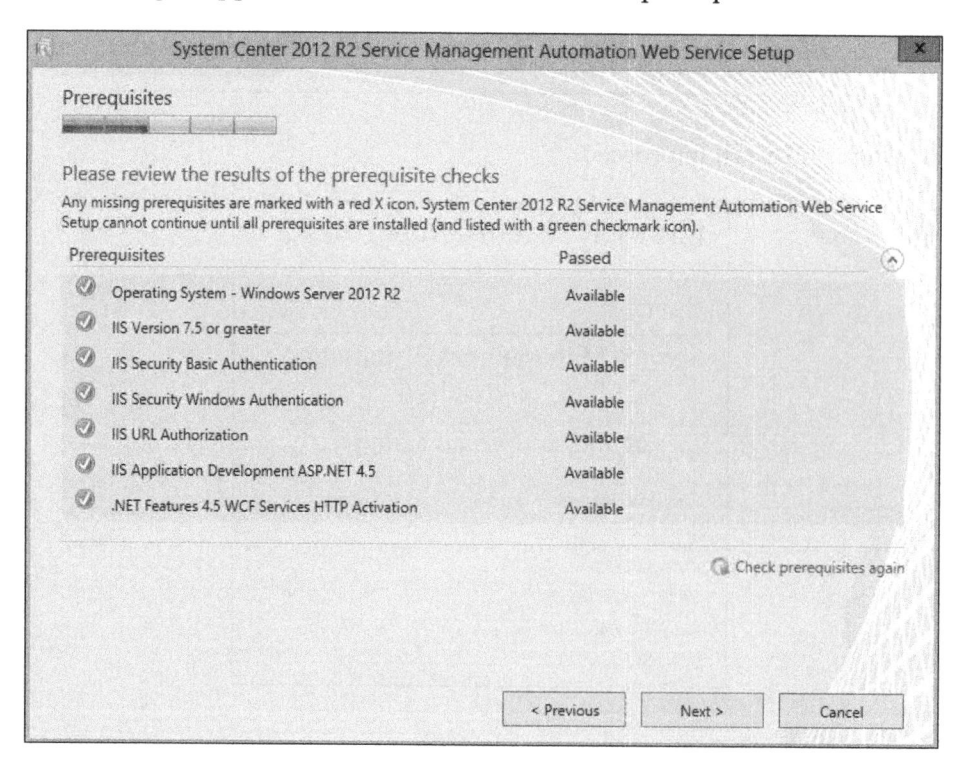

Chapter 9

8. Enter the database server connection information including the server name, port, database name, and credentials. Both Windows and SQL authentication can be used:

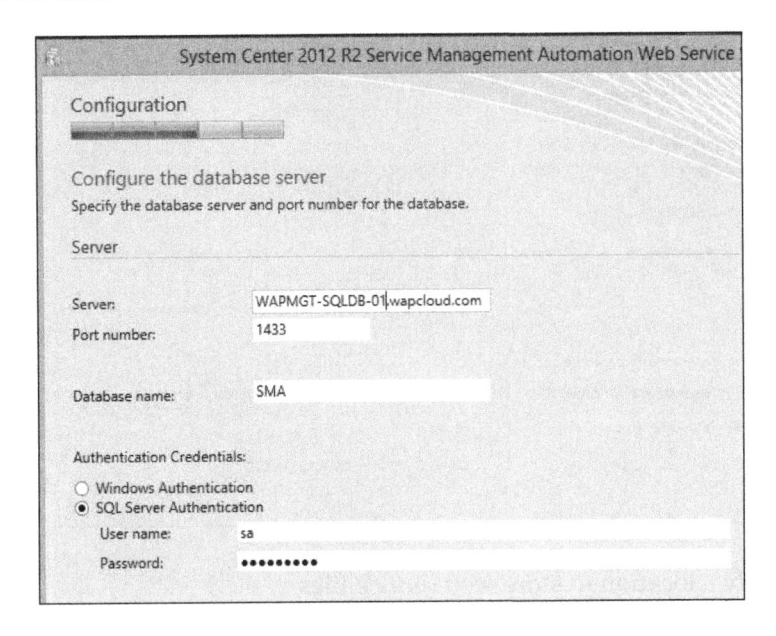

9. Specify security groups or users and credentials to run the web service application pool:

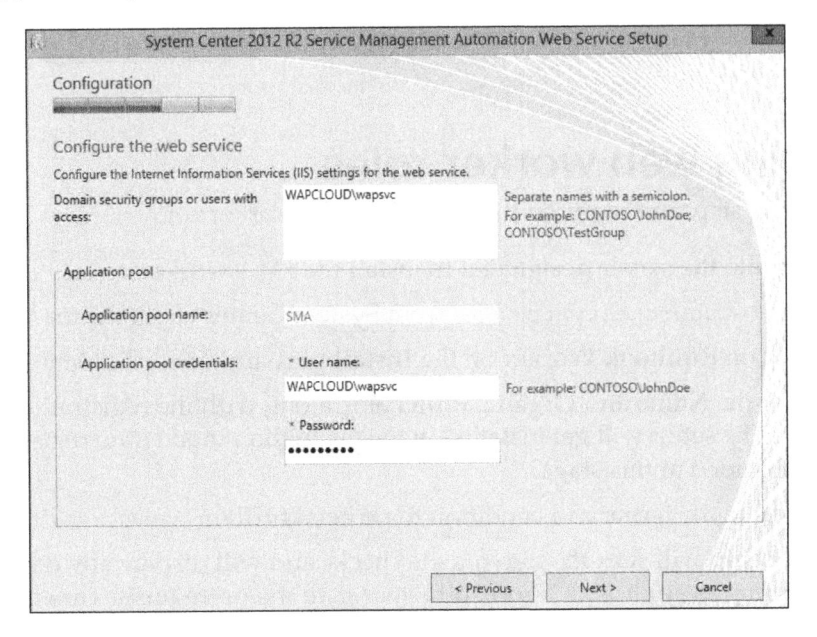

10. Specify the web service port and SSL certificate to use. The setup can also generate a self-signed certificate to use in test environments:

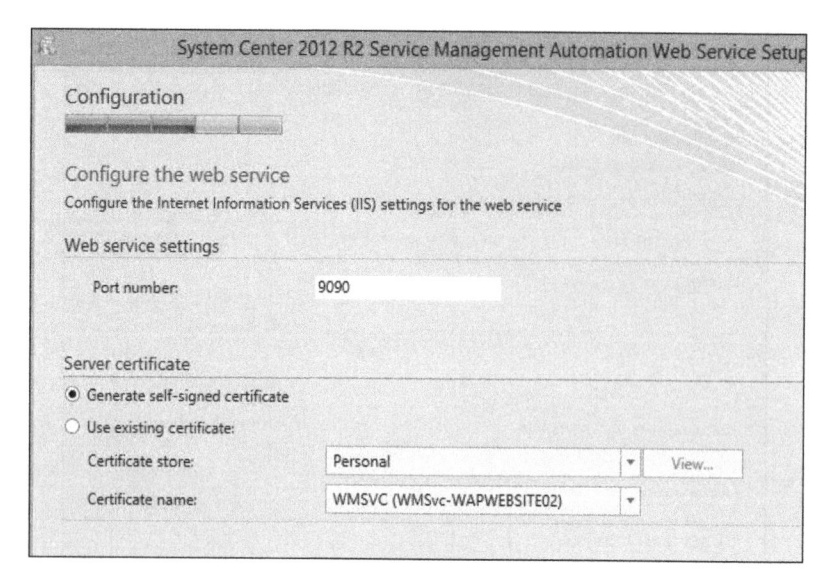

11. Specify a location to store web service files.
12. Specify choices for **CEIP** (**Customer Experience Improvement Program**) and Microsoft update.
13. Review the settings and click on **Install** to start the installation.
14. Click **Close** on the successful completion; the SMA web service is now installed.

Installing web worker roles

The following steps are required to install the SMA worker role:

1. Log into the server designated to install the SMA worker.
2. Start `SetupOrchestrator.Exe` from System Center Orchestrator Media.
3. Click on **Runbook Worker** on the **Install** page under Service Management.
4. Enter the **Name** and **Organization** name along with the registration key if any. The setup will get installed in the evaluation mode if no registration key is provided at this stage.
5. Agree to the terms and condition to proceed further.
6. The setup will start its prerequisite checks and will display any error or warning as applicable. Proceed further if all the prerequisites are met.

7. Enter the database server connection information including the server name, port, the database name, and credentials. Both Windows and SQL authentication can be used.
8. Specify the service account for running the SMA worker service:

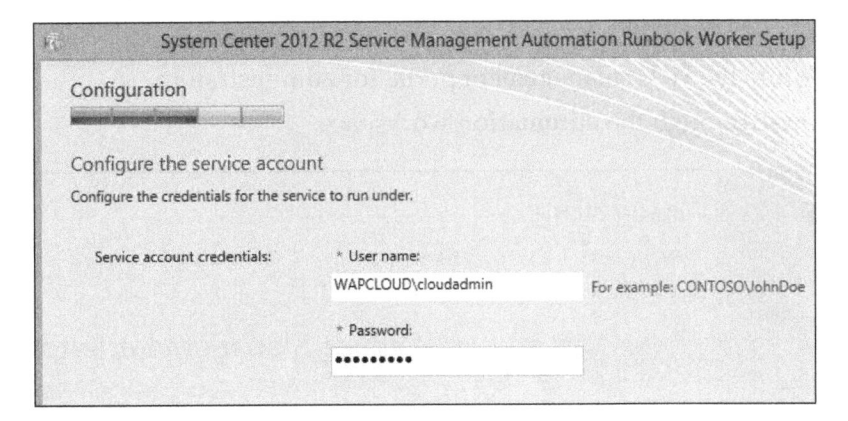

9. Specify a location to store worker files.
10. Specify choices for CEIP.
11. Review the setting and click on **Install** to start the installation.
12. Click on **close** upon successful completion. The SMA runbook worker is now installed.

The SMA PowerShell module can be installed in a similar manner on administrative endpoints.

Post installation tasks

Ensure to complete the following tasks to have a working SMA deployment for the WAP integration:

- Replace the self-signed certificate for SMA web services with trusted SSL in production environments.
- Verify the **SPF (Service Provider Foundation)** server trust the SSL certificate presented by SMA web service.

Integrating SMA with Windows Azure Pack

The following steps are required to integrate SMA with Windows Azure Pack by registering SMA endpoints:

1. Log into the WAP management portal for administrators.
2. Browse through the **automation** workspace:

3. Click on **Register the Service Management Automation Endpoint**.
4. Enter the SMA endpoint details along with some credentials:

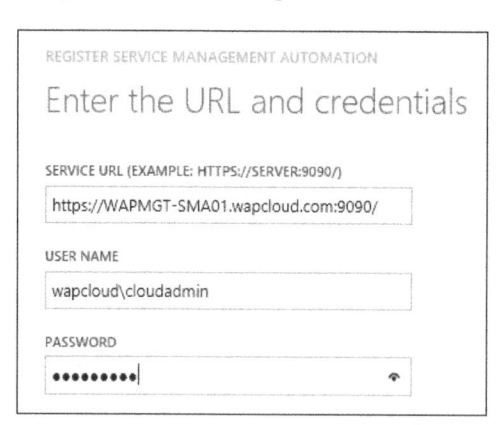

5. The SMA endpoint will be visible in the WAP portal upon a successful registration.

6. The **automation** workspace under the WAP portal can now be used for all operations related to SMA. The **DASHBOARD** page displays statuses and statistics about runbooks and jobs throughout the cloud. Similar dashboards can also be accessed per runbook:

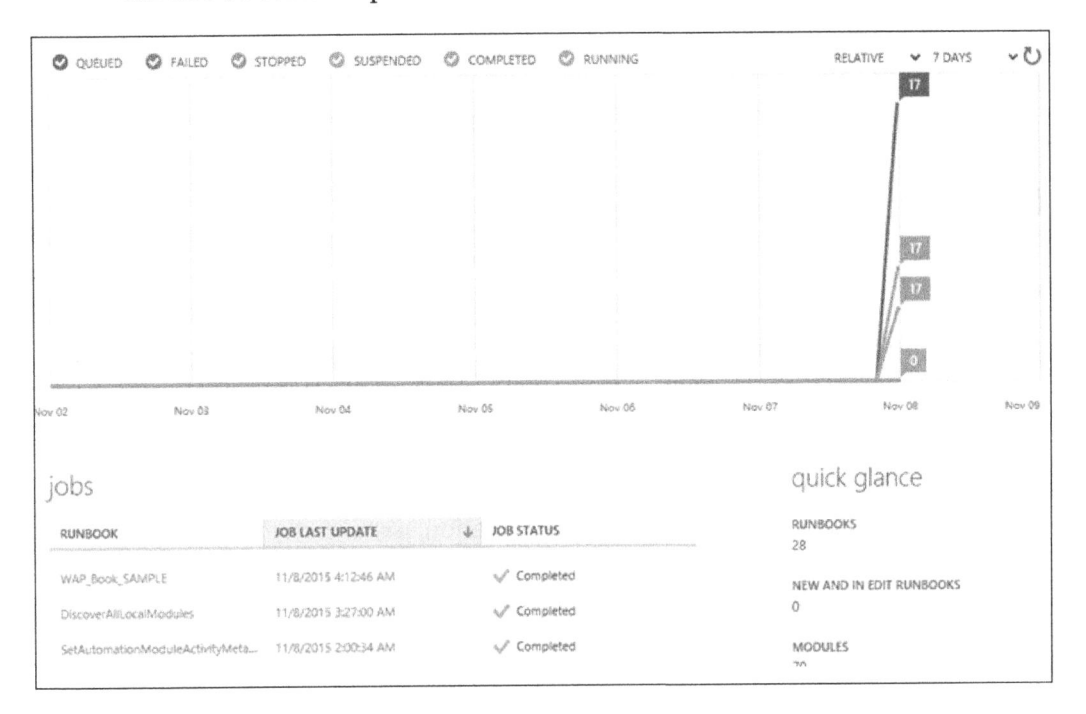

Dealing with SMA assets

Assets in a SMA-based automation solution for WAP provide global configurations and parameters that can be leveraged by runbooks. For example, it is very likely that any runbook being executed for VM cloud's operations may require VMM server connection info and credentials. In large environments having hundreds of runbooks, instead of defining VMM server connection information and credentials per runbook, these can be declared as assets and can be leveraged by all runbooks.

Declaring such variables at global level in asset also helps in handling changes at a later stage in a very smooth manner.

Assets in Windows Azure Pack automation include the following:

- Connections
- Credentials
- Variables
- Schedules
- Modules

Asset types and functionalities

The following are the types of assets and their functionalities:

- **Connections**: Connections include connectivity details and authorized credentials for common services used by runbooks. Examples include services such as SCVMM, Azure, or any other available services.
- **Credentials**: Credentials in WAP automation assets can be compared to Run As accounts in SCVMM. Credentials contain a username and password for accounts leveraged by runbooks for accessing, modifying, and managing resources across the cloud. WAP automation assets can store two types of credentials:
    - Windows PowerShell credentials
    - SSL certificates credentials

    Service providers can add multiple credentials depending upon the permission and usage required by runbooks.

- **Variables**: As implied by its name, variables can be used to store key values used by runbooks. Variables can be defined in the following format:
    - String
    - Integer
    - Boolean
    - Date time

    Variables having confidential values such as password can be encrypted for security.

- **Schedules**: This can be used to create a regular schedule for any runbook to execute; for example, a schedule can be created, which will initiate a runbook everyday at some specific time to collect statics data.

- **Modules**: This contains PowerShell modules, which can be used by runbooks to execute specific PowerShell cmdlets. Modules can be compared with integration packs in System Center Orchestrator.

  Modules help in managing all PowerShell modules in a central point without requiring installation at each worker role.

Adding and managing assets

The **ASSETS** tab under the automation workspace in the WAP management portal provides options to add or remove assets.

The following steps are required to add, delete, and modify assets:

1. Log into the WAP management portal for administrators.
2. Browse the **automation** workspace and the **ASSETS** tab.
3. By default, all the standard PowerShell modules are included in the WAP portal. Any additional module can be imported. Any existing module can be deleted by buttons available in the bottom pane:

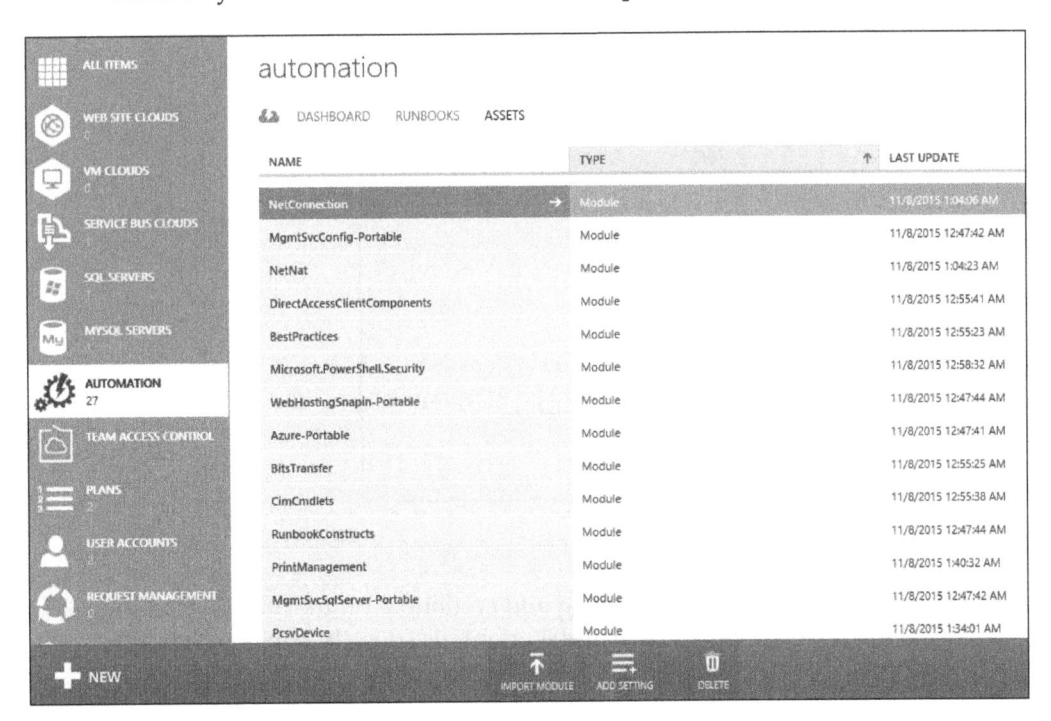

Automation and Authentication – Service Management Automation and ADFS

4. Click on **ADD SETTING** to add a new asset:

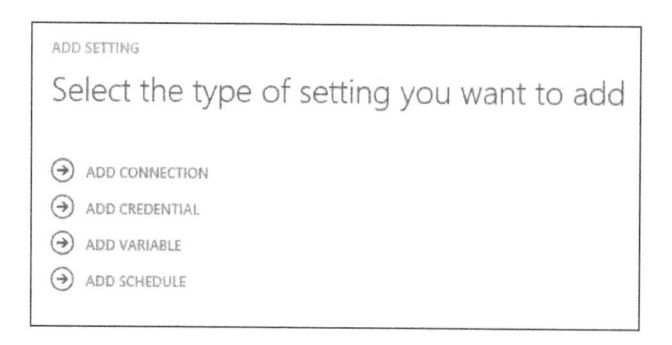

   ADD SETTING
   Select the type of setting you want to add
   → ADD CONNECTION
   → ADD CREDENTIAL
   → ADD VARIABLE
   → ADD SCHEDULE

5. Select the type of asset to be added and proceed further.
6. To create a connection asset, select a connection and provide connection details including connection type, name, hostname and credentials. By default, WAP supports the following connection types:

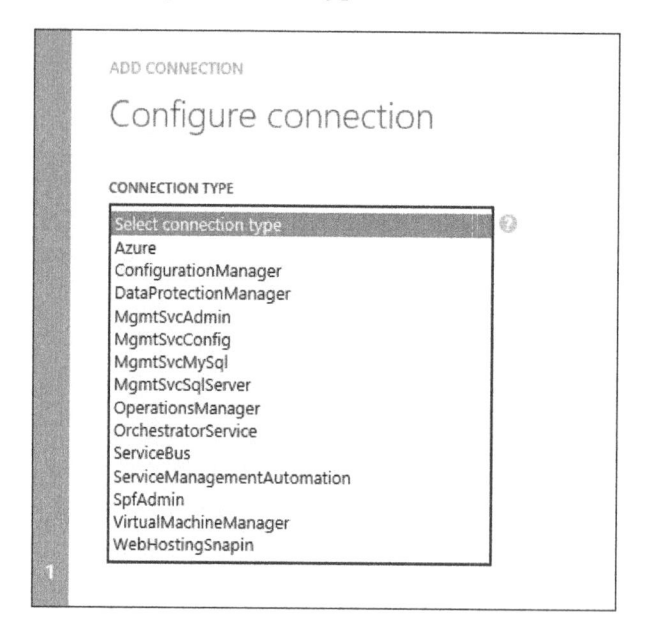

   ADD CONNECTION
   Configure connection

   CONNECTION TYPE
   Select connection type
   Azure
   ConfigurationManager
   DataProtectionManager
   MgmtSvcAdmin
   MgmtSvcConfig
   MgmtSvcMySql
   MgmtSvcSqlServer
   OperationsManager
   OrchestratorService
   ServiceBus
   ServiceManagementAutomation
   SpfAdmin
   VirtualMachineManager
   WebHostingSnapin

7. Add any credentials by selecting add credential on the add service page. Provide the credentials type and credentials friendly name and a username, password, or the SSL certificate as applicable:

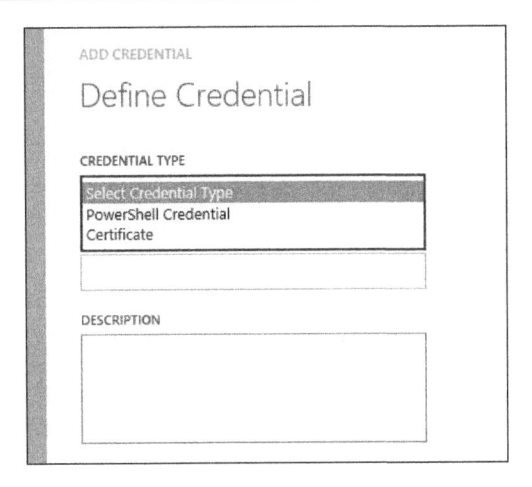

8. Add any variable by selecting add variable on the add service page provide the variable type, variable name, and value with an optional encryption:

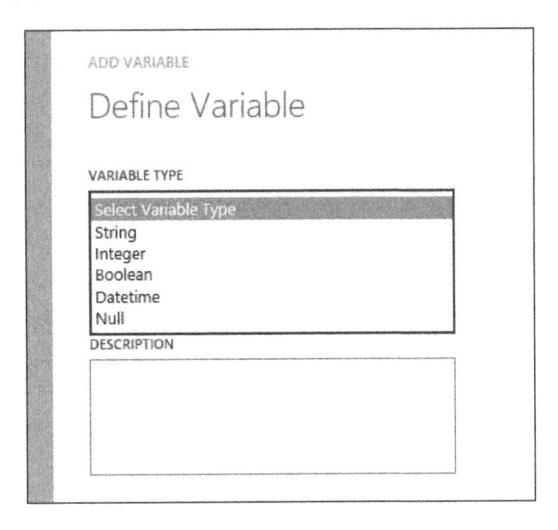

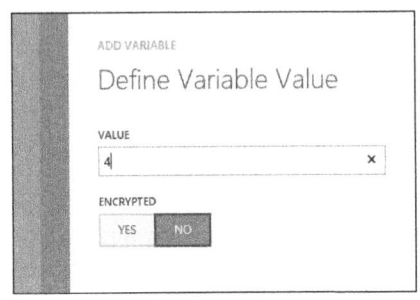

9. Add any schedule by selecting add schedule on the add service page. Provide a schedule name and schedule values including a type (one time or daily) and start time:

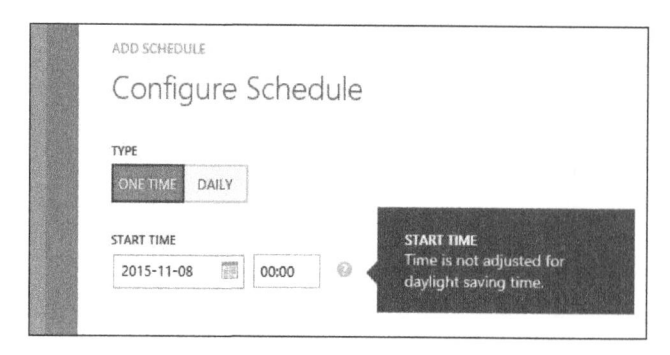

10. The created assets will now be visible in the **ASSETS** tab. They are ready for usage by the runbooks.

11. Clicking on any asset will display its configurations; for example, clicking on a module will display the module information along with PowerShell cmdlets. It will show the following screenshot:

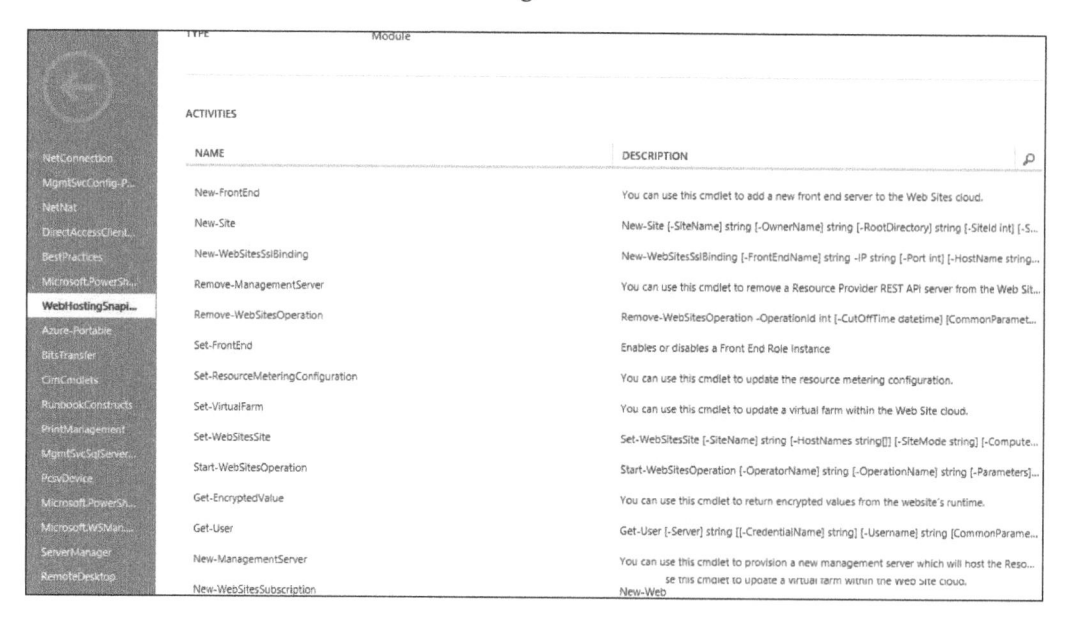

Additional assets can be created in a similar manner.

Dealing with SMA runbooks

SMA runbooks consist of PowerShell workflows, which include PowerShell cmdlets to perform specified tasks in an automated manner.

The Runbooks can be managed from the **RUNBOOKS** tab under the **automation** workspace WAP portal. Service providers can write PowerShell workflows and runbooks anywhere, and then import them in the WAP SMA.

The **RUNBOOKS** tab in the **automation** workspace provides functionality to perform the following basic operations on runbooks:

- Start the execution of any runbook
- Import a runbook to WAP (PS1 file)
- Export any existing runbook to the PS1 file on a local system
- Delete any existing runbook from WAP

Note that there is no GUI (drag and drop item) available for authoring runbooks such as System Center Orchestrator (SCO); it must be written manually in PowerShell workflows.

Sample runbooks

Windows Azure Pack along with SMA by default provides a few samples of runbooks that can be used and leveraged as a reference to author new runbooks.

The following steps outline the process to view and manage sample runbooks:

1. Log into the WAP management portal for administrators.
2. Browse the **automation** workspace and the **RUNBOOKS** tab.

Automation and Authentication – Service Management Automation and ADFS

3. Sample runbooks will be displayed. Click on any sample runbook to see its workflows and other configurations.

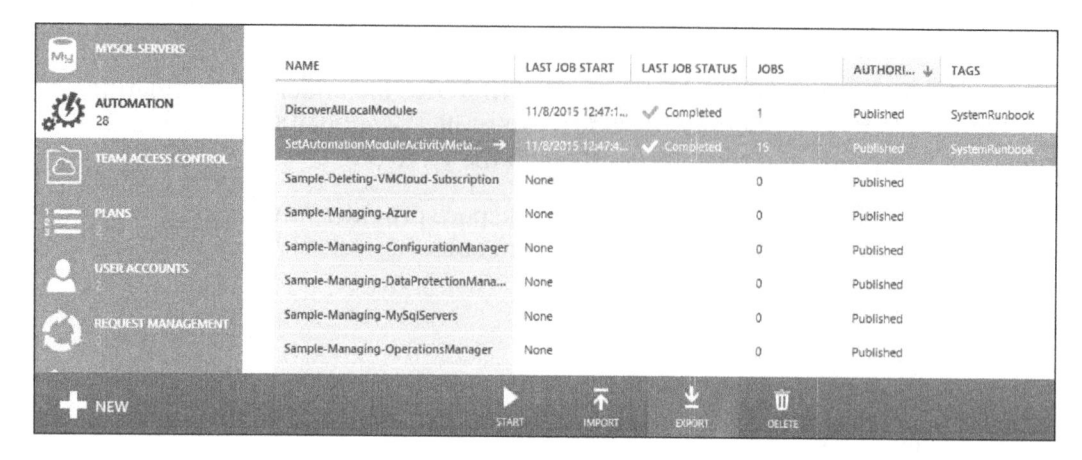

4. Any runbook can be started, imported, exported, and deleted using the buttons available in the bottom pane.

Creating a runbook

The following steps are required to create a runbook:

1. Log into the WAP management portal for administrators.
2. Browse the **automation** workspace and the **RUNBOOKS** tab.
3. Click on the **NEW** button, select **RUNBOOK** and **QUICK CREATE**:

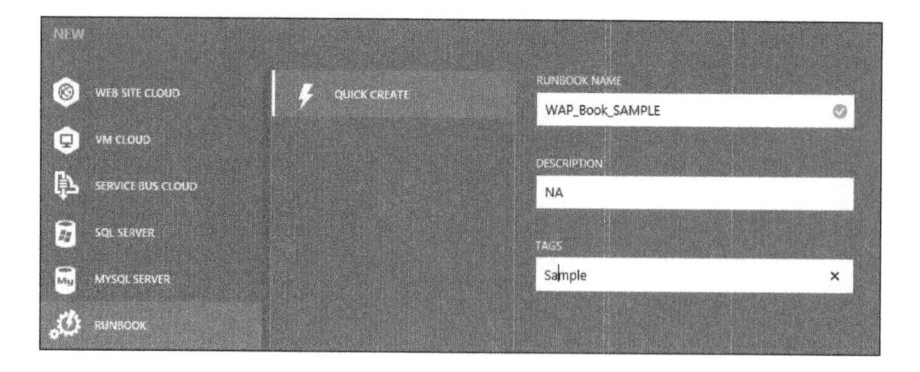

4. The newly created runbook will now be listed under the **RUNBOOKS** tab.
5. Click on **RUNBOOK NAME** to perform additional operations on the runbook including authoring and scheduling.

Authoring a runbook

Authoring a runbook involves writing PowerShell workflows for the runbook and managing runbook versions and modifications throughout the lifecycle.

Multiple tools can be leveraged by service providers to author a runbook:

- Windows PowerShell ISE
- Visual Studio IDE
- Windows Azure Pack management portal
- Any other source control or programming tool

While authoring runbooks in the Windows Azure Pack administrator portal, it can either be in the draft or published version. A published version is used by worker servers to execute the workload while initiating a runbook.

The following outlines the steps required to author a runbook in the Windows Azure Pack portal:

First, create runbook by following instructions given in the previous topic.

1. Select the newly created runbook and browse the **AUTHOR** workspace.
2. Click on **DRAFT**, and then the workflow writer will be available:

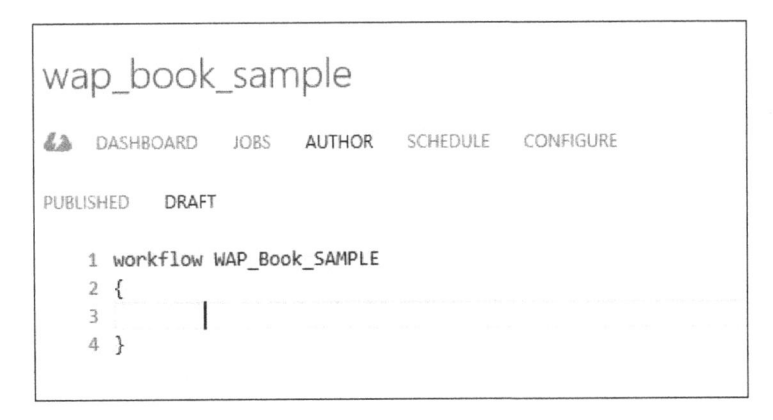

```
wap_book_sample

   DASHBOARD   JOBS   AUTHOR   SCHEDULE   CONFIGURE

PUBLISHED    DRAFT

   1 workflow WAP_Book_SAMPLE
   2 {
   3     |
   4 }
```

3. Follow the standard Microsoft PowerShell workflow writing guidelines to write the workflow for the runbook. See Microsoft documentation at https://azure.microsoft.com/en-in/documentation/articles/automation-powershell-workflow/ to learn more about writing PowerShell workflows.

4. The bottom pane buttons can be leveraged to add additional functionality into the runbook, such as adding another runbook (nesting) or adding any activity or assets.

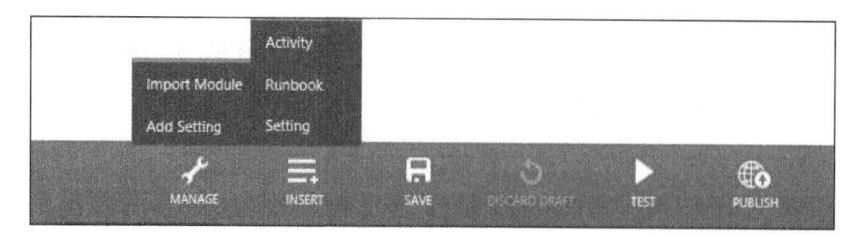

5. Clicking on **SAVE** will save the current version of the draft. Publishing will make this draft available for execution by SMA workers.

Using assets in runbook PowerShell workflows

SMA assets declared at global level can be used inside workflows by the following syntax:

- **Connection**: The following shows an example where connection declared in assets is being accessed in the PowerShell workflow:

  ```
  $SCVMMConnection = Get-AutomationConnection -Name "SCVMVMMConnection"
  $SCVMMServer = $SCVMMConnection.ComputerName
  $SCVMMUser = $SCVMMConnection.Username
  $SCVMMPassword = $SCVMMConnection.Password
  ```

- **Credentials**: The following PowerShell shows an example where credentials declared in assets are being accessed in the PowerShell workflow:

  ```
  $AccessCred = Get-AutomationPSCredential -Name "SampleCred"
  ```

- **Variable**: The following PowerShell shows an example where a variable declared in assets is being accessed in the PowerShell workflow:

  ```
  $ABCVar = Get-AutomationVariable -Name "SampleVAR"
  ```

Scheduling a runbook

Scheduling a runbook will automatically start executing the runbook as per the configured date, time, and frequency value. Schedules configured in assets can be attached with runbooks; custom schedules can also be created.

The following steps are required to author a runbook:

1. Select the runbook to be scheduled in the WAP portal and browse the **SCHEDULE** tab:

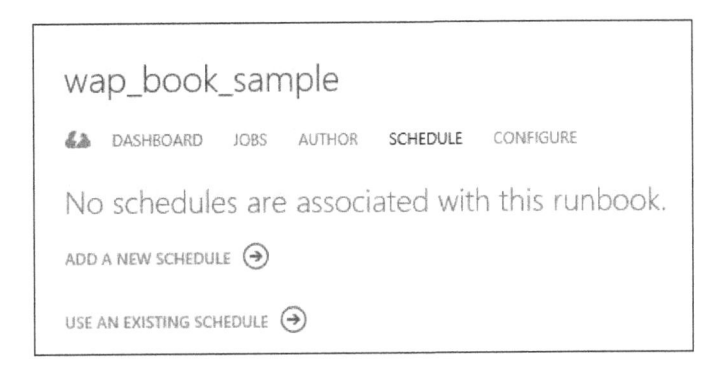

   ```
   wap_book_sample

   DASHBOARD   JOBS   AUTHOR   SCHEDULE   CONFIGURE

   No schedules are associated with this runbook.

   ADD A NEW SCHEDULE →

   USE AN EXISTING SCHEDULE →
   ```

2. Click on an existing schedule to the leverage schedule created in global assets. Click on **ADD A NEW SCHEDULE** to add a new schedule for this runbook.
3. Provide a schedule name and type (one time/daily) along with date and time to configure a new schedule.
4. Click on **Finish** to save the schedule configured for the runbook.

Dealing with jobs

Whenever a runbook execution is started, a corresponding job is created and assigned to a worker role for execution. The worker role stores jobs during runtime in a sandbox.

Using the Windows Azure pack portal **automation** workspace, we can see the status of jobs in real time and for historical data. Jobs can also be stopped, suspended, and resumed.

The following outlines the steps for viewing and dealing with runbooks:

1. The **RUNBOOKS** tab under the **automation** workspace displays the status for all runbooks in the WAP cloud:

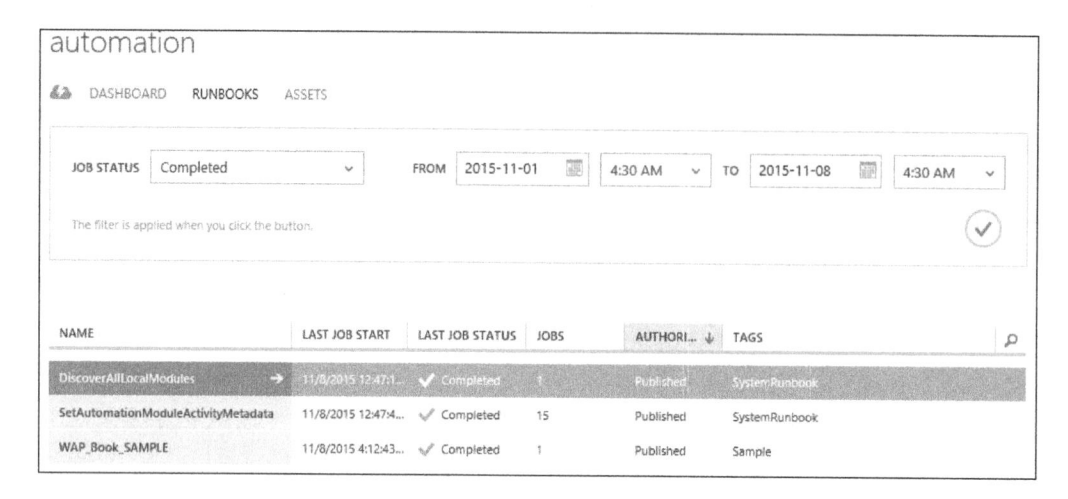

NAME	LAST JOB START	LAST JOB STATUS	JOBS	AUTHORI...	TAGS
DiscoverAllLocalModules	11/8/2015 12:47:1...	Completed	1	Published	SystemRunbook
SetAutomationModuleActivityMetadata	11/8/2015 12:47:4...	Completed	15	Published	SystemRunbook
WAP_Book_SAMPLE	11/8/2015 4:12:43...	Completed	1	Published	Sample

2. A job status per runbook can be accessed under the **JOBS** tab for each runbook page. Select the job status and timelines to see jobs status as per selected parameters.

Configuring the runbook logging

Windows Azure Pack provides multiple choices to cloud administrators for configuring logging levels and types for a runbook. Administrators can choose to enable or disable the following level of logging per runbook:

- Log Debug Records
- Log Verbose Records
- Log Progress Records

The following steps are required to configure logging options for a runbook:

1. Select the runbook and browse the configure tab.
2. Scroll down to the logging space and configure settings as per requirement; click on **SAVE** to save the changed configurations:

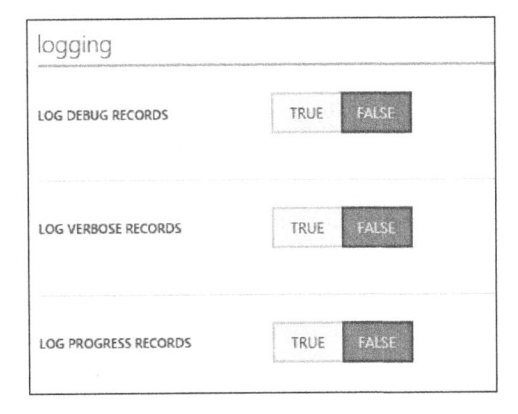

Linking runbooks with VM cloud actions

Linking runbooks with VM cloud operations enable executing a specified runbook only when a specific event or action occurs. Linking a runbook with actions helps in getting the required operations performed on objects as soon the objects gets created instead of waiting until the next runbook schedule.

The following steps are required to link the runbook with an action in VM clouds:

1. Log into the WAP portal for administrators and browse the **vm clouds** workspace.
2. Select the **AUTOMATION** tab:

3. Click on **LINK AN ACTION WITH A RUNBOOK**.

   WAP automation supports the following objects of VM clouds to link a runbook on the specific action:

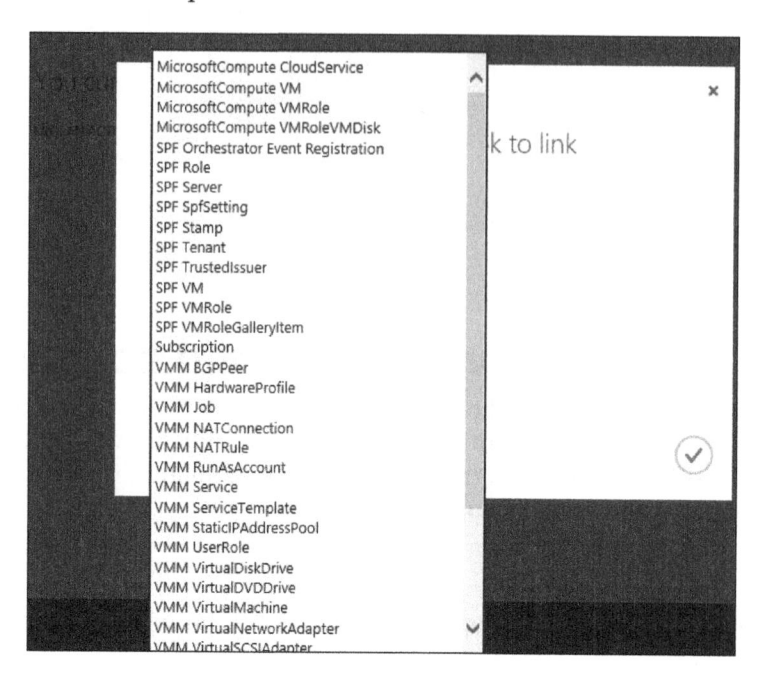

   ```
   MicrosoftCompute CloudService
   MicrosoftCompute VM
   MicrosoftCompute VMRole
   MicrosoftCompute VMRoleVMDisk
   SPF Orchestrator Event Registration
   SPF Role
   SPF Server
   SPF SpfSetting
   SPF Stamp
   SPF Tenant
   SPF TrustedIssuer
   SPF VM
   SPF VMRole
   SPF VMRoleGalleryItem
   Subscription
   VMM BGPPeer
   VMM HardwareProfile
   VMM Job
   VMM NATConnection
   VMM NATRule
   VMM RunAsAccount
   VMM Service
   VMM ServiceTemplate
   VMM StaticIPAddressPool
   VMM UserRole
   VMM VirtualDiskDrive
   VMM VirtualDVDDrive
   VMM VirtualMachine
   VMM VirtualNetworkAdapter
   VMM VirtualSCSIAdapter
   ```

4. Select **OBJECT**, **ACTION** and **RUNBOOK** to configure:

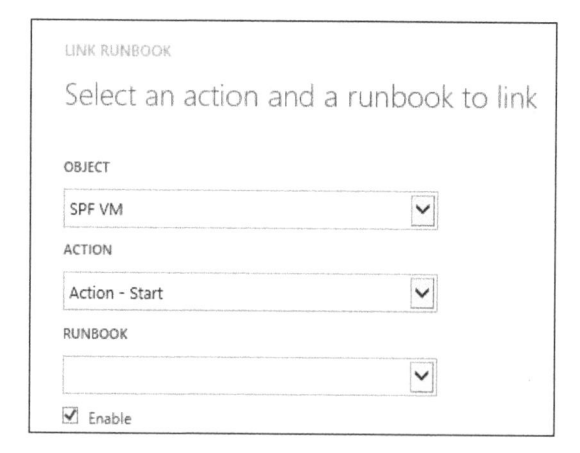

   LINK RUNBOOK

   Select an action and a runbook to link

   OBJECT

   SPF VM

   ACTION

   Action - Start

   RUNBOOK

   ☑ Enable

5. **Click** on **finish** to link the runbook with the selected action.

Enabling ADFS authentication for WAP portals

Windows Azure Pack standard installation includes authentication sites for both admin and tenant portals to leverage their default authentication mechanisms. Active directory provides authentication services worldwide. We can leverage AD features and capabilities by enabling our WAP portals to use ADFS for authentication.

This can enable service providers to authenticate tenant users against the tenant's own active directory hosted inside their on-premises infrastructure.

ADFS authentication architecture and overview – admin and tenant portals

By default, Windows Azure Pack portals are configured to use the following authentication mechanisms.

- The WAP management portal for administrators: Windows authentication
- The WAP management portal for tenants – ASP.NET provider

Active Directory Federations Services are used to simplify login and enable true SSO (single sign on) capabilities across the applications and services hosted anywhere (on-premises/public clouds). Using ADFS for authentication in Windows Azure Pack, cloud providers can secure and simplify authentication mechanisms for admins portals. For tenant portals, it will help in enabling single sign on for tenant users, leveraging a tenant's own active directory for authentication. The following diagram explains the authentication architecture for Windows Azure Pack with ADFS:

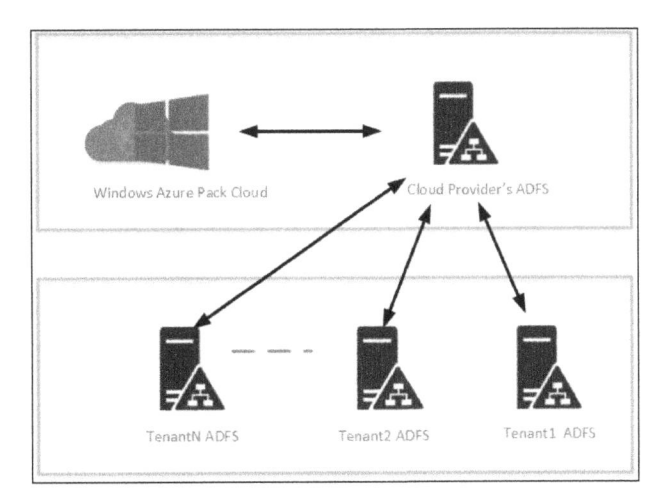

Implementing ADFS for the Windows Azure Pack cloud involves the following steps:

- Setting up ADFS farms (both cloud provides and tenants)
- Adding the tenant's ADFS as a claim provider to the cloud provider's ADFS
- Adding cloud provider's ADFS as a relying party to tenant's ADFS
- Adding the WAP portal (tenant/admin) as a relying party to the cloud provider's ADFS
- Adding the cloud provider's ADFS as a claim provider to the WAP tenant portal
- Testing and verifying the configuration

Setting up ADFS farms and configuring relationship between a provider's and tenant's ADFS service isn't covered in this book. See Microsoft ADFS documentation at `https://technet.microsoft.com/en-in/windowsserver/dd448613.aspx` to know more about ADFS.

Adding the WAP portal as a relying party

The following steps are required to add WAP portals as a relying party to the cloud provider's ADFS service. See *Chapter 3, Installing and Configuring Windows Azure Pack*, to learn more about the Windows Azure Pack architecture and role of these components:

1. Log into the ADFS server and open the ADFS console from the server manager.
2. Click on the **Add** relaying party trust.
3. Provide the federation metadata URL of the WAP server in the given format, that is, `https://manage.wapcloud.com/federationmetadata/2007-06/federationmetadata.xml`:

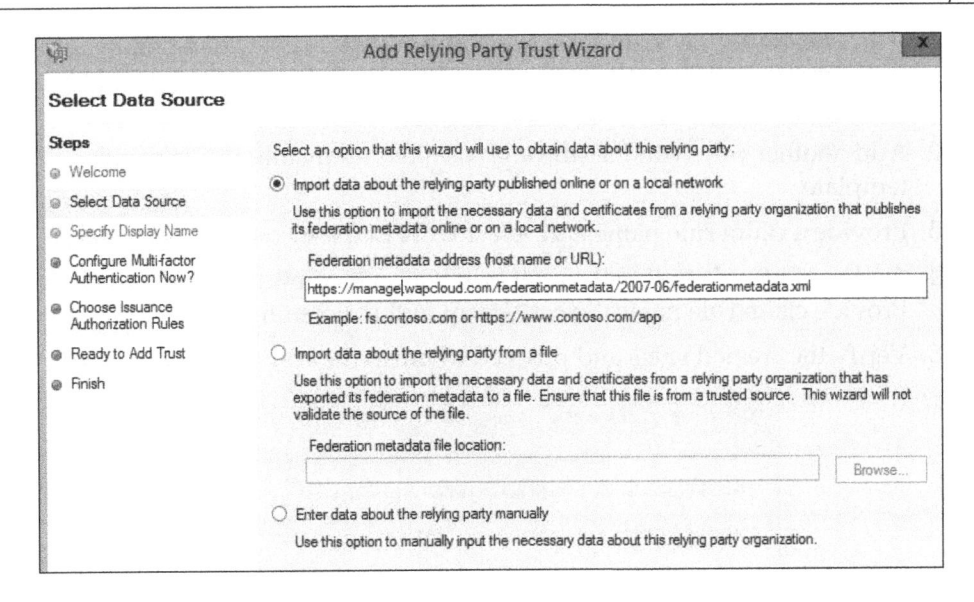

4. Specify **Display Name** and optional note.
5. Enable or disable the multi-factor authentication as per the service provider's decision.
6. Select **Permit** to allow all users to access this relying party.
7. On the **Finish** page, select the checkbox for **Edit claims rules**.
8. Add the rule with the setting called **Send LDAP Attributes as Claims**.
9. Provide a claim rule name and select **Active Directory** as **Attribute store**.
10. Map the User-Principal-Name LDAP attribute to the UPN called **Outgoing claim type**.

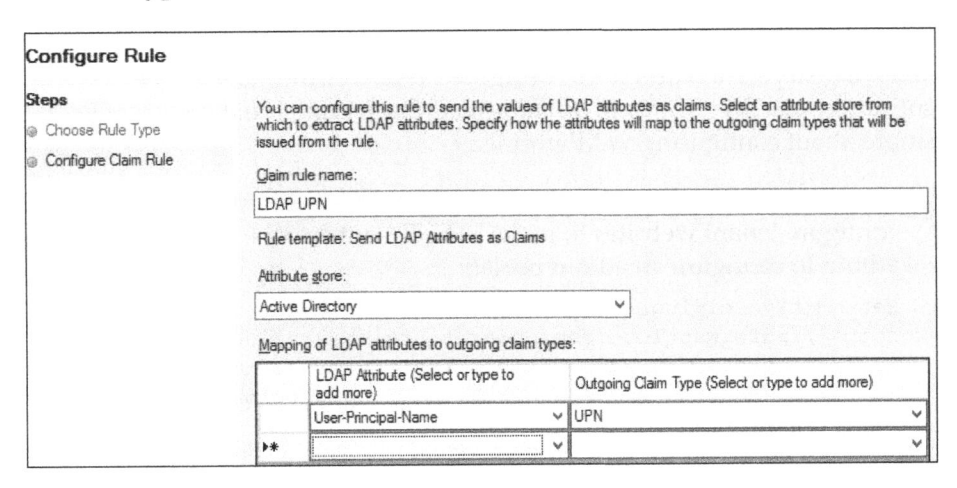

11. Add one more rule with the same configuration except changing the binding by mapping MapToken-Groups — Qualified by the domain name LDAP attribute to the group Outgoing claim type.
12. Add another rule with Passthrough or Filter an Incoming Claim rule template.
13. Provide a claim rule name and select **UPN** in the incoming claim type.
14. Add another rule to Passthrough or Filter an Incoming Claim template with Provide claim rule name. Select **Group** in the incoming claim type.
15. Verify the created rules and proceed to finish the configuration wizard.

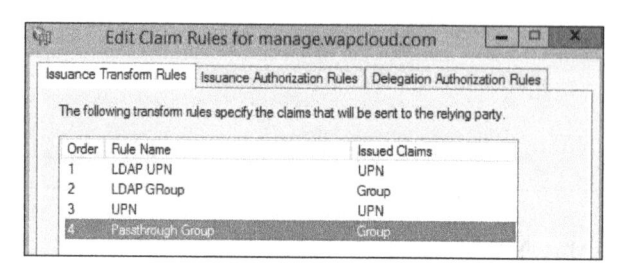

Order	Rule Name	Issued Claims
1	LDAP UPN	UPN
2	LDAP GRoup	Group
3	UPN	UPN
4	Passthrough Group	Group

Post this run to finish ADFS configurations along with the WAP website identifier:

```
Set-AdfsRelyingPartyTrust -TargetIdentifier'http://azureservices/
TenantSite'-EnableJWT $true
```

To get the identifier, run the following PowerShell. Provide the WAP portal party name in cmdlet:

```
Get-AdfsRelyingPartyTrust -Name "Party Name"
```

Configuring WAP websites to use ADFS

The following steps are required to configure WAP websites to use ADFS as the authentication site. See *Chapter 3, Installing and Configuring Windows Azure Pack*, to learn more about configuring WAP portals:

1. Execute the following PowerShell on the Windows Azure Pack server to configure tenant websites to use ADFS. Tenants can be replaced with an admin to configure an admin portal:

```
Set-MgmtSvcRelyingPartySettings -Target Tenant -MetadataEndpoint
https://adfs.wapcloud.com/FederationMetadata/2007-06/
FederationMetadata.xml -DisableCertificateValidation
-ConnectionString'Server=WAPMGT-SQLDB-01.wapcloud.com;User
Id=sa;Password=*******;'
```

2. Execute the following PowerShell on the Windows Azure Pack server to configure the Identity Provider to use ADFS:

```
Set-MgmtSvcIdentityProviderSettings -Target Membership
-MetadataEndpoint https://adfs.wapcloud.com/
FederationMetadata/2007-06/FederationMetadata.xml
-DisableCertificateValidation -ConnectionString'Server=WAPMGT-
SQLDB-01.wapcloud.com;User Id=sa;Password=*******;'
```

3. Execute the following PowerShell on the Windows Azure Pack server to configure the selected user as the administrator of WAP:

```
$adminuser = 'userap@domain.com'
$dbServer = 'WAPMGT-SQLDB-01.wapcloud.com'
$dbUsername = 'sa'
$dbPassword = 'SQL_Password'
$connectionString = [string]::Format('Server= {0} ;Initial
Catalog=Microsoft.MgmtSvc.Store;User Id={1};Password={2};',$dbServ
er, $dbUsername, $dbPassword)

Add-MgmtSvcAdminUser -Principal $adminuser -ConnectionString
$connectionstring
```

Post successful configuration, ADFS authentication can be verified by opening the WAP portal. The portal will automatically redirect the authentication to the ADFS page.

Summary

At the end of this chapter, we have completed building essential services for our WAP cloud solution. You learned about building a SMA solution for automating the WAP cloud resource provisioning, monitoring, and management. You learned about planning, installing, and configuring SMA. You learned about SMA assets and runbooks including authoring and managing runbooks.

We also covered using authentication capabilities of ADFS with Windows Azure Pack for admin and tenant portal authentication.

In the next chapter, we will look at the extensible architecture of the Windows Azure Pack cloud by learning about partner and third-party developed products for extending WAP capabilities and features.

10
Extending WAP Capabilities with Partners' Solutions

In the first chapter, you learned about the extension capabilities of Windows Azure Pack which provides flexibilities to facilitate custom cloud service offerings. In this chapter, we will be discussing about a few available extensions for WAP developed by Microsoft's partners and third-party vendors.

Along with partners' solutions, we will also take a look at Microsoft Azure Stack—a future on-premises cloud solution by Microsoft and Windows Azure Pack updates.

We will be covering the following topics in this chapter:

- Microsoft Azure Stack
- Windows Azure Pack Updates
- Windows Azure Pack Partner Ecosystem
- Offer VMware with WAP – vConnect by Cloud Assert
- Konube Integrator – connect with public clouds
- Apprenda – Enterprise PaaS Solutions
- BlueStripe's Performance Center for WAP
- Usage and billing by Cloud Assert
- Cloud Cruiser for WAP
- Request Management by GridPro
- Odin – WAP APS packages
- Cisco ACI – an application centric infrastructure
- 5nine cloud security
- Team access control for WAP
- Nutanix hyper-converged infrastructure for WAP clouds
- NetApp storage for Microsoft clouds

Microsoft Azure Stack

At Ignite April 2015, Microsoft announced the future release of an on-premises cloud platform named Microsoft Azure Stack; Azure Stack isn't the next version to Azure Pack. It works on a different architecture and enables a consistent experience to the Azure preview portal of Microsoft's public cloud.

During Ignite, Brad Anderson, Microsoft's corporate vice president for cloud and enterprise said:

> *"You've told us you want Azure — all of Azure — in your data centers. Azure Stack ... is literally us giving you all of Azure to run in your data centers."*

Along with Azure consistency, Azure Stack is expected to deliver built-in hybrid capabilities with MS Azure, which aren't available in the case of WAP.

Azure Stack doesn't include System Center components as a core mandatory requirement for IaaS services. Resource providers will communicate directly with fabric components including Windows Servers and Hyper-V. Azure Stack is expected to deliver more Azure-like services including infrastructure, VMs, storage (blob), networks, applications (Azure Service Fabric), web applications, service bus, Azure Resource Manager, and so on. Azure Stack isn't expected to deliver all the things that Azure carries, but the list will be definitely long while comparing Azure Stack with Windows Azure Pack.

Along with portal and APIs, Azure Stack is likely to have the following components in its architecture:

- Azure Resource Manager
- Network controller (Windows Server 2016)
- Azure-based compute, network, and storage services
- Windows-based compute, network. and storage fabric

Azure Resource Manager is a new service management API. It is used to manage resources such as VMs, networks, websites, and more. Tenants can create resource groups and add resources to enable **RBAC** (**Role based Access Control**). ARM consists of RBAC capabilities when it is compared to the Microsoft Azure Public cloud preview portal.

Microsoft Azure Stack will have a single portal for admins and tenants, and it will leverage any of the following authentication services:

- Azure Active Directory
- Windows Active Directory
- **Active Directory Federation Services (ADFS)**

At the time of writing this book, Azure Stack wasn't available for testing. It is expected to be delivered with the 2016 wave of Microsoft products.

It must be noted that Microsoft Azure Stack isn't a replacement for WAP, or it doesn't mean an end to WAP. WAP will continue to get updates as per its update system, which we will be discussing in the next topic; go to `http://www.microsoft.com/en-in/server-cloud/products/azure-in-your-datacenter/ to learn more about Azure Stack` for more information.

Windows Azure Pack updates

Microsoft continuously improves the Windows Azure Pack solution by adding new features and resolving issues since its first release. There is a per quarter update planned for WAP technologies, and usually, it is in line with System Center products updates that majorly include SCVMM and SPF. At the time of writing this book, the latest available update was Update rollup 8.

After Update rollup 4, enhancements and new features were added as per the feedback and suggestions received from customers and partners. If you want to submit an idea or suggestion for Windows Azure Pack features, go to `https://feedback.azure.com/forums/255259-azure-pack`. Windows Azure Pack is expected to support a future version of Windows Server and System Center in future updates.

The following KB article includes fixed issues and new enhancements added in Azure Pack updates respectively:

- **WAP Update Rollup 1**: `http://support.microsoft.com/kb/2924386`
- **WAP Update Rollup 2**: `http://support.microsoft.com/kb/2932946`
- **WAP Update Rollup 3**: `http://support.microsoft.com/kb/2965416`
- **WAP Update Rollup 4**: `http://support.microsoft.com/kb/2992027`
- **WAP Update Rollup 5**: `http://support.microsoft.com/kb/3023209`
- **WAP Update Rollup 6**: `http://support.microsoft.com/kb/3051166`

- **WAP Update Rollup 7**: http://support.microsoft.com/kb/3069121
- **WAP Update Rollup 7.1**: http://support.microsoft.com/kb/3091399
- **WAP Update Rollup 8**: https://support.microsoft.com/en-us/kb/3096392

Windows Azure Pack Partner Ecosystem

WAP, with its custom extension capabilities enables partner and third party vendors to develop solutions to add value in a WAP deployment. These solutions can include technologies from improving existing deployment to adding new features.

There are multiple solutions available today in the market to extend WAP capabilities; a few are the in-development phase. Partner solutions can be segregated under the following categories:

- **Infrastructure**: Infrastructure partners provide fabric components, such as server, storage, networks, and so on, to run the Windows Azure Pack management and the tenant's workload. Examples include infrastructure solutions for WAP from Nutanix and NetApp.
- **Resource providers**: These add new services to WAP cloud offering catalogues. Examples include VMware VM's offering via WAP by Cloud Assert's vConnect solution.
- **Integration**: These solutions are integrated with WAP deployment to provide insights, such as performance or service dashboards, chargeback, request management, and so on. Examples include billing and chargeback solutions by Cloud Cruiser.
- **Gallery items**: Gallery items provide a wide range of catalogues to choose for tenants; they include catalogues for VM clouds and WebSites. See *Chapter 4, Building VM Clouds and IaaS Offerings* and *Chapter 7, Delivering PaaS – WebSites Cloud and Service Bus*, to know more about gallery items.

We will be covering a few of the solutions developed by partners in the upcoming topics. Microsoft provides a developer's kit to start developing solutions for WAP. The development kit is available at https://msdn.microsoft.com/library/dn448665.aspx.

Offer VMware with WAP – vConnect by Cloud Assert

Windows Azure Pack can be used to offer virtual machines hosted on the VMware's server virtualization platform by leveraging vConnect by Cloud Assert. At the time of writing this book, VMware held the highest market share of the server virtualization market. vConnect helps organizations and service providers to use their existing VMware infrastructure to offer IaaS services to internal users and tenants.

vConnect offers tenants to provision and run virtual machines on VMware via VM templates. Provisioning configurations are defined at the VM templates level; parameters are defined by tenants in the self-service portal.

Along with virtual machines, vConnect also offers back up as a service by integrating with Veeam backup solutions.

vConnect offers the following capabilities while offering VMware via WAP:

- VMware vCenter integration with WAP
- Customized VM's templates for IaaS offerings
- VM snapshots support
- Backup using Veeam
- On-demand configuration
- User quotas and granual control

vConnect architectural components include the following:

- Windows Azure Pack with vConnect Admin Extension, Tenant extension, and API.
- vConnect Database(MS SQL)
- Machine hosting VMware vSphere PowerCLI
- VMware vSphere infrastructure
- VMware VM templates for IaaS catalogues
- WAP Plans and Subscription

To learn more about vConnect for WAP, go through `http://www.cloudassert.com/Solutions/VConnect`.

Konube Integrator – connect with public clouds

Konube Integrator allows Windows Azure Pack users and tenants to connect to their public clouds subscriptions via the WAP portal to provision and manage their resources. This enables a hybrid cloud experience for tenants. Organizations and service providers can leverage Konube Integrator to offer an integrated and homogeneous experience to their end users.

Konube Integrator supports the following connections to the public clouds subscription by users in their WAP portal:

- Microsoft Azure
- Amazon Web Services
- Rackspace

Rackspace connectivity is through OpenStack, enabling it to connect to other cloud providers based upon OpenStack.

Konube writes on their official website that Konube Integrator is built for all sizes of customers to solve hybrid and multi cloud challenges. If you are working with more than one cloud provider, be it your own cloud or a third-party cloud, you now have a solution to simplify your work flow. You can now deliver increased business agility through a simple interface and a single pane of glass across all your cloud resources to your end users.

Visit http://www.konube.com/ to learn more about Konube Integrator for Windows Azure Pack to know more.

Apprenda – Enterprise PaaS solutions

Apprenda is the leading Enterprise PaaS powering the next generation of software-defined enterprises, disrupting industries and winning with software.

Apprenda integrates with Windows Azure Pack to enable complete PaaS capabilities for modern .NET and Java applications. Apprenda services can be offered to tenant developers to create and manage N-Tier, cloud-enabled .NET applications that incorporate WCF, and Windows services via the Windows Azure Pack tenant portal.

Apprenda PaaS service integration with WAP enables the following services, offering capabilities for service providers:

- It will integrate WAP and Apprenda to turn your datacenter into a self-service platform for IT professionals and developers
- It will drive some real hybrid cloud scenarios across multiple private, public, and hosted clouds
- It will accelerate the development of websites and custom apps
- We can use cloud-enabled existing apps without rewriting them
- It provides a single pane of glass to manage your PaaS workloads through WAP
- It enables governance policies to allow applications to securely move between internal and external clouds

Go through `https://apprenda.com/lp/apprenda-in-windows-azure-pack/` and `https://apprenda.com/blog/video-how-apprenda-works-with-windows-azure-pack/` to learn more about Apprenda's solution for Windows Azure Pack.

BlueStripe's performance center for WAP

BlueStripe's performance center for Windows Azure Pack enables cloud administrators and tenants to perform end-to-end application monitoring and management using the WAP portal.

Performance center includes the following capabilities:

- Live performance dashboards for applications and application tiers
- Dynamic application and dependency maps visualizing the virtual infrastructure in use
- Tight integration into Windows Azure Pack workflow allowing for seamless movement from analysis to remediation

Performance center provider service provides flexibilities to define the level of capabilities available to tenants with WAP plans. Performance center architecture includes extensions for admin and tenant portals, BlueStripe Resource Provider, and FactFinder management servers.

A FactFinder management server is deployed as per subscription and can be used by the performance center to get statics from public clouds (MS Azure), any on-premises private cloud, or systems. The performance center can be leveraged by the tenant's application owners to set custom monitoring and dashboards including parameters such as response time. At the time of writing this book, Microsoft had acquired BlueStripe.

To learn more about BlueStripe's performance center for WAP, go through `https://channel9.msdn.com/Series/Windows-Azure-Pack-Partner-Solutions/04`.

Usage and billing by Cloud Assert

Cloud Assert provides a chargeback solution for Windows Azure Pack, which can be used to manage usage and billing for tenants and internal customers.

Cloud Assert writes following on their official website for usage and billing solutions:

Usage and billing solution enables Windows Azure Pack administrators to configure pricing for more than 100 plus resources, maintain multiple Pricing Profiles, integrate with billing systems, and generate invoices automatically based on real usage from end users.

It supports multiple scenarios including the following:

- **Plan Credits:** This is similar to Azure. Users can have an overall credit of say X amount, and they are free to use any resource for this X amount. Excess usage is automatically billed based on utilization.
- **Bundled Offers:** This is similar to popular service provider offerings. Users buy a bundle of resources in advance, such as X CPU, Y DB Size, and Z websites. Only usage that exceeds these including unit credits will be invoiced.
- **Pure Usage Based:** There will be no included credits at the plan or resource level. All the usage will be invoiced and based on metered resource values.

To know more about usage and billing by Cloud Assert, go through `http://www.cloudassert.com/Solutions/Usage`.

Cloud Cruiser for WAP

Cloud Cruiser offers financial management solutions for Windows Azure Pack to manage financial aspects for service providers and organizations. Cloud Cruiser is available in two mediums:

- Cloud Cruiser Express
- Cloud Cruiser Premium

Cloud Cruiser writes the following on its official websites with respect to the capabilities offered by respective editions.

Cloud Cruiser Express for Windows Azure Pack offers the following:

- View your cloud costs directly from within the WAP portal
- Automate chargeback and cloud billing for your Windows Azure Pack computing environment
- Gain control of your cloud spending with tenant budgets and automated alert notifications
- Be up and running in under 10 minutes with a streamlined Cloud Cruiser Express installed right from the Windows Azure Pack installer

Upgrading to Cloud Cruiser Premium for Windows Azure Pack offers the following:

- Scale your financial management capabilities to support larger deployments including more VMs, databases, and website instances
- Support a heterogeneous computing environment with additional Microsoft cloud products or other public, private, or traditional computing environments
- Add advanced financial management capabilities, such as customer and service analysis, profit management, demand forecasting, and more

To learn more about Cloud Cruiser for Windows Azure Pack, go through `http://www.cloudcruiser.com/partners/microsoft/`.

Request Management by GridPro

Request Management by GridPro allows Windows Azure Pack users to submit, track, and update incidents and requests for resources within Azure Pack. Request Management integrates with System Center Service Manager to provide these functionalities.

GridPro writes the following benefits of using Request Management for both organizations and service providers:

- Request Management and Service Management provisioning in a unified portal through Windows Azure Pack integration
- It enables users and tenants to submit, track and update incidents and requests
- It allows decision makers to approve requests, and it allows implementers to complete their tasks in the Windows Azure Pack portal
- It publishes new request offerings to users and tenants from the Service Manager 2012 Service Catalogue
- Service usage data collected can be used to monetize requests
- Enables hosters to offer higher value services built on Windows Azure Pack
- Usage data enables billing based on incidents and requests
- Claims-based authentication provides flexibility for user access
- It can easily manage resources by providing users with one single view, enabling them to perform predefined actions based upon the type of resource
- It is available in all 12 languages that Windows Azure Pack supports

To learn more about Request Management by GridPro, go through `http://www.gridprosoftware.com/en/products/requestmanagement`.

Odin – WAP APS packages

As Odin writes on their official website, Windows Azure Pack APS package provides complete support for Windows Azure Pack, enabling service providers to offer Windows Azure services based on their infrastructure. This APS package reduces the time to market to offer Windows Azure Pack services by automating billing, provisioning, and customer management.

When you deploy the Windows Azure Pack APS package with Service Automation, you will get a complete set of business capabilities as follows:

- Storefront integration
- Automated ordering and provisioning
- Customer self-service control panels
- Billing and service plan management
- Resource reporting and tracking
- Full reseller and white-label capability
- Ability to customize workflow to drive business processes with the greatest efficiency

To learn more about Odin's solution for Windows Azure Pack, go through http://www.odin.com/products/automation/services-and-applications/windows-azure-package/.

Cisco ACI – application centric infrastructure

Cisco ACI is designed to provide datacenter fabric to applications as per application requirements and business policies. ACI facilitates this in an application-centric way by enabling application-centric policies to host applications infrastructure such as VMs and networks on fabric.

Cisco integrates its ACI application policy framework with Microsoft technologies including Hyper, SCVMM, and Azure Pack. While it is integrated with WAP, ACI provides a self-service experience to tenants to choose policies for their networking requirements.

ACI enables this by developing an ACI custom resource provider and extensions for Windows Azure Pack.

The ACI architecture for enabling this solution involves the following components:

- Windows Azure Pack Solution (UR 5 or higher) with ACI resource provider's and extensions
- SCVMM logical networks
- Cisco APIC agent for Hyper-V — installed on all Hyper-V hosts
- WAP plans and subscriptions including ACI services

Along with network policies, ACI also enables access for layer 4 to 7 capabilities to tenants via products from Citrix and NetScaler. To learn and start implementing Cisco ACI with Windows Azure Pack, go through http://www.cisco.com/c/en/us/td/docs/switches/datacenter/aci/apic/sw/1-x/virtualization/b_ACI_Virtualization_Guide.html and http://www.cisco.com/c/en/us/solutions/collateral/data-center-virtualization/application-centric-infrastructure/white-paper-c11-732080.html.

5nine cloud security

5nine cloud security for Windows Azure Pack enables service providers to offer customer Security as a Service. It enables tenants to manage firewall configurations and protect their virtual machines running Windows or Linux

5nine adds two major capabilities for Windows Azure Pack including Virtual firewall and **IDS** (**Intrusion detection system**). These capabilities are delivered without installing agents inside virtual machines. Agentless solution ensures no performance hit on virtual machines.

5nine integrates with the virtual switch on Hyper-V to enable these capabilities. See the following links to learn more about 5nine cloud security for Windows Azure Pack:

`http://www.5nine.com/5nine-security-for-hyper-v-product.aspx#Azure`

`http://www.5nine.com/Docs/5nine_wap_extension_overview_en.pdf`

`http://www.5nine.com/Docs/5nineCloudSecurityAzurePack_Guide.pdf`

Team access control for WAP

Team access, controlled by Terawe, is a scoped access control (similar to RBAC) solution for Windows Azure Pack. Team access control enables scoped quota management and access control that enables administrators and team managers and members to use resources in a controlled yet flexible way. To learn more about team access control for WAP, go through `http://www.terawe.com/tac4wapack`.

Nutanix hyper-converged infrastructure for WAP clouds

Nutanix, a leader in the hyper-convergence market, has conducted functional testing for WAP workloads to their Web Scale virtual computing platform. To access reference architecture for running Windows Azure Pack cloud on Nutanix platform, go through `http://go.nutanix.com/microsoft-private-cloud-windows-azure-pack.html`.

A NetApp storage for Microsoft Clouds

The NetApp storage solution integrates with Microsoft Cloud OS, scaling from private to public clouds to accelerate deployment of cloud-based datacenter infrastructure, applications, and services. To learn more about NetApp solution for Microsoft cloud platforms, go through `http://www.netapp.com/us/solutions/cloud/microsoft-cloud/index.aspx`.

Summary

In this chapter, we discussed about Microsoft Azure Stack next platform by Microsoft for building clouds on-premise. You learned about the Windows Azure Pack updates system.

We covered the Windows Azure Pack Partner Ecosystem and discussed the offerings of solutions developed by partners to extend Windows Azure Pack capabilities.

With this chapter, our journey of building clouds with Windows Azure Pack has come to an end. In this book, you learned how to plan, implement, manage, and experience a cloud solution built using Microsoft technologies. If you did your own lab implementation following the course of the book, then by now, you must be ready with an enterprise class cloud offering IaaS, PaaS, and SaaS services.

Learning is a never ending process in this changing IT world.

I recommend `http://social.technet.microsoft.com/wiki/contents/articles/20689.the-azure-pack-wiki-wapack.aspx` to keep updated on Windows Azure Pack.

I recommend `http://blogs.technet.com/b/privatecloud/` to keep updated on other Microsoft cloud technologies.

Index

Symbol

5nine cloud security
 about 335
 reference links 336

A

account and subscriptions management operations, tenant
 about 194-196
 account, deleting 197
 co-admins, adding 196, 197
 management certificate, uploading 195
Active Directory Federation Services (ADFS) 11, 327
add-ons
 about 169, 170
 creating 173-180
 for MySQL DBaaS 284, 285
 for SQL 284, 285
 linking, to plan 182
 managing 173-181
ADFS authentication
 architecture 319
 enabling, for WAP portals 319
 implementing, for WAP 320
 overview 319
 URL 320
 WAP portal, adding as relying party 320-322
 WAP websites, configuring 322, 323
Application payload 139

Apprenda
 about 330
 PaaS service integration, with WAP 331
 URL 331
architecture, SMA
 about 293
 database 294
 PowerShell module 294
 runbook worker 294
 web service 293
architecture, WAP WebSites
 about 215
 cloud service roles 215
 database roles 216
assets, SMA
 adding 307-310
 dealing with 305
 managing 307-310
 types 306, 307
authentication sites
 about 11
 admin 11
 tenant 11
Azure Site Recovery
 URL 123

B

best practices, Hyper-V deployment
 about 36
 for installation 36, 37
 for machine deployment 39
 for networking 38
 for storage deployment 38

best practices, Hyper-V networking
  for cluster and mobility deployment 40
  for storage deployment 38
  for virtual machine deployment 39
building blocks, WAP cloud solution
  about 13
  custom resource provider 16
  DBaaS offering solution components 15
  IaaS offering, enabling 14
  Service Bus offering solution components 15
Business Continuity and Disaster Recovery (BCDR) 30

C

capabilities
  about 7
  automation 8
  custom offerings 8
  databases 8
  management portal for cloud admins 7
  management portal for tenants 7
  service bus 8
  service management REST API 7
  virtual machines 7
  virtual networks 8
  websites 8
capacity recommendations
  for file servers 218
  for SQL servers 218
  for WebSites Roles 217
Cisco application centric infrastructure (ACI)
  about 335
  components 335
  reference URLs 335
Cloud add-on
  planning 173
Cloud Assert
  about 332
  bundled offers 332
  plan credits 332
  pure usage based 332
  usage and billing solutions 332

cloud catalogue
  OS images, preparing 124
Cloud Cruiser
  about 333
  Express 333
  Premium 333
  URL 333
cloud deployment
  Nutanix hyper-converged infrastructure 336
  scaling 23, 24
  SCVMM cloud, building 116
cloud fabric infrastructure
  cloud hardware, sizing for private cloud 29
  cloud management infrastructure 35
  core MS Infrastructure, services planning 35
  hardware, selecting 28, 29
  hardware, sizing 29
  hypervisor's deployment options, selecting 31
  hypervisor's editions, selecting 31
  planning 28
  system center deployment options, selecting 33
  system center edition, selecting 33
  tenant workload infrastructure 35
cloud management DB
  SQL Server, deploying 42
  SQL Server, planning 42
cloud management fabric
  virtual machines, setting up 41, 42
cloud network fabric
  configuring, with SCVMM 63
  network virtualization 65, 66
  planning, with SCVMM 63
Cloud plans
  additional settings 172
  configurations 170
  custom settings 172
  gallery 171
  hardware profiles 171
  networks 171
  planning 170, 171
  resource provider offerings 170
  services 170

templates 171
usage limit 171
VM Cloud 170
VMM Management server 170
cloud service providers
requirements 6
WAP 5-10
cloud storage fabric
configuring, with SCVMM 74
planning, with SCVMM 74
CodePlex
URL 139
components 9-12
Console Connect
about 161
architecture 161, 162
deploying 163
deployment, securing 166
deployment, with SSL certificate 162
Remote Desktop Services Gateway, setting up 164, 165
trusted certificates, importing to management servers 163, 164
core MS Infrastructure services
Active Directory 35
DHCP 36
DNS 35
IPAM 36
NTP 35
PXE Boot server 36
credential encryption
DKM 58
DPAPI 58
customer address (CA) 65
Customer Experience Improvement Program (CEIP) 302
custom resource provider
solution components 16

D

Database as a Service (DBaaS)
about 3, 285, 286
access 286, 287
architectural components 265

database management operations 288
database provisioning 286, 287
plans, authoring 282
platform fabric, planning 266
solution components, MySQL 15
solution components, SQL 15
database roles, WAP websites
application database 216
run time database 216
service management API database 216
tenants DB 216
database
value, updating in Authentication Service Redirection 106
value, updating in Authentication Service Relay 106
value, updating in Portal FQDN configuration 106
DBaaS offerings
capabilities 264
dedicated database services 264, 265
dedicated groups 290
dedicated plans 290
dedicating 289
features 264
overview 264
plans 290
shared database services 264
VM Role gallery item 289, 290
DBaaS platform fabric
about 266
database server's groups, planning 266
DB QoS
enabling 278
Denial of Service (DOS) 237
deployment models
about 16
cloud deployment, scaling 23, 24
distributed deployment architecture 18, 19
Express deployment architecture 17, 18
minimal production deployment architecture 20-22
scaled Production deployment architecture 22

deployment models, SCVMM
  about 51
  distributed deployment 51
  high availability mode 52
  standalone deployment 51
deployment model, WAP
  Distributed Deployment Architecture 86
  Express Deployment Architecture 86
  review 85, 86
deployment options and editions, hypervisor
  Microsoft Hyper-V Server 2012 R2 32, 33
  right edition, selecting 32
  selecting 31
  Windows Server editions 31, 32
Distributed architecture
  WAP, installing 96, 97
distributed deployment architecture 18, 19
DNS names, WAP portal
  configuring 100, 101
DNS records
  websites, accessing 219
  website content, developing 219
  website content, publishing 219

E

Express
  deployment architecture 17, 18
  deployment, configuring 91-93
  installing 88-91

F

File Server Resource Manager (FSRM) 221
firewall ports requisites
  for WAP components 97, 98
functionalities 9-12

G

Gallery Resource Import (GIRT)
  about 114
  functionalities 148
  URL 148
  used, for dealing with gallery resource 148-151
  using 148
gallery resources
  developing 152-160
  developing, VM Role Authoring tool used 151, 152
  importing, in WAP 142
  obtaining, ways 139
  preparing, in SCVMM 142
  preparing, in WAP 142
  used, for building VM Role IaaS offering 140
GridPro
  Request Management, using 333

H

hardware, cloud fabric infrastructure
  sizing 29
  sizing, for private cloud 30
  sizing, for service provider cloud 30
high availability (HA) 86
hosting plan 169
Hyper-V
  adding, in host groups 62, 63
  cluster and mobility deployment best practices 40
  deployment, best practices 36
  storage deployment best practices 38, 39
hypervisor compute layer
  configuring, with SCVMM 59
  planning, with SCVMM 59

I

IaaS
  cloud solution components 14
  WAP, integrating with System Center Suite 24-26
IaaS virtual machine offerings
  about 129
  standalone virtual machine 129
  VM Role 130

Information Technology Infrastructure
    Library (ITIL) 26
installation
    best practices, for Hyper-V 37
    prerequisites, for SMA 297, 298
    prerequisites, for WAP 86, 87
Internet Information Services (IIS) 297

J

JavaScript Object Notation (JSON) 137

K

Konube Integrator
    about 330
    connections, to public clouds
        subscription 330
    URL 330

L

Linux OS virtual machine
    VHDX, preparing 128
logical networks, networking fabric
        configuration
    about 66, 67
    creating 67-69
    IP pool, creating 69, 70
    IP Pool , creating 70
    Virtualized VM Network, creating 70
    VM network, creating 71, 72

M

management operations, VM Role
    configure page 209
    dashboard page 207
    instances page 208
    performing 207
    scale page 208
management operations, WebSites cloud
    about 234, 235
    block list- IP filtering 238
    IP filtering 237
    IP SSL 239

monitoring 235
    platform credentials 238
    roles page 234
    settings, configuring 236, 237
    utilization dashboard 234
Microsoft Azure Stack
    about 326, 327
    URL 327
Microsoft Cloud OS
    vision 1, 2
    NetApp storage 336
Microsoft Operations Framework
        (MOF) 26
Microsoft Web Platform Installer
        (WEB PI)
    about 86, 96
    used, for downloading gallery
        items 140, 141
minimal production deployment
        architecture 20-22
MySQL DBaaS
    management operations 276, 277
MySQL Server
    adding, to groups 275, 276
    configuring 272-274
    DBaaS 271
    fabric deployment, planning 268
    groups, creating 274
    installing 272, 274
    URL 268, 272

N

NetApp storage
    for Microsoft Clouds 336
    URL 336
Network Address Translation
        (NAT) 197, 200
networking fabric configuration
    in SCVMM 66
    load balancers 73
    logical networks 66
    logical switches 73
    MAC address pool 73
    network service 73

port classifications 73
port profiles 73
VIP template 73
Network Virtualization using General Routing Encapsulation (NVGRE) mechanism 65
Nutanix hyper-converged infrastructure
for WAP clouds 336
URL 336

O

Odin
about 334
URL 335
Operating System Environment (OSE) 34
optional components
about 12
partner provided and custom offering extension 12
service bus extension 12
SQL and MySQL resource provider 12
usage extensions (API and collector) 12
Virtual Machines Cloud 12
WebSites cloud extension 12
options, for providing storage fabric
directly attached storage(DAS) 74
file storage (SMB 3.0) 75
scale out File Server 75
SMI-S or SMP providers, using 75
Software Defined Storage (Microsoft Storage Spaces) 75
traditional SAN arrays 74

P

Partner Ecosystem
development kit, URL 328
gallery items 328
infrastructure 328
integration 328
resource providers 328
performance center, BlueStripe
capabilities 331
for WAP 331
for WAP, URL 332

plan
add-on, linking 182
advertising 177-179
cloning 177-180
configuring 177, 178
creating 173-177
customized plans 172
designing 172
financials 173
for MySQL DBaaS, creating 282-284
for SQL, creating 282-284
managing 173
planning 169-172
public plans 172
publishing 177, 178
special services or features 173
standard packs plans 172
Platform as a Service (PaaS) 211
PowerShell module
installing 298-302
private cloud, organization
characteristics 4, 5
WAP 3-5
provider's address (PA) 65

Q

Quality of Service (QOS) 120

R

RDS Gateway server
registering 165
Request Management
benefits, by GridPro 334
by GridPro URL 334
resiliency recommendations
for file servers 217
for SQL servers 217
resource definition package
importing 146, 147
resource templates 279, 281
Role based Access Control (RBAC) 326
runbook worker, SMA
installing 298-302

S

scaled Production deployment
architecture 22
SCVMM
  cloud, creating 117-122
  host groups, creating 59-61
  host groups, planning 59, 60
  networking fabric, configuring 66
  registering, with WAP 114-116
  resource extension packages,
    importing 142, 143
  used, for configuring cloud network
    fabric 63-65
  used, for configuring cloud storage
    fabric 74
  used, for configuring hypervisor compute
    layer 59
  used, for planning cloud network
    fabric 63-65
  used, for planning cloud storage fabric 74
  used, for planning hypervisor compute
    layer 59
  virtual machine hosts, adding in host
    groups 62
SCVMM 2012 R2
  agent 51
  architecture 58, 59
  Cloud storage deployment options 74, 75
  database 51
  deploying 50
  installing 52
  library 51
  library server 51
  Management console 51
  Management server 50
  planning 50
  storage fabric, configuring 76-78
SCVMM 2012 R2 installation
  about 52
  post installation tasks 57
  prerequisite 52
  procedure 53-57
  software prerequisite 53

SCVMM cloud
  building, for WAP cloud 116
  creating 117-122
SCVMM management server
  deployment prerequisites 58
SCVMM virtual machine template
  creating, for standalone VM Cloud
    offerings 131-135
Server Core version 31
server roles, WebSites cloud service roles
  controller 215
  file server 215
  front end role 215
  management server 215
  publisher role 215
  web worker 215
Service Bus
  about 249
  architecture 251
  cloud farm, configuring 251-255
  cloud farm, installing 251-255
  cloud farm, registering, with
    WAP 255, 256
  features, provisioning 258, 259
  namespace, provisioning 258, 259
  plan, authoring 257
  queues 250queues, creating 260
  solution components 15
  tenant's experience 258
  topics 250, 251
  topics, creating 260
Service management API
  about 10
  Admin API 10
  Tenant API 10
  Tenant public API 10
Service Management Automation. *See* SMA
service management portals
  about 11
  management portal for administrators 11
  management portal for tenants 11
Service Provider Foundation. *See* SPF

SMA
  about 117, 130, 160
  architecture 292, 293
  assets, dealing with 305
  configuring 297
  infrastructure planning 295
  installation prerequisites 297
  installing 297
  integrating, with WAP 304, 305
  overview 292, 293
  post installation tasks 303
  PowerShell module, installing 298-302
  runbooks, dealing with 311
  runbook worker, installing 298-302
  web service, installing 298-302
  web worker roles, installing 302, 303
SMA assets
  adding 307-310
  functionalities 306
  managing 307-310
  types 306
  using, in PowerShell workflows 314
SMA infrastructure
  database 295
  planning 295
  planning, for availability 295
  planning, for performance and
     capacity 296
  serves, sizing 296
  virtual machines, for SMA servers 295
  web service role 295
  worker role 295
SMA runbooks
  authoring 313, 314
  creating 312
  dealing with 311
  jobs, dealing with 315, 316
  linking, with VM Cloud actions 317, 318
  logging configuration 316
  managing 311
  operations 311
  samples 311
  scheduling 315
SPF
  about 303
  Admin Web Service 78
  architecture 78
  deploying 78
  deployment options 78
  highly available scaled deployment 79
  planning 78
  Provider Service 79
  registering, with WAP 108-110
  standalone single server deployment 79
  Usage Service 79
  VMM Web Service 78
SPF 2012 R2 installation
  about 79
  post installation tasks 83
  prerequisites 80
  procedure 81, 82
  software prerequisites 80
SQL
  groups, creating 269-279
  management operations 276, 277
SQL DBaaS
  implementing 268
  SQL groups, creating 269, 270
  SQL Servers, adding to groups 270
SQL resource governor
  about 278
  implementing, for WAP 278
SQL Server
  adding, to groups 270, 271
  configuring, for cloud management DB 42
  creating 279
  database server version, selecting 42, 44
  deployment model 42-44
  fabric deployment, planning 267
  planning, for cloud management DB 42
  URL, for installation 268
SQL Server 2012 SP2
  configuring 45
  installing 45
  installing, procedure 45-49
  post installation tasks 50
SSL certificates
  Default Domain certificates 221
  obtaining, for WAP websites 102-104
  preparing 220
  publishing certificate 221

standalone virtual machine
  about 129, 201
  creating 201, 202
  management operations 203, 204
standalone VM Cloud offerings
  SCVMM virtual machine template, creating 131-135
standalone VM IaaS offerings
  building 131
  VM template functionality, testing 135-137
  VM templates, requisites 131
Storage Area Network (SAN) 74
storage fabric configuration, SCVMM
  parameters 76, 78
  storage classifications 76
  storage provider 76
subscription
  adding, to tenant's user account 188, 189
  administration portal 187
  management operations, performing 187, 188
  overview 187
sysprepped virtual disk
  preparing, for Windows OS virtual machine 126, 127
system center
  deployment options, selecting 33, 34
  editions 34
System Center Orchestrator (SCORCH) 26
system center products
  capabilities 25
  Operations Manager 25
  Service Management Automation 25
  Service Provider Foundation 24
  Virtual Machine Manager 25
System Center Suite
  WAP, integrating with 24, 25
System Center Virtual Machine Manager. *See* **SCVMM**

T

team access control
  for WAP, URL 336
tenant
  account management 191
  management operations, performing on accounts and subscriptions 194-197
  plan subscription 192, 193
  registration 191
  signing up 192, 193
  user accounts, creating 182, 183
  user accounts, managing 182

U

user accounts, tenants
  additional accounts management settings, configuring 186
  creating 182-184
  managing 182
  notification settings, configuring 184, 185
  rules, configuring 184-186

V

vConnect
  architectural components 329
  leveraging, by Cloud Assert 329
  URL 329
  VMware, offering via WAP 329
VHDX
  preparing, for Linux OS virtual machine 128
virtual hard disks properties, VM Role
  configuring 143, 144
  family name, configuring 145
  Familyname property 144
  Operating System property 144
  operating system property, configuring 144
  release property, configuring 145
  tags 144
  tags property, configuring 145
virtual machine, for tenants
  connecting, Console Connect used 161
  connecting, remote desktop connection used 161
virtual machine Role (VM Role)
  about 130
  architecture 137
  components 137
  creating 205, 206
  example kit 160

example kit, URL 160
flexibilities 130
gallery items 139
gallery resources 139
management operations 206-209
provisioning 205
resource definition packages 138
resources extension packages 138, 139
virtual hard disks properties,
   configuring 143
virtual machines
   deployment best practice, for
      Hyper-V 39, 40
   hosts, adding in host groups 62
   setting up, for cloud management
      fabric 41, 42
virtual network
   creating 197, 199
   extending 199, 200
   managing 197-200
VM Clouds
   overview 114
   requisites 117
   SMA runbooks, linking with 317, 318
VM gallery items
   gallery resource import tool 140
   VM Role authoring tool 139
VM images
   planning 125, 126
VM Role Authoring tool
   obtaining 152
   sample gallery resource,
      developing 152-160
   URL 152
   used, for developing VM Role gallery
      resource 151, 152
VM Role IaaS offering
   building, with gallery resources 140
VM template functionality
   testing 135-137

W

WAP
   about 2, 85
   add-on 169

capabilities 7, 8
Cloud Cruiser 333
Cloud plans 170
cloud solution building blocks 13
components 9-12
configuring 86
Console Connect 161
DBaaS offerings 264
deployment model, review 85, 86
deployment models 16
deployment, scaling considerations 24
features, URL 327
firewall ports requisites 97, 98
for cloud service providers 5, 6
for organization's private cloud 3-5
functionalities 9-12
installing 86
installing, in Distributed
   architecture 96, 97
installing, prerequisite 86, 87
integrating, with System Center
   Suite 24-26
offerings 7, 8
Partner Ecosystem 328
plan 169
RDS Gateway server, registering 165
SCVMM cloud, verifying 123
SCVMM Cloud, verifying 123, 124
SCVMM, registering with 114-116
SMA, integrating with 304, 305
SPF, registering with 108, 110
SQL resource governor, implementing 278
successful deployment, validating 94-96
team access control 336
updates 327
use cases 3
WebSites cloud, installation 219
WAP APS packages 334
WAP portal
   accessibility, customizing 98-100
   ADFS authentication, enabling 319
   certificates, customizing 98-100
   configuration, for using new URL 105
   configuration, for using ports 105
   configuration, for using SSL 105

[348]

database changes, updating 106, 107
DNS names, configuring 100, 101
portal customizations, verifying 108
SSL Certificates, obtaining 102-104
Service Bus
about 249
architecture 251
cloud farm, configuring 251-255
cloud farm, installing 251-255
cloud farm, registering, with
  WAP 255, 256
features, provisioning 258, 259
namespace, provisioning 258, 259
plan, authoring 257
queues 250
WAP WebSites
architecture 215
WebSites cloud
capabilities 212
configuring 222
controller, installing 222-228
DNS records, preparing 219
file servers, preparing 221
installation, preparing 219
installing 222
management operations 234
management servers, installing 222-228
overview 212
plans, authoring 239
platform, planning 216
solution components 14
solution components, PaaS offering 14
source control, configuring 232
source control, customizing 232
SQL server, preparing 220
SSL certificates, preparing 220
web gallery feed settings 233
web gallery feed settings, customizing 232
Windows servers, preparing 219
WebSites cloud, for service providers
application and framework support 213
automatic and self service 213
deployment and management 213
flexible service levels 213
granual QOS and metering 213
high density 212
hypervisor agnostic 213

multi tenancy 213
resilient distributed architecture 213
scalability 212
WebSites cloud, for tenants
about 242
deployment tools 214
flexible development 214
frameworks and programming options 214
management operations 245-249
provisioning and management 214
Quick Create option 243-245
scalability 214
self service 214
web app gallery 214-245
WebSites cloud offerings
plan, creating 240-242
Websites cloud plans
authoring 239
Basic mode 240
customized plans 240
Intro mode (free mode) 240
overview 239, 240
Reserved mode 240
standard plans 240
service models 239, 240
WebSites cloud platform
planning 216
planning, for capacity 217, 218
planning, for resiliency 216, 217
WebSites Management Server
front end, configuring 229-231
front end, installing 229-231
registering, with WAP 228, 229
WebSites server roles
domain, versus workgroup 218
web worker roles
installing 302, 303
Windows Azure Pack. *See* WAP
**Windows Management Instrumentation
  (WMI) 165**
Windows OS virtual machine
sysprepped virtual disk, preparing 126, 127
Windows Process Activation Service 215
**Windows Remote Management
  (WinRM) 221**
Windows Server Catalog 29

Thank you for buying
Building Clouds with Windows Azure Pack

About Packt Publishing

Packt, pronounced 'packed', published its first book, *Mastering phpMyAdmin for Effective MySQL Management*, in April 2004, and subsequently continued to specialize in publishing highly focused books on specific technologies and solutions.

Our books and publications share the experiences of your fellow IT professionals in adapting and customizing today's systems, applications, and frameworks. Our solution-based books give you the knowledge and power to customize the software and technologies you're using to get the job done. Packt books are more specific and less general than the IT books you have seen in the past. Our unique business model allows us to bring you more focused information, giving you more of what you need to know, and less of what you don't.

Packt is a modern yet unique publishing company that focuses on producing quality, cutting-edge books for communities of developers, administrators, and newbies alike. For more information, please visit our website at www.packtpub.com.

About Packt Enterprise

In 2010, Packt launched two new brands, Packt Enterprise and Packt Open Source, in order to continue its focus on specialization. This book is part of the Packt Enterprise brand, home to books published on enterprise software – software created by major vendors, including (but not limited to) IBM, Microsoft, and Oracle, often for use in other corporations. Its titles will offer information relevant to a range of users of this software, including administrators, developers, architects, and end users.

Writing for Packt

We welcome all inquiries from people who are interested in authoring. Book proposals should be sent to author@packtpub.com. If your book idea is still at an early stage and you would like to discuss it first before writing a formal book proposal, then please contact us; one of our commissioning editors will get in touch with you.

We're not just looking for published authors; if you have strong technical skills but no writing experience, our experienced editors can help you develop a writing career, or simply get some additional reward for your expertise.

Microsoft Windows Azure Development Cookbook

ISBN: 978-1-84968-222-0   Paperback: 392 pages

Over 80 advanced recipes for developing scalable services with the Windows Azure platform

1. Packed with practical, hands-on cookbook recipes for building advanced, scalable cloud-based services on the Windows Azure platform explained in detail to maximize your learning.
2. Extensive code samples showing how to use advanced features of Windows Azure blobs, tables and queues.
3. Understand remote management of Azure services using the Windows Azure Service Management REST API.

Windows Azure Programming Patterns for Start-ups

ISBN: 978-1-84968-560-3   Paperback: 292 pages

A step-by-step guide to create easy solutions to build your business using Windows Azure services

1. Explore the different features of Windows Azure and its unique concepts.
2. Get to know the Windows Azure platform by code snippets and samples by a single start-up scenario throughout the whole book.
3. A clean example scenario demonstrates the different Windows Azure features.

Please check **www.PacktPub.com** for information on our titles

Microsoft Azure IaaS Essentials

ISBN: 978-1-78217-463-9   Paperback: 170 pages

Design, configure, and build your cloud-based infrastructure using Microsoft Azure

1. Deploy both Windows-based and Linux-based virtual machines to Microsoft Azure.

2. Utilize SQL Server Azure to build a robust, highly available solution that can be recovered in the event of disaster for your important business applications.

3. A practical guide to configuring and creating a virtual network that expands your on-premises network into a cloud-based infrastructure.

Microsoft Azure Storage Essentials

ISBN: 978-1-78439-623-7   Paperback: 126 pages

Harness the power of Microsoft Azure services to build efficient cloud solutions

1. Get to grips with the features of Microsoft Azure in terms of Blob, Table, Queue, and File storage.

2. Learn the how and when of using the right storage service for different business use cases.

3. Make use of Azure storage services in various languages with this fast-paced and easy-to-follow guide.

Please check **www.PacktPub.com** for information on our titles